A CLASSICAL INTRODUCTION TO CRYPTOGRAPHY
Applications for Communications Security

A CLASSICAL INTRODUCTION TO CRYPTOGRAPHY
Applications for Communications Security

by

Serge Vaudenay
Swiss Federal Institute of Technologies (EPFL)

 Springer

Serge Vaudenay
Ch. de Riant-Mont 4
CH-1023 Crissier
Switzerland

Library of Congress Cataloging-in-Publication Data

A C.I.P. Catalogue record for this book is available
from the Library of Congress.

A CLASSICAL INTRODUCTION TO MODERN CRYPTOGRAPHY
Applications for Communications Security
by Serge Vaudenay
Swiss Fédéralel Institute of Technologies (EPFL)

05-14-07

ISBN-10: 0-387-25464-1   e-ISBN-10: 0-387-25880-9
ISBN-13: 978-0-387-25464-7   e-ISBN-13: 978-0-387-25880-5

Printed on acid-free paper.

Printed in the United States of America.

9 8 7 6 5 4 3 2 1   SPIN 11357582, 11426141

springeronline.com

To Christine and Emilien

Contents

Preamble

Cryptography is the *science of information and communication security*. It entered in mass product markets quite recently and every citizen from developed countries uses it daily. It is used for authentication and encryption (bank cards, wireless telephone, e-commerce, pay-TV), access control (car lock systems, ski lifts), payment (prepaid telephone cards, e-cash), and may become the fundamental instrument of democracy with the advent of e-voting systems. To master cryptographic tools becomes a requirement for most engineers. The present book aims at presenting fundamentals on modern cryptography.

Cryptography is a puzzling kaleidoscope where we have to face and use malice at the same time, to rationalize irrational behaviors, to prove unprovability, and to twist mathematics to make it fit applications. We easily switch from theoretical questions on elliptic curves to standardization problems such as how to represent a number in a communication protocol. One needs to juggle with assembly code on chips and distributed systems over the Internet. We are concerned about commercial aspects such as patents or mass products, as well as communication aspects since cryptography is more and more exposed in media, novels, and movies. Since I first started to work on cryptography, I always summarized how fun it was by the slogan *La crypto c'est rigolo!*[1] My wish is that the reader appreciates the malicious beauty of this puzzling science throughout this textbook.

When writing the preamble of textbooks, authors usually try to justify themselves for introducing yet-another-book. Actually, I had to set up a new course on cryptography. When looking around in the library, I realized that I had to write a new one myself. My motivation came from the following observations.

Education problem. I realized that *there is a substantial gap between state-of-the-art research on cryptography and standard applications.* Most of daily used standards are quite old (more than 5 years indeed!), new flaws are regularly discovered. At the time I am wrapping up the present textbook, the MD5 hash function (a 14-year-old standard which is used in most Internet protocols) has been broken, the stronger SHA-1 hash function (its small 10-year-old brother which is basically used in every other protocol) is in a very bad shape. Standards are being updated or completely replaced and have very short life span. Weaknesses are discovered in well-established standards such as PKCS#1v1.5 (12 years old), TLS 1.0 (6 years old), or IPSEC (7 years old). Furthermore, they are almost never built on strong notions of security. Even very young standards such as Bluetooth 1.2 (2 years old) rely on ad hoc and pragmatic security instead of protocols with (pretty well) proven security. Although we

---

[1] Crypto is fun!

know some strongly secure encryption schemes such as the Cramer-Shoup cryptosystem (7 years old), we still daily use PKCS#1v1.5. Although we know some efficient and provably secure message authentication codes in the perfect cipher model like OMAC (2 years old), we still use HMAC (8 years old) with heuristic security.

It is virtually impossible to teach standards which will be used in 5 years from now. Even techniques which look like the Graal of cryptographers at this time may become completely obsolete in a short time frame. Nevertheless, engineers who will be able to understand future standards and to assess the security impacts of cryptographic products must be trained. For this, I tried to present cryptography like *an evolutionary process*. I tried to suggest more questions than answers and to provide a critical taste. If the reader can ask the right questions after reading this book, it will have reached its goal.

A place for conventional cryptography. Most textbooks concentrate on public-key cryptography. It is actually conceptually more elegant and more adapted to formal treatments since the mathematics behind (number theory) are well studied and understood. Conventional cryptography uses more exotic math, . . . and actually more mess than math. It is actually quite hard to construct a mess theory in conventional cryptography since the mess is assembled in a more artistic than scientific way by experts in this field. Paradoxically, most mass products do not use public-key cryptography at all. Wireless communications such as GSM or Bluetooth use no prime numbers and actually require no such techniques. Once a secret key is established, applications such as SSL/TLS, IPSEC, or PGP no longer use public-key cryptography. So it seems that *most textbooks favor the part of cryptography that has tiny representativity in practice*. The present textbook is more balanced between conventional cryptography and public-key cryptography.

The two sides of cryptanalysis. Most authors present cryptanalysis as a kind of cryptographic hooliganism: cryptanalysis is for breaking nice cryptographic toys by any means. There is actually no rules for outlaws and one can even try to break a cryptographic scheme with dirty math and unchecked assumptions as long as experiment validates the attack. Actually, because of the gap between research and practice, most of the daily used standards are not built on solid foundations and are more likely to be broken by experts. However, cryptanalysis has a constructive side on which the expert tries to prove the robustness of cryptography. Unfortunately, an absolute proof is often impossible, and one must satisfy from "adversary models" and "proofs-by-reduction." *Adversary modelism and proof reductionism are the two main paradigms of security validation* at this time. This book tries to present a rigorous approach on cryptanalysis.

Cryptography for communication security. Most textbooks hide the communication models and objectives. Following Shannon, cryptography is a way to establish secure communications over insecure channels by using an extra hypothesis: a channel which already provides security. This channel is basically used to set up a confidential and authenticated symmetric key. Once set up, symmetric keys can be used to communicate securely (i.e., confidentially and in an authenticated way) over insecure channels by using conventional cryptography. Merkle reduces the extra channel hypothesis to the problem of communicating in an authenticated way: the extra channel no longer requires to protect confidentiality but only authentication. The reduction is further improved by using the Diffie–Hellman protocol. At last, following the Rivest–Shamir–Adleman (RSA) scheme, asymmetric keys can be set up once for all using this channel so that the extra channel is no longer required. In this book I tried to present secure communication as the ultimate goal of cryptography and to emphasize the usage of multiple channels with specific security properties.

This textbook presents cryptography in a classical way by following a chronological order. As a consequence, recent (strong) notions of security such as resistance to adaptive chosen ciphertext attacks (or "nonmalleability") are lately presented.

The science of cryptographic analysis requires an amazingly wide spectrum of mathematical background. One can be surprised to see that we extensively use complexity theory or number theory. I have tried to provide reminders and abstracts of the required knowledge. I have to apologize for those who will think that there is a too strong "Bourbaki taste" formalism here. Formalism is indeed useful. Sometimes, inability to provide a formal description is due to misconception, so having a formal picture brings some kind of confidence: it is a necessary (but unfortunately not sufficient) condition for catching the right concepts.

Using this Document

This document is the transcript of a course given at the Communication Systems Division of EPFL since 2001. In that course I tried to make a distinction between the material that students *must* know from the material covering more advanced topics in cryptography. The lectures are thus split into basic and advanced courses. Titles of sections which belong to the advanced material are preceded by the $\star$ symbol. At a first reading, the reader can thus focus on nonadvanced parts. Every chapter begins with a synthetic table of contents and ends with a few exercises. References are put in the Bibliography at the end of this document.

People who look for information about standards for implementation purposes may find some here. They are however strongly encouraged to refer to the source documents of the standards.

A companion exercise book with solutions is also available. In addition, some information (e.g. errata) is available on the Internet on.

http://www.vaudenay.ch/crypto/

As this manuscript may contain errors, readers who find some are encouraged to check the errata list and submit a report if necessary.

Additional Readings

Besides the present textbook, we recommend the following books. Further readings are suggested at the end of this book.

B. Schneier. *Applied Cryptography*. John Wiley & Sons, NY, 1996. (Ref. [159].)
　　French version: *Cryptographie Appliquée*. Vuibert, Paris, 1996.
　　This is an easy survey book. Since most of the technical details are omitted, this must not be used as a reference for technical concepts. It is also becoming a little outdated.

N. Ferguson, B. Schneier. *Practical Cryptography*. John Wiley & Sons, NY, 2003. (Ref. [67].)
　　This book may be used as a "cryptography for dummies": it may be a good starting point (or a definite ending point) for dummies.

D.R. Stinson. *Cryptography, Theory and Practice* (2nd Edition). CRC, NY, 2002. (Ref. [177].)
　　French version: *Cryptographie, Théorie et Pratique*. Vuibert, Paris, 2003.
　　An excellent introduction to cryptography (lecture notes of Douglas Stinson at the University of Waterloo).

N. Koblitz. *A Course in Number Theory and Cryptography*. Springer-Verlag, NY, 1994. (Ref. [102].)
　　A nice introduction to algorithmic number theory for cryptography.

V. Shoup. *A Computational Introduction to Number Theory and Algebra*. Online textbook, 2004. (Ref. [170].)
　　An outstanding ABC on number theory for beginner cryptographers. It really goes step by step.

Acknowledgments

I would like to thank people who helped prepare this document. In particular, I heartily thank my colleagues from LASEC, the Security and Cryptography Laboratory, especially Pascal Junod who was responsible for the exercises in the beginning of this course, and also Gildas Avoine, Thomas Baignères, Martine Corval, Matthieu Finiasz, Yi Lu, Jean Monnerat, as well as Claude Barral, Julien Brouchier, and Simon Künzli. I am also grateful to the EPFL students for working hard on the course and their extensive comments, especially Ramun Berger and Nicolas Dunais. I owe my gratitude to my peers for highly valuable comments: Eli Biham, Colin Boyd, Matt Franklin, Dieter Gollmann, Marc Joye, Willi Meier, David Naccache, Phong Nguyen, Raphael Phan, David Pointcheval, and Jacques Stern. Finally, I would like to thank Christine and Emilien for their permanent encouragement and love. This textbook is dedicated to them.

Serge Vaudenay

1

Prehistory of Cryptography

Content

Foundation: history, vocabulary, transpositions, substitutions
Basic ciphers: simple substitution, Vigenère, Vernam
Modern settings: digital communications, Kerckhoffs principles
★The Shannon Theory of secrecy: entropy, encryption model, perfect secrecy

Cryptography distinguishes itself from coding theory in the sense that the presence of random noise in the latter is replaced by malicious adversaries in the former. It uses a specific vocabulary and relies on some fundamental principles which are presented in this chapter. We also expose historical cases which are relevant for our analysis, and survey the Shannon Theory of secrecy which was an attempt to make cryptography rely on information theory. Unfortunately, the goals of achieving "perfect" secrecy were too ambitious and impossible to achieve in practice at a reasonable cost.

1.1 Foundations of Conventional Cryptography

1.1.1 The Origins of Cryptography

As an easy introduction, we can say that, strictly speaking, cryptography begins with history: with the origin of language writing. As an example, the Egyptians were able to communicate by written messages with hieroglyph. This code was the secret of a selected category of people: the scribes. Scribes used to transmit the secret of writing hieroglyph from father to son until the society collapsed. It was only several millenia later that this secret code was broken by Champollion.

Although Egyptian codes are quite anecdotal, history includes many other cryptographic usages.[1] Communication with secret codes was commonly required

for diplomacy: governments had to communicate with their remote embassies in suspicious environments,
during war: army headquarters had to communicate through hostile environments,
for individual or corporate privacy: some people wanted to be protected against their neighborhood (against jealous spouses, against dictatorships, etc.), companies wanted to protect their assets against competitors.

---

[1] See Ref. [173] for other examples, or Ref. [98] for references on history.

Most of these stories, however, used cryptography in a pedestrian way. This was the prehistory of cryptography. Most of the secret codes had a *security based on obscurity:* secret codes were dedicated to applications, and people who wanted to communicate securely had to choose their own secret code. Thus, all communication users had to be cryptographers. Modern cryptography history began with electrical communication technology to which this model was clearly not well suited.

Knowledge and science used to be limited to a small category of privileged people in ancient civilizations until education became accessible to everyone. Hopefully, education brings communication to people: most people in developed countries know (more or less) how to read and write in a common language (or even several ones) and most people have access to communication systems. It is furthermore impractical to invent a new language, or a new communication system, in order to provide secrecy. So we cannot use common communication systems in order to provide secrecy.

Language makes it feasible to encode any information into a standard message which consists of a character stream. Following the Shannon Separation Principle paradigm, we should definitely use an additional code in order to encode the standard message into a secret code. This process, called encryption, must be invertible, and the inversion should require a secret information.

1.1.2   Key Words

We list here a few key words. The reader may also use the Internet Security Glossary which was published by the Internet Society as the RFC 2828 informational standard (Ref. [168]).

- *Confidentiality, secrecy*: insurance that a given information cannot be accessed by unauthorized parties.
- *Privacy*: ability for a person to control how his personal information spreads in a community. This is often (improperly) used as a synonym of "secrecy."
- *Code*: a system of symbols (formally, a set of "words" called codewords) which represent information. Note that codes are not related to secrecy from this definition.
- *Coding theory*: science of code transformation which enables to send information through a communication channel in a reliable way. Usually, this theory focuses on noisy channels and tries to make the information recovery feasible to anyone (as opposed to cryptography which tries to make the information recovery feasible for authorized parties only).
- *Encode, Decode*: basic processes of coding theory: action to transform an information into a codeword, or to recover the information from a codeword.
- *Cryptography*: (originally) the science of secret codes, enabling the confidentiality of communication through an insecure channel. As opposed to coding theory which faces random noises, cryptography faces malicious adversaries. Now

"cryptography" has a wider sense, being defined as the science of information protection against unauthorized parties by preventing unauthorized alteration of use. Cryptographic algorithms are the mathematical algorithms which enforce protection.

- *Cipher*: (formally) secret code, enabling the expression of a public code by a secret one by making the related information confidential. This definition is different from the one in RFC 2828, namely, "a cryptographic algorithm for encryption and decryption."
- *Cryptographic system*: set of cryptographic algorithms which include ciphers and other cryptographic schemes.
- *Cryptosystem*: an abbreviation of "cryptographic system" which is not recommended in RFC 2828. It is mostly used for "public-key cryptosystem"[2] in which case it is a set of cryptographic algorithms that include algorithms for key pair generation, encryption, and decryption. It is also (improperly) used as a synonym of "cipher." Cipher is mostly used for symmetric key techniques.[3]
- *Cleartext*: information encoded by using a public code, i.e. available "in clear."
- *Plaintext*: input of an encryption algorithm (usually, a cleartext).
- *Ciphertext, cryptogram*: information encoded by a cryptographic system.
- *Encryption, encipherment, decryption, decipherment*: basic cryptographic processes: action to transform a plaintext into a ciphertext or the opposite. Note that purists make a subtle difference between decryption and decipherment as detailed below.
- *Decryption* (for purists): action to transform a ciphertext into a plaintext by an unauthorized party.
- *Decipherment* (for purists): action to transform a ciphertext into a plaintext by an authorized party.
- *Cryptanalysis, cryptographic analysis, cryptoanalysis*: theory of security analysis of cryptographic systems. Usually, this term is used in a negative way: for the insecurity analysis (by breaking the security of systems). This is a little misleading since this can also be used in a positive way: for security certification (by formal proof or reduction to problems which are known to be hard but not yet proven to be so).[4]
- *Breaking a cryptosystem*: proving the insecurity of a cryptosystem, for instance by exhibiting how to decrypt a message.
- *Cryptology*: science of cryptography and cryptanalysis (sometimes also steganography). Purists thus distinguish "cryptography" from its superset "cryptology." (The title of the present textbook may thus be a little misleading.)
- *Steganography*: science of information hiding. Here we do not want to protect the secrecy of an information only, we also want to make sure that any unauthorized party has no evidence that the information even exists (for instance, by watermarking).

---

[2] See Chapter 9.
[3] See Chapter 2.
[4] See, e.g., Chapter 4.

1.1.3   Transpositions, Substitutions, and Secret Keys

In the antiquity, Spartan warriors used to encrypt messages by using scytales. These were cylinders around which they wrapped a leather belt. Encryption was performed by writing the message on a leather belt along the axis of the cylinder and unwrapping the belt. Decryption was performed by wrapping the belt around a cylinder of the same diameter and reading along the axis.

Obviously, this encryption consists of changing the order of the characters in the message, according to a secret permutation called *transposition*.

Later in Rome, Caesar used another cryptographic system which consisted of replacing every character by the character which comes three positions later in the alphabet. Following the Latin alphabet of Caesar[5], the substitution was as follows.

```
a b c d e f g h i k l m n o p q r s t v x
D E F G H I K L M N O P Q R S T V X A B C
```

For instance, the plaintext `caesar` was encrypted into FDHXDV.[6] The Caesar Cipher generalizes into the *simple substitution cipher*: we encrypt by replacing every character by another one obtained by a secret permutation of the alphabet. We decrypt by replacing every character by another one obtained by the inverse permutation of the alphabet. The permutation is called a *substitution*.

The UNIX community is already familiar with the ROT13 substitution which shifts the alphabet by 13 positions as follows.

```
a b c d e f g h i j k l m n o p q r s t u v w x y z
N O P Q R S T U V W X Y Z A B C D E F G H I J K L M
```

This makes it an involution: rotating twice by 13 positions consists of rotating by 26 positions. Since 26 is the exact size of the alphabet, this rotation is a complete rotation which leads to no transform at all.

It is quite easy to break a simple substitution cipher by using frequencies of character in human language. We can, for instance, use the frequencies of characters in English texts as given in Fig. 1.1. We can also use frequent digrams or trigrams. Here

---

[5] Most textbooks on cryptography describe the Caesar cipher with a 26-character alphabet, which is a little anachronic. There were only 21 characters at this time. Characters Y and Z were foreign characters, used in order to transcript Greek words. Characters I and J were the same one, I. Characters U and V were also the same (V). Character W did not exist.

[6] Writing ciphertext with capital letters and plaintext with small letters is a common convention.

Letter	Probability	Letter	Probability	Letter	Probability
A	0.082	J	0.002	S	0.063
B	0.015	K	0.008	T	0.091
C	0.028	L	0.040	U	0.028
D	0.043	M	0.024	V	0.010
E	0.127	N	0.067	W	0.023
F	0.022	O	0.075	X	0.001
G	0.020	P	0.019	Y	0.020
H	0.061	Q	0.001	Z	0.001
I	0.070	R	0.060		

Figure 1.1. Frequencies of characters in english texts.

are the 30 most frequent digrams in decreasing order of likelihood:

```
TH,  HE,  IN,  ER,  AN,  RE,  ED,  ON,  ES,  ST,  EN,  AT,
TO,  NT,  HA,  ND,  OU,  EA,  NG,  AS,  OR,  TI,  IS,  ET,
IT,  AR,  TE,  SE,  HI,  and  OF.
```

Here are the 12 most frequent trigrams:

```
THE,  ING,  AND,  HER,  ERE,  ENT,  THA,  NTH,  WAS,  ETH,
FOR,  and  DTH.
```

Transposition and substitution are the two elementary operations which can be used to build up a cipher. Another important concept is the notion of key.

The Caesar Cipher was improved in the sixteenth century by Blaise de Vigenère. Here we consider every character as an integral residue modulo the size of the alphabet. This way, the Caesar Cipher can be considered as adding 3 to every characters. The Vigenère Cipher consists of using a word as a *secret key K*, splitting the messages into blocks of the the same length of the key, and adding characterwise the key onto every block.

As an example we encrypt `this is a dummy message` with the key ABC. Here we need to compute

```
      thi   sis   adu   mmy   mes   sag   e
  +   ABC   ABC   ABC   ABC   ABC   ABC   A

  =   TIK   SJU   AEW   MNA   MFU   SBI   E
```

and we obtain `TIKSJUAEWMNAMFUSBIE`. Note that adding A, B, and C corresponds to a translation by 0, 1, and 2 positions respectively in the alphabet. Translations are cyclic, e.g. $y + C = A$.

We notice important particular cases:

- when the key is of length 1, we obtain a simple substitution;
- when the key is as long as the message and the alphabet is binary, we obtained the Vernam cipher (one-time pad). (see Section 1.1.4.)

Given a sequence $x = x_1 x_2 \cdots x_n$ of characters x_i in an alphabet Z, we define the number n_c of indices i for which $x_i = c$, and the index of coincidence by

$$\text{Index} = \Pr_{I,J}[x_I = x_J | I < J] = \sum_{c \in Z} \frac{n_c(n_c - 1)}{n(n - 1)}$$

where I and J are two independent uniformly distributed elements of $\{1, \ldots, n\}$. The index of coincidence is invariant under substitution: if we encrypt x into another sequence by simple substitution, this will not change the index of coincidence. When n tends toward infinity, the index of coincidence only depends on the sequence distribution. For a sequence randomly taken from an English text, the index of coincidence is approximately 0.065. For sequences generated from a truly random distribution, this is approximately 0.038.

This index of coincidence can thus be used in order to break the Vigenère Cipher.

1: **for** all guesses for the length m of the secret key **do**
2:     put the ciphertext in an array with m columns
3:     check that the index of coincidence of each column is high
4: **end for**
5: check the key shifts between columns with mutual indices of coincidence

(Note that the guess for the length of the key can be speeded up by using the Kasiski Test.) The mutual index of coincidence between two sequences $x = x_1 x_2 \cdots x_n$ and $y = y_1 y_2 \cdots y_n$ is $\Pr_{I,J}[x_I = y_J]$. It should be high when the two sequences come from the same substitution.

With the example TIKSJUAEWMNAMFUSBIE, if we guess that $m = 3$ we can write

T	I	K
S	J	U
A	E	W
M	N	A
M	F	U
S	B	I
E		

and so we can compute the index of coincidence of TSAMMSE, IJENFB, and KUWAUI. (Note that this example is not so relevant because the ciphertext is too short.)

1.1.4   Vernam Cipher

With the industrial revolution, communications became automatic (with telegraph, radio, etc.). Encryption and decryption had to be performed by a cryptographic device. The telewriter used the Baudot code for which all characters are encoded into 5 bits. The *Vernam cipher* (1926) is defined by

- the plaintext is a bitstring: an element of $\{0, 1\}^n$
- the secret key is a uniformly distributed element of $\{0, 1\}^n$
- the ciphertext is $C_K(X) = X \oplus K$ where $\oplus$ is the bitwise XOR

The key is aimed at being used for only one plaintext. For this reason this cipher is also known as *one-time pad*. It was published in 1926 by Gilbert Vernam, from AT&T. (It was actually invented at the end of the First World War, but since the war was over, people did not get any more interest in it until 1926.) The security was formally proven by Shannon, by using the notion of perfect secrecy. Later on, the Vernam cipher was used for the red telephone between Moscow and Washington.

Note that the Vernam cipher uses a keyed substitution. It is a kind of Vigenère cipher with a binary alphabet and a one-time key.

The drawbacks of this cipher are that

- the key must be at least as long as the message,
- it becomes insecure if a key is used twice,
- the security result makes sense only when the key source is truly random,
- some pseudorandom keys may lead to insecure implementations,
- randomness is expensive.

The security of the Vernam cipher is indeed critically sensitive to the freshness requirement on the secret key. In the forties, the Soviet intelligence agency KGB was using the Vernam cipher, but was reusing some fragments of keys several times. This led the American counterpart NSA to decrypt messages in the famous VERONA project.

This cipher notably illustrates in a very nice visual way as shown by Moni Naor and Adi Shamir in Ref. [137]. Let us assume that the plaintext, the ciphertext, and the key are black-and-white images. These are indeed sequences of bits: a white pixel is a 0 bit and a black pixel is a 1 bit. We assume that we perform the encryption on a computer and that we next print the ciphertext and the key by representing bits with special square black-and-white patterns. We use a balanced black-and-white pattern, e.g. a 2×2 array with two white cells and two black cells. This pattern is used in order to represent 0 bit. The complement pattern is used in order to represent 1 bit. This step is called "pixel coding" (see Fig. 1.2). Now we can overlay the key onto the ciphertext. Nonoverlapping patterns will be complement patterns and will look completely black. As a matter of fact, they correspond to complement bits whose XOR is 1. Overlapping patterns will look gray from far away (see Fig. 1.3). They correspond to equal bits

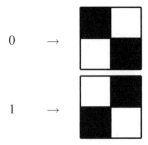

Figure 1.2. Pixel coding for visual cryptography.

whose XOR is 0. Hence we can visually decrypt. As an example, Fig. 1.4 shows a ciphertext, a key, and what we see from the overlay.

1.1.5   Enigma: Toward Industrial Cryptography

A famous example of an industrial encryption scheme is the Enigma machine which was used by the Germans during World War II.

We let π be a fixed permutation over the 26-character alphabet with the following properties:

- it has no fixed point ($\pi(x) \neq x$ for any x),
- it is an involution ($\pi(\pi(x)) = x$ for any x).

We let S be a set of five permutations over the alphabet. For $\alpha \in S$, we let α_i denote $\rho^{-i} \circ \alpha \circ \rho^i$ where ρ is the circular rotation over the alphabet by one position (ρ^i thus denotes the circular rotation over the alphabet by i positions). We let σ be any involution over the alphabet with the property that it has exactly six fixed points. We pick $\alpha, \beta, \gamma \in S$ pairwise different. We pick a number a.

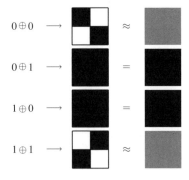

Figure 1.3. Visual pixel XOR.

Figure 1.4. Visual cryptography example.

For a plaintext $x = x_1, \ldots, x_m$ with $m < 26^3$, we let

$$y_i = \sigma^{-1} \circ \alpha_{i_1}^{-1} \circ \beta_{i_2}^{-1} \circ \gamma_{i_3}^{-1} \circ \pi \circ \gamma_{i_3} \circ \beta_{i_2} \circ \alpha_{i_1} \circ \sigma(x_i)$$

where $i_3 i_2 i_1$ are the last three digits of the basis 26 numeration of $i + a$. Finally, we let $y = y_1, \ldots, y_m$ be the ciphertext.

This is a mathematical definition of an electromechanical device. In practice, α, β, and γ are rotors that permute 26 electrical signals, α_i simply consists of α turned by i positions, S is a box of five rotors, π is a cabled permutation which sends back electrical signals, σ is a configurable wire connection, and a is the initial position of the rotors.

Here the secret consists of

- the specification of manufactured permutations like π and the five permutations of S,
- the choice of the initial offset a,
- the choice of σ.

Once again, we notice that the Enigma cipher consists of a keyed substitution. Here, the key is rather short.

Enigma was made to be "unbreakable," even if the enemy had the specifications (namely, the above description and $\pi, \alpha, \beta, \gamma$): the number of combination is so high (namely 26^3 times the number of possible wired permutation σ) that the enemy cannot obtain the key by exhaustive search. Poles reconstructed the Enigma machine before World War II and started to perform cryptanalysis. Their knowledge was given to the Allied forces when Poland was invaded.

Cryptanalysis starts with the following observation. The permutation which maps x_i onto y_i is an involution without any fixed point, and any two of these permutations which differ only on the choice of σ are isomorphic. The attack then starts by finding known plaintexts: messages always have predictable headers or footers, and we can rule wrong guesses out by checking that we have no fixed points. Then, we describe the observed sequence of input-output pairs and we describe it as a graph. If we guess the initial choice of a, we must obtain an isomorphic graph. An automatic process then exhaustively tries all possible a combinations (we have 26^3 of them). Handy analysis then ends up recovering σ.

Interestingly, the first programmable computer which was ever built (even before the ENIAC) was constructed in order to break ciphers like Enigma. Some dedicated machines called "bombes" (from the name of a Polish ice cream) were performing the exhaustive search on a. Alan Turing was a member of the team which built this machine and so this was indeed the first Turing machine. The reason why textbooks on computer science refer to ENIAC as the first computer is that the existence of these activities became to be publicly known only in the seventies.[7]

1.2 Roots of Modern Cryptography

1.2.1 Cryptographic Problems: The Fundamental Trilogy

In Anglo-Saxon literature, cryptography is usually illustrated by famous characters: Alice and Bob (A and B). For biblical reasons, the malicious adversary is usually female and called Eve. According to the (politically incorrect) folklore, Alice and Bob want to communicate securely (for instance, confidentially) and to protect against Eve. A Canadian rock band was even inspired to write a French song about it.[8]

Cryptography concentrates on three fundamental paradigms.

Confidentiality. The information should not leak to any unexpected party.
Integrity. The information must be protected against any malicious modification. (Example: integrity of communications, integrity of backups, etc.)
Authentication. The information should make clear who the author of it is. (Example: signature authentication, access control, etc.)

---

[7] For more references, see Ref. [91].
[8] "Les Tchigaboux," see http://www.iro.umontreal.ca/~crepeau/CRYPTO/Alice-Bob.html.

Some other cryptographic notions are also considered. They are dedicated to special problems. We make here a brief list which is far from exhaustive in order to suggest possible original problems in modern cryptography. It illustrates the rich variety of modern cryptographic problems.

Nonrepudiation. In the case of a dispute on the origin of the document, someone should be able to formally prove that he is not the author. This repudiation proof should be made impossible if he actually is the author.

Electronic payment. The notion of electronic coin should be protected against, for instance, double spending, because it is easy to copy digital information.

Anonymity. Privacy protection may require anonymity enforcement.

Electronic votes. Democracy protection requires that ballots should be anonymous, that a single person should not vote more than once, and that people should not be able to prove for whom they voted afterwards (otherwise they could be subject to threats or corruption).

Zero-knowledge. We want to make sure that no information leaks out of a security protocol.

1.2.2   Assumptions of Modern Cryptography

Cryptography in communication systems relies on some fundamental principles.

The n^2 Problem

In a network of n users, there is a number of potential pairs of users within the order of magnitude of n^2. Obviously we cannot make a dedicated secure channel between any pair of users. This means that we cannot invent a new cryptosystem for every pair of users.

We should better use a common cryptosystem, but enable the distinction between pairs of users by making them choose their own *secret key* like in the Vigenère cipher or the Enigma cipher. In addition, this paradigm benefits from the fact that not every user needs to be a mathematician in order to make a new cryptosystem.

We deduce a need for the cryptosystem to be shared among a large number of users, and a need for the cryptosystem to depend on an easily selectable parameter called a secret key.

The Kerckhoffs Principle

Assuming the cryptosystem is designed by a third party, from a third company, in a third country jurisdiction, since it is furthermore implemented in n points of a network, security should definitely not rely on the secrecy of the cryptosystem itself. The protection of the cryptosystem structure may be considered as an extra security protection, but should not be necessary for security.

Therefore, the security analysis of the cryptosystem must assume that the algorithm is public.

Note that despite what cryptographers regularly claim, the Kerckhoffs Principle does not mean that we should make the cryptosystem public.

Auguste Kerckhoffs, a French professor of grammar, stated other principles about cryptography in the nineteenth century, but this one is the most popular one.

The Moore Law

Secret keys can be tried exhaustively. With technological improvements, computers are faster and faster. Moore stated an empirical law which says that the speed of CPUs doubles every 18 months. If a cryptosystem is designed for long-term secrecy, the secret key must thus be long enough to resist exhaustive search using future technologies.

The Murphy Law

If there is a single security hole, the exposure of a cryptosystem will make sure that someone will eventually find it. Even if this person is honest, this discovery may ultimately leak to malicious parties. By extension we should keep in mind that security does not add up: systems are as secure as their weakest part.

1.2.3   Adversarial Models

For studying the security of a cryptosystem we must consider its whole environment. Security analysis identifies several famous threat models. Here are a few attack models against ciphers. We can, of course, consider any combination of them.

Ciphertext-only attack. The adversary tries to break the system by wiretapping the ciphertext messages.

Known plaintext attack. The adversary obtains the ciphertext and succeeds to get the corresponding plaintext in a way or another (for instance, if the plaintext is a standard message). She then tries to exploit this extra information to break the system.

Chosen plaintext attack. The adversary can play with the encryption device and submit appropriately chosen plaintexts, and get the corresponding ciphertexts in return. She then tries to exploit this experiment by breaking the system.

Chosen ciphertext attack. The adversary can play with the decryption device, and thus decrypt any chosen cryptogram. She then tries to exploit this experiment in order to decrypt other cryptograms without using this access model.

We distinguish adversary capabilities (as above) from adversary goals. In the case of attack models against ciphers, we can, for instance, consider *key recovery attacks* (in which the goal is to deduce the secret key) from a *decryption attack* (in which the goal is to decrypt a target ciphertext). It is thus quite important to describe the adversary models related to every cryptographic system.

1.2.4 Cryptography from Various Perspectives

On the Government Side: The Cold War

The military success of the Allies during World War II was partly due to cryptography, and as such, cryptography became highly estimated during the cold war. A famous implementation was the *red telephone* between Moscow and Washington DC. This was a kind of email service (not a real telephone) with encryption through a *one-time pad* (see Section 1.1.4).

United States and Russia had an opposite approach of intelligence. While Russia mainly used on-site physical agents, the United States started to develop a communication wiretapping industry. They created the NSA, the existence of which remained secret until very recently, and developed the Echelon network.[9] Echelon is aimed at listening to all electronic communications (telephone, radio, fax, satellite, cables, etc.), at automatically analyzing and filtering them, and at developing virtual agents which can trigger alerts.

Cryptography was considered as a war weapon and regulated as such: import–export organizations, salesmen, developers, researchers, publishers were controlled by government agencies in many countries (United States, France, etc.). Switzerland was one of the only cryptographic paradise where one could freely set up mirror companies for cryptographic products. In other countries, obscure agencies used to put vetoes on some sensitive research projects (like studying data integrity control algorithms), to lobby to forbid scientific publications (even the present textbook could have been classified as a war weapon and the book holder could have been prosecuted by a military court), and to classify some patent applications. Programs were set up in order to facilitate government inspection of private communications by *key escrow* (for instance, with the US *cliper chip* which has now disappeared).[10] There is indeed an equilibrium to find between individual privacy and national security, and governments used to clearly favor the latter. The situation has become much more liberal now and cryptography can be taught, studied, and used in private business.

On the Industry Side: Electronic Commerce

While cryptography research, development, and usage were restricted, there was a need for communication protection in civil environments. In the seventies, banking was using more and more electronic transactions and had to make them secure. At this time, the

---

[9] For more references on the NSA, see Ref. [22].
[10] This situation is described by Whitfield Diffie and Susan Landau in Ref. [60].

US Government made an encryption standard available (DES) to protect unclassified but sensitive data.[11]

Now, the rise of electronic commerce and mobile communication introduces a new need for security. Industries also need to protect industrial secrets and trades. Software manufacturers need to have secure and user-friendly license management tools. Artists and major companies had a severe revenue loss because of peer-to-peer media exchange platforms. More generally, most goods providers, not necessarily in the information technology sector, want to implement easy tracing tools such as tags using radio frequency identification (RFID) technology. It should be used in order to optimize logistic, but it is a threat to people's privacy at the same time.

On the Academic Side: Research in Cryptology

At the same time that the US Government was pushing for an encryption standard, the academic world in computer sciences was building complexity theory: the mathematical notion of *intractability*, *NP-completeness*, *one-way functions*, etc.[12] The mathematical notion of *complexity* became the natural root of information protection.

The academic world naturally discovered the notion of *public-key cryptography*[13]: we could encrypt with a public key, but decryption without a private key had to face a large complexity problem.[14]

On the People Side: Towards Civil Cryptography?

At the same time that governments and industry were developing security applications for their businesses, people also wanted to protect their activities. The PGP effort (Pretty Good Privacy) by some privacy protection activists illustrates the need to strengthen people's privacy by email encryption against governmental requirements.[15] Law enforcement, goods traceability, and license and media protection evolve in such a way that automatic applications can implement them. This typically violates people's privacy.

Even democracy management may be performed by machines since electronic voting is being developed. Obviously this must be done under very careful concern about the people's integrity. Since the present document is aimed at teaching cryptography, the author would like to make the reader aware of the risks of a possible technologic nightmare in preparation.

---

[11] See Chapter 2.
[12] See Chapter 8.
[13] See Chapter 9.
[14] For more details, see Ref. [175]. See also Ref. [116].
[15] See Chapter 12.

1.2.5   Methodology

Communication Channels

Communication channels have different kinds of attributes: cost, speed, availability, reliability, security. Here, reliability refers to resistance against random noise. We do not consider it since it is addressed by coding theory. So we implicitly consider that all communication channels perform a transmission in a reliable way: the sent information is always equal to the received one unless there is a malicious attack.

As we have seen, security may relate to the ability to provide confidentiality, integrity, or authentication. If we use basic telegraph through radio signal, speed is high, cost is low, but security is void. Availability is also high since ether is (in principle) always usable. If we now use the diplomatic case to transmit information (for instance, we give some information to an ambassador who is physically sent to the information destination), we have a low speed, a high cost, but a high security. Availability also depends on the airplane and the schedule of the ambassador. If we now use Enigma-encrypted radio signals, the speed is high, the cost is relatively low (the development of the Enigma machine is quickly amortized in wartime), and the security should have been high.

Note that we talk about communication channels in a broad sense: we are not only interested in moving some information from one place of a three-dimensional space to another. We are also interested in the fourth dimension (time): we also want to archive some information which can be used later. So an archive system can also be considered as a communication channel.

Reduction

Computer science is a matter of reduction: instead of solving a problem from scratch, we try to cut it into several subproblems, and reduce one problem to another one. Security is the same. As we will see later, it is impossible to consider that we can have a single communication channel which is cheap, fast, available, and secure. On the other hand, we can use expensive, slow, hardly available, but secure channels in order to transform a cheap, fast, available, and insecure channel into a cheap, fast, available, and secure one. In the next sections and chapters we will see how to do it by improving the security attributes.

1.3   ⋆The Shannon Theory of Secrecy

1.3.1   ⋆Secrecy of Communication

The purpose of encryption is to ensure communication secrecy. We assume that we want to communicate, which means to transmit information through a channel. The channel is not assumed to be secure.

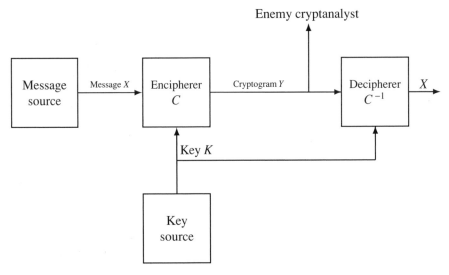

Figure 1.5. The Shannon encryption model.

Following the Shannon Theory, we do not encrypt fixed messages, but messages coming from a plaintext source. The plaintext source generates random texts according to some given probability distribution. For instance, with the distribution of plain English texts, the probability that the plaintext is `hello world` is much greater (particularly when the message is a textbook about a programming language) than the probability that it is `gbwiub oafp` (except maybe in some Vogon poetry).[16]

Following the Shannon Theory, a cipher is given by

1. a plaintext source (with the corresponding distribution),
2. a secret key distribution,
3. a ciphertext space,
4. a rule which transforms any plaintext X and a key K by a ciphertext $Y = C_K(X)$,
5. a rule which enables recovering X from K and $Y = C_K(X)$ as $X = C_K^{-1}(Y)$.

(see Fig. 1.5.) A more intuitive definition of a cipher includes

1. a plaintext space, a ciphertext space, a key space,
2. a key generation algorithm,
3. an encryption algorithm,
4. a decryption algorithm.

These definitions relate to *conventional cryptography*.

---

[16] See the *Hitch Hiker's Guide to the Galaxy* trilogy by Douglas Adams.

In this setting, the secret key K must still be transmitted in a secure way, so we need a secure channel. To summarize, in order to transmit a message securely, we first need to set up a key and transmit it securely. Is this a vicious circle? It is not for two reasons. Firstly, the key can be a very short piece of information and it can be easier to protect it than to protect the message. We can afford using an expensive channel in order to send a short key securely. Later on, we use an inexpensive channel in order to send long messages securely thanks to encryption. Secondly, even if the key is long (which is the case of the Vernam cipher), it still makes sense to use an expensive channel to transmit it securely. The secure channel may not be available all the time, or may have longer transmission delays (for instance, if this channel consists of shipping the key by airplane from Washington to Moscow). We can use it when available by anticipating that we will have to transmit a confidential document in the future. Later on, we can use any available channel with fast transmission. This makes the secure channel virtually available. We summarize this paradigm by saying that using an expensive, slow, hardly available, but confidential channel, we can transform any other channel into a confidential one by using the Shannon model of encryption.

1.3.2 *Entropy

Given a random variable X, we define the *entropy* by

$$H(X) = - \sum_x \Pr[X = x] \log_2 \Pr[X = x].$$

The *joint entropy* $H(X, Y)$ of two random variables is defined as the entropy of the joint variable $Z = (X, Y)$, i.e.

$$H(X, Y) = - \sum_{x,y} \Pr[X = x, Y = y] \log_2 \Pr[X = x, Y = y].$$

Note that X and Y are *independent* if and only if $\Pr[X = x, Y = y] = \Pr[X = x] \times \Pr[Y = y]$ for any x and y. We further define the *conditional entropy* $H(X|Y)$ as $H(X|Y) = H(X, Y) - H(Y)$, i.e.

$$H(X|Y) = - \sum_{x,y} \Pr[X = x, Y = y] \log_2 \Pr[X = x | Y = y].$$

Here are some basic facts on entropy.[17]

Theorem 1.1. *For any distribution, we have*

- $H(X, Y) \geq H(X)$ *with equality if and only if Y can be written $f(X)$*
- $H(X, Y) \leq H(X) + H(Y)$ *with equality if and only if X and Y are independent;*

---

[17] For more information, see the textbook by Cover and Thomas (Ref. [52]).

- *if* $\Pr[X = x] \neq 0$ *for at least n values of x then* $H(X) \leq \log_2 n$ *with equality if and only if all nonzero* $\Pr[X = x]$ *are equal to* $\frac{1}{n}$.

1.3.3 ⋆*Perfect Secrecy*

Perfect secrecy means that the *a posteriori* distribution of the plaintext X after we know the ciphertext Y is equal to the *a priori* distribution of the plaintext: the conditional distribution of X given Y is equal to the original distribution. Formally, for all x and y such that $\Pr[Y = y] \neq 0$, we have $\Pr[X = x | Y = y] = \Pr[X = x]$.

Theorem 1.2. *Perfect secrecy is equivalent to* $H(X|Y) = H(X)$ *and to the statistic independence between X and Y.*

Proof. We have

$$H(X|Y) = H(X, Y) - H(Y) \leq H(X)$$

with equality if and only if X and Y are independent. Thus $H(X|Y) = H(X)$ is equivalent to the independence of X and Y.

If we have perfect secrecy, then

$$\frac{\Pr[X = x, Y = y]}{\Pr[Y = y]} = \Pr[X = x | Y = y] = \Pr[X = x]$$

for any x and y, thus X and Y are independent, thus $H(X|Y) = H(X)$.

If now $H(X|Y) = H(X)$, and X and Y are independent, we have

$$\Pr[X = x | Y = y] = \frac{\Pr[X = x, Y = y]}{\Pr[Y = y]} = \Pr[X = x]$$

for any x and y; thus we have perfect secrecy.   □

Theorem 1.3 (Shannon 1949). *Perfect secrecy implies* $H(K) \geq H(X)$.

Proof. We first prove the intermediate property which holds in all cases: $H(Y) \geq H(X)$. First, we have $H(Y) \geq H(Y|K)$. We notice that the knowledge of K gives the same distribution for X and Y, thus $H(Y|K) = H(X|K)$. But since X and K are independent, we obtain $H(Y|K) = H(X)$. We thus have $H(Y) \geq H(X)$.

We now notice that when X is fixed, the knowledge of K determines Y. Furthermore, K and X are independent. Thus we have $H(Y, K|X) = H(K)$. Then we have $H(X, Y, K) \geq H(X, Y)$. Thus we have $H(K) \geq H(Y|X)$. If we have perfect secrecy, we have $H(Y|X) = H(X|Y) + H(Y) - H(X) = H(Y)$. Thus we have $H(K) \geq H(Y)$.

Hence we obtain $H(K) \geq H(X)$.   □

Corollary 1.4. *If X is an m-bit string and if we want to achieve perfect secrecy for any distribution of X, then the key must at least be represented with m bits.*

Proof. If we want to achieve perfect secrecy for any *a priori* distribution of X, we need to have $H(K) \geq H(X)$ for any distribution of X of m-bit strings. For the uniform distribution we obtain $H(K) \geq m$. Now if k is the key length, we know that for any distribution of K, we have $H(K) \leq k$. Thus we have $k \geq m$. $\square$

The corollary and the following result show that we cannot achieve perfect secrecy in a cheaper way than the Vernam cipher.

Theorem 1.5. *The Vernam cipher provides perfect secrecy for any distribution of the plaintext.*

Proof. Let $Y = X \oplus K$ be the ciphertext where X and K are independent bit strings of length n, and K is uniformly distributed. For any x and y, we have

$$\begin{aligned}
\Pr[X = x, Y = y] &= \Pr[X = x, K = x \oplus y] \\
&= \Pr[X = x] \times \Pr[K = x \oplus y] \\
&= \Pr[X = x] \times 2^{-n}.
\end{aligned}$$

By adding over all x we obtain that $\Pr[Y = y] = 2^{-n}$. We deduce that $\Pr[X = x | Y = y] = \Pr[X = x]$ for any x and y. $\square$

1.3.4 ⋆*Product Ciphers*

Given two ciphers C and C' defined by two secret key distributions K and K', we define the product cipher $C' \circ C$ with the product distribution on the secret key (K, K').

1.4 Exercises

Exercise 1.1. *Propose a way in order to break simple substitution ciphers.*

Exercise 1.2. *Friedrich Kasiski, a Prussian military officer, worked on the Vigenère cipher in the early nineteenth century and developed a famous test. The Kasiski Test consists of counting the number of occurrences of multigrams. (Multigrams are sub-words of the cryptogram. Example: digrams are multigrams of length two, trigrams are multigrams of length three, etc.) Explain how we can use the Kasiski Test in order to break the Vigenère cipher.*

Exercise 1.3. *Compute the mutual index of coincidence between two streams of English text transformed with the same random substitution.*

Compute the mutual index of coincidence between two streams of English text transformed with two independent random substitutions.

Exercise 1.4. *Let n be an integer. A Latin square of order n is an $n \times n$ array L with entries in $\{1, \ldots, n\}$ such that each integer appears exactly once in each row and each column of L. It defines a cipher over the message space $\{1, \ldots, n\}$ and the key space $\{1, \ldots, n\}$ in which the encryption of i under the key k is $L(k, i)$.*

Prove that a Latin square defines a cipher which achieves perfect secrecy if a key is used once and is uniformly distributed.

Exercise 1.5. *We assume that the plaintext*

```
conversation
```

is encrypted into the ciphertext

```
HIARRTNUYTUS
```

by using the Hill cipher. This cipher uses an $m \times m$ invertible matrix in $\mathbf{Z}_{26}$ as a secret key. First the messages are encoded into sequences of blocks of m $\mathbf{Z}_{26}$-integers. Each block is then separately encrypted by making a product with the secret matrix.

Recover m and the secret key by a known plaintext attack.

Exercise 1.6. *Product of Vigenère ciphers.*

1. *Given a fixed key length, prove that the set of all Vigenère encryption function defined by all possible keys of given length is a group.*
2. *What is the product cipher of two Vigenère ciphers with different key lengths?*

2

Conventional Cryptography

Content

DES: Feistel Scheme, S-boxes
Modes of operation: ECB, CBC, OFB, CFB, CTR, UNIX passwords
Classical designs: IDEA, SAFER K-64, AES
★Case study: FOX, CS-CIPHER
Stream ciphers: RC4, A5/1, E0
Brute force attacks: exhaustive search, tradeoffs, meet-in-the-middle

In Chapter 1 we saw the foundations of cryptography. Shannon formalized secrecy with the notion of entropy coming from information theory, and proved that secrecy was not possible unless we used (at least) the Vernam cipher. Except for the red telephone application, this is not practical. We can however do some cryptography by changing the model and relying on a computational ability. Before carefully formalizing computability in Chapter 8 we use an intuitive notion of complexity. Indeed, the need of an industry for practical cryptographic solutions pushed toward adopting an empirical notion of secrecy: a cryptographic system provides secrecy until someone finds an attack against it.

We recall that symmetric encryption relies on three algorithms:

- a key generator which generates a secret key in a cryptographically random or pseudorandom way;
- an encryption algorithm which transforms a plaintext into a ciphertext using a secret key;
- a decryption algorithm which transforms a ciphertext back into the plaintext using the secret key.

Symmetric encryption is assumed to enable confidential communications over an insecure channel assuming that the secret key is transmitted over an extra secure channel. Fig. 2.1 represents one possible use of this scheme. Here the secret key is transmitted from the receiver to the sender in a confidential way, and the adversary tries to get information from the ciphertext only.

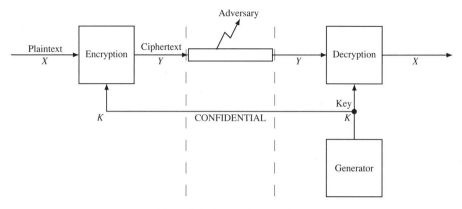

Figure 2.1. Symmetric encryption.

2.1 The Data Encryption Standard (DES)

DES is the Data Encryption Standard which was originally published by the NBS—National Bureau of Standards—a branch of the Department of Commerce in the USA.[1] After a call for proposals, DES was originally proposed as a standard by IBM, based on a previous cipher called LUCIFER developed by Horst Feistel. The US Government (and particularly the NSA) contributed to the development. DES was adopted as a standard and published in 1977 as a FIPS—Federal Information Processing Standard.[2] It was developed based on the need for security in electronic bank transactions. NIST did not renew the standard in 2004 and so the standard is now over. It is however still widely used.

In the seventies, the information technology business was mostly driven by hardware industry (and not by software and service companies). DES was intended for hardware implementations.

DES is a block cipher: it enables the encryption of 64-bit block plaintexts into 64-bit block ciphertexts by using a secret key. It is thus a family of permutations over the set of 64-bit block strings. Encryption of messages of arbitrary length is done through a mode of operation which is separately standardized (see Section 2.2).

The secret key is also a 64-bit string, but eight of these bits are not used at all. Therefore, we usually say that DES uses secret keys of length 56 bits.[3]

DES consists of a 16-round Feistel scheme. A Feistel scheme (named from the author of the previous cipher LUCIFER which was based on a similar structure) is a ladder structure which creates a permutation from a function. Actually, the input string is split into two parts of equal length, and the image of one part through a round function

---

[1] The NBS is now replaced by the NIST—National Institute of Standards and Technology.

[2] The standard has been updated several times. The 1999 version is available as Ref. [5].

[3] More precisely, the 64-bit key is represented as 8 bytes, and the most significant bit of every byte may be used for parity check.

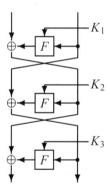

Figure 2.2. Function $\Psi(F^{K_1}, F^{K_2}, F^{K_3})$.

is XORed to the other part. We obtain two parts which are then exchanged (except in the final round). The round function uses subkeys derived from a secret key.

This elementary process is iterated, and the number of round function applications is called the number of rounds. We usually denote $\Psi(F_1, \ldots, F_r)$ the permutation obtained from an r-round Feistel scheme in which the round functions are $F_1, \ldots, F_r$. All F_i may come from a single function F with a parameter K_i defined by a subkey. We denote $F_i = F^{K_i}$. Fig. 2.2 illustrates a 3-round Feistel scheme. DES consists of 16 rounds.

More precisely, DES starts by a bit permutation IP, performs the Feistel cipher using subkeys generated by a key schedule, and finally performs the inverse of the IP permutation. This is illustrated in Fig. 2.3.

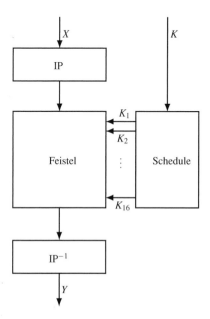

Figure 2.3. DES architecture.

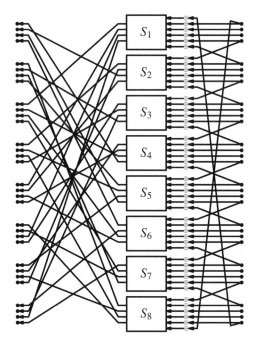

Figure 2.4. DES round function.

The round function of DES has a main 32-bit input, a 48-bit subkey parameter input, and a 32-bit output. For every round, the 48-bit subkey is generated from the secret key by a key schedule. Basically, every 48-bit subkey consists of a permutation and a selection of 48 out of the 56 bits of the secret key. As illustrated in Fig. 2.4, the round function consists of

- an expansion of the main input (one out of two input bits is duplicated) in order to get 48 bits,
- a XOR with the subkey,
- eight substitution boxes which transform a 6-bit input into a 4-bit output,
- a permutation of the final 32 bits (which can be seen as a kind of transposition).

The substitution boxes (called S-boxes) have a 6-bit input and a 4-bit output. We have eight S-boxes called $S_1, S_2, \ldots, S_8$. They are defined by tables in the standard. The tables however need to be read in a special way. For instance, S_3 is defined by

0	1	2	3	4	5	6	7	8	9	10	11	12	13	14	15
10	0	9	14	6	3	15	5	1	13	12	7	11	4	2	8
13	7	0	9	3	4	6	10	2	8	5	14	12	11	15	1
13	6	4	9	8	15	3	0	11	1	2	12	5	10	14	7
1	10	13	0	6	9	8	7	4	15	14	3	11	5	2	12

The 6-bit input $b_1b_2b_3b_4b_5b_6$ is split into two parts b_1b_6 and $b_2b_3b_4b_5$. The first part b_1b_6 indicates which line to read: 00 is the first line, 01 the second, 10 the third, and 11 the fourth. The second part $b_2b_3b_4b_5$ indicates which column to read in binary. For instance, 0101 is column 5. The entry is the 4-bit output in decimal, to be converted in binary. Hence the image of 001011 by S_3 is 0100 (4).

The DES key schedule is done by the following algorithm. We use two registers C and D of 28 bits. The 56 key bits from K are first split into C and D following a fixed bit selection table PC1. Each round then rotates the bits in C and D by r_i positions depending on the round number i. (The r_i's are also defined by a table.) Then another bit selection table PC2 takes 24 bits from each of the two registers and concatenates them in order to make a round key.

1:   $K \xrightarrow{\text{PC1}} (C, D)$
2:   **for** $i = 1$ to 16 **do**
3:      $C \leftarrow \text{ROL}_{r_i}(C)$
4:      $D \leftarrow \text{ROL}_{r_i}(D)$
5:      $K_i \leftarrow \text{PC2}(C, D)$
6:   **end for**

Here ROL_r is a circular rotation of r bits to the left. The r_i's are defined by

i	1	2	3	4	5	6	7	8	9	10	11	12	13	14	15	16
r_i	1	1	2	2	2	2	2	2	1	2	2	2	2	2	2	1

Note that the sum of all r_i's is 28 so that we can generate the round keys in the decryption ordering by starting with the same C and D and by running the loop backwards.

2.2 DES Modes of Operation

DES enables the encryption of 64-bit blocks. In order to encrypt plaintexts of arbitrary length, we have to use DES in a mode of operation. Several modes have been standardized for DES (ECB, CBC, OFB, CFB, CTR) in Ref. [6].

2.2.1 Electronic Code Book (ECB)

The plaintext x is split into 64-bit blocks $x_1, \ldots, x_n$, and the ciphertext y is the concatenation of encrypted blocks.

$$x = x_1 || x_2 || \cdots || x_n$$
$$y = C(x_1) || C(x_2) || \cdots || C(x_n)$$

(See Fig. 2.5.) There are a few security problems.

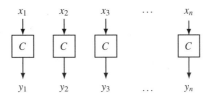

Figure 2.5. ECB mode.

Information Leakage by Block Collisions

If two plaintext blocks are equal (say $x_i = x_j$), then the two corresponding ciphertext blocks are equal. The equality relation is an information which leaks.

This would not be a problem if the plaintext blocks were totally random as the probability of equalities would be reasonably low. However, real plaintexts have lots of redundancy in practice, so equalities are frequent.

Integrity Issues

Although encryption is assumed to protect confidentiality, and not integrity, a third party can intercept the ciphertext and permute two blocks. The legitimate recipient of the modified ciphertext will decrypt the message correctly and obtain two permuted plaintext blocks.

Similarly, a block can be deleted, replaced by another one, *etc.* The plaintext is thus easily malleable by an adversary.

2.2.2 Cipher Block Chaining (CBC)

The plaintext x is split into 64-bit blocks $x_1, \ldots, x_n$, and the ciphertext y is the concatenation of blocks which are obtained iteratively. We have an initial vector IV which is a fake initial block. As illustrated in Fig. 2.6, encryption is performed by the following rules.

$$x = x_1 || x_2 || \cdots || x_n$$
$$y_0 = \text{IV}$$
$$y_i = C(y_{i-1} \oplus x_i)$$
$$y = y_1 || y_2 || \cdots || y_n$$

CBC decryption is easily performed by the following rules.

$$y = y_1 || y_2 || \cdots || y_n$$
$$y_0 = \text{IV}$$
$$x_i = y_{i-1} \oplus C^{-1}(y_i)$$
$$x = x_1 || x_2 || \cdots || x_n$$

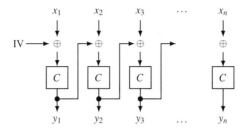

Figure 2.6. CBC mode.

The initial vector does not have to be secret. There are actually four different ways to use the IV.

1. Generate a pseudorandom IV which is given in clear with the ciphertext.
2. Generate a pseudorandom IV which is transmitted in a confidential way.
3. Use a fixed IV which is a known constant.
4. Use a fixed IV which is another part of the secret key.

The US standards recommend one of the two first solutions.

There are a few security problems.

Information Leakage by First Block Collisions

If for two different plaintexts the first blocks x_1 are the same and the IV is fixed, then there is still a leakage of the equality of these blocks. This is why we prefer having a random IV.

Integrity Issues

A third party can replace ciphertext blocks so that all but a few plaintext blocks will decrypt well. This may be an integrity problem.

2.2.3 Output Feedback (OFB)

The plaintext x is split into ℓ-bit blocks $x_1, \ldots, x_n$, and the ciphertext y is the concatenation of blocks which are obtained iteratively. We still have an initial vector IV. As depicted in Fig. 2.7, the encryption obeys the following rules.

$$x = x_1 || x_2 || \cdots || x_n$$
$$s_1 = \text{IV}$$
$$r_i = \text{truncL}_\ell(C(s_i))$$
$$s_{i+1} = \text{truncR}_{64}(s_i || r_i)$$

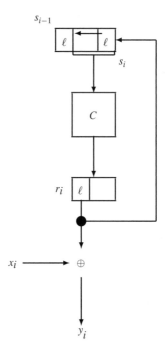

Figure 2.7. OFB mode.

$$y_i = x_i \oplus r_i$$
$$y = y_1 || y_2 || \cdots || y_n$$

Here truncL$_\ell$ truncates the ℓ leftmost bits, and truncR$_{64}$ truncates the 64 rightmost bits. When ℓ is set to the full block length (here 64 bits), the description of the OFB mode is quite simple as illustrated in Fig. 2.8. Note that it is not recommended to use ℓ smaller than the block length due to potential short cycles (see Ref. [57]).

Actually, the OFB mode can be seen as a pseudorandom generator mode which is followed by the one-time pad. Here IV must be used only once (otherwise the cipher is equivalent to a one-time pad with a key used several times). The IV does not have to be secret.

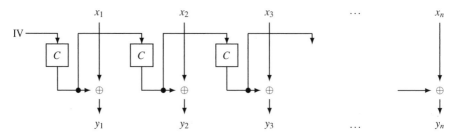

Figure 2.8. OFB mode with ℓ set to the block length.

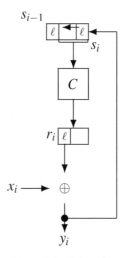

Figure 2.9. CFB mode.

2.2.4 Cipher Feedback (CFB)

The plaintext x is split into ℓ-bit blocks $x_1, \ldots, x_n$, and the ciphertext y is the concatenation of blocks which are obtained iteratively. We still have an initial vector IV. As depicted in Fig. 2.9, the encryption is according to the following rules.

$$
\begin{aligned}
x &= x_1 || x_2 || \cdots || x_n \\
s_1 &= \text{IV} \\
r_i &= \text{truncL}_\ell(C(s_i)) \\
y_i &= x_i \oplus r_i \\
s_{i+1} &= \text{truncR}_{64}(s_i || y_i) \\
y &= y_1 || y_2 || \cdots || y_n
\end{aligned}
$$

The simple version of the CFB mode with ℓ set to the block length (here 64 bits) is depicted in Fig. 2.10. As for the OFB mode and since the first block is encrypted by a one-time pad, IV need not be secret, but must be fresh (i.e. used only once).

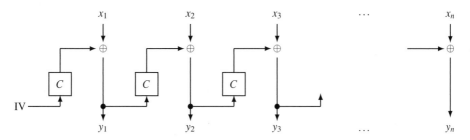

Figure 2.10. CFB mode with ℓ Set to the block length.

2.2.5 Counter Mode (CTR)

The plaintext x is split into ℓ-bit blocks $x_1, \ldots, x_n$, and the ciphertext y is the concatenation of blocks which are obtained iteratively. We use a sequence $t_1, \ldots, t_n$ of counters and the encryption is performed by

$$y_i = x_i \oplus \mathrm{truncL}_\ell(C(t_i)).$$

For a given key, all counters must be pairwise different. For this we can, for instance, let t_i be equal to the binary representation of $t_1 + (i - 1)$ so that each t_i "counts" the block sequence. The initial counter t_1 can either be equal to the latest used counter value stepped by one unit or include a nonce which is specific to the plaintext. In the latter case nonces must be pairwise different.

In Fig. 2.11 the CTR mode with ℓ set to the block length of C is depicted.

2.3 Multiple Encryption

DES relies on a secret key of 56 effective bits, which is rather short. To strengthen its security, people suggested to use multiple DES encryption with several keys.

2.3.1 Double Mode

A first proposal was to use a double mode following the regular product cipher:

$$\mathrm{Enc} = C_{k_1} \circ C_{k_2}$$

One security problem is that we may face meet-in-the-middle attacks (see Section 2.9.5). For this reason double modes are not recommended.

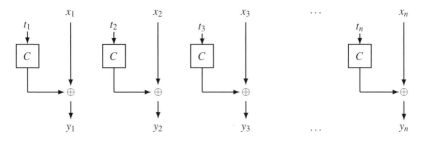

Figure 2.11. CTR mode with ℓ set to the block length.

2.3.2 Triple Mode

Since the double mode does not improve security so much, we use a standard triple mode. The regular triple-DES is defined by three 56-bit keys k_1, k_2, and k_3 by

$$\text{Enc} = C_{k_3} \circ C_{k_2}^{-1} \circ C_{k_1}.$$

(See Ref. [5].) In addition, three keying options are defined:

1. k_1, k_2, k_3 are three independent keys (the key length is thus 168 bits);
2. $k_1 = k_3$ and k_2 are two independent keys (the key length is thus 112 bits);
3. $k_1 = k_2 = k_3$ which is equivalent to DES in simple mode. (This is a kind of retrocompatibility with DES.)

Note that some advanced brute force attacks against triple modes exist as well.

2.4 An Application of DES: UNIX Passwords

A famous application of DES is the old UNIX CRYPT algorithm.[4] It is used for access control of users based on passwords.

Basically, the "encrypted" version of passwords is stored in a database /etc/passwd whose confidentiality was not originally meant to be ensured. Whenever a user types his login name and password, the system "encrypts" the password and compares it to the "encrypted" password stored in the corresponding record of the database. The encryption is based on modified DES due to the following observations (see Fig. 2.12).

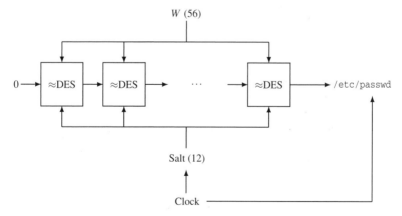

Figure 2.12. UNIX passwords.

---

[4] A summary of the specification can be found in Ref. [128], pp. 393–394.

- We do not want the security to rely on the secrecy of a critical secret key. Thus we want to make the decryption impossible even with full knowledge. Thus we use DES in a kind of a one-way mode: instead of computing $C(W)$ for a password W used as a plaintext, we compute $C_W(0)$ on the null plaintext with W used as a key. (W is truncated onto its first eight characters. It must consist of ASCII characters, thus 7-bit long, which makes 56 bits.)
- In order to make the exhaustive search more lengthy, we use a more complicated encryption. This can be tolerated for human user authentication as long as it does not require more than a fraction of a second. Thus we use 25 iterations of DES with the password used as a secret key.
- In order to prevent brute force attacks based on mass manufactured DES chips, we modify DES in order to make these chips unusable.
- In order to thwart attacks based on precomputed tables, the modification of DES involves a random 12-bit salt which is stored in clear with the encrypted password. Actually, some of the 48 bits of the expanded block are swapped depending on the salt. The 12-bit salt is generated from the system clock when the password is set up.

2.5   Classical Cipher Skeletons

Many block ciphers are described in the literature. We survey classical design skeletons.

2.5.1   Feistel Schemes

The Feistel scheme is the most popular block cipher skeleton. It is fairly easy to use a random round function in order to construct a permutation. In addition, encryption and decryption hardly need separate implementations.

An example is DES, described in Section 2.1.

Here are some possible generalizations of the Feistel scheme.

- We can add invertible substitution boxes in the two branches of the Feistel scheme (as done in the BLOWFISH cipher).
- We can replace the XOR by any other addition law. We do not necessarily need commutativity nor associativity: only regularity (like $a * x = a * y$ implies $x = y$).
- We do not need to have balanced branches. We may also have unbalanced ones (like in the BEAR and LION cipher).
- We can generalize the scheme so that it has more than two branches:
  - (a) round functions with one input and several outputs (like in MARS),
  - (b) round functions with several inputs and one output (like in MD4),
  - (c) round functions with several inputs and outputs.

The first three variants are illustrated in Fig. 2.13.

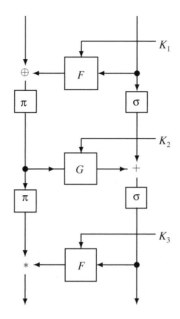

Figure 2.13. Variants of the Feistel scheme with two branches.

2.5.2   Lai–Massey Scheme

A famous block cipher which is not based on the Feistel scheme is the IDEA cipher. IDEA stands for International Data Encryption Algorithm. It follows two previous versions called PES (Proposed Encryption Standard) and IPES (Improved Proposed Encryption Standard). It was developed during the PhD studies of Xuejia Lai under the supervision of James Massey at the ETH Zürich. IDEA was published in Lai's thesis (Ref. [110]) in 1992. It is patented by Ascom and made freely available for noncommercial use.[5]

Like DES, IDEA is a block cipher for 64-bit blocks. IDEA uses much longer keys than DES as it allows for 128-bit keys. In the same way that DES was dedicated to hardware, IDEA was dedicated to software implementation on 16-bit microprocessors (which used to be a luxurious architecture in the early nineties). It makes an extensive use of the XOR, the addition modulo 2^{16}, and the product of nonzero residues modulo $2^{16} + 1$.

IDEA uses a structure similar to the Feistel scheme which can be called the Lai–Massey scheme. It also enables making a permutation from a function. It however requires a two-branch balanced structure and a commutative and associative law like the XOR operation. As depicted in Fig. 2.14, it simply consists of adding to both branches the output of a round function whose input is the difference of the two branches: a

---

[5] The commercial development of IDEA is currently managed by the company MediaCrypt.

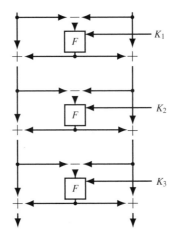

Figure 2.14. The Lai–Massey scheme.

(x_L, x_R) pair is mapped onto the (y_L, y_R) pair defined by

$$y_L = x_L + t$$
$$y_R = x_R + t$$

where $t = F(x_L - x_R)$. Note that this scheme is invertible by replacing the $+$ by $-$ and changing the order of the subkeys. Unfortunately, the Lai–Massey scheme cannot be used as is since the pair difference is an invariance: we have

$$x_L - x_R = y_L - y_R.$$

This is obviously an unsuitable property for security. For this reason we must insert (at least) a permutation σ as depicted in Fig. 2.15 and have

$$y_L = \sigma(x_L + t)$$
$$y_R = x_R + t$$

as it will be detailed in Section 2.6.1 for the FOX algorithms. When the permutation σ is such that $z \mapsto \sigma(z) - z$ is also a permutation, we say that σ is an *orthomorphism* for the $+$ law. We can demonstrate that when σ is an orthomorphism, then the Lai–Massey scheme provides security properties which are similar to those for the Feistel scheme. So the invariance of the basic Lai–Massey scheme is no longer a problem. In IDEA, key-dependent permutations (namely, products and additions) are used instead of a fixed σ.

IDEA consists of eight rounds. One round is as represented in Fig. 2.16. The $\cdot$ represents the multiplication modulo $2^{16} + 1$ to a subkey, the $+$ is the regular addition modulo 2^{16} to a subkey, $\oplus$ is the bitwise XOR, and MA is the Multiplication–Addition structure, which is depicted in Fig. 2.17. The MA structure also requires multiplication to subkeys. The addition law which is used in the Lai–Massey scheme of IDEA is the XOR.

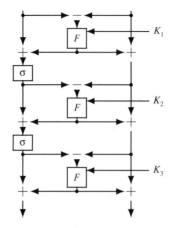

Figure 2.15. The Lai–Massey scheme with orthomorphism σ.

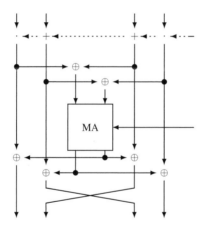

Figure 2.16. One round of IDEA.

Figure 2.17. The MA structure in IDEA.

2.5.3   Substitution–Permutation Network

Shannon originally defined the encryption as a cascade of substitutions (like the Caesar cipher, or like the S-boxes in DES) and permutations (or transpositions, like the Spartan scytales, or the bit permutation after the S-boxes in DES). Therefore, many block ciphers fit to the category of substitution–permutation networks. However, this term was improperly used in order to refer to cascade on invertible layers made from invertible substitutions of coordinate permutations. Feistel schemes and Lai–Massey schemes are not considered to belong to this category in general.

SAFER K-64 is an example of a substitution–permutation network. It was made by James Massey for Cylink and was published in 1993 (see Refs. [121, 122]). It encrypts 64-bit blocks with 64-bit keys and is dedicated to 8-bit microprocessors (which are widely used in embedded system, for instance in smart cards). It uses XORs and additions modulo 2^8. It also uses exponentiation in basis 45 in the set of residues modulo 257 and its inverse which are implemented with lookup tables.

SAFER K-64 is a cascade of six rounds which consists of

- a layer of XOR or addition to subkeys,
- a layer of substitutions (exponentiation or logarithms as above),
- a layer of XOR or addition to subkeys,
- three layers of parallel linear diffusion boxes which make an overall transformation similar to the fast Fourier transform.

(See Fig. 2.18.) Diffusion boxes consist of mappings denoted by 2-PHT which are linear with respect to the $\mathbf{Z}_{256}$ structure. They are represented with their inverse in Fig. 2.19.

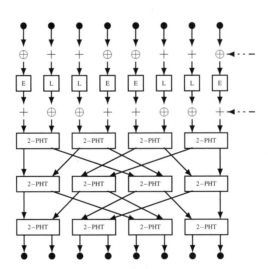

Figure 2.18. One round of SAFER.

$$u = 2x + y \bmod 256 \quad v = x + y \bmod 256 \qquad x = u - v \bmod 256 \quad y = 2v - u \bmod 256$$

Figure 2.19. Diffusion in SAFER.

2.6 Other Block Cipher Examples

2.6.1 ⋆FOX: A Lai–Massey Scheme

FOX is a family of block ciphers which was released in 2003 (see Refs. [96, 97]). It was designed by Pascal Junod and Serge Vaudenay for the MediaCrypt company. The family includes block ciphers with 64-bit and 128-bit blocks. Round numbers and key sizes are flexible. We use an integral number r of rounds between 12 and 255 and a key of k bits with an integral number of bytes, up to 256 bits. The name FOX64/k/r refers to the block cipher of the family characterized by 64-bit blocks, r rounds, and keys of k bits. Similarly, FOX128/k/r refers to the block cipher with 128-bit blocks. The nominal choices denoted by FOX64 and FOX128 refer to FOX64/128/16 and FOX128/256/16 respectively. Namely, we use $r = 16$ as a nominal number of rounds and a key length which corresponds to two blocks.

A key schedule processes the key K and a direction (either "encrypt" or "decrypt") and produces a sequence $RK_1, \ldots, RK_r$ of r round keys in this ordering if the direction is "encrypt" or the opposite if the direction is "decrypt." Encryption is performed through r rounds as depicted in Fig. 2.20. Every round processes a data block and a round key RK (whose size consists of two blocks) and produces another data block. The $r - 1$ first rounds have identical structure but the last round is a little different.

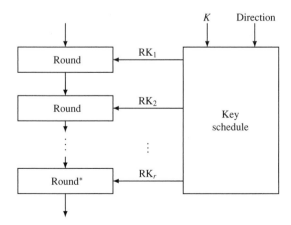

Figure 2.20. The FOX skeleton.

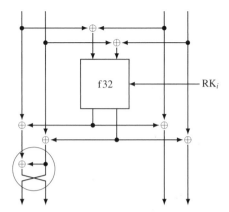

Figure 2.21. One round of FOX64 with an orthomorphism.

The FOX64 round is a Lai–Massey scheme as defined in Section 2.5.2 with the XOR as the addition law and an orthomorphism as depicted in Fig. 2.21. Note that branches in the Lai–Massey scheme are split into two in the figure, leading us to four branches in total. The orthomorphism appears in the bottom left branches (circled in the figure). It maps (a, b) onto $(b, a \oplus b)$ for the encryption and onto $(a \oplus b, a)$ for the decryption. The last round of FOX64 is the same Lai–Massey scheme without the orthomorphism. The FOX128 round is an extended Lai–Massey scheme with two orthomorphisms as depicted in Fig. 2.22. The last round omits the orthomorphisms. With this design we easily demonstrate that flipping the key schedule direction effects two permutations which are the inverse of each other.

Round functions are denoted $f32$ and $f64$ for FOX64 and FOX128 respectively. Those functions process a data of 32 and 64 bits respectively and a round key RK_i which is split into two halves RK_{i0} and RK_{i1}. As depicted in Figs. 2.23 and 2.24, RK_{i0} is first XORed to the input data. Then a byte-wise substitution is performed using a substitution box denoted S-box followed by a linear transform denoted mu4 and mu8

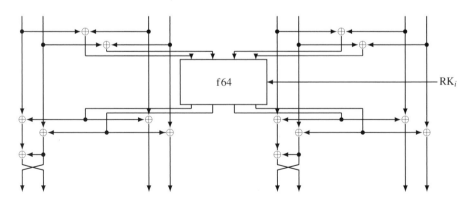

Figure 2.22. One round of FOX128 with orthomorphisms.

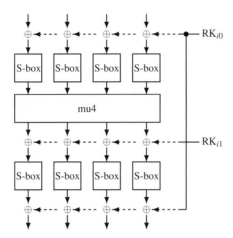

Figure 2.23. Round function f32 of FOX64.

respectively. Then RK_{i1} is XORed with the output of mu4 (or mu8) and another byte-wise substitution takes place. Finally, a last XOR to RK_{i0} is performed. Functions mu4 and mu8 are linear in the sense that they process vectors of bytes that are considered as elements of the finite field $GF(2^8)$ by multiplying them with a constant matrix.

The key schedule of FOX highly depends on the parameters. The main idea, as depicted in Fig. 2.25, consists of first padding the key with some constant in order to get a 256-bit key, then mixing those bytes in order to avoid trailing constant bytes, and obtain a 256-bit main key. This key is XORed to constants which are generated by a linear feedback shift register (LFSR) which can be clocked in one direction or the other. The XOR is then processed through a nonlinear (NL) function which produces a round key. There are some subtleties depending on the parameters.

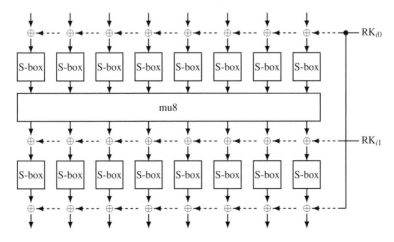

Figure 2.24. Round function f4 of FOX128.

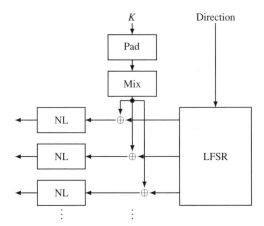

Figure 2.25. Key schedule of FOX.

- For FOX64 with key of length up to 128 bits, there is no real need for having a 256-bit main key and this actually induces a penalty for the implementation performances. Indeed we use a 128-bit main key and LFSR and NL functions updated accordingly.
- When the key has a "full size," i.e. $k = 256$, or $k = 128$ with FOX64, there is no need for padding and byte mixing. Indeed, we omit them. In order to avoid key schedule interference between several kinds of keys, we slightly modify NL.

It should be noted that NL is defined by using functions which are similar to encryption rounds. It was designed in order to be "one way" and to generate unpredictable round keys.[6]

2.6.2 ⋆CS-CIPHER: A Substitution–Permutation Network

Another example is the CS-CIPHER (CSC) which was developed by Jacques Stern and Serge Vaudenay at the Ecole Normale Supérieure for the company Communication & Systems. It was published in 1998 (see Refs. [176, 181]). It encrypts 64-bit blocks with keys of variable length from 0 to 128 bits and is dedicated to 8-bit microprocessors, and consists of eight rounds of fast Fourier transform (FFT)-like layers (see Fig. 2.26). The difference with SAFER is that this transform is not linear.

One round of CSC is an FFT-like layer with a mixing box M as an elementary operation. M has two input bytes and two output bytes. It includes a one-position bitwise rotation to the left (denoted ROTL), XORs (denoted with the $\oplus$ notation), a nonlinear permutation P defined by a table, and a special linear transform φ defined by

$$\varphi(x) = (\text{ROTL}(x) \text{ AND } 55) \oplus x$$

---

[6] See Ref. [96] for a complete description.

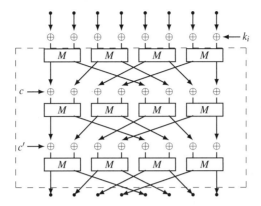

Figure 2.26. One round of CS-CIPHER.

where AND is the bitwise logical AND and 55 is an hexadecimal constant which is 01010101 in binary. We notice that φ is linear, and actually an involution since

$$\varphi(\varphi(x)) = (\text{ROTL}(\varphi(x)) \text{ AND } 55) \oplus \varphi(x)$$
$$= x.$$

Thus φ is a linear permutation. The permutation P is defined in order to be a nonlinear involution:

$$P(P(x)) = x.$$

We can then finally define M. Fig. 2.27 represents M with the XOR with subkey bytes at the input. It is easy to see that Fig. 2.28 represents the inverse transform where φ' is defined by

$$\varphi'(x) = (\text{ROTL}(x) \text{ AND } \text{aa}) \oplus x.$$

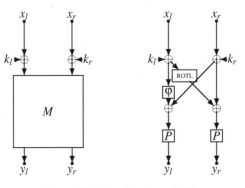

Figure 2.27. The mixing box of CSC.

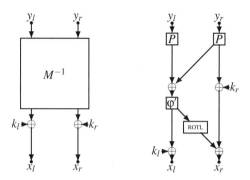

Figure 2.28. The invert mixing box of CSC.

For completeness we also provide a complete view of CSC in Fig. 2.29. We see that the key schedule is actually defined by a Feistel scheme.

2.7 The Advanced Encryption Standard (AES)

With the improvement of computer technology due to the Moore law, the security of DES is no longer appropriate for electronic commerce. The US Government decided to restart a standardization process called the Advanced Encryption Standard (AES)

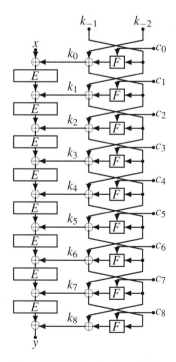

Figure 2.29. External view of CSC.

in 1997. This process was open: anyone was invited to submit a candidate and to send public comments. Fifteen candidates were accepted (a few other submissions did not meet the requirements and were rejected) in 1998. Based on public comments (and apparently on popularity), this pool was downsized to five finalists in 1999. In October 2000, one of these five algorithms was selected as the forthcoming standard: Rijndael (see Refs. [1, 54]).

Rijndael was designed by Joan Daemen (from the Belgium company Proton World International) and Vincent Rijmen. They both originated from the Catholic University of Leuven. Rijndael was designed for the AES process. Following the AES requirements, it encrypts 128-bit blocks with keys of size 128, 192, or 256. It is dedicated to 8-bit micro-processors. It consists of several rounds of a simple substitution–permutation network.

AES is based on the structure of SQUARE.[7] This design simply consists of writing the 128-bit message block as a 4×4 square matrix of bytes. (Formally, Rijndael tolerates other block sizes, but 128-bit was the target block size for AES.) Encryption is performed through 10, 12, or 14 rounds depending on whether the key size is 128, 196, or 256 bits. The number of rounds is denoted by Nr. Each round (but the final one) consists of four simple transformations:

1. SubBytes, a byte-wise substitution defined by a single table of 256 bytes,
2. ShiftRows, a circular shift of all rows (row number i of the matrix is rotated by i positions to the left for $i = 0, 1, 2, 3$),
3. MixColumns, a linear transformation performed on each column and defined by a 4×4 matrix of $GF(2^8)$ elements,
4. AddRoundKey, a simple bitwise XOR with a round key defined by another matrix.

The final round is similar, except for MixColumns which is omitted. The round keys are generated by a separate key schedule.

More formally, one block s is encrypted by the following process, in which w is the output subkey sequence from the key schedule algorithm.

AES encryption(s, W)
 1: **AddRoundKey**(s, W_0)
 2: **for** $r = 1$ to $Nr - 1$ **do**
 3: **SubBytes**(s)
 4: **ShiftRows**(s)
 5: **MixColumns**(s)
 6: **AddRoundKey**(s, W_r)
 7: **end for**
 8: **SubBytes**(s)
 9: **ShiftRows**(s)
 10: **AddRoundKey**(s, W_{Nr})

----

[7] SQUARE was designed by the same authors and Lars Knudsen in 1997 (see Ref. [55]).

The block s is also called state and represented as a matrix of terms $s_{i,j}$ for $i, j \in \{0, 1, 2, 3\}$. Terms are bytes, i.e. elements of a set Z of cardinality 256. SubBytes is defined as follows.

SubBytes(s)
   1: **for** $i = 0$ to 3 **do**
   2:     **for** $j = 0$ to 3 **do**
   3:        $s_{i,j} \leftarrow$ S-box$(s_{i,j})$
   4:     **end for**
   5: **end for**

Here S-box is the substitution table. Mathematically, it is a permutation of $\{0, 1, \ldots, 255\}$. ShiftRows is defined as follows.

ShiftRows(s)
   1: replace $[s_{1,0}, s_{1,1}, s_{1,2}, s_{1,3}]$ by $[s_{1,1}, s_{1,2}, s_{1,3}, s_{1,0}]$
       {rotate row 1 by one position to the left}
   2: replace $[s_{2,0}, s_{2,1}, s_{2,2}, s_{2,3}]$ by $[s_{2,2}, s_{2,3}, s_{2,0}, s_{2,1}]$
       {rotate row 2 by two positions to the left}
   3: replace $[s_{3,0}, s_{3,1}, s_{3,2}, s_{3,3}]$ by $[s_{3,3}, s_{3,0}, s_{3,1}, s_{3,2}]$
       {rotate row 3 by three positions to the left}

We define the set Z as the set of all the 256 possible combinations

$$a_0 + a_1.x + a_2.x^2 + \cdots + a_7.x^7$$

where $a_0, a_1, a_2, \ldots, a_7$ are either 0 or 1 and x is a formal term. Elements of Z are thus defined as polynomials of degree at most 7. AddRoundKey is defined as follows.

AddRoundKey(s, k)
   1: **for** $i = 0$ to 3 **do**
   2:     **for** $j = 0$ to 3 **do**
   3:        $s_{i,j} \leftarrow s_{i,j} \oplus k_{i,j}$
   4:     **end for**
   5: **end for**

Here the $\oplus$ operation over Z is defined as an addition modulo 2, i.e.

$$\left(\sum_{i=0}^{7} a_i.x^i\right) \oplus \left(\sum_{i=0}^{7} b_i.x^i\right) = \sum_{i=0}^{7} (a_i + b_i \bmod 2).x^i.$$

A multiplication $\times$ in Z is further defined as follows.

1. We first perform the regular polynomial multiplication.
2. We make the Euclidean division of the product by the $x^8 + x^4 + x^3 + x + 1$ polynomial and we take the remainder.
3. We reduce all its terms modulo 2.

Later in Chapter 6 we will see that this provides Z with the structure of the unique finite field of 256 elements. This finite field is denoted by $GF(2^8)$. This means that we can add, multiply, or divide by any nonzero element of Z with the same properties that we have with regular numbers. We can further define matrix operations with terms in Z. We can then define MixColumns as follows.

MixColumns(s)
1: **for** $i = 0$ to 3 **do**
2:    let v be the 4-dimensional vector with coordinates $s_{0,i}, s_{1,i} s_{2,i} s_{3,i}$
3:    replace $s_{0,i}, s_{1,i} s_{2,i} s_{3,i}$ by the coordinates of $M \times v$
4: **end for**

Here M is a 4×4-matrix over Z defined by

$$
M = \begin{pmatrix}
x & x+1 & 1 & 1 \\
1 & x & x+1 & 1 \\
1 & 1 & x & x+1 \\
x+1 & 1 & 1 & x
\end{pmatrix}.
$$

The substitution table S-box is defined by the inversion operation x^{-1} (except for $x = 0$ which is mapped to zero) in the finite field $GF(2^8)$. This operation has good nonlinear properties. In order to "break" the algebraic structure of this table, an affine transformation is added on this function.

The linear transformation in MixColumns is defined by a matrix following principles similar to the mixing box of CSC (see Section 2.6.2): whenever i input bytes of this linear transformation are modified, we make sure that this induces a modification of at least $5 - i$ output bytes.[8]

We complete the description of AES by outlining the key expansion. It is easier to consider W as a row sequence (i.e. four bytes) of length 4Nr starting by w_0 and up to w_{4Nr-1}. Hence

$$
W_i = [w_{4i}, w_{4i+1}, w_{4i+2}, w_{4i+3}].
$$

The key expansion proceeds with a key described as a sequence of Nk rows (i.e. Nk is either 4, 6, or 8) starting from key_0. The expansion works as follows.

---

[8] Equivalently, the set of all $(x, M(x))$ 8-byte vectors is an MDS code if M denotes the linear transformation, or in other words, M is a multipermutation.

KeyExpansion(key, Nk)
  1: **for** $i = 0$ to $Nk - 1$ **do**
  2:     $w_i \leftarrow key_i$
  3: **end for**
  4: **for** $i = Nk$ to $4 \times (Nr + 1) - 1$ **do**
  5:     $t \leftarrow w_{i-1}$
  6:     **if** $i \bmod Nk = 0$ **then**
  7:         replace $[t_0, t_1, t_2, t_3]$ by $[t_1, t_2, t_3, t_0]$ in t
  8:         apply S-box to the four bytes of t
  9:         XOR $x^{i/Nk-1}$ (raise the polynomial x to the power $i/Nk - 1$
              in $GF(2^8)$) to the first byte of t
 10:     **else if** $Nk = 8$ and $i \bmod Nk = 4$ **then**
 11:         apply S-box to the four bytes of t
 12:     **end if**
 13:     $w_i \leftarrow w_{i-Nk} \oplus t$
 14: **end for**

2.8   Stream Ciphers

2.8.1   *Stream Ciphers versus Block Ciphers*

All conventional encryption schemes that we have seen so far are block ciphers in the sense that they encrypt blocks of plaintexts. They are often opposed to stream ciphers which encrypt streams of plaintext on the fly. A stream cipher often encrypts streams of plaintext bits, or streams of plaintext bytes. This distinction is often misleading since block ciphers are used as well in a mode of operation so that they can encrypt streams of blocks. Nevertheless, we will call block cipher an encryption scheme in which the underlying primitive is defined on a large finite set (of "blocks") which cannot be enumerated exhaustively in practice. With this definition we cannot assimilate a bit or a byte to a block. Conversely, we call stream cipher an encryption scheme which can encrypt streams of information in a smaller finite set.

First of all we notice that we can transform a pseudorandom generator into a stream cipher. Stream ciphers are indeed often defined by a key-stream generator which is used as a one-time pad: instead of having a large random key for the Vernam cipher, we use a pseudorandom key which is generated as a key-stream.

We also notice that we can transform a block cipher into a stream cipher by using the CFB, or CTR mode, with a small parameter ℓ[9] (see Sections 2.2.3, 2.2.4, and 2.2.5).

2.8.2   *RC4*

RC4 is an encryption algorithm which was designed in 1987 by Ronald Rivest at MIT. It was kept as a commercial secret until it was disclosed in 1994. In particular there is no

---

[9] It is not recommended to do the same for OFB.

patent on RC4, but RC4 is a registered trademark of RSA Data Security. RC4 is widely used, for instance in SSL/TLS (see Section 12.3). In particular, some Internet browsers and servers may use RC4 as a default encryption algorithm for protected transactions.

RC4 works as a finite automaton with an internal *state*. It reads a plaintext as a byte stream and produces a ciphertext as a byte stream. Its heart is actually a key-stream generator which is used for the one-time pad algorithm. In an initialization stage, a secret key is processed without producing keys. The automaton ends up in an internal state which is thus uniquely derived from the secret key only. Then, every time unit, the automaton updates its internal state and produces a key byte which is XORed to a plaintext byte in order to lead to a ciphertext byte.

We consider the set $\{0, 1, \ldots, 255\}$ of all bytes. The internal state consists of two bytes i and j and a permutation S of this set which is encoded as an array $S[0], S[1], \ldots, S[255]$. All operations are done on bytes (i.e. additions are taken modulo 256).

In the initialization, we process a key which is represented as a sequence $K[0], K[1], \ldots, K[\ell - 1]$ of ℓ bytes. The internal state is first initialized as follows. Byte j is set to 0, and the permutation S is set to the identity, i.e. $S[i] = i$ for $i = 0, 1, \ldots, 255$. Key bytes are then iteratively processed, and the bytes i and j are reset to 0.

```
 1: j ← 0
 2: for i = 0 to 255 do
 3:     S[i] ← i
 4: end for
 5: for i = 0 to 255 do
 6:     j ← j + S[i] + K[i mod ℓ]
 7:     swap S[i] and S[j]
 8: end for
 9: i ← 0
10: j ← 0
```

The key size ℓ is typically between 5 and 16 bytes (i.e. between 40 and 256 bits).

It is important that we never use the same state twice. Thus, plaintexts are iteratively encrypted, which means that the initial state for a new plaintext is equal to the final state for the previous plaintext.

The key-stream generator works as follows. Every time unit, we perform the following sequence of instructions.

```
1: i ← i + 1
2: j ← j + S[i]
3: swap S[i] and S[j]
4: output S[S[i] + S[j]]
```

Thus we update i, j, and S, and we output a byte which is given by S at index $S[i] + S[j]$.

2.8.3 A5/1: GSM Encryption

A5/1 is another stream cipher which is part of the A5 family. It is used in the GSM mobile telephone networks. It is used in order to secure phone calls in the radio link from the mobile telephone to the base station. It was designed by the SAGE group of ETSI. The description of A5/1 is another trade secret, but the algorithm was reverse-engineered and published in the Internet. It is commonly admitted that this description is similar to the ETSI one.

A5/1 is also based on a finite automaton with an internal state. As depicted in Fig. 2.30, A5/1 is based on three LFSRs with a mutual clock control. The three registers R_1, R_2, R_3 contain 19, 22, and 23 bits respectively. The internal state thus has $19 + 22 + 23 = 64$ bits. Every time unit, some registers are clocked and some may not be clocked at all. When a register is clocked, it means that its content is shifted by one bit position and that a new bit is pushed. This new bit is the XOR of a few bits of the involved LFSRs.

More precisely, R_1 has 19 bits $R_1[0], \ldots, R_1[18]$. When R_1 is clocked, the content $R_1[0], \ldots, R_1[18]$ is replaced by b, $R_1[0], \ldots, R_1[17]$, i.e. R_1 is shifted by inserting a new bit b which is computed by

$$b = R_1[13] \oplus R_1[16] \oplus R_1[17] \oplus R_1[18].$$

R_2 has 22 bits $R_2[0], \ldots, R_2[21]$. When R_2 is clocked, it is similarly shifted by inserting a new bit

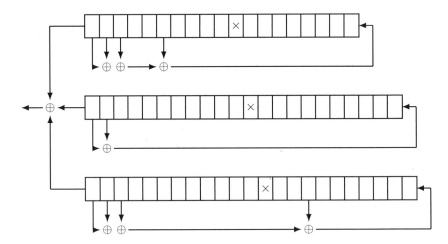

Figure 2.30. A5/1 automaton.

$$b = R_2[20] \oplus R_2[21].$$

R_3 has 23 bits $R_3[0], \ldots, R_3[22]$. When R_3 is clocked, it is similarly shifted by inserting a new bit

$$b = R_3[7] \oplus R_3[20] \oplus R_3[21] \oplus R_3[22].$$

In order to determine which registers to clock, we use three special bits called "clocking taps" from every register, namely $R_1[8]$, $R_2[10]$, and $R_3[10]$. We compute the majority bit among those three bits, and registers whose clocking tap agree with the majority are clocked. Consequently, we are ensured that at least two registers are clocked. All registers are clocked if the three clocking taps agree on the same bit.

Every time unit, a bit is output from this scheme. This output bit is the XOR of the leading bits, namely

$$R_1[18] \oplus R_2[21] \oplus R_3[22].$$

We use the generated key stream as in the one-time pad.

A5/1 also includes an initialization which generates the initial internal state from an encryption key and some GSM parameters. It is required that a new key is set up for any new frame of 114 bits. More precisely, the key is set up from a 64-bit secret key KC and a 22-bit frame number Count. This is indeed a kind of CTR mode. The usage of a secret key KC is thus limited. Because of the structure of the frame number in the GSM standard we can have at most 2.7 million frames for a single key, which corresponds to 4 hours of GSM communication.

The A5/1 initialization works as follows. The three registers are first set to zero. Then every bit of KC is processed in 64 clock cycles by XORing them to the first register cells and stepping all registers (i.e. the clock control is disabled). Every bit of the frame number Count is then processed in a similar way and the A5/1 automaton is run for 100 clock cycles with its clock control enabled (but output bits are discarded).

```
1: set all registers to zero
2: for i = 0 to 63 do
3:     R₁[0] ← R₁[0] ⊕ KC[i]
4:     R₂[0] ← R₂[0] ⊕ KC[i]
5:     R₃[0] ← R₃[0] ⊕ KC[i]
6:     clock all registers
7: end for
8: for i = 0 to 21 do
9:     R₁[0] ← R₁[0] ⊕ Count[i]
10:    R₂[0] ← R₂[0] ⊕ Count[i]
```

11:    $R_3[0] \leftarrow R_3[0] \oplus \text{Count}[i]$
12:    clock all registers
13: **end for**
14: **for** $i = 0$ to 99 **do**
15:    clock the A5/1 automaton
16: **end for**

2.8.4   E0: Bluetooth Encryption

E0 is another stream cipher which is used in the Bluetooth standard (see Ref. [18]).
As in A5/1, E0 is an automaton which generates keystreams which are simply XORed
to the plaintext as in the Vernam cipher. E0 generates one bit every clock cycle and
frames of 2745 bits. After a frame is generated, the E0 automaton is reset to another
state.

The state of the E0 automaton is described by the content of four linear feedback
shift registers $\text{LFSR}_1, \text{LFSR}_2, \text{LFSR}_3, \text{LFSR}_4$ of length $25, 31, 33, 39$ respectively, and
the content of two 2-bit registers c_{t-1} and c_t. Every clock cycle, the four registers are
clocked, c_t, is moved to c_{t-1}, and c_t is updated by using c_{t-1}, c_t, and the registers.

More precisely, one bit x_t^i is output from LFSR_i at every clock cycle. A summator
computes $y_t = x_t^1 + x_t^2 + x_t^3 + x_t^4$ and represents it in binary using three bits $y_t^2 y_t^1 y_t^0$.
The automaton outputs a new keystream bit $z_t = y_t^0 \oplus c_t^0$ where $c_t = c_t^1 c_t^0$. The new
value $c_{t+1} = c_{t+1}^1 c_{t+1}^0$ of c_t is computed by

$$c_{t+1}^1 = s_{t+1}^1 \oplus c_t^1 \oplus c_{t-1}^0$$
$$c_{t+1}^0 = s_{t+1}^0 \oplus c_t^0 \oplus c_{t-1}^1 \oplus c_{t-1}^0$$

where

$$s_{t+1} = \left\lfloor \frac{y_t + c_t}{2} \right\rfloor .$$

E0 is actually a little more complicated. E0 is based on two levels of the above
automaton as depicted in Fig. 2.31. Formally, the encryption algorithm E0 takes the
logical address BD_ADDR of the master (Bluetooth is based on master-slave protocols)
which is represented on 48 bits, the clock value of the master CLK which is represented
on 26 bits, and an encryption key K_c of 128 bits. The first level is used in order to
initialize the automaton for every frame. The second level generates frames with the
initialized automaton. Concretely, the encryption key K_c is first linearly shrunk and
then expanded into a 128-bit key so that the *effective* key length can be lowered for
regulation purposes. Then, the reexpanded encryption key, the master address, and the
master clock enter into the LFSR of the automaton which is clocked. After running
the automaton, 128 bits are output, which serve as the initial value of the second-level

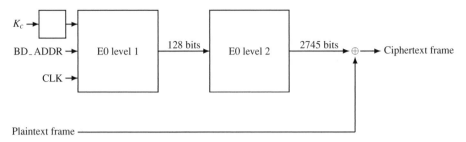

Figure 2.31. The E0 keystream generator.

automaton for producing the keystream frame. Frames are finally used as a keystream in the Vernam cipher.

E0 is very efficient in hardware. Its circuit is depicted in Fig. 2.32. The division by two at the output from the second summator simply consists of dropping one bit. Internal memory bit pairs for c_t and c_{t-1} are represented by the z^{-1} symbol as a clock time delay.

2.9 Brute Force Attacks

We now wonder what kind of security we can expect from symmetric encryption from a generic point of view. Namely, we wonder about performances of generic attacks using brute force which can apply to any encryption algorithm considered as a black box. Security will be measured in terms of the encryption parameters such as the key length and the message space size.

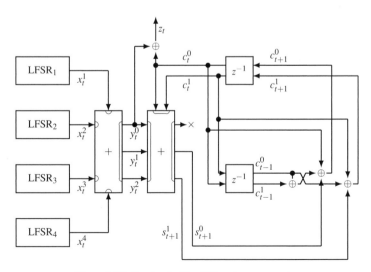

Figure 2.32. One level of the E0 keystream generator.

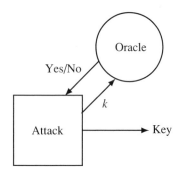

Figure 2.33. Key recovery with a stop test oracle.

2.9.1 Exhaustive Search

Exhaustive search consists of trying all possible keys exhaustively until it is the correct key. We can simplify the attack model by assuming that we have an oracle, which for each key K answers if it is correct or not. The attack is thus a machine which plays with the oracle in order to get some information out of it by sending queries (see Fig. 2.33). Without any more formal notion of a "machine," we can still define the complexity in terms of number of oracle calls.[10] In a cipher with a key space of N possible keys which are uniformly generated, we can prove that the best attack has a worst case complexity of N oracle calls and an average complexity of (about) $\frac{N}{2}$ oracle calls. Clearly, the best attack can be assumed to be deterministic (otherwise, we just take the machine which simulates the best deterministic behavior of the probabilistic machine), and does not query the oracle with twice the same question. Therefore, the best attack can be defined as an ordering of the candidates for the right key. The optimal ordering is defined by the *a priori* distribution of the target key.[11]

In practice we do not know the *a priori* distribution of the target. Thus, if we take a fixed ordering in order to try key candidates, we may fall into the worst case complexity. For this we randomize the ordering of the key candidates. Fig. 2.34 shows a program draft for this attack. In the worst case, the right key is the last one which is sent to the oracle. If the right key is the i-th candidate, the complexity is equal to i. Since the permutation σ is randomly chosen, the probability that the right key is the i-th queried one is $\frac{1}{N}$. Thus the average complexity is

$$\sum_{i=1}^{N} i \, \frac{1}{N} = \frac{N+1}{2}.$$

The ultimate security goal of a cipher with keys of n bits is to have a best attack of complexity $\Omega(2^n)$ with a "not-too-small" work factor.[12]

---

[10] In Chapter 8 we define a formal notion of machine and the notion of complexity of the computation.
[11] See Exercise 2.9 on p. 62.
[12] This Ω notation means that there exists a constant $c > 0$ called work factor such that for any n, the complexity is at least $c2^n$ elementary operations. The notion of complexity is formally defined in Chapter 8.

There is a trick in order to strengthen the security against exhaustive search: make a key schedule complicated. In general, the key schedule is legitimately used only once for many encryptions. Exhaustive search uses the key schedule many times. For instance, BLOWFISH has a complicated key schedule.

Input: an oracle $\mathcal{O}$, a set of possible keys $\mathcal{K} = \{k_1, \ldots, k_N\}$
Oracle interface: input is an element of $\mathcal{K}$, output is Boolean
1: pick a random permutation σ of $\{1, \ldots, N\}$
2: **for** all $i = 1$ to N **do**
3:     **if** $\mathcal{O}(k_{\sigma(i)})$ **then**
4:         yield $k_{\sigma(i)}$ and stop
5:     **end if**
6: **end for**
7: search failed

Figure 2.34. Exhaustive search algorithm.

We can wonder now what the hypothesis about the availability of the oracle really means in practice. We may only have some hints about the key. Namely, we can have some equations that the key must satisfy. Typically, we can assume that we have a plaintext–ciphertext pair so that the key must solve the equation which says that the plaintext encrypts into the ciphertext. Another typical situation is when we intercept a ciphertext and we know that the plaintext has some redundant information, e.g. the plaintext is an English text. If the equations are characteristic enough for the key, the unique solution is the right key candidate so that we can simulate the oracle by equation solution checking.

2.9.2   Dictionary Attack

Another brute force attack is the dictionary attack. A dictionary is a huge table which has been precomputed in order to speed up a key search. In practice, when one looks for the definition of a word, it is too expensive to do it by exhaustive search! For this a dictionary sorts all definitions by using an ordering on a key.

Here is a way to formalize a dictionary attack. We first precompute a list of many $(C_K(x), K)$ pairs for a fixed plaintext x. The first entry $C_K(x)$ is used as an index in order to sort the list as in a dictionary, and the second entry K is the "definition." Then, if we obtain a $C_K(x)$ value (by chosen plaintext attack), we directly have a list of suggested K values. Let M be the number of entries in the dictionary. If K is in a set of N possible keys, and uniformly distributed, the probability of success, i.e. the probability that it is in the dictionary, is M/N. When K is not uniformly distributed, we can focus on a dictionary of the most likely K values. This is done in practice when we try to crack passwords.

We now assume that we have T targets $C_K(x)$ instead of one: there are T secret keys that we try to attack simultaneously and we are interested in getting at least

Input: an encryption scheme C, a fixed message x
Preprocessing
1: **for** M different candidates K **do**
2:     compute $C_K(x)$
3:     insert $(C_K(x), K)$ in a dictionary
4: **end for**
5: output the dictionary
Attack
Attack input: T many values $y_i = C_{K_i}(x)$, a dictionary
6: **for** $i = 1$ to T **do**
7:     look at y_i in the dictionary
8:     **for all** $(C_K(x), K)$ with $C_K(x) = y_i$ **do**
9:         yield i, K
10:    **end for**
11: **end for**

Figure 2.35. Multitarget dictionary attack.

one. (Fig. 2.35 illustrates the program structure.) Let p be the probability of success. Assuming that the target K values are independent and uniformly distributed, we have $1 - p = (1 - M/N)^T$. Hence

$$p \approx 1 - e^{-MT/N}.$$

This becomes quite interesting when $M \approx T \approx \sqrt{N}$. Of course the probability of success increases substantially when the targets are not uniformly distributed and we focus on most likely candidates.

2.9.3 Codebook Attack

Yet another brute force attack is the codebook attack. . It consists of, first, collecting all $(C_K(x), x)$ pairs, then, upon reception of a y to decrypt, look for the entry in the collection for which $y = C_K(x)$. The whole collection of pairs is called the codebook.

2.9.4 ★Time–Memory Tradeoffs

An optimized way to perform exhaustive search is to use a large precomputed table and to make a compromise between time complexity and memory requirements. Here we must consider four parameters: the time to perform the precomputation, the size of the precomputed table, the probability of success when looking for a key, and the time complexity for looking for a key. For the latter parameter, we can also distinguish worst case complexity and average case complexity.

The original method for time-memory tradeoffs was proposed by Martin Hellman in 1980 in order to break DES (see Ref. [88]). We assume that we are looking for a key K for which we know a plaintext–ciphertext pair (x, y) with a fixed x. This fixed x is necessary to prepare the precomputed table. In practice this attack assumption makes sense when the adversary performs a chosen plaintext attack (in order to get y from x) or when the encryption protocol requires that the sender starts by encrypting this fixed message x. We further assume that for all k the bitstrings $C_k(x)$ have the same size which is larger than the key length so that it is likely that values of k for which $y = C_k(x)$ reduce to the unique solution $k = K$.

One first selects an arbitrary "reduction function" R which reduces a bitstring of the size of y to a key candidate $R(y)$. This leads to the definition of a function f

$$f(k) = R(C_k(x))$$

which maps a key candidate to another key candidate so that we can iterate it. The precomputation consists of making a table of m pairs $(k_{i,0}, k_{i,t})$ where all $k_{i,0}$ are randomly selected and $k_{i,t}$ is the t-th term of a sequence $k_{i,j}$ defined by

$$k_{i,j} = f(k_{i,j-1}).$$

(See Fig. 2.36.) In order to look for K once we are given y, we can apply R to y and repeatedly apply f until we find a value which matches one $k_{i,t}$ in the table. If we find one value $k_{i,t}$, we can get $k_{i,0}$ from the table and apply f repeatedly until we find $R(y)$ again. Note that if the total number of f applications reaches $t - 1$ without success we can give up and the attack fails. Otherwise we find a key k such that $f(k) = R(y)$. This may be due to $C_k(x) = y$, which leads to $K = k$. Otherwise the attack fails. Figs. 2.37 and 2.38 with ℓ set to 1 illustrate this method.

$$
\begin{array}{c|c|ccccccccccc|c|cc}
\cline{2-2}\cline{14-14}
 & k^1_{1,0} & \overset{f_1}{\mapsto} & k^1_{1,1} & \overset{f_1}{\mapsto} & k^1_{1,2} & \overset{f_1}{\mapsto} & k^1_{1,3} & \overset{f_1}{\mapsto} & \cdots & \overset{f_1}{\mapsto} & k^1_{1,t-1} & \overset{f_1}{\mapsto} & k^1_{1,t} & & (k^1_{1,t}, k^1_{1,0}) \\
 & k^1_{2,0} & \overset{f_1}{\mapsto} & k^1_{2,1} & \overset{f_1}{\mapsto} & k^1_{2,2} & \overset{f_1}{\mapsto} & k^1_{2,3} & \overset{f_1}{\mapsto} & \cdots & \overset{f_1}{\mapsto} & k^1_{2,t-1} & \overset{f_1}{\mapsto} & k^1_{2,t} & & (k^1_{2,t}, k^1_{2,0}) \\
T_1: & k^1_{3,0} & \overset{f_1}{\mapsto} & k^1_{3,1} & \overset{f_1}{\mapsto} & k^1_{3,2} & \overset{f_1}{\mapsto} & k^1_{3,3} & \overset{f_1}{\mapsto} & \cdots & \overset{f_1}{\mapsto} & k^1_{3,t-1} & \overset{f_1}{\mapsto} & k^1_{3,t} & \Rightarrow & (k^1_{3,t}, k^1_{3,0}) \\
 & \vdots & & \vdots & & \vdots & & \vdots & & \vdots & & \vdots & & \vdots & & \vdots \\
 & k^1_{m,0} & \overset{f_1}{\mapsto} & k^1_{m,1} & \overset{f_1}{\mapsto} & k^1_{m,2} & \overset{f_1}{\mapsto} & k^1_{m,3} & \overset{f_1}{\mapsto} & \cdots & \overset{f_1}{\mapsto} & k^1_{3,t-1} & \overset{f_1}{\mapsto} & k^1_{m,t} & & (k^1_{m,t}, k^1_{m,0}) \\
\cline{2-2}\cline{14-14}
\end{array}
$$

$$\vdots$$

$$
\begin{array}{c|c|ccccccccccc|c|cc}
\cline{2-2}\cline{14-14}
 & k^\ell_{1,0} & \overset{f_\ell}{\mapsto} & k^\ell_{1,1} & \overset{f_\ell}{\mapsto} & k^\ell_{1,2} & \overset{f_\ell}{\mapsto} & k^\ell_{1,3} & \overset{f_\ell}{\mapsto} & \cdots & \overset{f_\ell}{\mapsto} & k^\ell_{1,t-1} & \overset{f_\ell}{\mapsto} & k^\ell_{1,t} & & (k^\ell_{1,t}, k^\ell_{1,0}) \\
 & k^\ell_{2,0} & \overset{f_\ell}{\mapsto} & k^\ell_{2,1} & \overset{f_\ell}{\mapsto} & k^\ell_{2,2} & \overset{f_\ell}{\mapsto} & k^\ell_{2,3} & \overset{f_\ell}{\mapsto} & \cdots & \overset{f_\ell}{\mapsto} & k^\ell_{2,t-1} & \overset{f_\ell}{\mapsto} & k^\ell_{2,t} & & (k^\ell_{2,t}, k^\ell_{2,0}) \\
T_\ell: & k^\ell_{3,0} & \overset{f_\ell}{\mapsto} & k^\ell_{3,1} & \overset{f_\ell}{\mapsto} & k^\ell_{3,2} & \overset{f_\ell}{\mapsto} & k^\ell_{3,3} & \overset{f_\ell}{\mapsto} & \cdots & \overset{f_\ell}{\mapsto} & k^\ell_{3,t-1} & \overset{f_\ell}{\mapsto} & k^\ell_{3,t} & \Rightarrow & (k^\ell_{3,t}, k^\ell_{3,0}) \\
 & \vdots & & \vdots & & \vdots & & \vdots & & \vdots & & \vdots & & \vdots & & \vdots \\
 & k^\ell_{m,0} & \overset{f_\ell}{\mapsto} & k^\ell_{m,1} & \overset{f_\ell}{\mapsto} & k^\ell_{m,2} & \overset{f_\ell}{\mapsto} & k^\ell_{m,3} & \overset{f_\ell}{\mapsto} & \cdots & \overset{f_\ell}{\mapsto} & k^\ell_{3,t-1} & \overset{f_\ell}{\mapsto} & k^\ell_{m,t} & & (k^\ell_{m,t}, k^\ell_{m,0}) \\
\cline{2-2}\cline{14-14}
\end{array}
$$

Figure 2.36. Table for Time–Memory tradeoff.

Input: an encryption scheme C, a fixed message x
Parameter: ℓ, m, t
Preprocessing
1: **for** $s = 1$ to ℓ **do**
2:    pick a reduction function R_s at random and define $f_s : k \mapsto R_s(C_k(x))$
3:    **for** $i = 1$ to m **do**
4:        pick k' at random
5:        $k \leftarrow k'$
6:        **for** $j = 1$ to t **do**
7:            compute $k \leftarrow f_s(k)$
8:        **end for**
9:        insert (k, k') in table T_s
10:   **end for**
11: **end for**

Figure 2.37. Time–Memory tradeoff (Preprocessing).

Attack
Attack input: $y = C_K(x)$
1: **for** $s = 1$ to ℓ **do**
2:    set i to 0
3:    set k to $R_s(y)$
4:    **while** T_s contains no $(k, .)$ entry and $i < t$ **do**
5:        increment i
6:        $k \leftarrow f_s(k)$
7:    **end while**
8:    **if** T_s contains a $(k, .)$ entry **then**
9:        get the (k, k') entry from table T_s
10:      **while** $C_{k'}(x) \neq y$ and $i < t$ **do**
11:        increment i
12:        $k' \leftarrow f_s(k')$
13:      **end while**
14:      **if** $C_{k'}(x) = y$ **then**
15:        yield k'
16:      **end if**
17:    **end if**
18: **end for**
19: abort: the attack failed

Figure 2.38. Time-Memory tradeoff (Attack).

We can estimate the number of pairwise different $k_{i,j}$ in one table as follows.

$$E\left(\#\{k_{i,j}; 1 \le i \le m, 0 \le j < t\}\right) = \sum_{i=1}^{m} \sum_{j=0}^{t-1} \Pr\left[k_{i,j} \notin \{k_{i',j'}; i' < i \text{ or } j' < j\}\right].$$

(We do not count the end value of each chain.) Let $\text{Fresh}_{i,j}$ be the event $\left[k_{i,j} \notin \{k_{i',j'}; i' < i \text{ or } j' < j\}\right]$. Since $k_{i,j} = f(k_{i,j-1})$, we have $\text{Fresh}_{i,j} \subseteq \text{Fresh}_{i,j-1}$. Furthermore, we have

$$\Pr\left[\text{Fresh}_{i,j} | \text{Fresh}_{i,j-1}\right] \ge 1 - \frac{it}{2^n}.$$

Hence we have

$$\Pr\left[\text{Fresh}_{i,j}\right] \ge \left(1 - \frac{it}{2^n}\right)^{j+1}.$$

We deduce that the expected number of keys per table is greater than

$$\sum_{i=1}^{m} \sum_{j=0}^{t-1} \left(1 - \frac{it}{2^n}\right)^{j+1}.$$

The probability of success for looking for K is the probability that K is one of the keys in the table. Thus we have

$$p \ge 2^{-n} \sum_{i=1}^{m} \sum_{j=0}^{t-1} \left(1 - \frac{it}{2^n}\right)^{j+1}.$$

As the table gets larger, some chain will eventually collide and merge, which prevents the number of keys per table from increasing. So it may be preferable to keep many small tables. Figs. 2.37, and 2.38 illustrate the multitable version. Obviously the precomputation complexity is $P = \ell m t$ encryptions and reductions. The time complexity of the attack is $T = \ell t$ encryptions and reductions in the worst case, and $T_e = \frac{\ell}{2} t$ in the average case (for success only). The memory size is about $M = \ell m$ blocks. The probability p of success is such that

$$p \ge 1 - \left(1 - 2^{-n} \sum_{i=1}^{m} \sum_{j=0}^{t-1} \left(1 - \frac{it}{2^n}\right)^{j+1}\right)^{\ell}.$$

We let $x = 2^{\frac{n}{3}}$ and $1 - e^{-L}$ be the right-hand term of the p inequality. For $\ell = \lambda x$, $m = \mu x$, and $t = \tau x$, when $\mu \tau \ll x$, we have

$$L = -\lambda x \log\left(1 - x^{-3} \sum_{i=1}^{\mu x} \sum_{j=0}^{\tau x - 1} \left(1 - \frac{it}{x^2}\right)^{j+1}\right)$$

$$\approx \frac{\lambda}{x^2} \sum_{i=1}^{\mu x} \sum_{j=0}^{\tau x-1} \left(1 - \frac{i\tau}{x^2}\right)^{j+1}$$

$$= \frac{\lambda}{\tau} \sum_{i=1}^{\mu x} \frac{1}{i} \left(1 - \left(1 - \frac{i\tau}{x^2}\right)^{\tau x}\right)\left(1 - \frac{i\tau}{x^2}\right)$$

$$\approx \frac{\lambda}{\tau} \sum_{i=1}^{\mu x} \frac{1}{i} \left(1 - e^{-\frac{i\tau^2}{x}}\right)$$

$$\approx \frac{\lambda}{\tau} \int_0^{\mu\tau^2} \frac{1 - e^{-t}}{t} \, dt.$$

(Note that this is equivalent to $\frac{\lambda}{\tau} \log(\mu\tau^2)$ when $\mu\tau^2$ increases, so that $p \geq 1 - (\mu\tau^2)^{-\frac{\lambda}{\tau}}$ when μ and τ are large enough.) With $\ell \approx m \approx t \approx 2^{\frac{n}{3}}$ we obtain $P \approx 2^n$, $T \approx M \approx 2^{2n/3}$, and $p \geq 0.549$.

There exist several improvements of this technique, e.g. using the notion of "distinguished points." The most efficient so far uses the notion of "rainbow tables" and is due to Philippe Oechslin (see Ref. [142]). Here, instead of using many tables with one reduction function in each, we use a larger table with many reduction functions (see Fig. 2.39). We define

$$k_{i,j} = f_j(k_{i,j-1}).$$

The algorithm is depicted in Figs. 2.40, 2.41.

Here we make sure that no chains collide in the precomputation. This induces an overhead in the precomputation. At the i-th iteration the probability for a new chain to collide is approximately $1 - e^{-t\frac{i-1}{2^n}}$, so the precomputation complexity is

$$P \approx \sum_{i=1}^{m} te^{t\frac{i-1}{2^n}} = t\frac{e^{\frac{mt}{2^n}} - 1}{e^{\frac{t}{2^n}} - 1} \approx 2^n \left(e^{\frac{mt}{2^n}} - 1\right).$$

The probability of a key being in a column is $m.2^{-n}$ so

$$p = 1 - (1 - m.2^{-n})^t$$

$$T: \begin{array}{|c|ccccccc|c|}
\hline
k_{1,0} & \xrightarrow{f_1} & k_{1,1} & \xrightarrow{f_2} & k_{1,2} & \xrightarrow{f_3} & k_{1,3} & \xrightarrow{f_4} \cdots \xrightarrow{f_{t-1}} & k_{1,t-1} & \xrightarrow{f_t} & k_{1,t} \\
k_{2,0} & \xrightarrow{f_1} & k_{2,1} & \xrightarrow{f_2} & k_{2,2} & \xrightarrow{f_3} & k_{2,3} & \xrightarrow{f_4} \cdots \xrightarrow{f_{t-1}} & k_{2,t-1} & \xrightarrow{f_t} & k_{2,t} \\
k_{3,0} & \xrightarrow{f_1} & k_{3,1} & \xrightarrow{f_2} & k_{3,2} & \xrightarrow{f_3} & k_{3,3} & \xrightarrow{f_4} \cdots \xrightarrow{f_{t-1}} & k_{3,t-1} & \xrightarrow{f_t} & k_{3,t} \\
\vdots & & \vdots & & \vdots & & \vdots & & \vdots & & \vdots \\
k_{m,0} & \xrightarrow{f_1} & k_{m,1} & \xrightarrow{f_2} & k_{m,2} & \xrightarrow{f_3} & k_{m,3} & \xrightarrow{f_4} \cdots \xrightarrow{f_{t-1}} & k_{3,t-1} & \xrightarrow{f_t} & k_{m,t} \\
\hline
\end{array}
\begin{array}{c}
(k_{1,t}, k_{1,0}) \\
(k_{2,t}, k_{2,0}) \\
\Rightarrow \quad (k_{3,t}, k_{3,0}) \\
\vdots \\
(k_{m,t}, k_{m,0})
\end{array}$$

Figure 2.39. Rainbow table.

Input: an encryption scheme C, a fixed message x

Parameter: m, t

Preprocessing

1: **for** $j = 1$ to t **do**
2:     pick a reduction function R_j at random and define $f_j : k \mapsto R_j(C_k(x))$
3: **end for**
4: **for** $i = 1$ to m **do**
5:     **repeat**
6:         pick k' at random
7:         $k \leftarrow k'$
8:         **for** $j = 1$ to t **do**
9:             compute $k \leftarrow f_j(k)$
10:         **end for**
11:     **until** T contains no $(k, .)$ entry
12:     insert (k, k') in table T
13: **end for**

Figure 2.40. Time–Memory tradeoff with a rainbow table (Preprocessing).

$$\approx 1 - e^{-\frac{mt}{2^n}}.$$

The time complexity of the attack is $T = \frac{t^2}{2}$ encryptions and reductions in the worst case, and $T_e = \frac{t^2}{8}$ in the average case (for success only). The memory size is about $M = m$ blocks. With $m = 2^{\frac{2n}{3}}$ and $t = (\log 2)2^{\frac{n}{3}} \approx 0.693 \times 2^{\frac{n}{3}}$ we obtain $P \approx 2^n$, $M \approx 2^{\frac{2n}{3}}$, $T \approx 0.240 \times 2^{\frac{2n}{3}}$, and $p \approx \frac{1}{2}$. This is a substantial improvement.

To summarize brute force generic attacks, we list in the following table the *essential* complexity of each part of the attack for a probability of success close to one.

Strategy	Preprocessing	Memory	Time
Exhaustive search	1	1	N
Dictionary attack	N	N	1
Tradeoffs	N	$N^{\frac{2}{3}}$	$N^{\frac{2}{3}}$

2.9.5 Meet-in-the-Middle Attack

In order to strengthen DES, people first tried to make a simple product with itself, resulting in a double-DES (see Section 2.3.1). More generally, we have

$$C_{K_1 K_2}(X) = C''_{K_2}\left(C'_{K_1}(X)\right).$$

Attack

Attack input: $y = C_K(x)$

1: **for** $i = t$ down to 1 **do**
2:      set k to $R_i(y)$
3:      **for** $j = i$ to t **do**
4:          $k \leftarrow f_j(k)$
5:      **end for**
6:      **if** T contains one $(k, .)$ entry **then**
7:          get the (k, k') entry from table T
8:          **for** $s = 1$ to $i - 1$ **do**
9:              $k' \leftarrow f_s(k')$
10:         **end for**
11:         **if** $C_{k'}(x) = y$ **then**
12:             yield k'
13:             abort: the attack succeeded
14:         **end if**
15:     **end if**
16: **end for**
17: abort: the attack failed

Figure 2.41. Time–Memory tradeoff with a rainbow table (Attack).

If C' and C'' have key spaces of N' and N'' keys respectively, the ultimate security goal is to have a security related to a minimal complexity of $N = N' \times N''$. This goal is not achieved as shown by the following attack. The attack is called "meet-in-the-middle attack" and was devised by Ralph Merkle and Martin Hellman in 1981 (see Ref. [133]).

As illustrated in Fig. 2.42, let us consider a known plaintext attack: we know a (x, y) pair such that $y = C_{K_1 K_2}(x)$. The meet-in-the-middle attack consists of making a table of all possible $C_{K_1}(x)$ (which is of size N'), and for all possible K_2, in computing $C_{K_2}^{-1}(y)$ and looking for the value in the table. This will suggest a list of possible $K_1 K_2$ keys which can be tried with other known plaintexts (see Fig. 2.43). The complexity is $N' + N''$ instead of N. Therefore doubling the structure is not a good paradigm for strengthening the security.

2.10 Exercises

Exercise 2.1. *Prove that*

$$\mathrm{DES}_{\overline{K}}(\overline{x}) = \overline{\mathrm{DES}_K(x)}.$$

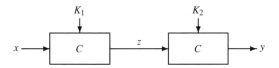

Figure 2.42. Meet-in-the-Middle.

Input: two encryption schemes C' and C'' with two corresponding sets
   of possible keys $\mathcal{K}'$ and $\mathcal{K}''$, an (x, y) pair with $y = C''_{K_2}(C'_{K_1}(x))$
1: **for** all $k_1 \in \mathcal{K}'$ **do**
2:     compute $z = C'_{k_1}(x)$
3:     insert (z, k_1) in a hash table (indexed with the first entry)
4: **end for**
5: **for** all $k_2 \in \mathcal{K}''$ **do**
6:     compute $z = C''^{-1}_{k_2}(y)$
7:     **for** all (z, k_1) in the hash table **do**
8:         yield (k_1, k_2)
9:     **end for**
10: **end for**

Figure 2.43. Meet-in-the-middle attack.

Deduce a brute force attack against DES with average complexity 2^{54} DES encryptions.[13]

Exercise 2.2. *We say that a DES key K is weak if DES_K is an involution. Exhibit four weak keys for DES.*

Exercise 2.3. *We say that a DES key K is semi-weak if it is not weak and if there exists K' such that*

$$\mathrm{DES}_K^{-1} = \mathrm{DES}_{K'}.$$

Exhibit four semi-weak keys for DES.[14]

Exercise 2.4. *In CBC Mode, show that an opponent can replace one ciphertext block so that the decryption will let all plaintext blocks but x_i and x_{i+1} unchanged.*

Exercise 2.5. *Describe how the OFB decryption is performed.*

Describe how the CFB decryption is performed.

Exercise 2.6. *Prove that the multiplication over nonzero residues modulo $2^{16} + 1$ defines a group operation over a set of 2^{16} elements.*

We represent nonzero residues modulo $2^{16} + 1$ with their modulo 2^{16} reduction. (This means that "1" represents 1, "2" represents 2, etc., and "0" represents 2^{16}.)

Explain how to efficiently implement this operation in software from regular CPU operations. (This operation is used in IDEA.)

Exercise 2.7. *Show that $x \mapsto (45^x \bmod 257) \bmod 256$ is a permutation over $\{0, \ldots, 255\}$. (This permutation is used as a substitution box in SAFER K-64.)*

---

[13] This exercise was inspired by Ref. [89].
[14] This exercise was inspired by Ref. [89].

Exercise 2.8. *We want to break a keyed cryptographic system. We assume we have access to an oracle which on each queried key answer whether or not the key is correct. We iteratively query the oracle with randomly selected keys (in an independent way). Compute the expected complexity (in term of oracle queries) in general, and when the distribution of the key is uniform. How can we improve the attack?*

Exercise 2.9. *We assume that we have an oracle which for any of the N possible keys K answers if it is correct or not.*

If the a priori distribution of the keys is not uniform but known by the adversary, what is the best algorithm for finding the key with the oracle? Prove that its complexity relates to the guesswork which is defined by

$$W(K) = \sum_{i=1}^{N} i . \Pr[K = k_i]$$

where all possible keys $k_1, \ldots, k_N$ are sorted such that the $\Pr[K = k_i]$ sequence is decreasing.[15]

As an example, let us consider a pseudorandom generator which generates an element x of $\{0, 1, \ldots, p - 1\}$ uniformly for a given prime number p. In order to get a random n-bit string, we consider $K = x \bmod 2^n$.

1. *Compute $W(K)$ for $p > 2^n$. Example: $n = 64$ and $p = 2^{64} + 13$.*
2. *Compute $W(K)$ for $p < 2^n$. Example: $n = 64$ and $p = 2^{64} - 59$.*
3. *Let $\Delta = |p - 2^n|$. Express $W(K)$ in terms of Δ and compare both cases.*

Exercise 2.10. *Explain how to make a dictionary attack against UNIX passwords. What is the complexity?*

Exercise 2.11. *We assume that we have an oracle which for any of the N possible keys K answers if it is correct or not.*

If the a priori distribution of the keys is not uniform but known by the adversary, what is the best memoryless algorithm for finding the key with the oracle? Prove that its complexity relates to the Renyi entropy of coefficient $\frac{1}{2}$ which is defined by

$$H_{\frac{1}{2}}(K) = \left(\sum_{i=1}^{N} \sqrt{\Pr[K = k_i]} \right)^2$$

where $k_1, \ldots, k_N$ is the list of all possible keys.[16]

[15] This exercise was inspired by Ref. [123].
[16] This exercise was inspired by Ref. [39].

3

Dedicated Conventional Cryptographic Primitives

Content

Hash functions: MD5, SHA, SHA-1
Generic attack against hash funtions: birthday paradox
⋆Analysis of hash functions: dedicated attack against MD4
Message authentication codes: CBC-MAC, HMAC
⋆Pseudorandom generator: congruential generator

In Chapter 2 we saw several conventional encryption algorithms. They were dedicated to *confidentiality*. In this chapter we study other conventional cryptographic primitives that are dedicated to *integrity*, *authentication*, and *randomness*.

3.1 Cryptographic Hashing

3.1.1 Usage

In computer science, hash functions are used in order to arrange a database so one of its element can be accessed very efficiently. An entry is usually a pair (x, y) where x is the entry label and y is data. It is stored at the location $h(x)$ in the database. Later on, if we want to have access to data related to the label x, we just look at the location $h(x)$. Problems arise when we have two different labels x and x' such that $h(x) = h(x')$. This is called a *collision*. Efficient hash functions are functions whose domain space is small and whose *expected* number of collisions is small in practical applications.

In cryptography, hash functions are used to protect the *integrity* of data: instead of protecting the integrity of data of arbitrary length, we want to concentrate on protecting the integrity of really small bitstrings. Thus, we need to hash the data onto a string of fixed length which is called the *hashed value*, or the *message digest*, or the *fingerprint*, or even (improperly) the *cyclical redundancy check* (CRC). CRCs are used for error detection, but "cryptographic CRCs" are different: here the adversary is assumed to be malicious and no longer a random noise process. Assuming we succeed in protecting the integrity of the hashed value, we can detect if the data has been modified by hashing it again and comparing the two hashed values. We can thus use an expensive integrity channel in order to provide integrity over an insecure channel (see Fig. 3.1).

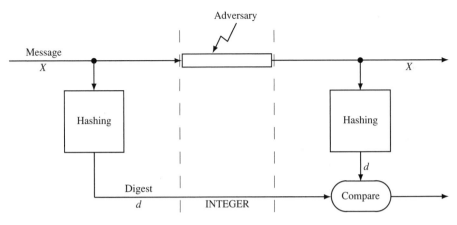

Figure 3.1. Integrity channel.

Cryptographic hash functions are sometimes called *manipulation detection codes* (MDC).

For security, we have to ensure that a change in the data content without a change in the hashed result is an impossible scenario. Actually, the forgery of two different data with the same hashed value must be intractable. Therefore, we need the collisions to be intractable. We improperly say that the hash function is *collision-free*. This qualification is improper because collisions do exist. They are simply hard to find. A more correct way is to say that it is *collision-resistant*. The difference between cryptographic hash functions and regular hash functions (which are used in the hash table data structure) is that collisions are intractable for a malicious adversary instead of just being unlikely events.

Cryptographic hash functions are also used for *commitment*. Someone who wants to commit on data x without revealing it (for instance a bid for a contract) can just reveal $h(x||r)$ where r is a random string. He can later open the commitment by revealing x and r. In this case, we need the hash function to be one-way: we need that given $h(x||r)$, it is intractable to recover x or any information about x.

3.1.2   Threat Models

As we had several classical attack models for block ciphers (like known or chosen plaintext attacks), here are three important attack models for cryptographic hash functions.

First preimage attack: from a fixed y we try to get x such that $h(x) = y$.
Second preimage attack: from a fixed x we try to get $x' \neq x$ such that $h(x) = h(x')$.
Collision: we try to get $x' \neq x$ such that $h(x) = h(x')$.

Depending on the application, these attack models are relevant or not.

In the integrity protection scenario, the goal of the adversary is to replace a given message x by another message x' with the same hashed value. This clearly corresponds to the second preimage attack.

In the commitment scenario, the participant who commits to x may try to cheat by replacing x by a different x' with the same hashed value before opening the commitment. In this case he has control on x so he can also choose it. Hence this corresponds to the collision attack scenario. The other participant of the commitment scheme may try to retrieve information about x from the commitment. This is a kind of first preimage attack.

So, as we can see, many security properties may be required for hash functions depending on the threat model.

As usual, it is pretty hard to formally define these security properties. From the viewpoint of complexity theory, we should consider families of hash functions instead of a single one engraved in stone. In practice, the hash function is really fixed and we consider an intuitive notion of security.

3.1.3   From Compression to Hashing

A classical cryptographic hash function design, due independently to Ralph Merkle and Ivan Damgård, consists of iterating a *compression function*. As with encryption, which can be based on a block cipher by using a mode of operation, we can construct a cryptographic hash function from a compression function. Here, a compression function is a function which takes fixed length inputs and returns a fixed length output (which is shorter than the total input length).

For instance, the MD5 cryptographic compression function (see below) has two inputs, H of length 128 bits and B of length 512 bits, and outputs a 128-bit string. As depicted in Fig. 3.2, hashing an arbitrary length message M proceeds as follows.

1. We pad M with one bit equal to 1, followed by a variable number of zero bits, and 64 bits encoding the length of M in bits, so that the total length of the padded message is the smallest possible multiple of 512 (see Fig. 3.3). Let $\bar{M}$ denote the *padded message*.
2. We cut $\bar{M}$ into a sequence of 512-bit blocks $B_1, \ldots, B_n$.
3. We let $H_0 = \text{IV}$, a fixed *initial value*.

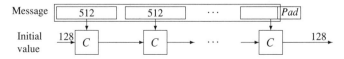

Figure 3.2. The Merkle–Damgård scheme.

Figure 3.3. Padding in the Merkle–Damgård scheme.

4. For $i = 1, \ldots, n$, we let $H_i = C(H_{i-1}, B_i)$.
5. We define $H_n = h(M)$.

We notice that this construction restricts to messages of size less than 2^{64} bits. In practice this is not a problem since this represents $2'097'152$ Tera Bytes, which cannot be managed with current technology.

Theorem 3.1 (Merkle–Damgård 1989 [56, 130]). *With the above construction, if the compression function C is collision-resistant, then the hash function h is collision-resistant as well.*

Proof. If we can construct a collision for the hash function $h(M) = h(M')$, let $\bar{M} = B_1, \ldots, B_n$ and $\bar{M}' = B_1', \ldots, B_{n'}'$. We also define H_i and H_j' following the above scheme. We have $H_n = H_{n'}'$. Thus we have $C(H_{n-1}, B_n) = C(H_{n'-1}', B_{n'}')$. Either this is a collision on the compression function, or the inputs are equal. If this is the case, then we have $B_n = B_{n'}'$, but since the last block includes the length of the messages, M and M' have the same length, thus $n = n'$. We also have $H_{n-1} = H_{n-1}'$, thus $C(H_{n-2}, B_{n-1}) = C(H_{n-2}', B_{n-1}')$. We continue the proof the same way. Since the messages are different, we must have $B_i \neq B_i'$ at some point. Thus we must get a collision on the compression function. ☐

3.1.4 Example of MD5

MD5 is a famous cryptographic hash function example. It is widely used in Internet applications. It was designed by Ronald Rivest at MIT in 1991 and published as the RFC 1321 Internet standard in 1992 (Ref. [157]). It hashes arbitrary length bitstrings onto 128 bits. MD5 stands for "Message Digest," and is based on a previous algorithm, MD4. It uses the Merkle-Damgård construction from a $128 \times 512 \rightarrow 128$ compression function.[1]

The compression function is made from an "encryption function" by the Davies-Meyer scheme: given an "encryption function" C_0 which maps a 128-bit value $H = (A, B, C, D)$ and a 512-bit key block B into a 128-bit value, we define

$$C(H, B) = C_0(H, B) + (A, B, C, D)$$

where the addition here is the word-wise addition modulo 2^{32}.

---

[1] Note that some collisions on MD5 were exhibited at the CRYPTO'04 conference by Xiaoyun Wang and Xuejia Lai. This means that MD5 should no longer be considered as a secure hash function and should be replaced in most existing standards.

The encryption C_0 consists of four rounds as depicted in Fig. 3.4: the message block (key block) is permuted into a sequence $x_0, \ldots, x_{15}$ following a permutation which depends on the round number, and every of the four input words is sequentially transformed through a generalized four-branch Feistel scheme. Each transformation is defined by a box with a main input a, a key input x, and three side inputs b, c, and d as shown in Fig. 3.5.

The output of the transformation box is

$$\text{ROTL}^{\alpha_{i,j}}(a + f_i(b, c, d) + x + k_{i,j}) + b$$

where $\alpha_{i,j}$ and $k_{i,j}$ are defined by a table, ROTL is the bitwise rotation to the left (by a number of position specified as a superscript), and f_i is a bitwise Boolean function defined by

$$f_1(b, c, d) = \text{if } b \text{ then } c \text{ else } d$$
$$f_2(b, c, d) = \text{if } d \text{ then } b \text{ else } c$$
$$f_3(b, c, d) = b \text{ XOR } c \text{ XOR } d$$
$$f_4(b, c, d) = c \text{ XOR } (b \text{ AND } (\text{NOT } d))$$

where the "if ... then ... else" function is defined by

$$\text{if } b \text{ then } c \text{ else } d = (b \text{ AND } c) \text{ OR } ((\text{NOT } b) \text{ AND } d).$$

3.1.5 Examples of SHA and SHA-1

SHA is another famous cryptographic hash function example. SHA stands for "Secure Hash Algorithm". It was published by the US Government as the FIPS 180 standard (Ref. [15]) in 1993. It is based on MD5 and is mainly used in digital signature schemes. It hashes onto 160 bits and uses the Merkle-Damgård construction from a $160 \times 512 \rightarrow 160$ compression function. The original version was replaced by a slightly different one, SHA-1, in 1995 (see the FIPS 180-1 standard, Ref. [16], which is now superseded by the FIPS 180-2 standard, Ref. [17]). There was no justification for this replacement (just a mention about security problems). However, Florent Chabaud and Antoine Joux, from the French Department of Defense, publicly raised a weakness of the original SHA which seemed to have disappeared in SHA-1 (see Ref. [43]). Antoine Joux later announced to have found a collision on the original SHA.[2] As for MD5, the compression functions of SHA and SHA-1 are made from an "encryption function" by the Davies-Meyer scheme: given an "encryption function" C_0 which maps 160-bit value $H = (A, B, C, D, E)$ and a 512-bit key block $B = (x_0, \ldots, x_{15})$ into a 160-bit

---

[2] The collision was announced at the CRYPTO'04 conference, surprisingly at the same time that a collision on MD5 was found.

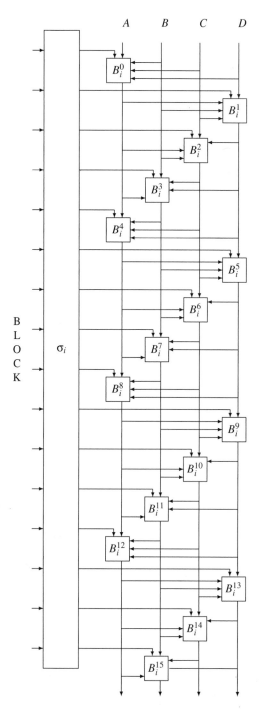

Figure 3.4. One round of MD5.

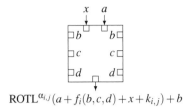

$$\text{ROTL}^{\alpha_{i,j}}(a + f_i(b,c,d) + x + k_{i,j}) + b$$

Figure 3.5. Transformation box in MD5.

value, we define

$$C(H, B) = C_0(H, B) + (A, B, C, D, E)$$

where the addition here is the word-wise addition modulo 2^{32}.

The encryption C_0 consists of four rounds, each consisting of 20 transformation steps. The message block (key block) is expanded following a linear relation, and every of the five input words is sequentially transformed through a generalized five-branch Feistel scheme. Each transformation is defined by a box with a main input a, a key input x, and four side inputs b, c, d, and e. More precisely, C is defined by the algorithm depicted in Fig. 3.6.

Input: an initial hashed value a, b, c, d, e, a message block $x_0, \ldots, x_{15}$
Output: a hash a, b, c, d, e
  1: **for** $i = 16$ to 79 **do**
  2:    $x_i \leftarrow \text{ROTL}^1 (x_{i-3} \text{ XOR } x_{i-8} \text{ XOR } x_{i-14} \text{ XOR } x_{i-16})$
  3: **end for**
  4: **for** $i = 1$ to 4 **do**
  5:    **for** $j = 0$ to 19 **do**
  6:       $t \leftarrow \text{ROTL}^5(a) + f_i(b, c, d) + e + x_{20(i-1)+j} + k_i$
  7:       $e \leftarrow d$
  8:       $d \leftarrow c$
  9:       $c \leftarrow \text{ROTL}^{30}(b)$
10:       $b \leftarrow a$
11:       $a \leftarrow t$
12:    **end for**
13: **end for**
14: $a \leftarrow a + a_{\text{initial}}$
15: $b \leftarrow b + b_{\text{initial}}$
16: $c \leftarrow c + c_{\text{initial}}$
17: $d \leftarrow d + d_{\text{initial}}$
18: $e \leftarrow e + e_{\text{initial}}$

Figure 3.6. Compression in SHA-1.

Each transformation layer uses an f_i function and a k_i constant. f_i is a bitwise Boolean function defined by

$$f_1(b, c, d) = \text{if } b \text{ then } c \text{ else } d$$
$$f_2(b, c, d) = b \text{ XOR } c \text{ XOR } d$$
$$f_3(b, c, d) = \text{majority}(b, c, d)$$
$$f_4(b, c, d) = b \text{ XOR } c \text{ XOR } d$$

where the majority function is defined by

$$\text{majority}(b, c, d) = (b \text{ AND } c) \text{ OR } (c \text{ AND } d) \text{ OR } (d \text{ AND } b).$$

(As a Boolean function, if two bits out of b, c, and d are equal, then majority(b, c, d) is equal to that bit.)

As previously mentioned, the difference between SHA and SHA-1 is little. SHA has exactly the same compression function except for the "key schedule" which is replaced by

1: **for** $i = 16$ to 79 **do**
2:     $x_i \leftarrow x_{i-3} \text{ XOR } x_{i-8} \text{ XOR } x_{i-14} \text{ XOR } x_{i-16}$
3: **end for**

with the ROTL rotation missing!

For completeness we mention that the the US standard on secure hash algorithms also includes four other algorithms called SHA224, SHA256, SHA384, and SHA512 (see Ref. [17]). These four algorithms are quite similar, and are more complex variants of SHA-1. The message digest length is 224, 256, 384, and 512 bits respectively. SHA384 and SHA512 work with 64-bit words instead of 32-bit words, and cut messages in blocks of 1024 bits instead of 512.

3.2 The Birthday Paradox

If the hashed value is of size n, regular brute force preimage or second preimage attacks require 2^n hash computations: we iteratively pick a random x until we find a solution. The probability that the complexity is exactly i (which means that the i-th trial succeeds, and all previous ones fail) is $(1 - 2^{-n})^{i-1}2^{-n}$. Thus, the average complexity in terms of number of hash computations is

$$\sum_{i=1}^{+\infty} i(1 - 2^{-n})^{i-1}2^{-n} = 2^n.$$

Collisions are easier to find with the attack in Fig. 3.7, thanks to the *birthday paradox*. This paradox simply notices that if we pick 23 people, by assuming that their

> **Input**: a cryptographic hash function h onto a domain of size N
> **Output**: a pair (x, x') such that $x \neq x'$ and $h(x) = h(x')$
> 1: **for** $\theta \sqrt{N}$ many different x **do**
> 2:   compute $y = h(x)$
> 3:   **if** there is a (y, x') pair in the hash table **then**
> 4:   yield (x, x') and stop
> 5:   **end if**
> 6:   add (y, x) in the hash table
> 7: **end for**
> 8: search failed

Figure 3.7. Collision search with the birthday paradox.

birthdays are independent and uniformly distributed among 365 days, then at least two of them are likely to share the same birthday. It can be mathematically expressed as follows.

Theorem 3.2. *If we pick independent random numbers in* $\{1, 2, \ldots, N\}$ *with uniform distribution* $\theta \sqrt{N}$ *times, we get at least one number twice with probability*

$$1 - \frac{N!}{N^{\theta\sqrt{N}}(N - \theta\sqrt{N})!} \xrightarrow[N\to+\infty]{} 1 - e^{-\frac{\theta^2}{2}}.$$

For $N = 365$, we obtain the following figures.

$\theta\sqrt{N}$	10	15	20	25	30	35	40
θ	0.52	0.79	1.05	1.31	1.57	1.83	2.09
Probability	12%	25%	41%	57%	71%	81%	89%

So we can find a collision on a hash function by hashing random numbers until the list of hashed values have a collision. If we want to find a collision on MD5 which uses 128-bit hashed values, we thus use $\theta.2^{64}$ MD5 computations.

Proof. The probability that we have no collision is the number of ordered subsets of $\{1, \ldots, N\}$ of cardinality $\theta\sqrt{N}$, which is $N!/(N - \theta\sqrt{N})!$, divided by the number of sequences of numbers of length $\theta\sqrt{N}$, which is $N^{\theta\sqrt{N}}$.

We approximate the probability by using the Stirling Approximation[3]

$$n! \underset{n\to+\infty}{\sim} \sqrt{2\pi n}\, e^{-n} n^n.$$

---

[3] The $\sim$ notation means that there is equality between both sides with a proportional coefficient which tends toward 1 when n tends toward infinity.

Hence

$$1 - p = \frac{N!}{N^{\theta\sqrt{N}}(N - \theta\sqrt{N})!}$$

$$\sim \left(1 - \frac{\theta}{\sqrt{N}}\right)^{-N+\theta\sqrt{N}} e^{-\theta\sqrt{N}}$$

$$= \exp\left[-\theta\sqrt{N} + (-N + \theta\sqrt{N})\log\left(1 - \frac{\theta}{\sqrt{N}}\right)\right]$$

We now use $\log(1 - \varepsilon) = -\varepsilon - \frac{\varepsilon^2}{2} + o(\varepsilon^2)$

$$1 - p \sim \exp\left[-\theta\sqrt{N} + (-N + \theta\sqrt{N})\log\left(1 - \frac{\theta}{\sqrt{N}}\right)\right]$$

$$\sim \exp\left[-\frac{\theta^2}{2} + o(1)\right]$$

which means it tends towards $e^{-\frac{\theta^2}{2}}$.   □

A simpler way to express the birthday paradox consists of estimating the number of collisions. If we take a sequence $X_1, \ldots, X_n$ of independent uniformly distributed random variables in $\{1, \ldots, N\}$, the number of collisions is

$$C = \sum_{i=1}^{n-1} \sum_{j=i+1}^{n} 1_{X_i = X_j}$$

and we have $\Pr[X_i = X_j] = \frac{1}{N}$, so the expected number of collisions is

$$E(C) = \frac{n(n-1)}{2} \times \frac{1}{N}$$

and for $n = \theta\sqrt{N}$, we have $E(C) \sim \frac{\theta^2}{2}$. The variance is $V(C) \sim \frac{\theta^2}{2}$ as well.

Here, the analysis is quite easy when the complexity is fixed, but there is no real need, in practice, for upper-bounding it by $\theta\sqrt{N}$ as in Fig. 3.7. The general analysis is the subject of Exercise 3.3.

For completeness we provide a similar result which is used in order to find collisions between two separated lists (for instance, if we want to find a male–female couple of people with the same birthday).

Theorem 3.3. *If we make two sequences of length $\theta_1\sqrt{N}$ and $\theta_2\sqrt{N}$ by picking independent random numbers in $\{1, 2, \ldots, N\}$ with uniform distribution, we get at least* *one common number in the two sequences with probability*

$$p \xrightarrow[N \to +\infty]{} 1 - e^{-\theta_1 \theta_2}.$$

Proof. Let $N_1 = \theta_1 \sqrt{N}$, $N_2 = \theta_2 \sqrt{N}$, and let us consider the independent random variables with uniform distribution $X_1, \ldots, X_{N_1}, Y_1, \ldots, Y_{N_2}$ in $\{1, \ldots, N\}$. We want to compute

$$p = \Pr[\exists i, j \ X_i = Y_j].$$

Let C be the cardinality of $\{X_1, \ldots, X_{N_1}\}$. We have

$$1 - p = \sum_{c=1}^{N_1} \Pr[C = c] \left(1 - \frac{c}{N}\right)^{N_2}.$$

Since c is always less than N_1, we have

$$1 - p \geq \left(1 - \frac{N_1}{N}\right)^{N_2} \xrightarrow[N \to +\infty]{} e^{-\theta_1 \theta_2}.$$

On the other hand, let α_N be such that $\alpha_N \longrightarrow +\infty$ and $\alpha_N = o(\sqrt{N})$. We truncate the above sum to $c = N_1 - \alpha_N$. We have

$$1 - p \leq \left(1 - \frac{N_1 - \alpha_N}{N}\right)^{N_2} + \Pr[C < N_1 - \alpha_N].$$

The first term tends toward $e^{-\theta_1 \theta_2}$ since $\alpha_N = o(\sqrt{N})$. It remains to prove that $\Pr[C < N_1 - \alpha_N]$ is negligible.

Let

$$D = \sum_{i<j} 1_{X_i = Y_j}.$$

We have $\Pr[C < N_1 - \alpha_N] \leq \Pr[D > \alpha_N]$. Obviously we have $E(D) = \frac{N_1(N_1-1)}{2N}$. Since all $1_{X_i = X_j}$ are pairwise independent, we can also compute the variance

$$V(D) = \frac{N_1(N_1 - 1)}{2N} \left(1 - \frac{1}{N}\right).$$

Now from the Chebyshev Inequality we have

$$\Pr[D > \alpha_N] \leq \frac{V(D)}{(\alpha_N - E(D))^2}.$$

Since $E(D)$ tends toward a constant, it is negligible compared to α_N. Since $V(D)$ tends toward a constant, this probability tends toward zero. □

To summarize, when using a hash function which hashes down to n bits, brute force attacks have the following complexities.

- Preimage attacks (first and second preimage attacks) have complexity 2^n.
- Collision attacks have complexity $2^{\frac{n}{2}}$.

3.3 ⋆A Dedicated Attack on MD4

The birthday paradox provides a generic way to attack hash functions in order to forge collisions. These generic attacks are always possible, and their complexity depends on the output size. For MD5, the output hash length is of 128 bits, so birthday-paradox-based attacks have a complexity of the order of 2^{64}. The ideal goal of conventional cryptographic primitives is to have no better attacks.

However, the particular design of some primitives may lead to some dedicated attacks. Here we exhibit an attack of this type against a simplified version of MD4.

MD4 is a hash function which is similar to MD5, but with the following differences.[4]

- MD4 has three rounds (instead of four for MD5).
- f_2 is defined by

$$f_2(b, c, d) = (b \text{ AND } c) \text{ OR } (c \text{ AND } d) \text{ OR } (d \text{ AND } b)$$

  which is the majority function.
- The output of the transformation box does not add b any more.

The MD4 permutations are defined as follows.

$$\sigma_1 = \begin{pmatrix} 0 & 1 & 2 & 3 & 4 & 5 & 6 & 7 & 8 & 9 & 10 & 11 & 12 & 13 & 14 & 15 \\ 0 & 1 & 2 & 3 & 4 & 5 & 6 & 7 & 8 & 9 & 10 & 11 & 12 & 13 & 14 & 15 \end{pmatrix}$$

$$\sigma_2 = \begin{pmatrix} 0 & 1 & 2 & 3 & 4 & 5 & 6 & 7 & 8 & 9 & 10 & 11 & 12 & 13 & 14 & 15 \\ 0 & 4 & 8 & 12 & 1 & 5 & 9 & 13 & 2 & 6 & 10 & 14 & 3 & 7 & 11 & 15 \end{pmatrix}$$

$$\sigma_3 = \begin{pmatrix} 0 & 1 & 2 & 3 & 4 & 5 & 6 & 7 & 8 & 9 & 10 & 11 & 12 & 13 & 14 & 15 \\ 0 & 8 & 4 & 12 & 2 & 10 & 6 & 14 & 1 & 9 & 5 & 13 & 3 & 11 & 7 & 15 \end{pmatrix}$$

This means, e.g., that $\sigma_2(8) = 2$. The constants $k_{i,j}$ actually do not depend on j and are defined by

$$k_1 = 0, \quad k_2 = \text{5a827999}, \quad k_3 = \text{6ed9eba1}$$

---

[4] MD4 was presented at the CRYPTO'90 conference. See Ref. [156].

in hexadecimal. Rotations $\alpha_{i,j}$ depend on i and j mod 4 only and are defined as follows.

i	j mod 4			
	0	1	2	3
1	3	7	11	19
2	3	5	9	13
3	3	9	11	15

For instance, $\alpha_{3,6} = 11$.

In the dedicated attack we simplify MD4 by suppressing the final round, so that we have two rounds instead of three. This example is meant to be illustrative only since this does not lead to any attack against the full MD4 itself.

A useful building block for information diffusion in conventional cryptographic primitives is the notion of *multipermutation*.[5] Intuitively, a multipermutation is a function with multiple inputs and multiple outputs with the property that modifying one or several inputs of the function has the influence of modifying a maximal number of outputs from the computation. Concretely, if a function f has p inputs and q outputs, modifying r inputs must have the influence of modifying at least $q - r + 1$ outputs. For instance, if $p = q = 4$, modifying r inputs leads to modifying at least $5 - r$ outputs. The linear transform M of MixColumns in the Advanced Encryption Standard (AES) has this property. If $p = q = 2$, modifying r inputs leads to modifying at least $3 - r$ outputs. The mixing box M of CS-CIPHER has this property. If $p = 3$ and $q = 1$, modifying $r = 1$ input must lead to the modification of the output. The f_1 and f_2 functions of MD4 do not have this property as shown below.

Indeed, we observe that we can control modifications on a single input of f_1 or f_2 as follows. For any a, the function $f_1(11 \cdots 1, a, \cdot)$ is a constant equal to a. The functions $f_1(00 \cdots 0, \cdot, a)$ and $f_1(\cdot, a, a)$ have the same property. Similarly, the functions $f_2(a, a, \cdot)$, $f_2(a, \cdot, a)$, and $f_2(\cdot, a, a)$ have the same property. From these properties we deduce that for any transformation box in the second round, if the main input is 0, if the key input is $-k_2$ (the constant of the second round), and if two out of the three other registers are 0, then the output remains 0.

The permutation σ_1 of the first round is in fact the identity permutation: the key values are used in their original ordering. Therefore, provided that $x_0, \ldots, x_{11}$ are fixed, it is easy to choose x_{12}, x_{13}, and x_{14} so that the content of the A, C, and D registers are all 0 (see Fig. 3.8a).

---

[5] Multipermutations were first proposed by Claus Schnorr and Serge Vaudenay (Ref. [162]). A more complete study is available in Ref. [179].

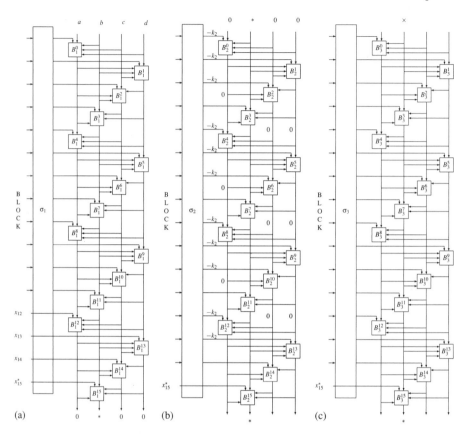

Figure 3.8. Dedicated attack against MD4. (a) First round, (b) second round, and (c) third round.

The permutation σ_2 of the second round is such that $x_{12}, x_{13}, x_{14}, x_{15}$ are the key values used in the B register. Therefore, if all other values are set to $-k_2$, and x_{12}, x_{13}, x_{14} are chosen in order to achieve the above property, we make sure that the content of the A, C, and D registers remains zero (see Fig. 3.8b). This property holds for any choice of x_{15}.

We can consider the output of the second round as a random function of x_{16} for which three registers are always zero. Randomness is thus limited to 32 bits. Considering the birthday paradox, we can deduce a collision after 2^{16} trials: we obtain two different key blocks for which the output after the second round is the same. This breaks MD4 reduced to its first two rounds (see Fig. 3.9).

We can even look at what happens in the third round with this attack. The permutation σ_3 of the third round is such that x_{16}, the only modified key value, is used in the last transformation box (see Fig. 3.8c). Therefore, the two key blocks x and x' which collide after the second round have the property that MD4(x) and MD4(x') only differ in their second 32-bit quarter. In optimizing this attack, we can find two key blocks for which the MD4 digests differ in one single bit, which is quite remarkable. (If digest

Output: two message blocks x and x'
1: **for** $i = 0, 1, 2, 4, 5, 6, 8, 9, 10, 12, 13$ **do**
2:     $x_{\sigma_2^{-1}(i)} \leftarrow -k_2$
3: **end for**
4: $x_{11} \leftarrow$ random $\{$we have defined $x_0, \ldots, x_{11}\}$
5: initialize a, b, c, d to the initial hash value
6: **for** $i = 0$ to 11 **do**
7:     $(a, d, c, b) \leftarrow (d, c, b, \text{ROTL}^{\alpha_{i,1}}(a + f_1(b, c, d) + x_i + k_1))$
8: **end for**
9: **for** $i = 12$ to 14 **do**
10:     $x_i \leftarrow -(a + f_1(b, c, d) + k_1)$
11:     $(a, d, c, b) \leftarrow (d, c, b, 0)$
12: **end for** $\{$we now have defined all x_i but $x_{16}\}$
13: $b_0 \leftarrow a$ $\{b_0, x_0, \ldots, x_{14}$ define a function g as detailed below$\}$
14: look for a collision $g(x_{15}) = g(x'_{15})$
15: define $x'_i = x_i$ for $i = 0, \ldots, 14$
16: output x and x' and exit

Function $g(x_{15})$:
1: initialize a, c, d to 0
2: $b \leftarrow \text{ROTL}^{\alpha_{15,1}}(b_0 + x_{15} + k_1)$
3: **for** $i = 0$ to 15 **do**
4:     $(a, d, c, b) \leftarrow (d, c, b, \text{ROTL}^{\alpha_{i,2}}(a + f_2(b, c, d) + x_{\sigma_2(i)} + k_2))$
5: **end for**
6: return b

Figure 3.9. Dedicated attack against MD4.

values are compared by human beings, a modification in one bit out of 128 may not be noticed!)

These attacks against MD4 were further improved by Hans Dobbertin, a mathematician from the German Intelligence Agency, who showed how to build full collisions (see Refs. [61, 62]). As depicted in Fig. 3.10, the main idea consists of keeping track of a single bit flip in the message block. Indeed, we consider two messages such that the least significant bit of x_{12} is flipped. This message modification starts influencing the computation at the output of the B_1^{12} box. The first part of the analysis consists of looking for some entering values of the A, B, C, and D registers before this box and some values of $x_0, x_4, x_8, x_{12}, x_{13}, x_{14}$, and x_{15} which are the only values which are used up to the B_2^3 box. All those values must be such that the influence of flipping the bit of x_{12} leads to flipping only two bits of the A, B, C, and D registers, namely the bit of 2^{25} in B and the bit of 2^5 in C. This part of the attack is based on solving some equations. The second part of the analysis consists of picking some random matching $x_1, x_2, x_3, x_5, x_6, x_7, x_9, x_{10}, x_{11}$ so that we get the right content of the A, B, C, and D registers before the B_1^{12} box. The third part of the analysis consists of expecting that those two bit flips in B and C have a controlled propagation behavior as depicted in Fig. 3.10, they do not propagate to A and D and only two bits are flipped in total. Since

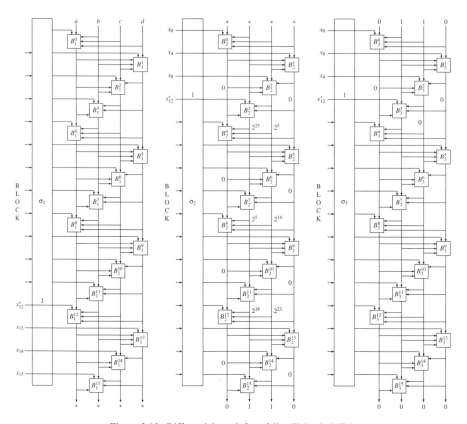

Figure 3.10. Differential graph for a full collision in MD4.

the flipped bit of B is rotated by 13 positions in B_2^7, B_2^{11}, and B_2^{15}, it arrives in the least significant position before B_3^3 where x_{12} enters again. Similarly, the flipped bit of C is rotated by 9 positions in B_2^6, B_2^{10}, and B_2^{14}, it also arrives in the least significant position before B_3^2 where the flipped bit of B can be used to cancel it. Indeed, we estimate that those bit flips propagate as explained with a probability which is roughly $2^{-21} \times \left(\frac{3}{4}\right)^7 \times 2^{-2} \approx 2^{-26}$. (The 2^{-21} is for preventing the propagation of one flipped bit from one register to the other, the $\left(\frac{3}{4}\right)^7$ is for preventing the propagation of one flipped bit in a carry in an addition, and the 2^{-2} is for the final cancellation of the flipped bits.) This means that we should obtain a collision after about 2^{26} trials once we run the MD4 computation.

3.4 Message Authentication Codes

3.4.1 Usage

Message authentication codes are called MACs. They can guarantee the authenticity of a document in an insecure channel. If we want to do this with a cryptographic hash function, the hashed value must be transmitted through a secure channel which

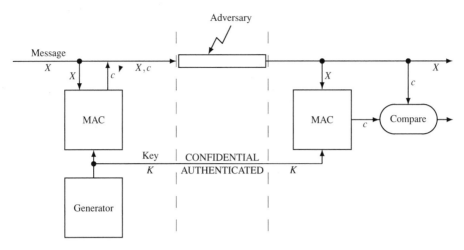

Figure 3.11. Authentication channel.

guarantees the authenticity. As it is done for encryption, we can separate the usage of this channel from the transmission of the document by using it to transmit a secret key and no message dependent value. Once the key is set up, the transmission of the hashed value is replaced by the transmission of the MAC through the insecure channel. We can thus use an expensive authentication channel in order to provide authentication over an insecure channel (see Fig. 3.11).

Note that message authentication implicitly includes message integrity and is thus a little stronger. It is a common mistake to mix up both and to speak about message integrity when we want to speak about message authentication. One reason may be that we want to reserve the noun "authentication" for peer authentication rather than message authentication.

The MAC is thus computed (from the message and the secret key) by a function which is improperly called MAC. It usually works like a cryptographic hash function with a key.

3.4.2   Threat Model

We want to protect ourselves against an adversary who has already seen several pairs (M, c) where c is the MAC for M, and who wants to create a pair (M, c) with a new M (which is not authentic) and a valid MAC (which would pass the authenticity check). Like for encryption, the pairs can be obtained by known or chosen message attacks (see Fig. 3.12).

Note that we concentrate on the authentication of single messages but we do not address integrity of a communication session: as long as messages are authenticated, we

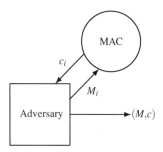

Figure 3.12. Adversarial model for message authentication codes.

cannot suspect them for having been sent to the recipient by an adversary since it must have been generated by the legitimate user. An adversary may however try to swap, erase, or replay some MAC-ed messages in a communication session. This is typically thwarted by adding a sequence number within the message, as it will be illustrated in Chapter 12.

3.4.3 MAC from Block Ciphers: CBC-MAC

A famous construction for MAC is the CBC-MAC construction. A first idea for this construction is to take the last encrypted block of the CBC encryption of the message as a MAC.

This idea is however not secure. Let us assume that we know three pairs (M_1, c_1), $(M_2, c_2), (M_3, c_3)$ such that M_1 and M_3 have the same length and M_2 is the concatenation of M_1 and another message. Let us denote $M_2 = M_1||B||M_2'$ where B is a single message block. If C denotes the block cipher (with an unknown key), the encrypted block of M_2 which matches B is

$$C(B \oplus c_1).$$

We define $B' = B \oplus c_1 \oplus c_3$ and $M_4 = M_3||B'||M_2'$. The encrypted block of M_4 which matches B' is

$$C(B' \oplus c_3) = C(B \oplus c_1),$$

which is the same encrypted block as that of M_2. Therefore, all encrypted blocks for M_4 after B' will be equal to the encrypted blocks for M_2 after B. Hence the last encrypted block of M_2 is equal to the last encrypted block of M_4, which means that the MAC of M_4 is c_2. We can thus forge a new valid pair (M_4, c_2).

Following a second idea called "Encrypted MAC (EMAC)," one can encrypt the last encrypted block of the CBC encryption with another key. We still have an attack which uses the birthday paradox. If the opponent gets $\theta \sqrt{N}$ valid pairs (where N is the number of possible MACs and θ is a constant which defines the probability of success

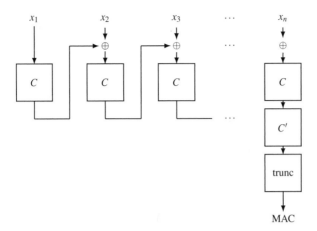

Figure 3.13. Encrypted CBC-MAC.

of the attack), which is $1 - e^{-\theta^2/2}$, he is likely to observe a collision: he gets a pair (M_1, c) and a pair (M_2, c) with the same MAC c. If the opponent can now request the MAC corresponding to a message $M_3 = M_1 || M_3'$ obtained by concatenating M_1 with any M_3', he will get (M_3, c'). He will then be able to create a new pair (M_4, c') with $M_4 = M_2 || M_3'$. This attack is essentially optimal as the result in the next section shows.

A third idea consists of dropping a few bits to avoid collision attacks (see Fig. 3.13), e.g. truncating the MAC to the first half of the bits. This is actually the ISO/IEC 9797 standard (Ref. [11]) MAC algorithm.

One problem remains: how to handle messages whose lengths are not multiples of the block size? For this, three constructions called XCBC, RMAC, and TMAC has been proposed. Furthermore, the key length in the previous constructions looks unnecessarily long. A final variant called OMAC as "One-key CBC MAC" has been proposed as a new standard (see Ref. [94]). OMAC is actually a family of MAC algorithms whose OMAC1 seems to be the favorite instance at this time. An instance of the family is defined by two constants Cst_1 and Cst_2, a MAC length t, and a function H which maps a message block and a constant to a message block. Given a message block L, we let H_L denote the function which maps the remaining constant to a message block. OMAC works as follows. Let us assume that we are given a MAC key K and a message $M = x_1 || x_2 || \cdots || x_n$ where all x_i (except x_n) are full message blocks and the length of x_n is at most the size of a full message block.

1. Let L be the encryption of the zero block, i.e. the message block whose all bits are set to zero. Compute $H_L(\mathrm{Cst}_1)$ and $H_L(\mathrm{Cst}_2)$. (Note that this step can be preprocessed for a given key K since it does not depend on the message M.)
2. If x_n has not the full block length, concatenate it with a bit 1 followed by as many bits as necessary (if any) to reach the block length. In the latter case, we say that the message was padded.

3. If x_n was not padded, replace it by $x_n \oplus H_L(\mathrm{Cst}_1)$. If x_n was padded, replace it by $x_n \oplus H_L(\mathrm{Cst}_2)$.
4. Compute the regular CBC-MAC of $x_1||x_2|| \cdots ||x_n$.
5. Truncate it to its t leftmost bits and obtain the MAC of M.

In the OMAC1 instance, H is defined in the finite field $\mathrm{GF}(2^n)$ where n is the block length. Concretely, blocks are n-bit strings which represent a polynomial in the variable u whose coefficients are binary and read in descending order from the coefficient of u^{n-1} (the leftmost bit) to the constant coefficient (the rightmost bit). The addition of polynomials corresponds to the XOR of bitstrings. The multiplication of a polynomial represented by the bitstring B by u is obtained from B by dropping the leftmost bit and concatenating a zero bit, then by XORing the result to a constant if the dropped bit is 1. The constant is, in hexadecimal, $\texttt{0x000000000000001b}$ if $n = 64$ and $\texttt{0x00000000000000000000000000000087}$ if $n = 128$. These rules and field properties fully define a multiplication law over n-bit strings. Finally, $H_L(x)$ is the multiplication of L by x, Cst_1 is the bitstring representing u, i.e. $\texttt{0x00}\cdots\texttt{02}$, and Cst_2 is the bitstring representing u^2, i.e. $\texttt{0x00}\cdots\texttt{04}$. Note that we only have to compute $L \times u$ and $L \times u^2$, which means that we just have to multiply L by the constant u twice. Implementation of the full $\mathrm{GF}(2^n)$ arithmetics is not necessary. So finally, we can get rid of all these algebraic aspects (which will be made clearer in Chapter 6) and define the operation $y \leftarrow x \times u$ by

1. take x;
2. drop the leftmost bit and insert a new bit zero to the right;
3. if the dropped bit was 1, XOR with $\texttt{0x00}\cdots\texttt{1b}$ for $n = 64$ and $\texttt{0x00}\cdots\texttt{87}$ for $n = 128$;
4. get y.

In OMAC1, $H_L(\mathrm{Cst}_1)$ is defined by $L \times u$, and $H_L(\mathrm{Cst}_2)$ is defined by $H_L(\mathrm{Cst}_1) \times u$.

3.4.4 ⋆Analysis of CBC-MAC

To illustrate the CBC-MAC constructions from the previous section, we provide here a security analysis of the encrypted CBC-MAC, i.e. the EMAC construction. Assuming that the block encryption with the first key is denoted C_1 and that the final block double encryption with the two keys is denoted C_2, EMAC matches the construction in the following theorem.

Theorem 3.4. *Given two independent uniformly distributed random permutations C_1 and C_2 on $\mathcal{M}$ of cardinality N, let us define*

$$\mathrm{MAC}(x_1, \ldots, x_\ell) = C_2(C_1(\cdots C_1(C_1(x_1) \oplus x_2) \oplus \cdots \oplus x_{\ell-1}) \oplus x_\ell).$$

We assume that the MAC function is implemented by an oracle, and we consider an (adaptive) adversary who can send queries to the oracle with a limited total length of q:

if $M_1, \ldots, M_d$ denote the finite block sequences on $\mathcal{M}$ which are sent by the adversary to the oracle, we assume that the total number of blocks is less than q. The purpose of the adversary is to output a message M which is different from all M_i together with its MAC value c. The probability of success of any adversary (i.e. the probability that the MAC value is correct) is smaller than

$$\frac{q(q+1)}{2} \times \frac{1}{N-q} + \frac{1}{N-d}.$$

Note that this is less than q^2/N when $4 \leq q \leq N/4$.

When $q = \theta\sqrt{N}$, this is approximately $\frac{\theta^2}{2}$ (which is greater than $1 - e^{-\frac{\theta^2}{2}}$). Therefore, if the total length of all authenticated messages is negligible against $\sqrt{N}$, there is no better way than brute force attack to get collisions on the CBC-MAC (provided that C_1 and C_2 are perfectly random!).

Proof. First of all, we can assume without loss of generality that all M_i are pairwise different. The next step consists of transforming the adversary into a *nonadaptive* collision finder against a hash function H defined by

$$H(x_1, \ldots, x_\ell) = C_1(\cdots C_1(C_1(x_1) \oplus x_2) \oplus \cdots \oplus x_{\ell-1}) \oplus x_\ell.$$

Let $\mathcal{A}$ be the adversary against the MAC function. We define a collision finder $\mathcal{B}$ against H as follows.

1. We pick a random permutation C_2.
2. We simulate $\mathcal{A}$. Every time that $\mathcal{A}$ tries to send a query M_i to the oracle, we answer $c_i = c_2(H(M_i))$ to $\mathcal{A}$ ($i = 1, \ldots, d$). The simulation ends when $\mathcal{A}$ issues a pair (M, c) or fails.
3. If $\mathcal{A}$ failed, we send $M_1, \ldots, M_d$ to oracle H. If it outputs no collision, then $\mathcal{B}$ fails; otherwise it succeeds.
4. If $\mathcal{A}$ issues a forged pair (M, c) and if c is different from all the c_i's, then $\mathcal{B}$ fails. Otherwise we send $M_1, \ldots, M_d, M$ to oracle H. If it outputs no collision, then $\mathcal{B}$ fails; otherwise it succeeds.

Let E_s be the event that $\mathcal{A}$ succeeds when run with the MAC oracle. Let $p_s = \Pr[E_s]$. We will prove that $\mathcal{B}$ succeeds with a probability p, which is at least $p_s - \frac{1}{N-d}$. Then we conclude using Lemma 3.5 given later.

When running $\mathcal{A}$ with the MAC oracle, let E_c be the event that some queries collide, i.e. that $\text{MAC}(M_i) = \text{MAC}(M_j)$ for some $1 \leq i < j \leq d$. Clearly, $H(M_i) = H(M_j)$, so $\mathcal{B}$ will succeed.

Provided that E_c does not occur, the distribution of $c_1, \ldots, c_d$ in the simulation is exactly the same as the distribution of the $\text{MAC}(M_i)$ values. Hence the simulation of

$\mathcal{A}$ succeeds with probability at least $\Pr[E_s|\overline{E_c}]$. Let E_p be the event that the output c is equal to one answer c_i from the oracle. If E_p occurs then $\mathcal{B}$ succeeds. We have proven that $\mathcal{B}$ succeeds with probability

$$p \geq \Pr[E_c] + \Pr[E_s \cap E_p|\overline{E_c}]\Pr[\overline{E_c}].$$

If neither E_c nor E_p occurs, then either $H(M) = H(M_i)$ for some i and $\mathcal{A}$ fails, or $H(M)$ is new but the probability that $C_2(H(M)) = c$ is equal to $\frac{1}{N-d}$. Therefore the probability that $\mathcal{A}$ succeeds is at most $\frac{1}{N-d}$. We have

$$\Pr[E_s \cap \overline{E_p}|\overline{E_c}] \leq \frac{1}{N-d}$$

hence

$$p \geq \Pr[E_c] + \left(\Pr[E_s|\overline{E_c}] - \frac{1}{N-d}\right)\Pr[\overline{E_c}]$$

thus $p \geq p_s - \frac{1}{N-d}$. $\qquad\qquad\square$

Lemma 3.5. *Given one uniformly distributed random permutation C on $\mathcal{M}$ of cardinality N, let us define*

$$H(x_1, \ldots, x_\ell) = C(\cdots C(C(x_1) \oplus x_2) \oplus \cdots \oplus x_{\ell-1}) \oplus x_\ell.$$

We assume that the H function is implemented by an oracle, and we consider a non-adaptive adversary who can send queries to the oracle with a limited total length of q: if $M_1, \ldots, M_d$ denote the finite sequences on $\mathcal{M}$ which are sent by the adversary to the oracle, we assume that the total length is less than q. The purpose of the adversary is to output two different sequences among all the queried one with the same H value. The probability of success of any adversary is smaller than

$$\frac{q(q+1)}{2} \times \frac{1}{N-q}.$$

Proof. Let $M_i = m_{i,1}||\ldots||m_{i,q_i}$. We assume that the M_i's are pairwise different. We let E denote the event that we have $H(M_i) = H(M_j)$ for some $i \neq j$.

We define

$$U_{i,j} = C(\cdots C(C(m_{i,1}) + m_{i,2}) \cdots + m_{i,j-1}) + m_{i,j}$$

which is an intermediate value which is used to compute $\text{MAC}(M_i)$. We call "collision" an event $U_{i,j} = U_{r,s}$. This collision is trivial if $m_{i,1}||\ldots||m_{i,j} = m_{r,1}||\ldots||m_{r,s}$ (it will happen for any C) and nontrivial otherwise (it will depend on C). We let Coll denote the event that a nontrivial collision occurs.

We call "inversion" the event Inv that $C(U_{i,j}) = 0$ for some i, j.

The E event is clearly included in Inv $\cup$ Coll: if $U_{i,q_i} = U_{r,q_r}$, then either $m_{i,q_i} \neq m_{r,q_r}$ and it is a nontrivial collision, or it reduces to $U_{i,q_i-1} = U_{r,q_r-1}$ and we can iterate. Thus $\Pr[E] \leq \Pr[\text{Inv}] + \Pr[\text{Coll}]$.

In order to determine an upper bound on $\Pr[\text{Inv}]$, we can transform the collision attack against MAC into an inversion attack against C: we say that it succeeds whenever $C(U_{i,j}) = 0$ for some i and j. Clearly $\Pr[\text{Inv}]$ is the probability of success of this attack. But the probability that any adaptive attack against C finds a preimage of 0 after q queries is less than $\frac{q}{N-q}$: once the attack has submitted i queries, C is bound to i input/output pairs, but since C is uniformly distributed, the encryption of any new block is uniformly distributed among all other possible outputs, thus it is the zero block with probability $\frac{1}{N-i}$ which is less than $\frac{1}{N-q}$ when i is less than q. Thus $\Pr[\text{Inv}] \leq \frac{q}{N-q}$.

The remaining part of the proof is devoted to finding the upper bound of $\Pr[\text{Coll}]$.

We let $\mathcal{U}$ be the set of all $U_{i,j}$-indices, which means the set of all (i, j) such that $1 \leq i \leq d$ and $1 \leq j \leq q_i$. For $A \subseteq \mathcal{U}$ we let $c(A)$ be

$$c(A) = \{(i, j); \exists (r, s) \in A \ i = r \text{ and } j \leq s\}.$$

Thus $c(A)$ is the set of the indices of all $U_{i,j}$ which are required in order to compute all $U_{r,s}$ values for $(r, s) \in A$. We define an ordering on the set $2^{\mathcal{U}}$ of all subsets of $\mathcal{U}$ by

$$A \leq B \iff A \subseteq c(B).$$

A is less than B if all indices in A are required to compute the indices in B.

We let I be the set of all pairs of indices of potential nontrivial collisions $U_{i,j} = U_{r,s}$, namely the set of all pairs $\{(i, j), (r, s)\}$ of $\mathcal{U}$-elements such that $m_{i,1}\|\ldots\|m_{i,j} \neq m_{r,1}\|\ldots\|m_{r,s}$. For $\{(i, j), (r, s)\} \in I$ we let $\text{Coll}_{i,j,r,s}$ be the event of the collision $U_{i,j} = U_{r,s}$ (which is necessarily nontrivial since $\{(i, j), (r, s)\} \in I$), and we let $\text{MinColl}_{i,j,r,s}$ be the complementary, in $\text{Coll}_{i,j,r,s}$, of the union of all $\text{Coll}_{i',j',r',s'}$ for $\{(i', j'), (r', s')\} \in I$ and $\{(i', j'), (r', s')\} < \{(i, j), (r, s)\}$: we have a collision $U_{i,j} = U_{r,s}$ with no lower nontrivial collision $U_{i',j'} = U_{r',s'}$. We easily notice that the nontrivial collision event Coll is the union of all nontrivial minimal collisions:

$$\text{Coll} = \bigcup_{\{(i,j),(r,s)\} \in I} \text{MinColl}_{i,j,r,s}.$$

We have at most $\frac{q(q-1)}{2}$ terms in I. Hence

$$\Pr[\text{Coll}] \leq \frac{q(q-1)}{2} \max_{\{(i,j),(r,s)\} \in I} \Pr[\text{MinColl}_{i,j,r,s}].$$

(We need this inequality because it is easier to upper bound the probability of a nontrivial collision when we know that there is no sub-nontrivial collisions.)

For $\{(i, j), (r, s)\} \in I$, let us consider the $\text{MinColl}_{i,j,r,s}$ event. We assume without loss of generality that $s \leq j$. Since we have no previous collision we must have $m_{i,j} \neq m_{r,s}$. We cannot have $j = 1$ (otherwise $s = j = 1$, but $C(m_{i,1}) = C(m_{r,1})$ is either trivial or impossible). Thus $j > 1$ and the event is

$$C(U_{i,j-1}) \oplus m_{i,j} = U_{r,s}.$$

If we have a collision $U_{i,j-1} = U_{i',j'}$ with $(i, j - 1) \neq (i', j')$ and $(i', j') \in c(\{(i, j), (r, s)\})$, it must be trivial (otherwise the $U_{i,j} = U_{r,s}$ collision is not minimal) which means $j' = j - 1$, $i' = r$, and $m_{i,1}||\ldots||m_{i,j-1} = m_{r,1}||\ldots||m_{r,j-1}$. If $s < j$ we have $U_{i,j} = U_{r,s}$ and $U_{r,s} = U_{i,s}$ thus $U_{i,j} = U_{i,s}$ which is nontrivial, which contradicts the minimality of the initial collision. Thus we must have $s = j$, but the trivial collision $U_{i,j-1} = U_{r,j-1}$ make a nontrivial collision $U_{i,j} = U_{r,s}$ impossible. Therefore $U_{i,j-1}$ is equal to no $U_{i',j'}$ for $(i', j') \in c(i, j, r, s) \setminus \{(i, j - 1)\}$.

This implies that the marginal distribution of $C(U_{i,j-1})$ with the knowledge of all previous $U_{i',j'}$ and their C-images is uniform among a set of at least $N - q + 1$ elements. Hence $\Pr[\text{MinColl}_{i,j,r,s}] \leq \frac{1}{N-q}$. Finally,

$$\Pr(E) \leq \frac{q}{N-q} + \frac{q(q-1)}{2} \times \frac{1}{N-q} = \frac{q(q+1)}{2} \times \frac{1}{N-q}$$

$\square$

3.4.5   ⋆*MAC from Stream Ciphers*

Traditional hash functions must have improbable collisions. A traditional way to study regular hash functions in computer science is to consider the function as a random variable: we do not have a fixed hash function, but a family of hash functions, and we pick one at random. Hence we must consider the probability that $H(x) = H(y)$ for any different x and y, over the distribution of H. Following Carter and Wegman in Ref. [42], we say that a random hash function H is *ε-universal* if for any $x \neq y$ we have

$$\Pr[H(x) = H(y)] \leq \varepsilon.$$

We say that it is ε-*strongly-universal* if for any $x \neq y$ and any a and b we have

$$\Pr[H(x) = a, H(y) = b] \leq \frac{\varepsilon}{\#\mathcal{D}}$$

where $\mathcal{D}$ is the output domain of H.

A MAC algorithm is actually a random hash function whose distribution is defined by the secret key choice. We can construct a secure MAC from a universal hash function by simply encrypting the output with the Vernam cipher.

Theorem 3.6 (Wegman–Carter 1981 [184]). *Let $(h_K)_{K \in_U \mathcal{K}}$ be a family of hash functions over the output domain $\{0, 1\}^m$ defined by a random key K which is chosen uniformly at random in a key space $\mathcal{K}$. We assume that this family is ε-strongly-universal. Given K and a sequence of keys $K_1, K_2, \ldots$, which are independent and uniformly distributed over $\{0, 1\}^m$, we define a MAC algorithm which changes the key for every new message. Namely, the MAC of the message x_i of sequence number i is defined by*

$$c_i = h_K(x_i) \oplus K_i$$

An authenticated message is a triplet (x_i, i, c_i), where c_i is computed as above. No chosen message attack can forge a new authenticated message with a probability of success greater than ε.

Hugo Krawczyk improved this result as follows.

Theorem 3.7 (Krawczyk 1994 [108]). *Following the same notations, we say that h is ε-XOR-universal if for any $x \neq y$ and any a we have*

$$\Pr[h_K(x) \oplus h_K(y) = a] \leq \varepsilon.$$

The previous theorem still holds when the strong-universality hypothesis is replaced by XOR-universality.

Clearly, a ε-strongly universal hash function is ε-XOR-universal, so this result is stronger.

Proof. At the end, the adversary knows d authenticated messages (x_i, i, c_i) for $i = 1, \ldots, d$ and forges (x, j, c) with $x \neq x_i$ for any i. The K and K_j keys are conditioned to the knowledge of all (x_i, i, c_i).

If j is not in the $[1, d]$ interval, then K_j is uniformly distributed and independent from this information, so the probability that c is a valid MAC of (x, j) is 2^{-m}. (Note that if h is ε-XOR-universal, then ε must be greater than 2^{-m}, so c is valid with probability less than ε.)

If j is in the interval $[1, d]$, the probability of success is

$$\Pr[h_K(x) \oplus K_j = c | h_K(x_j) \oplus K_j = c_j, I]$$

where $I = \{h_K(x_i) \oplus K_i = c_i; i \in [1, d], i \neq j\}$. Because of the distribution of $K_1, \ldots, K_{j-1}, K_{j+1}, \ldots, K_d$, we can easily see that I is useless in the above probability. Finally we have

$$\Pr[h_K(x) \oplus K_j = c | h_K(x_j) \oplus K_j = c_j] = \Pr[h_K(x) \oplus h_K(x_j)$$
$$= c \oplus c_j | h_K(x_j) \oplus K_j = c_j] \leq \varepsilon$$

since K_j is independent from K. $\qquad\square$

Note that this construction generalizes by defining the MAC of x as being $h_K(x)$ encrypted using a stream cipher (instead of the Vernam cipher).

As an example of XOR-universal hash function family, we provide here a construction based on linear feedback shift registers (LFSR) called LFSR Toeplitz hash function, which is due to Hugo Krawczyk (see Ref. [108]). Given two parameters m and n, we define a hash function h_K from $\{0, 1\}^n$ to $\{0, 1\}^m$ based on a key $K = (p, s^0)$ where $s^0 = (s_0, \ldots, s_{m-1})$ is a bitstring of length m and p defines a polynomial $p(x) = p_0 + p_1 x + \cdots + p_m x^m$ of degree m, with coefficients in GF(2), and which is irreducible. (Note that this implies $p_0 = p_m = 1$.) We define an LFSR as a finite automaton whose state at time t is a bitstring $s^t = (s_t, \ldots, s_{t+m-1})$ of length m and which is updated following the connection polynomial $p(x)$, i.e. we have the following recursion formula:

$$s_{t+m} = \bigoplus_{j=0}^{m-1} p_j s_{t+j}.$$

The LFSR is first initialized to s^0 defined by K. Hashing a message $x_0, \ldots, x_{n-1}$ of n bits simply consists of XORing the states s^t, which correspond to a time t for which $x_t = 1$:

$$h_K(x_0, \ldots, x_{n-1}) = \bigoplus_{\substack{0 \leq t < n \\ x_t = 1}} s^t.$$

We can prove that given a fixed m and n, the family of all h_K hash functions is ε-XOR-universal with $\varepsilon = n \times 2^{1-m}$.

3.4.6   MAC from Hash Functions: HMAC

Making a hash function from a MAC algorithm is quite trivial: we just need to take a constant key. However, we need to keep in mind that MAC does not usually protect against collision attacks.

We can also make a MAC from cryptographic hash functions. The following construction, called HMAC, is due to Mihir Bellare, Ran Canetti, and Hugo Krawczyk. It has been published as the Internet standard RFC 2104 (Ref. [109]).

We assume that we are given a cryptographic hash function H which internally processes messages by blocks of B bytes and produces a digest of L bytes. For instance, if H is SHA-1, we have $B = 64$ and $L = 20$. We further use a parameter t which is the required size of the MAC in bytes. We require that t is at least 4 and at most the output size of H. Computing the MAC of a message m with a key K works as follows.

1. If K has more than B bytes, we first replace K by $H(K)$. (Having a key of such a long size does not increase the security.) Note that $H(K)$ has L bytes.
2. We append zero bytes to the right of K until it has exactly B bytes.
3. We compute
$$H(K \oplus \text{opad}||H(K \oplus \text{ipad}||m))$$
where ipad and opad are two fixed bitstrings of B bytes. The ipad consists of B bytes equal to $0\text{x}36$ in hexadecimal. The opad consists of B bytes equal to $0\text{x}5\text{c}$ in hexadecimal.
4. We truncate the result to its t leftmost bytes. We obtain $\text{HMAC}_K(m)$.

We can prove that if $H(K \oplus \text{ipad}||m)$ defines a secure MAC on fixed-length messages and if H is collision-resistant, then HMAC is a secure MAC on variable-length messages with two independent keys. However, we do not have any result on $H(K \oplus \text{ipad}||m)$. More precisely, here is the security result.

Theorem 3.8 (Bellare–Canetti–Krawczyk 1996 [24]). *Let H be a hash function which hashes onto ℓ bits. Given $K_1, K_2 \in \{0, 1\}^\ell$ we consider the following MAC algorithm.*

$$\text{MAC}_{K_1, K_2}(m) = H(K_2||H(K_1||m))$$

Assuming that H is collision-resistant and that $m \mapsto H(K_2||m)$ is a secure MAC algorithm for messages m of fixed length ℓ, then MAC is a secure MAC algorithm for messages of arbitrary length.

Hence, provided that HMAC is indistinguishable from the construction in this theorem, HMAC is a secure MAC algorithm as well.

Proof. In order to avoid confusion, we call $m \mapsto H(K_2||m)$ the small MAC and MAC_{K_1, K_2} the big MAC. We assume that we have an adversary $\mathcal{A}$ for the big MAC. We construct an adversary $\mathcal{A}'$ for the small MAC by simulation as follows.

1. We pick a random K_1 and we simulate $\mathcal{A}$.
2. Every time $\mathcal{A}$ sends a query X_i to the oracle, we compute $H(K_1||X_i)$ and we query the small MAC oracle with the result. We get c_i which is returned to $\mathcal{A}$ as the answer to the query.

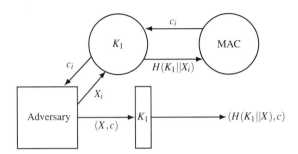

Figure 3.14. Adversary reduction by simulation in HMAC.

3. When $\mathcal{A}$ terminates by giving a forged (X, c) pair, we compute $H(K_1||X)$. If the result is equal to one previously computed $H(K_1||X_i)$, then this provides a collision on H. But this was assumed to be infeasible. Hence, $H(K||X)$ is different from all previously queried $H(K_1||X_i)$, and $(H(K_1||X), c)$ is thus a forgery for the small MAC.

The simulation is depicted in Fig. 3.14.   □

3.4.7   An Authenticated Mode of Operation

We conclude on message authentication codes with an example of mode of operation which combines encryption and MAC at the same time. Namely, those combined modes of operation can be used to achieve confidential communications which need to have strong integrity and authentication protection. They are called *authenticated modes of operation*. Several authenticated modes of operation exist. The most popular one at this time is called *counter with CBC-MAC* (CCM). It is designed to be used with AES or any other block cipher which uses 128-bit blocks.

As its name suggests, the CCM mode combines the CTR mode and CBC-MAC. Roughly speaking, the authenticated encryption of a message m is made by first computing the raw CBC-MAC T of m, and then encrypting $T||m$ in CTR mode. The attacks that we have seen on the raw CBC-MAC are thwarted by the encryption of the output tag.

More precisely, the CCM uses two parameters: the size M (in bytes) of the CBC-MAC tag T which must be even and lie between 4 and 16, and the size L (in bytes) of the field which will encode the message length, which must lie between 2 and 8. Note that M and L are encoded using 3 bits each, namely by the binary expansion of $\frac{M-2}{2}$ and $L - 1$ respectively. The value $L = 1$ is reserved.[6]

---

[6] For instance, future applications using messages whose length encoding (in bytes) requires more than 8 bytes (i.e. whose length is larger than 256^8 bytes, or 2^{34} GB) may later use this value.

A plaintext m is processed together with a key K to be used with the block cipher, a nonce N of $15 - L$ bytes, and an additional authenticated data a which is not meant to be encrypted. For instance, a can be a sequence number in a communication session, or a packet header to be authenticated.

To compute the CBC-MAC tag T with an empty a, we first compute a 128-bit block B_0, we then split m into a block sequence $B_1, \ldots, B_n$ (if necessary, the last block B_n is padded with zero bytes to make a full 128-bit block), we compute the raw CBC-MAC of $B_0 || B_1 || \ldots || B_n$, and we take the M leftmost bytes T of the result. The initial block B_0 is formatted by

$$B_0 = \text{flag} || N || \ell(m)$$

where N is the nonce (of $15 - L$ bytes), $\ell(m)$ is the length (in bytes) of m (of L bytes), and flag is a byte which is formatted by

$$\text{flag} = 0 || \text{adata} || M || L$$

where M and L are the encodings of the respective parameters on two 3-bit strings, adata is a bit set to zero when the data a is of length zero. The leading bit 0 is reserved. When the data a is of nonzero length, adata is set to one and a few blocks are inserted between B_0 and B_1. Those blocks consist of the encoding of the length of a followed by a, then padded, if necessary, with zero bytes so that it can split into an integral number of blocks. The encoding rule for the length of a depends on the size of a. For instance, when a consists of at most 65,279 bytes, the length of a is encoded on 2 bytes.

Following a counter mode, we construct a sequence of counter blocks $A_0, A_1,$ $A_2, \ldots$ by formatting them by

$$A_i = \text{flag} || N || i$$

where N is the nonce (of $15 - L$ bytes), i is the counter (encoded with L bytes), and flag is a byte whose three rightmost bits encode L and all others are basically set to zero.

To encrypt T, we XOR it to the first M bytes of $C_K(A_0)$ where C is the block cipher. To encrypt the message m, we XOR it to the first $\ell(m)$ bytes of $C_K(A_1) || C_K(A_2) || \cdots$. Processing m finally yields the concatenation of the two ciphertexts.

Decryption is quite straightforward from M, K, and N. Note that we can decrypt on the fly. We can also compute the CBC-MAC on the fly and do the final check with the decrypted T.

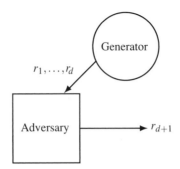

Figure 3.15. Adversarial model for a pseudorandom generator.

3.5 Cryptographic Pseudorandom Generators

3.5.1 *Usage and Threat Model*

Regular probabilistic algorithms use pseudorandom generators. They usually have to look like random to statistical tests. Secure application also need randomness, like simply choosing a secret key. Cryptographic pseudorandom generators need to be robust against malicious adversaries who will try to predict new random generations as depicted in Fig. 3.15.

For instance, if we use the Vernam cipher with a secret key generated by a cryptographic pseudorandom generator, we do not want an adversary who can perform a known plaintext attack to be able to predict the next key, otherwise the encryption is not secure against a known plaintext attack.

3.5.2 *⋆Congruential Pseudorandom Generator*

A famous pseudorandom generator which was first proposed for secure applications is the congruential pseudorandom generator. A general version of it is defined by a parameter k and k functions $\varphi_1, \ldots, \varphi_k$ from $\mathbf{Z}^k$ to $\mathbf{Z}$. The pseudorandom generator is defined by a secret modulus m, secret coefficients $\alpha_1, \ldots, \alpha_k$, and a secret initial state $s_1, \ldots, s_k$. The time counter is initially set to $i = k$. For a new generation, we first increment i and output

$$s_i = \sum_{j=1}^{k} \alpha_j \varphi_j(s_{i-k}, \ldots, s_{i-1}) \bmod m.$$

This pseudorandom generator is quite weak as shown by Joan Boyar and Hugo Krawczyk (see Refs. [36, 106, 107]). Assuming that an adversary has seen

$s_{i-k}, \ldots, s_{i-1}$, he can compute a vector defined by

$$B_i = \begin{pmatrix} \varphi_1(s_{i-k}, \ldots, s_{i-1}) \\ \varphi_2(s_{i-k}, \ldots, s_{i-1}) \\ \vdots \\ \varphi_k(s_{i-k}, \ldots, s_{i-1}) \end{pmatrix}.$$

Once he gets more than k vectors, say for instance $B_1, \ldots, B_i$, he can deduce a linear relationship

$$\gamma_i B_i = \sum_{j=0}^{i-1} \gamma_j B_j$$

with integral coefficients $\gamma_1, \ldots, \gamma_i$. Now since we know that s_i is a scalar product between B_i and a secret constant vector modulo a secret modulus m, we deduce that

$$\gamma_i s_i \equiv \sum_{j=0}^{i-1} \gamma_j s_j \pmod{m}.$$

This is used to get an estimate of m by the difference

$$\gamma_i s_i - \sum_{j=0}^{i-1} \gamma_j s_j.$$

More precisely, we attack the generator as depicted in Fig. 3.16. Here $\bar{m}$ is a multiple of m, which approximates m with increasing precision. After a few steps, we get $\bar{m} = m$, and we can recover the α_i by solving a linear system modulo m.

3.5.3 Practical Examples

We mention three practical cryptographic pseudorandom generators.

First, we notice that the OFB mode and CTR mode of block ciphers consist of transforming the block cipher into a pseudorandom generator to be used with the Vernam cipher. The OFB and CTR modes thus already define how to make a pseudorandom generator from a block cipher.

Second we mention the ANSI X9.17 standard generator (Ref. [2]) based on Triple-DES: The generator uses a timestamp and an internal seed. The new generation r is

Input: $B_0, B_1, \ldots$
Output: m

1: start with $i = k + 1$
2: **repeat**
3:     get a linear relationship $\gamma_i B_i = \sum_{j=0}^{i-1} \gamma_j B_j$ with integers
       $\gamma_0, \ldots, \gamma_i$ with a gcd equal to 1
4:     compute $x = \sum_{j=0}^{i-1} \gamma_j s_j$
5:     pick $\bar{m} = x - \gamma_i s_i$
6:     **repeat**
7:         increment i
8:         **if** $\bar{m} \neq 0$ **then**
9:             get a linear relationship $\gamma_i B_i \equiv \sum_{j=0}^{i-1} \gamma_j B_j \pmod{\bar{m}}$ with
               integers $\gamma_0, \ldots, \gamma_i$ with a gcd equal to 1 and where γ_i is a
               factor of $\bar{m}$
10:            compute $x = \sum_{j=0}^{i-1} \gamma_j s_j \bmod \bar{m}$
11:            replace $\bar{m}$ by the gcd of $\bar{m}$ and $x - \gamma_i s_i$
12:        **end if**
13:    **until** $\bar{m}$ is stable or equal to 0
14: **until** $\bar{m} \neq 0$
15: output $\bar{m}$

Figure 3.16. Attack on the linear congruential pseudorandom generator.

defined by

$$J = \text{Enc}(\text{timestamp})$$
$$r = \text{Enc}(J \oplus \text{Seed})$$

and the seed is replaced by

$$\text{NextSeed} = \text{Enc}(J \oplus r).$$

Finally we mention the *Yarrow-160* dedicated generator as proposed by John Kelsey, Bruce Schneier, and Niels Ferguson from the Counterpane System Company (see Ref. [101]). Here, there are two layers of pseudorandom generators. In the bottom layer, the generation is simply $\text{Enc}_K(\text{counter})$, where counter is incremented after each generation and K is a pseudorandom secret generated by the upper layer. This key is changed regularly (every 10 generations in Yarrow-160). In the upper layer, the generated key is simply the hashed value of a counter and an "entropy accumulator." This accumulator is fed, for instance, by all interrupt information from the hardware which are supposed to be random, with odd distribution. The aim of this generator is to accumulate the randomness and to convert it to a random key with a purer distribution. This is an example of a nondeterministic pseudorandom generator. A similar approach was adopted for Linux in the `random.c` library.

Some other ad hoc examples will be seen in Chapter 12.

3.6 Exercises

Exercise 3.1. *We modify MD5 by suppressing the padding scheme (we pad with 0 bits only). Exhibit a collision.*

Exercise 3.2. *We modify MD5 by suppressing the Davies-Meyer scheme: C is C_0. Prove that we can mount an inversion attack within a complexity of 2^{64}: for any target digest h, we can find a message m for which MD5(m) = h.*

(Hint: perform a meet-in-the-middle attack.)

Exercise 3.3. *We iteratively pick random elements in $\{1, 2, \ldots, N\}$ in an independent and uniformly distributed way until we obtain a collision. Compute the expected number of trials.*

Exercise 3.4. *Let x be a set. We call (p, q)-multipermutation on X any function f from X^p to X^q with the following property: for any two different tuples $(x_1, \ldots, x_{p+q})$ such that*

$$(x_{p+1}, \ldots, x_{p+q}) = f(x_1, \ldots, x_p)$$

at least $q + 1$ coordinates take different values.

Show that f_1 and f_2 in MD4 are not $(3, 1)$-multipermutations. Show that f_3 is a $(3, 1)$-multipermutation.

Show that the 2-PHT transform in SAFER is not a $(2, 2)$-multipermutation. Show that the M function in CSC is a $(2, 2)$-multipermutation.[7]

Exercise 3.5. *Let **K** be a finite field of order k. We define $H(x) = Ax$ for a random variable A uniformly distributed in **K**.*

Show that H is $\frac{1}{k}$-universal. Is it strongly-universal? How would you modify H to make it so?

We now consider $\mathbf{K} = \{0, 1\}^\ell$ as a finite field of order 2^ℓ. Show that H is $2^{-\ell}$-XOR-universal.

---

[7] This exercise was inspired by Ref. [179].

4

★Conventional Security Analysis

Content

★**Attack methods:** differential cryptanalysis, linear cryptanalysis
★**Security analysis:** nonlinearity, Markov ciphers
★**Security strengthening:** indistinguishability, dedicated construction, decorrelation

Previous chapters presented brute force attacks and dedicated attacks. This chapter investigates classical general attack methods for conventional cryptographic algorithms (namely, differential and linear cryptanalysis), and different ways to strengthen the security in primitive design or to estimate the resistance against attacks. For further readings we recommend the tutorial Ref. [90] of Howard Heys on differential and linear cryptanalysis.

4.1 ★Differential Cryptanalysis

The idea of differential cryptanalysis is originally due to Eli Biham and Adi Shamir from the Weizmann Institute in Israel.[1] It assumes a *chosen plaintext attack* model: the adversary can play with the encryption device as a black box, submitting chosen plaintexts and getting ciphertexts in return (see Fig. 4.1). The aim of the attack is to recover the secret key.

The basic idea of differential cryptanalysis is to investigate differential behaviors: we submit pairs of random plaintext blocks the difference of which is a fixed value a. We then look at the corresponding ciphertext difference until it is a fixed value b. A first analysis phase consists of looking for good a and b values in a heuristic way. A crucial quantity is the differential probability defined by

$$\mathrm{DP}^f(a, b) = \Pr[f(X + a) = f(X) + b]$$

where f is the encryption function and X is a uniformly distributed random variable. The higher this probability is, the more efficient the attack is. Additional dedicated tricks enable the analysis of complicated ciphers by using differentials on simplified variants.

We illustrate the differential cryptanalysis paradigm by the example of DES reduced to eight rounds instead of sixteen.

[1] See Refs. [28–31].

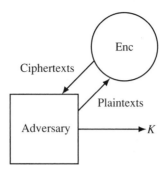

Figure 4.1. Chosen plaintext attack.

Let f be the five first rounds of DES and let us define a and b in hexadecimal by

$$a = 405\text{c}0000\ 04000000, \quad b = 04000000\ 405\text{c}0000$$

The following heuristic analysis suggests that

$$\text{DP}^f(a, b) \approx 2^{-13.4}$$

which we summarize by

$$405\text{c}0000\ 04000000 \xrightarrow[\text{DP}\approx 2^{-13.4}]{f} 04000000\ 405\text{c}0000.$$

In order to trace how this difference propagates throughout the DES design, we will analyze the S-boxes input and output differences. Hexadecimal notations are convenient for the 64-bit blocks. However, since S-boxes have inputs of 6 bits, it is more convenient to represent the 48-bit input differences in octal: any two consecutive octal digits represent the input of a single S-box.

Assuming that the input difference of the right half of the first round is 04000000 in hexadecimal, this corresponds to the input of the first round function. After the expansion, the difference is $00\ 10\ 00\ 00\ 00\ 00\ 00\ 00$ in octal (see Fig. 4.2). This means that the input of S_2 is the only modified one. Next we observe that

$$\text{DP}^{S_2}(10, \text{a}) = \frac{1}{4}$$

which means that an input difference of 10 in S_2 will lead to an output difference of a in hexadecimal (1010 in binary) with probability $\frac{1}{4}$. After the permutation in the round function, we obtain an output difference of 40080000 in hexadecimal. This means that the round function F of DES is such that

$$\text{DP}^F(04000000, 40080000) = \frac{1}{4}.$$

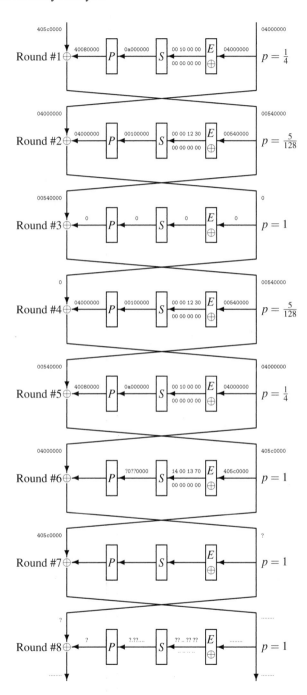

Figure 4.2. Differential cryptanalysis of DES reduced to eight rounds.

The output difference of 40080000 XORs onto the difference of $405c0000$ of the left half of the DES input. We obtain a difference of 00540000. Therefore, after the first round, we have a difference of $04000000\ 00540000$ with probability $\frac{1}{4}$.

If this holds, the input difference of 00540000 of the second-round function leads to an input difference (in octal) of $00\ 00\ 12\ 30\ 00\ 00\ 00\ 00$ to the S-boxes. From the definition of S_3 and S_4 we obtain that

$$\mathrm{DP}^{S_3}(12, 1) = \frac{10}{64}, \quad \mathrm{DP}^{S_4}(30, 0) = \frac{16}{64}.$$

We thus obtain an output difference of 00100000 from the S-boxes with probability $\frac{10}{64} \times \frac{16}{64} = \frac{5}{128}$. After the permutation, this difference becomes 04000000. This means that

$$\mathrm{DP}^{F}(00540000, 04000000) = \frac{5}{128}.$$

The output difference of 04000000 finally XORs onto the difference of 04000000, which therefore vanishes. Hence, after the second round, we have a difference of $00540000\ 00000000$ with probability $\frac{1}{4} \times \frac{5}{128} = \frac{5}{512}$.

The input difference of zero in the third-round function leads to an output difference of zero with probability 1. Therefore, after the third-round, we have a difference of $00000000\ 00540000$ with probability $\frac{5}{512}$.

In the fourth round, we can use the same property as that in the second round, namely

$$\mathrm{DP}^{F}(00540000, 04000000) = \frac{5}{128}.$$

Thus after the fourth round, we have a difference of $00540000\ 04000000$ with probability $\frac{5}{512} \times \frac{5}{128} = \frac{25}{2^{16}}$.

In the fifth round, we can use the same property as that in the first round, namely

$$\mathrm{DP}^{F}(04000000, 40080000) = \frac{1}{4}.$$

The 40080000 XORs onto 00540000 and leads to $405c0000$. Hence, after the fifth round, we have a difference of $04000000\ 405c0000$ with probability $\frac{25}{2^{16}} \times \frac{1}{4} = \frac{25}{2^{18}} \approx 2^{-13.4}$. This explains where the announced five-round differential characteristic comes from.

If x and $x + a$ are plaintext blocks such that this characteristic holds, we call $(x, x + a)$ a *right pair*. Otherwise we call it a *wrong pair*. The above heuristic analysis shows that we have at least a fraction of $2^{-13.4}$ of right pairs.

After the expansion in the sixth round, the input difference of 405c0000 leads to an input difference of

$$14\ 00\ 13\ 70\ 00\ 00\ 00\ 00$$

for the S-boxes: the input difference of S_2, S_5, S_6, S_7, and S_8 are zero. Thus the output difference of these S-boxes is zero. The output difference of these S-boxes in the eighth round is XORed to (1) the output differences of the same S-boxes in the sixth round (thus zero) and (2) the corresponding bits from the input difference in the sixth round, which are known (provided that we have a right pair) in order to produce some ciphertext-difference bits. Thus we can compute the inputs of the corresponding S-boxes in the eighth round and the output differences for the right pairs. Next we can try all possible corresponding key bits (six per S-box, which gives 30 bits) in order to suggest some 30-bit combinations.

In Fig. 4.2, unknown differences are represented by question marks, and computable values (from the ciphertext pairs) are represented by dots. Thus for each ciphertext pair, we compute two vectors of 30 bits which are the inputs of S_2, S_5, S_6, S_7, S_8 before the XOR with the subkey and one vector of 20 bits which is the output difference of these S-boxes, provided that we have a right pair. Each of these vector triplets will be consistent with some 30-bit subkey vector.

Now we use counters for every 30-bit combination. Namely, we make N experiments in which we query $(x, x + a)$ pairs. For each pair we increment the counter of suggested combinations. At the end we hope the right combination to have been suggested many times in order to distinguish it (see Fig. 4.3).

The right combination is suggested for every right pair. So it is at least suggested with probability $p_1 \approx 2^{-13.4}$ for each experiment. Its counter will thus eventually be in the range of $Np_1 \pm \sqrt{Np_1}$. This is called the *signal*.

Any other combination is suggested with probability $p_2 \approx 2^{-20}$. Their counters are thus eventually in the range of $Np_2 \pm \sqrt{Np_2}$ and are considered as *noise*.

The *signal over noise ratio* is thus $p_1/p_2 = 100$, which is high enough. We still need to choose N such that

$$\sqrt{Np_2} < \sqrt{Np_1} \ll N(p_1 - p_2)$$

in order to separate the two distributions, which means $N \gg 1/p_1 \approx 2^{13.4}$.

Precomputation:
1: for $i = 2,5,6,7,8$, $u, u' \in \{0, \ldots, 63\}$ and $v \in \{0, \ldots, 15\}$ initialize
   a set $\text{SubCandidate}_{i,u,u',v}$ to the empty set
2: for $i = 2,5,6,7,8$, for $u, u', k \in \{0, \ldots, 63\}$, insert k in the set
   $\text{SubCandidate}_{i,u,u',S_i(u \oplus k) \oplus S_i(u' \oplus k)}$

Attack:
3: collect N pairs (x, y) and $(x \oplus a, y')$ of plaintext-ciphertext pairs and
   let y_R (resp. y_L) denote the right (resp. left) half of y, as well as for
   y'
4: **for** each pair **do**
5:    compute $u = E(y_R)$ and $u' = E(y'_R)$ and $v = P^{-1}(y_L \oplus y'_L \oplus 04000000)$
6:    make the set product Candidate of all $\text{SubCandidate}_{u_i,u'_i,v_i}$ for
      $i = 2,5,6,7,8$ where u_i (resp. u'_i) denotes the i-th 6-bit packet
      of u (resp. u') and v_i denotes the i-th 4-bit packet of v, *i.e.*
      suggest in Candidate all 30-bit subkeys $k_2 k_5 k_6 k_7 k_8$ for which
      $k_i \in \text{SubCandidate}_{u_i,u'_i,v_i}$
7:    for all k in Candidate, increment a counter n_k
8: **end for**
9: sort all possible 30-bit subkeys k in decreasing order of n_k
10: for each possible 30-bit subkey k, exhaustively look at all the re-
    maining 26 bits and try the corresponding key

Figure 4.3. Differential cryptanalysis of eight-round DES.

After this attack we recover 30 out of the 48 bits of the eighth subkey. The missing
$56 - 30 = 26$ bits can be found with an exhaustive search, whose cost is negligible
against the cost of recovering these 30 bits. Therefore we have a chosen plaintext attack
against eight rounds of DES which enables the discovery of the full key after a number
of plaintext pairs with the order of magnitude of $2^{13.4}$. The complexity is essentially
in obtaining the corresponding ciphertexts and managing 2^{30} counters. (This last cost
can be efficiently decreased by using further dedicated algorithmic tricks.)

The initial development of differential cryptanalysis techniques made possible to
break reduced versions of DES (as we have just shown) and some DES-like block
ciphers. Later, the cryptanalysis technique was improved and optimized. This led to an
attack on the full DES which requires 2^{47} chosen plaintexts to be successful. Interestingly, the attack is scalable in the sense that having fewer chosen plaintexts leads to
an attack with a reduced probability of success. Biham and Shamir have also shown
in 1991 that many slight modifications in the design of the S-boxes (even swapping
two existing S-boxes) lead to an impressive complexity breakdown (see Ref. [31]).
This suggests that the designers of DES indeed tried to make differential attacks as
hard as possible. Later, Don Coppersmith, one member of the original DES design
team at IBM, released in 1994 a technical report (Ref. [48]) explaining that DES was
made in order to optimally resist differential cryptanalysis attacks. This shows that the
research development of American standardization bodies was indeed 15 years ahead
of its time in the early seventies. However, because of the massive growth of industrial

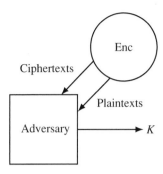

Figure 4.4. Known plaintext attack.

and academic activities in cryptography, it is likely that this gap, if still positive, has substantially reduced.

4.2 ⋆Linear Cryptanalysis

A dual idea to differential cryptanalysis was invented by Mitsuru Matsui at Mitsubishi Electronic (see Ref. [124, 125]) based on previous works from Henri Gilbert and his colleagues of France Telecom (see Ref. [74, 75, 178]) and by the independent discovery of anomalies in the S-boxes of DES by Matt Franklin and Adi Shamir.[2] It has been called *linear cryptanalysis*. In this method, instead of trying to keep track of difference propagation by chosen plaintext attacks, we try to keep track of Boolean information which is linearly obtained by a known plaintext attack: if we get one $(x, C(x))$ pair, we make a statistical analysis of the Boolean information $L(x, C(x))$ and deduce some information on the secret key (see Fig. 4.4).

We remind that all scalar linear mappings can be represented by a dot product with a constant vector: given $x \in \{0, 1\}^m$ and a linear mapping $\varphi : \{0, 1\}^m \to \{0, 1\}$ there exists a unique a such that for any x we have

$$\varphi(x) = a \cdot x = a_1 x_1 \oplus a_2 x_2 \oplus \cdots \oplus a_m x_m.$$

The first step of linear cryptanalysis on a function f thus consists of finding some good a and b vectors in a heuristic way so that $(a \cdot X) \oplus (b \cdot f(X))$ is a biased random variable. A crucial quantity is thus

$$\Pr[a \cdot X = b \cdot f(X)].$$

For normalization reasons, which will be made clear in the next sections, we define

$$\mathrm{LP}^f(a, b) = (2 \Pr[a \cdot X = b \cdot f(X)] - 1)^2$$

[2] See Ref. [165]. The Reference to the Master Thesis of Franklin can be found in the same reference.

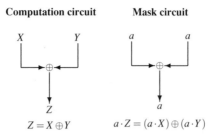

Figure 4.5. Dual circuit of a XOR gate.

over the uniform distribution of X. In a second step, we collect many $(x_i, f(x_i))$ pairs for $i = 1, \ldots, N$ and we use the biased Boolean information in order to recover some statistical information.

Let us start with a few preliminaries.

We assume that a keyed function f from $\{0, 1\}^p$ to $\{0, 1\}^q$ is described by a circuit which contains only substitution boxes, XOR gates, key gates, and duplicate gates. The circuit is an acyclic directed graph which can be represented into layers such that all gate inputs in some layer i are outputs from gates in layer $i - 1$. Layer 1 includes p input bits of f and key gates. The last layer includes q output bits of f. Starting from the output of f, we consider $b \cdot f(x)$. This means that we consider a bit mask b applied to the last layer of the circuit. This mask indicates which output bits from the layer we are considering to XOR together. We can now propagate the mask by applying the following rules.

- If the mask includes a bit u which is output from a XOR gate with inputs v and w, the mask on the previous layer will include v and w (see Fig. 4.5).
- If the mask includes two bits u and v which are output from a duplicate gate with input w, the mask on the previous layer will not include w (see Fig. 4.6 with $a = b$).
- If the mask includes one and only one bit which is output from a duplicate gate with input w, the mask on the previous layer will include w (see Fig. 4.6 with $a \neq b$).

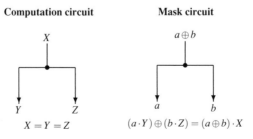

Figure 4.6. Dual circuit of a duplicate gate.

Computation circuit   **Mask circuit**

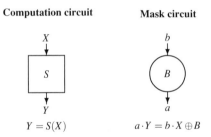

$$Y = S(X) \qquad\qquad a \cdot Y = b \cdot X \oplus B$$

Figure 4.7. Dual circuit of a substitution box.

- If the mask includes some output bits from a substitution box S, namely some $\beta \cdot S(u)$, the mask on the previous layer will include some $\alpha \cdot u$ so that the correlation between $\alpha \cdot u$ and $\beta \cdot S(u)$ is significant. We let $B = (\alpha \cdot u) \oplus (\beta \cdot S(u))$ be the bias bit which is associated to this substitution box (see Fig. 4.7).

Piling up all propagations, we obtain that

$$(b \cdot f(x)) \oplus (a \cdot x) = (c \cdot k) \oplus \bigoplus_i B_i$$

where k is the key vector and the B_i's are all bias vectors that we met in the substitution boxes.

Let us now introduce the following lemma.

Lemma 4.1 (Piling-up lemma). *For any Boolean variable B we define* $\mathrm{LP}(B) = (2 \Pr[B = 0] - 1)^2$. *Let $B_1, \ldots, B_n$ be n independent random variables. We have*

$$\mathrm{LP}(B_1 \oplus \cdots \oplus B_n) = \mathrm{LP}(B_1) \times \cdots \times \mathrm{LP}(B_n).$$

To prove this, we simply observe that $\mathrm{LP}(B) = (E((-1)^B))^2$, that $(-1)^{\alpha \oplus \beta} = (-1)^\alpha (-1)^\beta$, and we use the independence of the B_i's.

Going back to the propagation of masks, we now assume that the input of f is a random variable X and that the key k is fixed. We further make the heuristic assumption that all B_i's are independent. We obtain from the piling-up lemma that

$$\mathrm{LP}^f(a, b) = \prod_i \mathrm{LP}(B_i).$$

Hence, by making sure that all $\mathrm{LP}(B_i)$ are large, then the product $\mathrm{LP}^f(a, b)$ will be large. We also have to make sure that the number of B_i biases is as low as possible. This means that we have as few "active substitution boxes" as possible. Unfortunately there exists no general way to find these efficient a and b masks, nor to approximate $\mathrm{LP}^f(a, b)$ with the above techniques. We only have heuristic ways to find it.

As an illustration we consider eight rounds of DES. As depicted in Fig. 4.8, the output mask after the seventh round is

$$b = 21040080\ 00008000$$

and the input mask is

$$a = 01040080\ 00011000$$

so that if f is the function which maps a plaintext into the output from the seventh round, we have

$$(a \cdot x) \oplus (b \cdot f(x)) = \text{cste} \oplus B_1 \oplus B_3 \oplus B_4 \oplus B_5 \oplus B_7$$

where cste is a constant bit which depends on the key and the B_i's are bias bits in round i. Note that B_1, B_3, B_5, and B_7 are bias bits around the S_5 substitution box of DES whereas B_4 is a bias bit around S_1. Due to the piling-up lemma we obtain

$$\text{LP}^f(a, b) = \left(\frac{16 \times 10 \times 2 \times 20 \times 20}{32^5} \right)^2 = \left(\frac{125}{2^{15}} \right)^2 \approx 2^{-16}.$$

Note that f consists of the first seven rounds. The last round of eight-round DES is a little special since we will use the ciphertext and a guess for some key bits in order to compute the input of S_1, to deduce the output of S_1, and to subtract the bit masked by 00008000 from the ciphertext. This would lead us to the output from the seventh round, provided that the guess for the key bits is correct. This means that we have indeed a characteristic property of the right guess: for each guess κ of the 6 bits which are used in order to compute the input of S_1 in the last round, we can make statistics on the random bit $(a \cdot x) \oplus (b \cdot f(x))$, where $b \cdot f(x)$ is computed from $C(x)$ and κ. If guess κ is not correct, this random bit is approximately a uniformly distributed one. If guess κ is correct, this random bit has a bias LP approximately equal to $\lambda = 2^{-16}$.

More concretely, let X be a uniformly distributed random variable which represents a plaintext, and let $Y = C(X)$ be the ciphertext after we have reduced DES to eight rounds with an unknown secret key. We let U be equal to the 6 bits of the right half of Y which will input to S_1 in the last round after a XOR with 6 key bits. We also let V be a bit equal to

$$V = (a \cdot X) \oplus (b_L \cdot Y_R) \oplus (b_R \cdot Y_L)$$

where $b = b_L b_R$ and $Y = Y_L Y_R$, i.e. b_L (resp. b_R) denotes the left (resp. right) half of b and the same for Y.

If κ is the right guess for the 6 bits of the key, we are interested in the bit

$$W^\kappa = V \oplus (b_R \cdot P(S_1(U \oplus \kappa)||0000000))$$

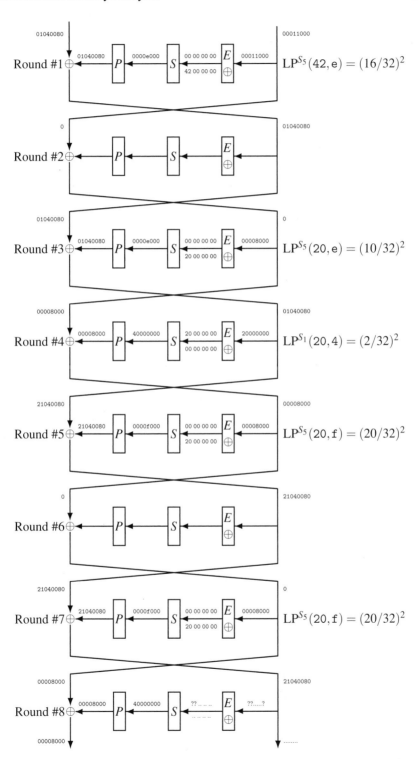

Figure 4.8. Linear cryptanalysis of DES reduced to eight rounds.

where P is the permutation in the DES round function and $||$ denotes the concatenation. This means that we consider the output bits of S_1 only. If κ is correct then $\Pr[W^\kappa = 1] = \frac{1}{2} + \frac{1}{2}(-1)^\beta\sqrt{\lambda}$, where β is an unknown constant that depends on some key bits. Collecting N independent samples (X_i, Y_i) of (X, Y) for $i = 1, \dots, N$, we compute N independent samples W_i^κ of W^κ. Let c^κ be the number of i's such that $W_i^\kappa = 1$. Clearly, the expected value of $\frac{c^\kappa}{N} - \frac{1}{2}$ is $\frac{1}{2}(-1)^\beta\sqrt{\lambda}$ and the variance is $\frac{1}{4N} - \frac{1}{4N}\lambda$. We make approximations to the first order of $\sqrt{\lambda}$, i.e. we neglect λ so that the standard deviation is approximately $\frac{1}{2\sqrt{N}}$. As N increases, the central limit theorem states that

$$\Pr\left[\frac{c^\kappa}{N} - \frac{1}{2} < \frac{t}{2\sqrt{N}}\right] \approx \frac{1}{\sqrt{2\pi}}\int_{-\infty}^t e^{-\frac{\left(x-(-1)^\beta\sqrt{\lambda N}\right)^2}{2}}\,dx.$$

We deduce that

$$\Pr\left[\left|\frac{c^\kappa}{N} - \frac{1}{2}\right| < \frac{t}{2\sqrt{N}}\right] \approx \frac{1}{\sqrt{2\pi}}\int_{-t}^t e^{-\frac{\left(x-(-1)^\beta\sqrt{\lambda N}\right)^2}{2}}\,dx$$

$$= \frac{1}{\sqrt{2\pi}}\int_0^t e^{-\frac{\left(x-(-1)^\beta\sqrt{\lambda N}\right)^2}{2}}\,dx + \frac{1}{\sqrt{2\pi}}\int_0^t e^{-\frac{\left(x+(-1)^\beta\sqrt{\lambda N}\right)^2}{2}}\,dx$$

$$= \frac{2}{\sqrt{2\pi}}e^{-\frac{\lambda N}{2}}\int_0^t e^{-\frac{x^2}{2}}\cosh\left(x\sqrt{\lambda N}\right)\,dx.$$

If κ is not the right guess, we can compute W_i^κ and c^κ by the same formula and we can approximate the expected value and standard deviation of $\frac{c^\kappa}{N} - \frac{1}{2}$ by 0 and $\frac{1}{2\sqrt{N}}$ respectively. A similar analysis leads to

$$\Pr\left[\left|\frac{c^\kappa}{N} - \frac{1}{2}\right| < \frac{t}{2\sqrt{N}}\right] \approx \frac{2}{\sqrt{2\pi}}\int_0^t e^{-\frac{y^2}{2}}\,dy.$$

Let $g^\kappa = \left|c^\kappa - \frac{N}{2}\right|$ be the grade for a guess κ. Let T be the triangle $\{(x, y) \in \mathbf{R}^2 ; x \geq y \geq 0\}$. We obtain that the probability that the grade of the right candidate is smaller than the grade of a given bad candidate is approximately

$$p = 1 - \frac{2}{\pi}e^{-\frac{\lambda N}{2}}\iint_T e^{-\frac{x^2+y^2}{2}}\cosh\left(x\sqrt{\lambda N}\right)\,dx\,dy.$$

This is a decreasing function in terms of $r = \lambda N$, which runs from $p = \frac{1}{2}$ (for $\lambda = 0$) to $p = 0$ (for $\lambda = +\infty$). We have

$$p = 1 - \frac{2}{\pi}e^{-\frac{r}{2}}\iint_T e^{-\frac{x^2+y^2}{2}}\cosh(x\sqrt{r})\,dx\,dy$$

$$= 1 - \frac{1}{\pi}\iint_T e^{-\frac{(x-\sqrt{r})^2+y^2}{2}}\,dx\,dy - \frac{1}{\pi}\iint_T e^{-\frac{(x+\sqrt{r})^2+y^2}{2}}\,dx\,dy.$$

Let us write this sum as $p = 1 - p_1 - p_2$. In the second integral we let $x = -\sqrt{r} + \rho \cos\theta$ and $y = \rho \sin\theta$. Variable θ is between 0 and $\frac{\pi}{4}$ in T. Then ρ goes from $\sqrt{2r}/(2 \cos(\theta + \pi/4))$ to $+\infty$. Hence

$$p_2 = \frac{1}{\pi} \int_0^{\frac{\pi}{4}} \left(\int_{\frac{\sqrt{2r}}{2\cos\left(\theta+\frac{\pi}{4}\right)}}^{+\infty} \rho e^{-\frac{\rho^2}{2}} \, d\rho \right) d\theta$$

$$= \frac{1}{\pi} \int_0^{\frac{\pi}{4}} e^{-\frac{r}{4\cos^2\left(\theta+\frac{\pi}{4}\right)}} \, d\theta.$$

In the first integral we let $x = \sqrt{r} + \rho \cos\theta$ and $y = \rho \sin\theta$. Variable θ is between 0 and π in T. When θ is between 0 and $\frac{\pi}{4}$, then ρ goes from 0 to $+\infty$. When θ is between $\frac{\pi}{4}$ and π, then ρ goes from 0 to $-\sqrt{2r}/(2 \cos(\theta + \pi/4))$.

$$p_1 = \frac{1}{4} + \frac{1}{\pi} \int_{\frac{\pi}{4}}^{\pi} \left(\int_0^{-\frac{\sqrt{2r}}{2\cos\left(\theta+\frac{\pi}{4}\right)}} \rho e^{-\frac{\rho^2}{2}} \, d\rho \right) d\theta$$

$$= \frac{1}{4} + \frac{1}{\pi} \int_{\frac{\pi}{4}}^{\pi} \left(1 - e^{-\frac{r}{4\cos^2\left(\theta+\frac{\pi}{4}\right)}} \right) d\theta$$

$$= 1 - \frac{1}{\pi} \int_{\frac{\pi}{4}}^{\pi} e^{-\frac{r}{4\cos^2\left(\theta+\frac{\pi}{4}\right)}} \, d\theta.$$

When adding p_1 and p_2, by using the symmetry of $\cos^2(\theta + \frac{\pi}{4})$ around $\theta = \frac{\pi}{4}$ we obtain

$$p = \frac{1}{\pi} \int_{\frac{\pi}{2}}^{\pi} e^{-\frac{r}{4\cos^2\left(\theta+\frac{\pi}{4}\right)}} \, d\theta$$

$$= \frac{1}{\pi} \int_{\frac{-\pi}{4}}^{\frac{\pi}{4}} e^{-\frac{r}{4\cos^2\theta}} \, d\theta$$

By using the symmetry of $\cos\theta$ around $\theta = 0$ we obtain

$$p = \frac{2}{\pi} \int_0^{\frac{\pi}{4}} e^{-\frac{r}{4\cos^2\theta}} \, d\theta$$

Clearly, when $0 \le \theta \le \frac{\pi}{4}$ we have $\cos^2\theta \in [\frac{1}{2}, 1]$. Therefore

$$\frac{1}{2} e^{-\frac{r}{2}} \le p \le \frac{1}{2} e^{-\frac{r}{4}}.$$

Having a number of bad candidates equal to B, we deduce that the expected rank R of the right candidates is such that

$$\frac{B}{2} e^{-\frac{\lambda N}{2}} \le R \le \frac{B}{2} e^{-\frac{\lambda N}{4}}.$$

Attack:

1: initialize 2^7 counters $n_{u,v}$ to zero for all possibles 6-bit values u and all possible bits v.

2: collect n plaintext-ciphertext (x, y) pairs,

3: **for** each (x, y) pair **do**

4:    set u to the 6 leading bits of the expansion $E(y_R)$ of y_R in the round function

5:    $v \leftarrow (a \cdot x) \oplus (b_L \cdot y_R) \oplus (b_R \cdot y_L)$

6:    increment $n_{u,v}$

7: **end for**

8: **for** all possible κ **do**

9:    compute
$$c^\kappa = n - \sum_{u,v} n_{u,v \oplus (b_R \cdot (P(S_1(u \oplus \kappa)||0000000)))}$$

10: **end for**

11: sort all possible κ in decreasing order of $|c^\kappa - \frac{n}{2}|$,

12: do an exhaustive search by using the sorted list for κ.

Figure 4.9. Linear cryptanalysis of eight-round DES.

Thus, in order to be the top candidate, it suffices to have

$$N = \frac{4}{\lambda} \log \frac{B}{2}.$$

Here we have roughly $B = 2^6$ bad candidates, so the right candidate for κ will be the top one in the sorted list of graded candidates for $N = \frac{13.86}{\lambda}$. Since $\lambda \approx 2^{-16}$ we deduce that $N = 2^{20}$ is far enough.

The complete algorithm is depicted in Fig. 4.9. In order to avoid computing c^κ with a loop of N iterations for the 2^6 possible values of κ, we can first preprocess the N samples into some counters so that each κ requires a little computation from these counters in order to compute c^κ. As we can see, the complete algorithm includes several phases.

1. A collecting phase of complexity N in which we preprocess the samples into the counters.
2. An analysis phase of complexity 2^6 in which we grade each candidate κ.
3. A sorting phase of similar complexity in which we sort all candidates.
4. A searching phase in which we look for the key using the information obtained from the analysis.

Here, the last phase requires a complexity of 2^{50} when the right candidate is top-ranked. This complexity can be substantially decreased by applying a similar analysis based on another characteristic so that we recover some other bits of the key. For instance, once we have recovered the key bits corresponding to S_1 in the final round, we can look for the key bits corresponding to S_5 in the first round. Here the bias of the characteristic is even larger since we cancel the $(16/32)^2$ factor. This leads to 6 additional bits on the key so that only 44 are missing. Further improvements and experiments show that using $N = 2^{21}$ we recover the full key within a few seconds of computations with a success rate of 99%. This attack can further be improved in order to break the full DES by using 2^{43} known plaintexts (see Ref. [125]).

4.3 ⋆Classical Security Strengthening

4.3.1 ⋆Nonlinearities

In order to measure the nonlinearity of a function f we define

$$\mathrm{DP}^f(a, b) = \Pr[f(X + a) = f(X) + b]$$
$$\mathrm{DP}^f_{\max} = \max_{a \neq 0, b} \mathrm{DP}^f(a, b)$$
$$\mathrm{LP}^f(a, b) = (2 \Pr[a \cdot X = b \cdot f(X)] - 1)^2$$
$$\mathrm{LP}^f_{\max} = \max_{a, b \neq 0} \mathrm{LP}^f(a, b)$$

where the probabilities hold over the uniform distribution of the random variable X. The nonlinearity for differential cryptanalysis corresponds to DP, and the nonlinearity for linear cryptanalysis corresponds to LP. $\mathrm{DP}^f(a, b)$ actually corresponds to the probability of the $a \rightarrow b$ differential characteristic for f. $\mathrm{LP}^f(a, b)$ corresponds to the LP bias of the $a \cdot x \oplus b \cdot f(x)$ bit. DP and LP are connected with the discrete Fourier transform.

Theorem 4.2. *If $f : \{0, 1\}^p \rightarrow \{0, 1\}^q$, for any $a \in \{0, 1\}^p$ and $b \in \{0, 1\}^q$ we have*

$$\mathrm{LP}^f(a, b) = 2^{-p} \sum_{\alpha, \beta} (-1)^{(a \cdot \alpha) + (b \cdot \beta)} \mathrm{DP}^f(\alpha, \beta)$$
$$\mathrm{DP}^f(a, b) = 2^{-q} \sum_{\alpha, \beta} (-1)^{(a \cdot \alpha) + (b \cdot \beta)} \mathrm{LP}^f(\alpha, \beta)$$

Proof. We first notice that

$$1_{a \cdot x = b \cdot f(x)} = \frac{(-1)^{(a \cdot x) + (b \cdot f(x))} + 1}{2}$$

thus

$$\mathrm{LP}^f(a, b) = \left(2^{1-p} \sum_{x \in \{0,1\}^p} 1_{a \cdot x = b \cdot f(x)} - 1 \right)^2$$

$$= \left(2^{-p} \sum_{x \in \{0,1\}^p} (-1)^{(a \cdot x) + (b \cdot f(x))} \right)^2$$

$$= 2^{-2p} \sum_{x, y \in \{0,1\}^p} (-1)^{(a \cdot (x \oplus y)) + (b \cdot (f(x) \oplus f(y)))}.$$

We can now sum over all possible values for $x \oplus y = \alpha$ and $f(x) \oplus f(y) = \beta$ by counting the number of (x, y) pairs that satisfy these relations. It is $2^p \mathrm{DP}^f(\alpha, \beta)$. So we obtain

$$\mathrm{LP}^f(a, b) = 2^{-p} \sum_{\alpha, \beta} (-1)^{(a \cdot \alpha) + (b \cdot \beta)} \mathrm{DP}^f(\alpha, \beta)$$

Next we compute

$$2^{-q} \sum_{\alpha, \beta} (-1)^{(a \cdot \alpha) + (b \cdot \beta)} \mathrm{LP}^f(\alpha, \beta)$$

$$= 2^{-q} \sum_{\alpha, \beta} (-1)^{(a \cdot \alpha) + (b \cdot \beta)} 2^{-p} \sum_{u, v} (-1)^{(\alpha \cdot u) + (\beta \cdot v)} \mathrm{DP}^f(u, v)$$

$$= 2^{-p-q} \sum_{u, v} \mathrm{DP}^f(u, v) \sum_{\alpha, \beta} (-1)^{((a \oplus u) \cdot \alpha) + ((b \oplus v) \cdot \beta)}.$$

The last sum is nonzero only for $a = u$ and $b = v$ in which case it is 2^{p+q}. Thus we obtain the second relation. $\qquad \square$

4.3.2 ⋆Characteristics and Markov Ciphers

Differential cryptanalysis is essentially heuristic. In order to make a formal study, we need to have a good model for the underlying primitives. One model, based on Markov ciphers, is due to Xuejia Lai, James Massey, and Sean Murphy.

Definition 4.3 (Lai–Massey–Murphy [111]). *A random permutation C over a group G is called a Markov cipher on G if for any $a, b, x \in G$ we have*

$$\Pr[C(x + a) - C(x) = b] = E\left(\mathrm{DP}^C(a, b)\right)$$

where the probability and the expectation hold over the distribution of the permutation C.

A basic example is $C(x) = C_0(x + K)$ where C_0 is a random permutation and K is an independent uniformly distributed key in a group.

The name "Markov cipher" refers to Markov chains. We recall that a Markov chain is a sequence $X_1, X_2, \ldots$ of "oblivious" random variables, which means that for any i and any $a_1, \ldots, a_i$ we have

$$\Pr[X_i = a_i | X_1 = a_1, \ldots, X_{i-1} = a_{i-1}] = \Pr[X_i = a_i | X_{i-1} = a_{i-1}].$$

The probability that $X_i = a_i$ only depends on the "recent past" $X_{i-1} = a_{i-1}$. A Markov chain is homogeneous if for any a and b the probability

$$\Pr[X_i = b | X_{i-1} = a]$$

does not depend on i. (Transition probabilities do not depend on "time.") The following property links Markov ciphers and Markov chains.

Theorem 4.4. *Let $C_1, \ldots, C_r$ be independent Markov ciphers on a group G, let x_1 and x_2 be two plaintexts, and let $Y_j^i = C_i \circ \cdots \circ C_1(x_j)$ for $j = 1, 2$ and $\Delta Y^i = Y_2^i - Y_1^i$ for $i = 1, \ldots, r$. The sequence $\Delta Y^0, \ldots, \Delta Y^r$ is a Markov chain. If the distribution of the C_i's is the same, the Markov chain is furthermore homogeneous.*

Proof. Let E be the event $\{\Delta Y^1 = \omega_1, \ldots, \Delta Y^{i-2} = \omega_{i-2}\}$ We have

$$\Pr[\Delta Y^i = \omega_i | \Delta Y^{i-1} = \omega_{i-1}, E]$$
$$= \sum_y \Pr[\Delta Y^i = \omega_i, Y_1^{i-1} = y | \Delta Y^{i-1} = \omega_{i-1}, E]$$
$$= \sum_y \Pr[C_i(y + \omega_{i-1}) - C_i(y) = \omega_i] \Pr[Y_1^{i-1} = y]$$

due to the independence between Y^{i-1} and C_i. This last probability is equal to $E(\mathrm{DP}^{C_i}(\omega_{i-1}, \omega_i))$ due to the definition of Markov ciphers. Therefore we have

$$\Pr[\Delta Y^i = \omega_i | \Delta Y^{i-1} = \omega_{i-1}, E] = \Pr[\Delta Y^i = \omega_i | \Delta Y^{i-1} = \omega_{i-1}].$$

The homogeneous property is trivial. □

The Markov cipher notion is a good model for differential cryptanalysis, as the following result shows.

Theorem 4.5. *With the notations of the previous theorem, we now consider x_1 and x_2 as random, independent, and uniformly distributed. For any differential characteristic $\Omega = (\omega_0, \ldots, \omega_r)$ we have*

$$E \left(\Pr_{x_1, x_2} [\Delta y^i = \omega_i, i = 1, \ldots, r | \Delta y^0 = \omega_0] \right) = \prod_{i=1}^r E \left(\mathrm{DP}^{C_i}(\omega_{i-1}, \omega_i) \right)$$

where the expectations are over the distribution of the ciphers.

We notice that the probability of the left-hand term is the probability of the differential characteristic, which depends on the key, and we take the expectation over the distribution of the key. People usually make the hypothesis of *Stochastic equivalence*, which says that what holds on average over the keys holds for any key, so that we can remove the expectations in the above result and have

$$\Pr_{x_1, x_2} [\Delta y^i = \omega_i, i = 1, \ldots, r | \Delta y^0 = \omega_0] \approx \prod_{i=1}^r \mathrm{DP}^{C_i}(\omega_{i-1}, \omega_i).$$

Proof. The ratio between the two shifted first terms of the equation is

$$\frac{\Pr[\Delta y^i = \omega_i, i = 1, \ldots, r | \Delta y^0 = \omega_0]}{\Pr[\Delta y^i = \omega_i, i = 1, \ldots, r-1 | \Delta y^0 = \omega_0]}$$

$$= \Pr[\Delta y^r = \omega_r | \Delta y^i = \omega_i, i = 0, \ldots, r-1]$$

$$= \Pr[\Delta y^r = \omega_r | \Delta y^{r-1} = \omega_{r-1}]$$

$$= E\left(\mathrm{DP}^{C_r}(\omega_{r-1}, \omega_r)\right).$$

So applying this equality with different r's, we obtain the result.   □

We can add up all characteristics with the same ω_0 and ω_r and obtain the following result.

Theorem 4.6. *Let $C_1, \ldots, C_r$ be independent Markov ciphers on $\{0, 1\}^m$. For any differential or linear characteristic (ω_0, ω_r), we have*

$$E\left(\mathrm{DP}^{C_r \circ \cdots \circ C_1}(\omega_0, \omega_r)\right) = \sum_{\omega_1, \ldots, \omega_{r-1}} \prod_{i=1}^{r} E\left(\mathrm{DP}^{C_i}(\omega_{i-1}, \omega_i)\right)$$

$$E\left(\mathrm{LP}^{C_r \circ \cdots \circ C_1}(\omega_0, \omega_r)\right) = \sum_{\omega_1, \ldots, \omega_{r-1}} \prod_{i=1}^{r} E\left(\mathrm{LP}^{C_i}(\omega_{i-1}, \omega_i)\right)$$

where the expectations are over the distribution of the ciphers.

The above result links the probability of what is called a *multipath characteristic* (ω_0, ω_r) with *single-path characteristics* $(\omega_0, \ldots, \omega_r)$. There is indeed a cumulative effect, although one single-path characteristic is often overwhelming.

4.3.3   ⋆*Theoretical Differential and Linear Cryptanalysis*

Classical studies of differential and linear cryptanalysis say that the complexity is roughly the inverse of the appropriate DP or LP coefficient. Hence a classical (and heuristic) argument for the security of block ciphers consists of proving that there are no high DP or LP coefficients. We can prove the equivalence between the DP and LP coefficients and the complexity of the attacks in a more formal way. For this we need to have a model of the attacks. Here we use the model in terms of a distinguisher.

As depicted in Fig. 4.10, a distinguisher is an algorithm which plays with a random oracle and which ultimately outputs 0 or 1. Given a distribution over random oracles, we can compute the probability that the algorithm outputs 1. We say that the algorithm distinguishes a distribution from another if the probabilities are far away.

Distinguishers are classical tools for measuring randomness. They are also called *Turing tests*.

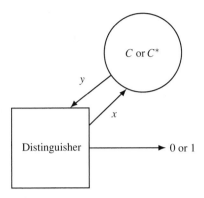

Figure 4.10. Distinguisher between C and C^*.

We say that a block cipher is secure if it cannot be distinguished from a truly random permutation. This is actually a quite strong model of security since if we can break a block cipher by decrypting a fresh ciphertext, we can *a fortiori* distinguish it from a truly random permutation by checking that the decryption is correct with the oracle.

Distinguishers are also the basic tool for differential and linear cryptanalysis. Linear cryptanalysis actually uses an approximation with an unexpectedly large bias which can be used to distinguish the cipher from a truly random permutation. Similarly, differential cryptanalysis uses a differential characteristic with an unexpectedly large probability.

We can modelize a differential distinguisher as depicted in Fig. 4.11.

Theorem 4.7. *Given two random permutations C and C^* over the same message space $\{0, 1\}^m$, where C^* is uniformly distributed, we let $\mathrm{Adv}\,(C, C^*)$ be the difference in the probability that the above distinguisher outputs 1 when the oracle implements the distributions of C and C^*. We have*

$$|\mathrm{Adv}\,(C, C^*)| \leq \max\left(\frac{n}{2^m - 1}, n E\left(\mathrm{DP}^C(a, b)\right)\right).$$

Therefore the attack is meaningless until the number of chosen plaintext pairs n reaches the order of magnitude of $1/E(\mathrm{DP}^C(a, b))$.

> **Parameters:** a complexity n, a characteristic (a, b)
> **Oracle:** a permutation c
> 1: **for** i from 1 to n **do**
> 2:   pick uniformly a random X and query for $c(X)$ and $c(X + a)$
> 3:   if $c(X + a) = c(X) + b$, output 1 and stop
> 4: **end for**
> 5: output 0

Figure 4.11. Differential distinguisher.

Proof. We let $p^C = \mathrm{DP}^C(a, b)$ be the probability of the characteristic (which depends on the secret key). Given a distribution C, the probability that the distinguisher outputs 1 is

$$E\left(1 - (1 - p^C)^n\right)$$

over the distribution of C. Since we have $1 - (1 - x)^n \leq nx$, this is less than $n.E(p^C)$. Now since $|p - p^*| \leq \max(p, p^*)$, we obtain that

$$\mathrm{Adv}(C, C^*) \leq n.\max\left(E(p^C), E(p^{C^*})\right).$$

Finally, we have

$$E\left(p^{C^*}\right) = E\left(\mathrm{DP}^{C^*}(a, b)\right)$$

$$= \mathop{E}_{C^*}\left(\Pr_X\left[C^*(X + a) = C^*(X) + b\right]\right)$$

$$= \mathop{E}_{X}\left(\Pr_{C^*}\left[C^*(X + a) = C^*(X) + b\right]\right)$$

$$= \frac{1}{2^m - 1}.$$

This concludes the proof. $\square$

Linear distinguishers can be modelized as depicted in Fig. 4.12. Here is a useful lemma in order to analyze the advantage.

Lemma 4.8. *For the distinguisher of Fig. 4.12 we let p^c be the probability that the output is 1 given an oracle c. We let p_0 be the probability that it outputs 1 when the counter is incremented with probability $\frac{1}{2}$ in each iteration instead of querying the oracle. We have*

$$|p^c - p_0| \leq 2\sqrt{n.\mathrm{LP}^c(a, b)}.$$

Proof. We first express the probability p^c that the distinguisher accepts c. Let N_i be the random variable defined as being 1 or 0 depending on whether or not we have $X \cdot a = c(X) \cdot b$ in the i-th iteration depending on the random variable X. All N_i's

---

Parameters: a complexity n, a characteristic (a, b), a set $\mathcal{A}$
Oracle: a permutation c
  1: initialize the counter value u to zero
  2: **for** i from 1 to n **do**
  3:     pick a random X with a uniform distribution and query for $c(X)$
  4:     if $X \cdot a = c(X) \cdot b$, increment the counter u
  5: **end for**
  6: if $u \in \mathcal{A}$, output 1, otherwise output 0

Figure 4.12. Linear distinguisher.

are independent and with the same 0-or-1 distribution. Let z be the probability that $N_i = 1$. We also define $\theta = 2z - 1 = \sqrt{LP^c a, b}$. We thus mean to prove that $|p^c - p_0| \leq 2\theta \sqrt{n}$. We have

$$p^c = \sum_{u \in \mathcal{A}} \binom{n}{u} z^u (1-z)^{n-u}$$

and

$$p^c - p_0 = \sum_{u \in \mathcal{A}} \binom{n}{u} \left(z^u (1-z)^{n-u} - \frac{1}{2^n} \right).$$

We would like to upper-bound $|p^c - p_0|$ over all possible $\mathcal{A}$ depending on z. Since z and $1 - z$ play a symmetric role, we assume without loss of generality that $z \geq \frac{1}{2}$. For $z = \frac{1}{2}$, the result is trivially true, so from now on we assume that $z > \frac{1}{2}$. Since $z^u (1-z)^{n-u}$ is an increasing function in terms of u we have

$$|p^c - p_0| \leq \sum_{u=k}^{n} \binom{n}{u} \left(z^u (1-z)^{n-u} - \frac{1}{2^n} \right)$$

where k is the smallest integer u such that the difference in parenthesis is nonnegative, i.e.

$$k = 1 + \left\lfloor n \frac{\log \frac{1}{2} - \log(1-z)}{\log z - \log(1-z)} \right\rfloor.$$

Replacing u by $\frac{n}{2}$ in the same expression in parenthesis we obtain a negative difference. Hence $k \geq \frac{n+1}{2}$. Similarly, replacing u by $n.z$, the expression in parenthesis turns out to be an increasing function in terms of z, which is 0 for $z = \frac{1}{2}$. Since $z > \frac{1}{2}$ we obtain that $k \leq \lceil n.z \rceil$. Therefore $\frac{n-1}{2} \leq k - 1 \leq (n-1)z + z$.

If $n = 1$, we have $k = 1$; thus $\max_{\mathcal{A}} |p^c - p_0| = z - \frac{1}{2}$ and so the result holds. If $n = 2$, we have $k \geq \frac{3}{2}$; thus $k = 2$ and

$$\max_{\mathcal{A}} |p^c - p_0| = \left(z - \frac{1}{2} \right) \left(z + \frac{1}{2} \right) \leq \frac{3}{2} \left(z - \frac{1}{2} \right)$$

and so the result holds as well. We now concentrate on $n \geq 3$.

We use the following identity.[3]

$$\sum_{u=k}^{n} \binom{n}{u} z^u (1-z)^{n-u} = k \binom{n}{k} \int_0^z t^{k-1} (1-t)^{n-k} \, dt.$$

[3] This identity was found in Ref. [155]. We can easily prove it by taking the derivative in terms of z.

We obtain

$$\max_{\mathcal{A}} |p^c - p_0| \leq k \binom{n}{k} \int_{\frac{1}{2}}^{z} t^{k-1}(1-t)^{n-k}\, dt \tag{4.1}$$

and thus

$$|p^c - p_0| \leq k \binom{n}{k} \left(z - \frac{1}{2}\right) \max_{t \in [0,1]} \left(t^{k-1}(1-t)^{n-k}\right).$$

The maximum is obtained for $t = \frac{k-1}{n-1}$; hence,

$$|p^c - p_0| \leq k \binom{n}{k} \left(z - \frac{1}{2}\right) \frac{(k-1)^{k-1}(n-k)^{n-k}}{(n-1)^{n-1}}.$$

Let $x = 2\frac{k-1}{n-1} - 1$. We have $k - 1 = \frac{n-1}{2}(1+x)$ and $n - k = \frac{n-1}{2}(1-x)$. We have $0 \leq x \leq 1$ and

$$|p^c - p_0| \leq k \binom{n}{k} \left(z - \frac{1}{2}\right) \frac{1}{2^{n-1}} \left((1+x)^{1+x}(1-x)^{1-x}\right)^{\frac{n-1}{2}}.$$

Note that by using $k \binom{n}{k} = n \binom{n-1}{k-1}$ and the Stirling approximation, we obtain that this bound is asymptotically equal to $\frac{\theta \sqrt{n}}{\sqrt{2\pi}}$ and so the bound we want to prove is not so loose.

We can easily prove that $(1+x)^{1+x}(1-x)^{1-x} \leq 2^{2x^2}$. Hence,

$$|p^c - p_0| \leq k \binom{n}{k} \left(z - \frac{1}{2}\right) \frac{1}{2^{n-1}} 2^{(n-1)x^2}.$$

Since $k - 1 \leq (n-1)z + z$, we have $x \leq \theta + \frac{\theta}{n-1} + \frac{1}{n-1} = \frac{n\theta + 1}{n-1}$. Thus,

$$|p^c - p_0| \leq \theta \times \left[k \binom{n}{k} \frac{1}{2^n}\right] \times 2^{\frac{(n\theta+1)^2}{n-1}}.$$

For $n = 3$, we have $k \binom{n}{k} \frac{1}{2^n} \leq \frac{3}{4}$; thus,

$$|p^c - p_0| \leq 2\theta \sqrt{n} \times \frac{1}{2\sqrt{3}} \times \frac{3}{4} \times 2^{\frac{(3\theta+1)^2}{n-1}}.$$

For $\theta \leq \frac{1}{2\sqrt{3}}$, we obtain $|p^c - p_0| \leq 2\theta \sqrt{n}$ and this remains true even for $\theta > \frac{1}{2\sqrt{3}}$. We now concentrate on $n \geq 4$.

The $\binom{n}{k}$ term is upper-bounded by $\binom{n}{r}$ with $r = \lceil \frac{n}{2} \rceil$. Furthermore, we have

$$\binom{n}{r} \frac{1}{2^n} \le \prod_{i=1}^{r} \left(1 - \frac{1}{2i} \right)$$

with equality when n is even. Then

$$\log \left(\binom{n}{r} \frac{1}{2^n} \right) \le \sum_{i=1}^{r} \log \left(1 - \frac{1}{2i} \right)$$

$$\le -\frac{1}{2} \sum_{i=1}^{r} \frac{1}{i}$$

$$\le -\frac{1}{2} \int_{1}^{r+1} \frac{dt}{t}$$

$$\le -\frac{1}{2} \log(r + 1)$$

$$\le -\frac{1}{2} \log \frac{n}{2} + 1$$

and therefore

$$\binom{n}{k} \frac{1}{2^n} \le \sqrt{\frac{2}{n+2}}.$$

Now we have

$$k \binom{n}{k} \frac{1}{2^n} = n \binom{n-1}{k-1} \frac{1}{2^n} \le \frac{n}{2} \sqrt{\frac{2}{n+1}} \le \sqrt{\frac{n}{2}}.$$

We deduce

$$|p^c - p_0| \le 2\theta \sqrt{n} \times 2^{\frac{(n\theta+1)^2}{n-1} - \frac{3}{2}}.$$

When $\theta \sqrt{n} < \frac{1}{2}$ and $n \ge 4$ we have $\frac{(n\theta + 1)^2}{n-1} - \frac{3}{2} < 0$, and so we obtain $|p^c - p_0| \le 2\theta \sqrt{n}$. When $\theta \sqrt{n} \ge \frac{1}{2}$, this also holds since the right-hand side of the inequality is greater than 1 and the left-hand side is a difference between two probabilities. This proves the upper bound.   □

Now here is the advantage of linear distinguishers.

Theorem 4.9 (Vaudenay 2003 [183]). *Given two random permutations C and C^* over the same message space $\{0, 1\}^m$, where C^* is uniformly distributed, we let $\mathrm{Adv}(C, C^*)$ be the difference in the probability that the linear distinguisher of complexity n (as* *depicted in Fig. 4.12) outputs 1 when the oracle implements the distributions of C and C*. We have*

$$\text{Adv}\,(C, C^*) \leq 3\sqrt[3]{n.E\left(\text{LP}^C(a, b)\right)} + 3\sqrt[3]{\frac{n}{2^m - 1}}.$$

Therefore, the attack is meaningless until the number of known plaintexts n reaches the order of magnitude of

$$n \approx 1/E\left(\text{LP}^C(a, b)\right).$$

Proof. We first notice that the advantage is zero when $a = 0$ or $b = 0$, so the bound holds. Let us now assume that $a \neq 0$ and $b \neq 0$. We now take a random permutation C with the corresponding Z and p^C as in the previous lemma. Let $\delta = E((2Z - 1)^2)$. (Note that $\delta = E(\text{LC}^C(a, b))$.) When $|2Z - 1| \leq \alpha$, we have

$$|p^C - p_0| \leq 2 \times \alpha\sqrt{n}.$$

Since $(2Z - 1)^2$ is positive, the probability that $|2Z - 1|$ is greater than α is less than $\frac{\delta}{\alpha^2}$. Hence

$$|p - p_0| \leq 2 \times \alpha\sqrt{n} + \frac{\delta}{\alpha^2}$$

for any α.

Let us now fix $\alpha = \left(\frac{\delta}{\sqrt{n}}\right)^{\frac{1}{3}}$. We obtain $|p - p_0| \leq 3 \times \sqrt[3]{\delta n}$.

We recall that $\delta = E\left(\text{LP}^C(a, b)\right)$. Since $a \neq 0$ and $b \neq 0$ we finally note that $E\left(\text{LP}^{C^*}(a, b)\right) = \frac{1}{2^m - 1}$ and so we can have

$$|p^* - p_0| \leq 3\sqrt[3]{\frac{n}{2^m - 1}}.$$

Finally, we use the fact that $|p - p^*| \leq |p - p_0| + |p^* - p_0|$.   □

4.3.4   ⋆Ad hoc Construction

We define

$$\text{EDP}^C_{\max} = \max_{a \neq 0, b} E\left(\text{DP}^C(a, b)\right)$$

$$\text{ELP}^C_{\max} = \max_{a, b \neq 0} E\left(\text{LP}^C(a, b)\right).$$

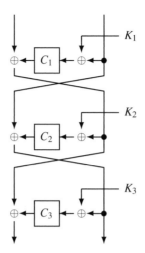

Figure 4.13. Nyberg–Knudsen construction.

Theorem 4.10 (Nyberg–Knudsen 1992 [141]). *Given three independent random permutations C_1, C_2, C_3 such that for all i we have $\mathrm{EDP}^{C_i}_{\max} \le p$, we let K_1, K_2, K_3 be three independent random half-blocks, and we define $\bar{C}_i(x) = C_i(x + K_i)$. We have*

$$\mathrm{EDP}^{\Psi\ (\bar{C}_1, \bar{C}_2, \bar{C}_3)}_{\max} \le p^2$$

Similarly, if $\mathrm{ELP}^{C_i}_{\max} \le p$ for $i = 1, 2, 3$, we have

$$\mathrm{ELP}^{\Psi\ (\bar{C}_1, \bar{C}_2, \bar{C}_3)}_{\max} \le p^2$$

This proves that the three-round Feistel scheme of Fig. 4.13 is "provably secure" against differential and linear cryptanalysis provided that the maximal EDP and ELP of round functions are low.

Proof. We let

$$X = V \oplus \bar{C}_1(W)$$
$$Y = W \oplus \bar{C}_2(X)$$
$$Z = X \oplus \bar{C}_3(Y)$$

$((V, W)$ is the input of $\Psi(\bar{C}_1, \bar{C}_2, \bar{C}_3)$ and (Z, Y) is the output). We have

$$\mathrm{EDP}^{\Psi(\bar{C}_1, \bar{C}_2, \bar{C}_3)}(vw, zy) = \Pr[\Delta Y = y, \Delta Z = z | \Delta V = v, \Delta W = w]$$
$$= \sum_x \Pr \dots \Delta X = x, \Delta Y = y, \Delta Z = z | \Delta V = v, \Delta W = w \dots$$
$$= \sum_x \mathrm{EDP}^{C_1}(w, x \oplus v) \mathrm{EDP}^{C_2}(x, y \oplus w) \mathrm{EDP}^{C_3}(y, z \oplus x).$$

We consider $vw \neq 0$. If $w \neq 0$ and $y \neq 0$, we can upper-bound $\text{EDP}^{C_1}(w, x \oplus v)$ and $\text{EDP}^{C_3}(y, z \oplus x)$ by p. Then we have

$$\text{EDP}^{\Psi(\bar{C}_1, \bar{C}_2, \bar{C}_3)}(vw, zy) \leq p^2 \sum_x \text{EDP}^{C_2}(x, y \oplus w)$$

which is 0 because C_2 is a permutation. If $w \neq 0$ and $y = 0$, we have

$$\text{EDP}^{\Psi(\bar{C}_1, \bar{C}_2, \bar{C}_3)}(vw, zy) = \text{EDP}^{C_1}(w, z \oplus v)\text{EDP}^{C_2}(z, y \oplus w)$$

which is less than p^2. The $w = 0$ and $y \neq 0$ case is similar. Finally, if $w = y = 0$, the $x = v$ term is the only remaining one, and the $\text{EDP}^{C_2}(x, y \oplus w)$ term must be zero because $x = v \neq 0$ and $y \oplus w = 0$ and C_2 is a permutation. $\square$

As an application, Kaisa Nyberg and Lars Knudsen invented the PURE cipher.[4] Its core is defined as a three-round Feistel cipher with round functions

$$F_K(x) = f(g(E(x) + K))$$

where $f : \text{GF}(2^{33}) \rightarrow \{0, 1\}^{32}$ consists of discarding one bit, $E : \{0, 1\}^{32} \rightarrow \text{GF}(2^{33})$ is an injective linear mapping, and $g : \text{GF}(2^{33}) \rightarrow \text{GF}(2^{33})$ is defined by $g(x) = x^3$. We can prove that $\text{EDP}_{\max} \leq 2^{-61}$ and $\text{ELP}_{\max} \leq 2^{-61}$.

The PURE cipher is provably secure against differential and linear cryptanalysis. This is however an ad hoc construction which is weak against another attack: the *interpolation cryptanalysis*. Let us consider $r = r' + 1$ rounds. Let $F_i = F_{K_i}$ and $C = \Psi(F_1, \ldots, F_{r'})$. For $X = (A_1, \ldots, A_{32}, c_1, \ldots, c_{32})$ with constant values c_i, let $Y = C(X) = (B_1, \ldots, B_{64})$. A classical result of the finite field theory tells us that $x \mapsto x^2$ is a linear function. Hence, every output bit of $g : x \mapsto x^3$ can be expressed as a multivariable polynomial of degree 2 in terms of input bits. For $i \geq 32$, B_i is a Boolean function of $A_1, \ldots, A_{32}$ with algebraic degree at most $2^{r'-2}$ if $r' - 2 \leq 32$. (This means that B_i can be expressed as a polynomial in terms of A_j's with a total degree at most $2^{r'-2}$.) If $\{X_1, \ldots, X_{2^{2r'-2}}\}$ is an affine space with dimension $2^{r'-2} + 1$, and $Y_j = C(x_j)$, then $\bigoplus Y_j = 0$ from the property of polynomial functions (see the lemma below). This property enables us to make a distinguisher between r' rounds and a truly random permutation (see Ref. [95]).

Lemma 4.11. *Let $f(x_1, \ldots, x_n)$ be a polynomial of total degree d over a field $\mathbf{K}$. If A is a subset of $\mathbf{K}^n$ with an algebraic structure of affine space of dimension $d + 1$, then*

$$\sum_{(x_1, \ldots, x_n) \in A} f(x_1, \ldots, x_n) = 0.$$

This can easily be proved by induction.

---

[4] This is the topic of Exercise 4.3 on p. 132.

A distinguisher between $r' = r - 1$ rounds and a random permutation can be transformed into a key recovery attack against r rounds. For instance, here is an attack on $r = 6$ rounds.

1: pick $c_1, \ldots, c_{32}$
2: pick an affine space $\{X_j = (A_{1,j}, \ldots, A_{32,j}, c_{1,j}, \ldots, c_{32,j})\}$ of dimension $2^{r'-2} + 1 = 9$
3: get $Y_j = C(X_j) = (Y_j^L, Y_j^R)$
4: find K_r such that $\bigoplus_j Y_j^L = \bigoplus_j f(Y_j^R \oplus K_r)$

We notice that the affine space consists of $2^9 = 512$ elements. The worst number of operations in Step 4 is thus 512 times the number of possible round keys which is 2^{33}. We thus have an attack of complexity 2^{42}. More generally, an attack against r rounds would have led to a complexity of $2^{33} \times 2^{2^{r-3}+1}$ elementary operations. When $r < 8$, this is better than the codebook attack.

Another way to use the Nyberg–Knudsen Theorem consists of having an iterative construction. This was the idea of Mitsuru Matsui who invented the MISTY cipher (see Refs. [126, 127]). A variant of MISTY (KASUMI) is used in the UMTS mobile telephone network (see Ref. [9]).

4.4 ⋆Modern Security Analysis

Although the design of modern block ciphers started in the seventies, all approaches we have seen so far are essentially empirical or heuristic. We cannot formally guarantee the security against any attack. Even when we restrict ourselves to differential and linear attacks, we always need to rely on some heuristic hypothesis in order to estimate the best characteristics. One exception though: the ad hoc construction based on the Nyberg–Knudsen result we have seen in Section 4.3.4. This construction however does not provide so much flexibility for the design, and even introduces other potential weaknesses. For this reason conventional cryptography seems to be bound to remain an art which is only accessible to experts. In this section we investigate new ways to formally address the problem. These results are an attempt to build up a theory for block ciphers in order to move from an artistic status to a scientific status.

4.4.1 ⋆Distinguishability Security Model

Indistinguishability is a strong notion of security for block ciphers. Formally, a *distinguisher* is a machine which plays with an oracle and ultimately outputs 0 or 1. (The notion of "machine" depends on the computational model. In Chapter 8, we will define the notion of *Turing machine*.) We measure the ability to distinguish a random oracle from another by the *advantage*, which is the difference between the expected output with both random oracles. The actual power of the machine depends on the security model. Using the notion of Turing machine, we can limit the time or memory complexity. It can also be *deterministic* or *probabilistic*, but this is no real limitation as the complexity is not bounded.[5] Usually, we only limit the number of *oracle calls*.

In this section we consider two important security models. We consider distinguishers which have to prepare all their queries to the oracle at the same time and with a limited number of oracle calls d. These are called *nonadaptive* distinguishers. In practice, they correspond to attacks which can play with an encryption device within a limited time period so that they have no time to prepare their questions in an adaptive way. We also consider distinguishers which are limited to d oracle calls, but which can make their queries depend on the oracle feedback from the previous ones. These are called *adaptive* distinguishers. We let Cl_{na}^d and Cl_a^d be the class of all nonadaptive and adaptive distinguishers, respectively.

We measure the resistance against a class of distinguishers Cl by the best advantage. Formally, if C and C^* are two random oracles, we define

$$\text{BestAdv}_{\text{Cl}}(C, C^*) = \max_{T \in \text{Cl}} \left(E(T^C) - E(T^{C^*}) \right)$$

where T^C denotes the output of the distinguisher T when interacting with the random oracle C. Most of distinguisher classes are symmetric in the sense that if a distinguisher T is in the class, then the opposite distinguisher $1 - T$ is also in the class. Therefore, there is no need for looking at the absolute value of the advantage.

We can motivate the notion of indistinguishability from an ideal function as one of the strongest security requirements for all conventional cryptographic primitives. In the case of a block cipher C, for instance, when an adversary is able to decrypt a ciphertext after having queried $d - 1$ chosen plaintexts, he can *a fortiori* use this attack in order to distinguish C from a truly random permutation C^* within d queries: if the ciphertext decrypts correctly, then the oracle implements C. Hence, if the block cipher C is indistinguishable from C^* within d queries, then the encryption is safe when used at most d times.

Similarly, if an adversary can forge an authenticated message after $d - 1$ queries to a MAC algorithm F, he can distinguish F from a truly random function F^* within d queries. So if F is indistinguishable from F^*, then the MAC function F is secure when used at most d times.

On the hash function side, we can prove that when we are given a truly random oracle function F^*, then we cannot find collisions in F^* essentially better than by doing a birthday paradox attack, and we cannot perform first or second preimage attacks against F^* essentially better than by doing exhaustive search. Therefore, under the assumption that a hash function can be simulated by a random oracle which is indistinguishable from F^*, a hash function is also a secure hash function.

---

[5] See Chapter 8.

Finally, indistinguishability from a truly random source is also a way to define *randomness*: a pseudorandom generator is secure if it is indistinguishable from a truly random generator. Clearly, if we can predict some nontrivial information about the next generation of a pseudorandom source, then we can distinguish it from a random one. The converse is also true: if we can distinguish a pseudorandom source from a random one with a minimal number d of generations, then from the $d - 1$ first generations we can predict that the d-th one will be the one for which the distinguisher yields 1. Indistinguishability is indeed often used as a synonym for randomness.

4.4.2   ⋆*The Luby–Rackoff Result*

In trying to analyze the security of DES, Michael Luby and Charles Rackoff proved that the Feistel cipher can actually generate a good pseudorandom permutation if the underlying round functions are random and we have at least three rounds. The result formally, which was publicly presented in 1986, states the following.

Theorem 4.12 (Luby–Rackoff 1986 [119]). *Let* F_1^*, F_2^*, F_3^* *be three independent random functions on* $\{0, 1\}^{\frac{m}{2}}$ *with uniform distribution. We have*

$$\mathrm{BestAdv}_{\mathrm{Cl}_a^d}(\Psi(F_1^*, F_2^*, F_3^*), F^*) \leq d^2.2^{-\frac{m}{2}}$$
$$\mathrm{BestAdv}_{\mathrm{Cl}_a^d}(\Psi(F_1^*, F_2^*, F_3^*), C^*) \leq d^2.2^{-\frac{m}{2}}$$

where F^* *(resp.* C^**) is a uniformly distributed random function (resp. permutation) on* $\{0, 1\}^m$. *The results would still hold if we replaced the XOR of the Feistel schemes by any (quasi)group operation.*

Proof. Following the Feistel scheme $F = \Psi(F_1^*, F_2^*, F_3^*)$, we let

$$x_i = (z_i^0, z_i^1)$$
$$z_i^2 = z_i^0 + F_1^*(z_i^1)$$
$$y_i = (z_i^4, z_i^3).$$

We let E be the event $z_i^3 = z_i^1 + F_2^*(z_i^2)$ and $z_i^4 = z_i^2 + F_3^*(z_i^3)$ for $i = 1, \ldots, d$. We thus have $[F]_{x,y}^d = \Pr[E]$. We now define

$$\mathcal{Y} = \{(y_1, \ldots, y_d); \forall i < j \ \ z_i^3 \neq z_j^3\}.$$

We can easily check that $\mathcal{Y}$ fulfills the requirements of Lemma 4.14 below. Firstly we have

$$\#\mathcal{Y} \geq \left(1 - \frac{d(d-1)}{2}2^{-\frac{m}{2}}\right)2^{md}$$

thus we let $\epsilon_1 = \frac{d(d-1)}{2}2^{-\frac{m}{2}}$. Second, for $y \in \mathcal{Y}$ and any x (with pairwise different entries), we need to consider $[F]_{x,y}^d$. Let E^2 be the event that all z_i^2's are pairwise different over the distribution of F_1^*. We have

$$[F]_{x,y}^d \geq \Pr[E|E^2]\Pr[E^2].$$

For computing $\Pr[E|E^2]$ we know that z_i^3's are pairwise different, as for the z_i^2's. Hence $\Pr[E|E^2] = 2^{-md}$. It is then straightforward that $\Pr[E^2] \geq 1 - \frac{d(d-1)}{2}2^{-\frac{m}{2}}$, which is $1 - \varepsilon_2$. We thus obtain from Lemma 4.14 (given later) that $\mathrm{BestAdv}_{\mathrm{Cl}_a^d}(F, F^*) \leq d(d-1)2^{-\frac{m}{2}}$. From Lemma 4.14 it is straightforward that $\mathrm{BestAdv}_{\mathrm{Cl}_a^d}(C^*, F^*) \leq \frac{1}{2}d(d-1)2^{-m}$. We thus obtain $\mathrm{BestAdv}_{\mathrm{Cl}_a^d}(F, C^*) \leq d^2 2^{-\frac{m}{2}}$ for $d \leq 2^{1+\frac{m}{2}}$. Since BestAdv is always less than 1, it also holds for larger d. $\qquad\square$

4.4.3 $\star$Decorrelation

The notion of decorrelation of a function provides a nice algebraic interpretation of the best advantage in terms of distribution distance (see Ref. [183]).

Given a random function F from a set A to a set B, we first define the real matrix $[F]^d$ as a $A^d \times B^d$-type matrix (the rows are numbered by input d-tuples, and the columns are numbered by output d-tuples) for which the $((x_1, \ldots, x_d), (y_1, \ldots, y_d))$-entry is

$$[F]_{(x_1,\ldots,x_d),(y_1,\ldots,y_d)}^d = \Pr[F(x_1) = y_1, \ldots, F(x_d) = y_d].$$

A random function F is aimed at being compared to a canonical ideal random function F^*. For instance, if F is a block cipher, the canonical ideal random function is a uniformly distributed random permutation. Given a distance D on the vector space of $A^d \times B^d$-type real matrices, we define the d-wise decorrelation bias of F by

$$\mathrm{Dec}^d(F) = D([F]^d, [F^*]^d).$$

Different distances will define various decorrelation notions.

We take a simple example with $A = \{0, 1, 2\}$ and $B = \{0, 1\}$ with $F(x) = (K.x^2 + K.\lfloor\frac{K+x}{2}\rfloor + x + 1) \bmod 2$ for K uniformly distributed in $\{1, 2, 3, 4\}$. Here is the table of all possible F functions.

K	$f(0)$	$f(1)$	$f(2)$
1	1	0	0
2	1	0	1
3	0	1	1
4	1	0	1

For $d = 1$ we use the following probability table that defines $[F]^1$.

	$y = 0$	$y = 1$
$x = 0$	1/4	3/4
$x = 1$	3/4	1/4
$x = 2$	1/4	3/4

For $d = 2$ we use the following probability table which defines $[F]^2$.

	$(y_1, y_2) = (0, 0)$	$(y_1, y_2) = (0, 1)$	$(y_1, y_2) = (1, 0)$	$(y_1, y_2) = (1, 1)$
$(x_1, x_2) = (0, 0)$	1/4	0	0	3/4
$(x_1, x_2) = (1, 0)$	0	3/4	1/4	0
$(x_1, x_2) = (2, 0)$	0	1/4	1/4	1/2
$(x_1, x_2) = (0, 1)$	0	1/4	3/4	0
$(x_1, x_2) = (1, 1)$	3/4	0	0	1/4
$(x_1, x_2) = (2, 1)$	1/4	0	1/2	1/4
$(x_1, x_2) = (0, 2)$	0	1/4	1/4	1/2
$(x_1, x_2) = (1, 2)$	1/4	1/2	0	1/4
$(x_1, x_2) = (2, 2)$	1/4	0	0	3/4

Therefore if we write rows and columns in this order we have

$$[F]^1 = \begin{pmatrix} 1/4 & 3/4 \\ 3/4 & 1/4 \\ 1/4 & 3/4 \end{pmatrix}, \quad [F]^2 = \begin{pmatrix} 1/4 & 0 & 0 & 3/4 \\ 0 & 3/4 & 1/4 & 0 \\ 0 & 1/4 & 1/4 & 1/2 \\ 0 & 1/4 & 3/4 & 0 \\ 3/4 & 0 & 0 & 1/4 \\ 1/4 & 0 & 1/2 & 1/4 \\ 0 & 1/4 & 1/4 & 1/2 \\ 1/4 & 1/2 & 0 & 1/4 \\ 1/4 & 0 & 0 & 3/4 \end{pmatrix}$$

We can compare F with a uniformly distributed F^* for which

$$[F^*]^1 = \begin{pmatrix} 1/2 & 1/2 \\ 1/2 & 1/2 \\ 1/2 & 1/2 \end{pmatrix}, \quad [F^*]^2 = \begin{pmatrix} 1/2 & 0 & 0 & 1/2 \\ 1/4 & 1/4 & 1/4 & 1/4 \\ 1/4 & 1/4 & 1/4 & 1/4 \\ 1/4 & 1/4 & 1/4 & 1/4 \\ 1/2 & 0 & 0 & 1/2 \\ 1/4 & 1/4 & 1/4 & 1/4 \\ 1/4 & 1/4 & 1/4 & 1/4 \\ 1/4 & 1/4 & 1/4 & 1/4 \\ 1/2 & 0 & 0 & 1/2 \end{pmatrix}$$

Decorrelation has nice properties which come from its algebraic definition. For instance we can use the triangular inequality. When D is defined by a matrix norm,[6] decorrelation is multiplicative: if the canonical ideal random function associated with a random permutation is a uniformly distributed random permutation, then the decorrelation of a product of independent random permutations is at most equal to the product of the decorrelation of each permutation. Let C_1 and C_2 be two independent random permutations over a set A. They are compared to a uniformly distributed random permutation over A. Because of the independence between C_1 and C_2, we have

$$[C_2 \circ C_1]^d = [C_1]^d \times [C_2]^d.$$

Then we notice that

$$[C_1]^d \times [C^*]^d = [C^* \circ C_1]^d = [C^*]^d$$

and

$$[C^*]^d \times [C_2]^d = [C_2 \circ C^*]^d = [C^*]^d$$

because $C^* \circ C_1$, $C_2 \circ C^*$, and C^* have exactly the same distribution. Hence

$$\left([C_1]^d - [C^*]^d\right) \times \left([C_2]^d - [C^*]^d\right) = [C_2 \circ C_1]^d - [C^*]^d$$

which leads us to

$$\mathrm{Dec}^d(C_2 \circ C_1) \leq \mathrm{Dec}^d(C_1) \times \mathrm{Dec}^d(C_2).$$

We now show the relationship between best advantage and decorrelation.

Theorem 4.13 (Vaudenay 2003 [183]). *We let $|||.|||_\infty$ be the matrix norm associated to the infinity norm:*

$$|||A|||_\infty = \max_{x_1,x_2,\ldots,x_d} \sum_{y_1,y_2,\ldots,y_d} |A_{(x_1,x_2,\ldots,x_d),(y_1,y_2,\ldots,y_d)}|.$$

For any F and its canonical ideal version F^* we have

$$\mathrm{BestAdv}_{\mathrm{Cl}_{na}^d}(F, F^*) = \frac{1}{2}\mathrm{Dec}_{|||.|||_\infty}^d(F).$$

Similarly, there exists a matrix norm $||.||_a$ which provides the same result for Cl_a^d:

$$\mathrm{BestAdv}_{\mathrm{Cl}_a^d}(F, F^*) = \frac{1}{2}\mathrm{Dec}_{||.||_a}^d(F).$$

---

[6] A matrix norm is a norm such that $||A \times B|| \leq ||A||.||B||$.

This matrix norm $||.||_a$ is defined by

$$||A||_a = \max_{x_1} \sum_{y_1} \max_{x_2} \sum_{y_2} \cdots \max_{x_d} \sum_{y_d} |A_{(x_1,x_2,\ldots,x_d),(y_1,y_2,\ldots,y_d)}|.$$

Proof. Since the distinguishers are not computationally bounded, they can be assumed to be deterministic (equivalently, we take the initial random tape which maximizes the advantage). For nonadaptive distinguishers, this means that the queries $x_1, \ldots, x_d$ are constant, and the distinguisher is characterized by an acceptance set A of many y's where $y = (y_1, \ldots, y_d)$. The probability that the distinguisher outputs one (over the distribution of the oracle) turns out to be $\sum_{y \in A} [F]_{x,y}^d$ for $x = (x_1, \ldots, x_d)$. The advantage is thus

$$\sum_{y \in A} \left([F]_{x,y}^d - [F^*]_{x,y}^d \right).$$

This is maximal when A consists of all y's such that the difference in the parenthesis is positive, and when x maximizes this sum. Now since the complete sum over all possible y's is zero, this sum is exactly half of the sum of all absolute values.

For adaptive distinguishers, we apply the same method by induction on d: we consider that the distinguisher queries a constant x_1, and we define a distinguisher limited to $d - 1$ queries depending on y_1. Assuming that the best of these distinguishers have an advantage of

$$\frac{1}{2} \max_{x_2} \sum_{y_2} \cdots \max_{x_d} \sum_{y_d} \left| [F]_{x,y}^d - [F^*]_{x,y}^d \right|$$

where x_1 and y_1 are constants, the advantage of the overall distinguisher will need to sum over all y_1, and to maximize the quantity over x_1. □

The following lemma is a tool for bounding the decorrelation. It means that if $[F]_{x,y}^d$ is close to $[F^*]_{x,y}^d$ for all x and almost all y, then the decorrelation bias of F is small.

Lemma 4.14. *Let d be an integer. Let F be a random function from a set $\mathcal{M}_1$ to a set $\mathcal{M}_2$. We let $\mathcal{X}$ be the subset of $\mathcal{M}_1^d$ of all $(x_1, \ldots, x_d)$ with pairwise different entries. We let F^* be a uniformly distributed random function from $\mathcal{M}_1$ to $\mathcal{M}_2$. We know that for all $x \in \mathcal{X}$ and $y \in \mathcal{M}_2^d$ the value $[F^*]_{x,y}^d$ is a constant $p_0 = (\#\mathcal{M}_2)^{-d}$. We assume there exist a subset $\mathcal{Y} \subseteq \mathcal{M}_2^d$ and two positive numbers ε_1 and ε_2 such that*

- $\#\mathcal{Y} p_0 \geq 1 - \varepsilon_1$
- $\forall x \in \mathcal{X} \, \forall y \in \mathcal{Y} [F]_{x,y}^d \geq [F^*]_{x,y}^d (1 - \varepsilon_2).$

Then we have $\text{BestAdv}_{\text{Cl}_a^d}(F, F^*) \leq \varepsilon_1 + \varepsilon_2.$

Proof. We use the characterization of $\mathrm{Dec}^d_{||.||_a}$ in terms of best adaptive distinguisher. We let $\mathcal{A}$ be a distinguisher between F and F^* limited to d oracle calls with maximum advantage. As discussed previously, we can assume without loss of generality that the distinguisher is deterministic, and that all queries to the oracle are pairwise different (we can simulate the distinguisher by replacing repeated queries by dummy queries). The behavior of $\mathcal{A}$ is deterministically defined by the oracle responses $y = (y_1, \ldots, y_d)$. We let x_i denote the i-th query defined by y. It actually depends on $y_1, \ldots, y_{i-1}$ only. We let $x = (x_1, \ldots, x_d)$ which is assumed to be in $\mathcal{X}$. We let A be the set of all y for which $\mathcal{A}$ outputs 0. It is straightforward that

$$\mathrm{Adv}_{\mathcal{A}}(F, F^*) = -\sum_{y \in A} \left([F]^d_{x,y} - [F^*]^d_{x,y} \right).$$

Next we have

$$\mathrm{Adv}_{\mathcal{A}}(F, F^*) \leq \sum_{\substack{y \in A \\ y \in \mathcal{Y}}} \varepsilon_2 [F^*]^d_{x,y} + \sum_{\substack{y \in A \\ y \notin \mathcal{Y}}} [F^*]^d_{x,y}.$$

By relaxing the y in the first sum, we observe that it is upper-bounded by ϵ_2. (We just have to add the y_j's backward, starting by adding all y_d's, then y_{d-1}, etc.) For the second sum, we recall that all x_i's are pairwise different, so $[F^*]^d_{x,y}$ is always equal to p_0. This sum is thus less than ε_1.   □

Finally, the following result shows the relationship between the decorrelation of order 2 and the resistance against differential and linear cryptanalysis. This demonstrates that although it is hard to construct a cryptographic primitive with proven low decorrelation bias to a high order d, focusing on the order $d = 2$ already provides decent security results.

Theorem 4.15 (Vaudenay 2003 [183]). *Let C be a random permutation over $\{0, 1\}^m$ compared with a uniformly distributed random permutation C^*. We have*

$$\mathrm{EDP}^C_{\max} \leq \frac{1}{2^m - 1} + \mathrm{BestAdv}_{\mathrm{Cl}^2_a}(C, C^*)$$

$$\mathrm{ELP}^C_{\max} \leq \frac{1}{2^m - 1} + 4\mathrm{BestAdv}_{\mathrm{Cl}^2_a}(C, C^*)$$

where C^* is a uniformly distributed random permutation.

Proof. By straightforward computations we obtain that

$$E(\mathrm{DP}^C(a, b)) = 2^{-m} \sum_{\substack{x_1, x_2 \\ y_1, y_2}} 1_{\substack{x_2 = x_1 + a \\ y_2 = y_1 + b}} [C]^2_{(x_1, x_2), (y_1, y_2)}$$

for any a and b, thus

$$E(\mathrm{DP}^C(a, b)) \leq 2^{-m} \sum_{\substack{x_1, x_2 \\ y_1, y_2}} 1_{\substack{x_2 = x_1 + a \\ y_2 = y_1 + b}} [C^*]^2_{(x_1, x_2),(y_1, y_2)} + \mathrm{BestAdv}_{\mathrm{Cl}_a^2}(C, C^*).$$

The first term is then $E(\mathrm{DP}^{C^*}(a, b))$ which is at most $\frac{1}{2^m - 1}$.

For the ELP result, we first notice that $2 \Pr_X[X \cdot a = C(X) \cdot b] - 1 = E\left((-1)^{X \cdot a + C(X) \cdot b}\right)$, and we express $\mathrm{LP}^C(a, b)$ as

$$\mathrm{LP}^C(a, b) = E\left((-1)^{(X_1 \oplus X_2) \cdot a + (C(X_1) \oplus C(X_2)) \cdot b}\right)$$

where X_1 and X_2 are independent uniformly distributed random variables. We have

$$E(\mathrm{LP}^C(a, b)) = 2^{-2m} \sum_{\substack{x_1, x_2 \\ y_1, y_2}} (-1)^{(x_1 \oplus x_2) \cdot a + (y_1 \oplus y_2) \cdot b} [C]^2_{(x_1, x_2),(y_1, y_2)}.$$

The contribution of terms for which $x_1 = x_2$ is equal to 2^{-m}. Considering that C is a permutation, we can concentrate on $x_1 \neq x_2$ and $y_1 \neq y_2$. Then we split the remaining sum into four groups depending on the two bits $(x_1 \cdot a \oplus y_1 \cdot b, x_2 \cdot a \oplus y_2 \cdot b)$. Let Σ_{b_1, b_2} be the sum of all probabilities for which the two bits are (b_1, b_2), $x_1 \neq x_2$, and $y_1 \neq y_2$. We have

$$E(\mathrm{LP}^C(a, b)) = 2^{-m} + 2^{-2m} \Sigma_{0,0} - 2^{-2m} \Sigma_{0,1} - 2^{-2m} \Sigma_{1,0} + 2^{-2m} \Sigma_{1,1}.$$

As a result of symmetry we have $\Sigma_{0,1} = \Sigma_{1,0}$. Furthermore, the sum of the four sums is $2^m(2^m - 1)$. Hence

$$E(\mathrm{LP}^C(a, b)) = 2^{-m} + 2^{-2m} \times 2^m(2^m - 1) - 4 \times 2^{-2m} \Sigma_{0,1}.$$

We deduce

$$E(\mathrm{LP}^C(a, b)) = 1 - 2^{2-2m} \sum_{\substack{x_1 \neq x_2 \\ y_1 \neq y_2}} 1_{\substack{x_1 \cdot a = y_1 \cdot b \\ x_2 \cdot a \neq y_2 \cdot b}} [C]^2_{(x_1, x_2),(y_1, y_2)}.$$

Finally, we obtain

$$E(\mathrm{LP}^C(a, b)) - E(\mathrm{LP}^{C^*}(a, b)) = -2^{2-2m} \sum_{\substack{x_1 \neq x_2 \\ y_1 \neq y_2}} 1_{\substack{x_1 \cdot a = y_1 \cdot b \\ x_2 \cdot a \neq y_2 \cdot b}} \left([C]^2_{(x_1, x_2),(y_1, y_2)} - [C^*]^2_{(x_1, x_2),(y_1, y_2)}\right)$$

$$\leq 4\mathrm{BestAdv}_{\mathrm{Cl}_a^2}(C, C^*).$$

which leads us to the stated result by straightforward computations. $\qquad \square$

4.5 Exercises

Exercise 4.1. *Given a function* $f : \{0, 1\}^p \to \{0, 1\}^q$ *we define*

$$DP^f(a, b) = \Pr[f(X + a) = f(X) + b]$$
$$LP^f(a, b) = (2\Pr[a \cdot X = b \cdot f(X)] - 1)^2$$

where X is uniformly distributed in $\{0, 1\}^p$. Give an algorithm for computing the whole table of DP^f in $O(2^{p+q})$ steps.[7] Give an algorithm for computing the whole table of LP^f in $O((p + q)2^{p+q})$ steps.

Exercise 4.2. *Prove that if $f : \{0, 1\}^p \to \{0, 1\}^q$, the following bounds hold.*

Bound	Name of eq. case	Necessary condition for eq.
$DP^f_{max} \geq 2^{-q}$	PN	$p \geq 2q, p$ even
$DP^f_{max} \geq 2^{1-p}$	APN	$p \leq q$ or $(p, q) = (2, 1)$
$LP^f_{max} \geq 2^{-p}$	B	$p \geq 2q, p$ even
$LP^f_{max} \geq u(p, q)$	AB	$p = q, p$ odd

where

$$u(p, q) = 2^{1-p}\left(1 + \frac{(2^{q-p} - 1)(2^{p-1} - 1)}{2^q - 1}\right).$$

Equality cases are called Perfect Nonlinear (PN), Almost Perfect Nonlinear (APN), Bent (B), and Almost Bent (AB). In addition, prove that B is equivalent to PN and that AB is equivalent to APN.[8]

Exercise 4.3. *We define*

$$
\begin{array}{lll}
f : GF(2^{33}) \to \{0, 1\}^{32} & \text{linear mapping} \\
g : GF(2^{33}) \to GF(2^{33}) & g(x) = x^3 \\
E : \{0, 1\}^{32} \to GF(2^{33}) & \text{linear mapping}
\end{array}
$$

where f consists of discarding 1 bit, and E is injective, and

$$F_K(x) = f(g(E(x) + K))$$

---

[7] This O notation means that there exists a constant $c > 0$ such that for any p and q, the complexity of this algorithm is at most $c2^{p+q}$ elementary operations. The notion of complexity is formally defined in Chapter 8.

[8] This exercise was inspired by Ref. [44].

for $K \in GF(2^{33})$.

Prove that $DP_{max}^g = LP_{max}^g = 2^{-32}$.

Deduce that for any K we have $DP_{max}^{F_K} \leq 2^{-31}$ and $LP_{max}^{F_K} \leq 2^{-31}$.

Deduce that for a Feistel cipher with at least three rounds with the above round function, we have $EDP_{max} \leq 2^{-61}$ and $ELP_{max} \leq 2^{-61}$. (This is used in order to construct the PURE cipher which was invented by Kaisa Nyberg and Lars Knudsen.)[9]

Exercise 4.4. *Let $C : \{0, 1\}^m \to \{0, 1\}^m$ be a random permutation. We compare C to a uniformly distributed permutation. Show that*

1. *the property $Dec^d(C) = 0$ does not depend on the choice of the distance on the matrix space,*
2. *if $Dec^1(C) = 0$, then the cipher C provides perfect secrecy for any distribution of the plaintext,*
3. *if $Dec^2(C) = 0$, then C is a Markov cipher.*

Exercise 4.5. *Let $C : \{0, 1\}^m \to \{0, 1\}^m$ be a random permutation. We compare C to a uniformly distributed permutation. We consider decorrelation defined by the adaptive norm ($\|.\|_a$).*

1. *Prove that $Dec^{d-1}(C) \leq Dec^d(C)$.*
2. *Prove that $0 \leq Dec^d(C) \leq 2$.*

Exercise 4.6. *Let $C, C^* : \{0, 1\}^m \to \{0, 1\}^m$ be random permutations. We assume that C^* is uniformly distributed. Show that*

1. *C is ε-strongly universal implies $2BestAdv_{Cl_a^2}(C, C^*) \leq \varepsilon$,*
2. *C is ε-strongly universal implies $EDP_{max}^C \leq \varepsilon$,*
3. *C is ε-XOR universal implies $EDP_{max}^C \leq \varepsilon$.*

Exercise 4.7. *Let $f_K : \{0, 1\}^m \to \{0, 1\}^m$ be a function defined by a random key K in a key space $\mathcal{K}$. We compare f_K to a uniformly distributed function.*

1. *Prove that if $Dec^d(f_K) = 0$, then $\#\mathcal{K} \geq 2^{md}$.*
2. *Show that for $f_K(x) = x \oplus K$, we obtain $Dec^1(f_K) = 0$.*
3. *Propose a construction for f_K such that $Dec^d(f_K) = 0$ and $\#\mathcal{K} = 2^{md}$.*

Exercise 4.8. *Prove that for any independent random function $F_1, \ldots, F_r$ on $\{0, 1\}^{\frac{m}{2}}$ such that*

$$BestAdv_{Cl_a^d}(F_i, F^*) \leq \varepsilon$$

[9] This exercise was inspired by Ref. [141].

we have

$$\text{BestAdv}_{\text{Cl}_a^d}(\Psi(F_1, \ldots, F_r), C^*) \leq \frac{1}{2} \left(2d^2 . 2^{-\frac{m}{2}} + 6\varepsilon \right)^{\lfloor \frac{r}{3} \rfloor}.$$

By using the previous exercises, propose a construction for a Feistel cipher C such that

$$\text{BestAdv}_{\text{Cl}_a^d}(C, C^*) \leq 2d^4 . 2^{-m}.$$

Design a new block cipher.[10]

---

[10] This exercise was inspired by Ref. [183].

5

Security Protocols with Conventional Cryptography

Content

Password access control: UNIX passwords, basic HTTP, PAP
Challenge–response protocols: digest HTTP, CHAP
One-time passwords: Lamport scheme, S/Key
Key distribution: Needham–Schroeder, Kerberos, Merkle puzzles
Authentication chains: Merkle signature scheme, timestamps
Case study: GSM network, Bluetooth network

In this chapter we look at several examples of protocols which use conventional cryptography. As we can see, the most important problems are peer authentication and key distribution. Once these problems are solved, the conventional cryptographic primitives that we have seen in previous chapters can be used in order to build up secure communications, e.g. establish communication sessions between a client and a server which preserve confidentiality, integrity, authentication, and in which no adversary can replay, reorder, or erase messages.

5.1 Password Access Control

The most intuitive way to perform access control is to request a password as depicted in Fig. 5.1. When a client wishes to connect to a server, they can proceed as follows.

1. The client first sends an access request to the server.
2. The server acknowledges and sends a password request to the client.
3. The client sends his password to the server.
4. The server checks the correctness of the password and either provides or denies access to the client.

Here, the password does not need to be kept in memory: the server only keeps a message digest (using a hash function) of the password. This is an interesting property for security since this protects against potential damages when the memory content is stolen.

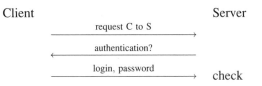

Figure 5.1. Password access control.

5.1.1   UNIX Passwords

UNIX passwords are a famous example that we saw in Section 2.4. Here, the client is a user (or a UNIX process whose permissions are associated to the user) and the server is a workstation.

Here the server must keep a database of "encrypted" (through a one-way function) passwords. The one-way encryption is purposely slow in order to slow down access control attacks.

5.1.2   Basic Access Control in HTTP

Another example of password access control, which is taken from RFC 2617 (Ref. [69]), is used in the HTTP protocol. Here the client is a browser who wishes to have access to a protected document called uniform resource identifier (URI) from a Web site. There are two access control protocols: one is called *basic* and the other is called *digest* (the latter is detailed in Section 5.2). In the basic protocol, the server must keep a database of (realm-value,userid,password) triplets, where realm-value indicates one "part" of the HTTP server, userid is the identification string of a user, and password is simply the password.

Upon a URI request to a server, the server sends a challenge

```
WWW-Authenticate: basic realm="⟨realm-value⟩"
```

Then the client must send credentials

```
Authorization: basic ⟨basic-credentials⟩
```

where basic-credentials is the string

⟨userid⟩:⟨password⟩

which is encoded according to the base64 algorithm.[1] If the (realm-value, userid, password) triplet is correct, the server can respond to the URI request. Otherwise it

---

[1] This encoding scheme simply consists of encoding bitstrings into byte sequences in which only 6 bits in every byte are used. This is in order to avoid escape characters which might be interpreted by processes as special instructions.

sends an error message

```
HTTP/1.0 401 Unauthorized
```

and sends the challenge again.

If the browser tries to connect to the URI and receives an access control request to which it does not know how to respond, it yields a dialog box urging the user to fill out the userid and password fields. Usually, these are kept in memory during the session of the browser so that the server can send many access control requests during the same session. This is why users are often requested to close the browser after the session so that no other user can access the same URI.

5.1.3 PAP Access Control in PPP

A similar example is one of the two access control protocols provided in the Point to Point Protocol (PPP) which enables the remote connection of a machine to a network. These two access control protocols are PPP Authentication Protocol (PAP) and Challenge-Handshake Authentication Protocol (CHAP), which will be discussed in Section 5.2. Both are detailed in RFC 1334 (Ref. [118]).

The PAP protocol is quite similar to the basic access control in HTTP.

5.2 Challenge–Response Protocols

The password access control protocol obviously provides low security since passwords may be intercepted by a third party (unless the communication channel protects confidentiality, which can be the case with the SSL protocol as discussed in Section 12.3).

In this section we have better access control protocols in which the client never sends a password in clear to the server. It actually proves that he has the password by replying to some random challenges as depicted in Fig. 5.2. This is not always feasible when the client is a human being. It is however quite easy to implement when the client is a machine.

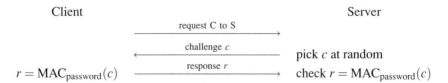

Figure 5.2. Challenge–Response access control.

The drawback of this method is that the server database needs to keep the passwords (i.e. not only the hashed values). It must therefore be strongly protected.

5.2.1 Digest Access Control in HTTP

The digest access control is an alternative to the basic protocol which is also described in RFC 2617 (Ref. [69]). We describe here the main features of the digest protocol without giving details for all parameters.

Upon a URI request to a server, the server sends a challenge

```
WWW-Authenticate: digest
                  realm="⟨realm-value⟩"
                  [domain="⟨URI⟩"]
                  nonce="⟨base64 nonce-value⟩"
                  [opaque="⟨base64 opaque-value⟩"]
                  [stale=true]
                  [algorithm=MD5]
                  [qop="⟨comma-separated list of auth or auth-int or token⟩"]
```

(Lines between [ ] are optional.) The realm-value works as in the basic access authentication scheme. The nonce-value is a one-time generated value (preferably encoded with base64). The opaque-value is only to be returned in the credentials. (It is quite convenient for servers who send several challenges to several clients at the same time: they can easily figure out which response corresponds to which challenge.) The `stale=true` string indicates that the nonce-value is now stale and that the client must send other credentials with a new nonce without querying the password again to the user. The qop-value suggests the quality of protection scheme.

We can use any standard hash function H and MAC KD. Default for H is MD5 and

$$KD_K(x) = H(K||``:"||x)$$

where $||$ denotes the concatenation operation.

The client then must send credentials

```
Authorization: digest
               username="⟨username-value⟩"
               realm="⟨realm-value⟩"
               nonce="⟨base64 nonce-value⟩"
               uri="⟨digest-uri⟩"
               response="⟨32lhex request-digest-value⟩"
               [algorithm=MD5]
```

[cnonce="⟨base64 cnonce-value⟩"]
[opaque="⟨base64 opaque-value⟩"]
[message-qop="⟨qop-value⟩"]
[nc=⟨8lhex nc-value⟩]

The algorithm and opaque-value must be the same as in the challenge. The qop-value must be in the suggested list from the challenge. Here 32lhex and 8lhex means 32 or 8 lowercase hexadecimal digits. Credentials must respond to the challenge following the computation below.

Computation of request-digest-value: if qop-value is auth (as for authentication) or auth-int (as for authentication with integrity protection), then

$$\text{request-digest-value} = KD_{H(A1)}(\langle\text{nonce-value}\rangle{:}\langle\text{nc-value}\rangle{:}\langle\text{cnonce-value}\rangle{:}$$
$$\langle\text{qop-value}\rangle{:}H(A2))$$

otherwise

$$\text{request-digest-value} = KD_{H(A1)}(\langle\text{nonce-value}\rangle{:}H(A2))$$

where $A1$ and $A2$ are computed as detailed below.
Computation of $A1$: if algorithm is MD5 then

$$A1 = \langle\text{username-value}\rangle{:}\langle\text{realm-value}\rangle{:}\langle\text{passwd}\rangle$$

and if algorithm is MD5-sess (as for MD5-hashed $A1$ for the whole session), then

$$A1 = H(\langle\text{username-value}\rangle{:}\langle\text{realm-value}\rangle{:}\langle\text{passwd}\rangle){:}\langle\text{nonce-value}\rangle{:}$$
$$\langle\text{cnonce-value}\rangle$$

where the hash value is computed once for the session (so that it does not compromise the confidentiality of passwd).
Computation of $A2$: if qop-value is auth then

$$A2 = \langle\text{Method}\rangle{:}\langle\text{digest-uri-value}\rangle$$

and if qop-value is auth-int then

$$A2 = \langle\text{Method}\rangle{:}\langle\text{digest-uri-value}\rangle{:}H(\langle\text{entity-body}\rangle)$$

where Method, digest-uri-value, and entity-body are part of the HTTP/1.1 standard.

As in the basic protocol, the server checks the correctness of the response and provides or denies access to the client.

5.2.2   CHAP Access Control in PPP

Challenge–Handshake Authentication Protocol (CHAP) is an alternative to the simple User-Password PPP Authentication Protocol (PAP) in RFC 1334 (Ref. [118]).

While initiating a PPP connection, or at any time during the PPP session, authentication with CHAP is required. Then CHAP packets are exchanged, encapsulated in PPP Data Link Layer frames. A CHAP packet consists of

$$Code||Identifier||Length||Data$$

where Code is a byte equal to 1, 2, 3, or 4, Identifier is a byte, and Length is the length of Data encoded on two bytes, i.e. it lies between 0 and 65535. The Identifier bytes are used to identify different simultaneous PPP sessions.

First the authenticator (PPP server) sends a CHAP packet with code 1 (challenge). Then the peer sends back a CHAP packet with code 2 (response). For the challenge and response, the Data consists of

$$Data = ValueSize||Value||Name$$

where Name is used to identify a Name-secret pair in an access control database and ValueSize is the size of Value encoded on one byte. The correct answer is defined by

$$Value_2 = H(Identifier||secret||Value_1)$$

where $Value_i$ is the value field of the packet with code i for $i = 1, 2$. Packets with code 3 and 4 indicate success and failure in the access control, respectively.

5.3   One-Time Password

Besides requiring the server to keep the passwords, the challenge-response protocols still face security problems when a challenge is repeated: if the adversary collected many challenge-response pairs, she can send multiple parallel service requests until she gets a challenge for which she knows the answer. We can prevent this by introducing an artificial delay for each access (this may substantially slow down this kind of attack), keeping track of aborted access requests, or having large challenges so that it will never be repeated. Equivalently, the challenge can be a counter value instead of a random value. In this case we can talk about *one-time passwords*: passwords which are used only once.

5.3.1   Lamport Scheme

One of the first one-time password cryptographic schemes was designed by Leslie Lamport at the time the notion of one-wayness was invented (see Ref. [113]). Basically, the Lamport scheme consists of several parts.

The password generation. The client is given a seed password w, and the server is given a pair $(f^n(w), n)$ associated with this client. Here, f is a one-way function.

The access control scheme. When the client wants to access the server for the i-th time, he sends $w_i = f^{n-i}(w)$ to the server. The server then checks that $f(w_i)$ is the first entry of the pair of the clients, retrieves the second entry which is necessarily $n - i + 1$, and replaces this pair by $(w_i, n - i)$ in the database.

With this scheme, the number of accesses is limited to n. The server only has to make one f computation. The client can implement a time–memory tradeoff: either he keeps all $f^i(w)$ in memory and does not have to compute anything (if the client is a human being, he can keep a sheet of passwords), or he only keeps w and makes on average $\frac{n}{2}$ f-computations per access, or stores m different passwords and makes on average $\frac{n}{2m}$ f-computations per access.

5.3.2   S/Key and OTP

The Bellcore company developed a popular one-time software based on the Lamport scheme: S/Key, which has also been published as an Internet document RFC 1760 (Ref. [85]). This was later transformed into an Internet standard: the one-time password (OTP) system RFC 2289 (Ref. [86]).

In this standard, the one-way f function is MD5 by default. It can also be SHA-1 or MD4.

In addition to the format of transmission, this standard provides an interesting way to represent passwords in a humanly readable way: the 64-bit password is first expanded into 66 bits with a checksum. Then it is split into six 11-bit packets. Each packet is encoded into a word given by a 2048-word dictionary of at most four alphabetical characters. Thus, a 64-bit password is represented by six humanly readable short words.

In OTP, the user gives his password w (more precisely a secret pass-phrase of at least 10 characters) to the OTP generator. The generator generates a random seed s which consists of 1–16 lowercase alphanumerical characters. It then hashes w concatenated with s and reduces it to 64 bits using a standard function (see Ref. [86]). This produces a string $S = H(w, s)$. (The purpose of the seed is to diversify the pass-phrase, since it may very well be the case that the same pass-phrase is used in different applications by a particular individual.) The generator then computes $p_i = H^{N-i}(S)$ for $i = 0, \ldots, N$ with a given integer N and gives them to the user together with s. The OTP generator also sends $p_0 = H^N(S)$ and s to the server and discards everything from its memory. The server keeps the last 64-bit one-time password p, a sequence integer i which is first set to 1, and s in memory with integrity protection.

When the user wants to access the server, the server sends a challenge

$$\texttt{otp-}\langle\text{algorithm}\rangle\ \langle\text{sequence integer}\rangle\ \langle\text{seed}\rangle$$

where seed is s and algorithm specifies on which algorithm H is based. The user then cross-checks that the sequence integer is correct and sends p_i to the server. The server rejects the user if $H(p_i) \neq p$. Otherwise, the server accepts, replaces p by p_i, and increments i. Note that the user can either recompute p_i from the seed and his pass-phrase or keep a list of all p_i's.

5.4 Key Distribution

Access control is a typical example of security protocols which involve conventional cryptography. Another important example is key agreement, key transmission, key distribution, or more generally key establishment. In many security applications, we need to share secret keys (as for conventional encryption, MAC, access control) over an insecure channel. Sometimes, one party needs to transmit its key to the other in a secure way. But sometimes, both parties only need to agree on a fresh common secret key.[2]

When two parties who do not share any common secret want to agree on a secret key with conventional cryptography, they need to use services from a third party. Many protocols require a *key distribution center* (KDC) which share a secret key with every participant.

5.4.1 The Needham–Schroeder Authentication Protocol

In the Needham–Schroeder protocol, a client C wants to access a server S so S has to be able to authenticate C (see Ref. [138]). The server does not have a database with all potential clients though. They use an authentication server (AS),[3] which is assumed to share a secret key with each individual. For instance, C and AS share a key K_C, S and AS share a key K_S, etc.

When C wants to access S, he first sends a request for authentication with S to AS in clear with a *nonce* N. A nonce is a random number which should be used once ("nonce" is a contraction of "number" and "once"). Then, AS replies to C with a message encrypted with K_C, which includes a fresh key K, the identity I_S of S, the nonce N, and a *ticket* $C_{K_S}(K, I_C)$ which includes K and the identity I_C of C. C can then send the ticket $C_{K_S}(K, I_C)$ to S. S can decrypt it, authenticate himself by sending $C_K(N)$, and C authenticates himself by replying $C_K(N + 1)$ (see Fig. 5.3).

Here, the fresh key K is generated by AS in order to secure the communication between C and S. AS makes sure that only C and S are able to retrieve it by using the encryption with K_C and K_S. The ticket sent by C to S must be generated by AS since

---

[2] We refer to Boyd and Mathuria (Ref. [37]) for a complete treatment on authenticated key establishment protocols.

[3] Here, "authentication server" is another terminology for "key distribution center."

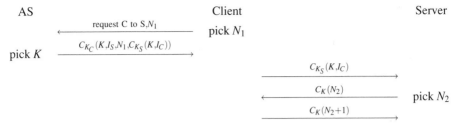

Figure 5.3. The Needham–Schroeder authentication protocol.

it is encrypted with K_S. (Nobody else should be able to encrypt with this key, so this seemingly suggests that symmetric encryption is used to provide authentication here.) So S is sure that C requested the ticket to AS, and that AS generated K for both of them.

This protocol, made in 1978, is important for historical reasons. It suffers, however, from the following drawback, and it is no longer recommended. The problem here is that when K gets leaked to an adversary because of a careless user, she can replay the ticket message $C_{K_S}(K, I_C)$ and thus impersonate C to S. The real problem is that S has no means to be ensured that K is fresh. Actually, this protocol was originally aimed at protecting against network outsiders. But the real problem comes from careless insiders. Several improvements of this protocol have been proposed, including the protocol which is used in Kerberos.

5.4.2 Kerberos

Kerberos is an improvement of the Needham–Schroeder authentication protocol. Two versions are currently well spread: Kerberos Version 4 and Kerberos Version 5. The latter was adopted as the Internet standard RFC 1510 (Ref. [105]). While the basic Kerberos protocol works as depicted in Fig. 5.4, the complete protocol works as follows. When a client wants to authenticate to a given server, the protocol proceeds as follows (see Fig. 5.5).

1. The client sends a request to the authentication server (AS), also called the Kerberos server.
2. The AS sends a credential—encrypted with the secret key of the client—to the client, together with a *grant*—encrypted with the secret key of the TGS. The TGS is the ticket granting server who issues short-term tickets. Both the credential and the grant include one selected mid-term key K_0, which is assumed to be fresh, and a timestamp. This key is to be shared by the client and the TGS only.
3. The client sends a request to the TGS with the grant.
4. The TGS sends a credential—encrypted with the secret key of the client—to the client, together with a *ticket*—encrypted with the secret key of the server.

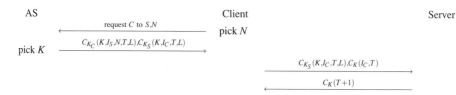

Figure 5.4. Basic Kerberos key establishment protocol.

This ticket includes a timestamp T and a lifetime period L. In order to avoid a session key compromise, the timestamp is assumed to be the present time, and the lifetime is assumed to be short.

5. The client sends the ticket to the server together with an *authenticator*. This authenticator is encrypted with the session key and corresponds to the $C_K(N)$ in the Needham–Schroeder protocol.
6. The server replies with another authenticator.

The initial authentication request includes the identity of the client and the identity of the server. It may also include various options for the ticket, among which the following are a few:

- *Renewable ticket*: The ticket has a short validity period but may be renewed (long-term tickets are dangerous because they can be stolen);
- *Postdated ticket*: postdated tickets are dangerous (because they can be stolen before they are used), and so they are explicitly marked as postdated, and security policy of servers may decide to accept or reject it;
- *Proxiable ticket*: when the client wants to pass a proxy to the server to perform a remote request on its behalf;

Of course, the AS may abort the protocol by an error message.

One problem with this protocol is that all individuals must have (relatively loosely) synchronous clocks.

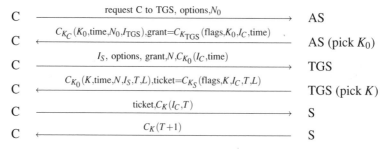

Figure 5.5. The Kerberos authentication protocol.

5.4.3 ⋆Merkle Puzzles

In 1978, Ralph Merkle published a paper (Ref. [129]) which explains how to perform confidential communication when the two parties do not share any secret, which is the basic problem of public-key cryptography.[4] Here, we assume that the two parties communicate over a channel which already provides authenticity and that they want to agree on a common secret key.

We use the notion of *puzzle*: a puzzle is defined by (y, c) and consists of recovering a key r such that $C_r^{-1}(y)$ is a triplet (n, k, c) where C is an encryption function. We assume that doing an exhaustive search takes a complexity of $\Theta(N)$ for a given parameter N. We also use a one-way function g, which is used as a pseudorandom generator.

We assume that N, C, and g are defined. The Merkle key establishment protocol works as follows between A and B.

1. A takes a random c, s_1, s_2. A takes N random r_i. A computes $n_i = g(s_1, i)$, $k_i = g(s_2, n_i)$, $y_i = C_{r_i}(n_i, k_i, c)$. A sends c and all y_i to B.
2. B picks a random i and solves the i-th puzzle. He recovers n_i and k_i. B sends n_i to A.
3. A gets $k_i = g(s_2, n_i)$. A and B now share the k_i secret key.

(See Fig. 5.6.) The time complexity for A and B is $O(N)$. If an adversary wants to recover k_i without knowing i, she must solve all puzzles until n_i is correct, which takes $\Omega(N^2)$.

5.5 ⋆Authentication Chains

We put here some applications of conventional cryptography which are a little more exotic. They illustrate how hash functions can be chained.

5.5.1 ⋆Merkle Tree

Before public-key cryptography was invented, researchers tried to invent the notion of *digital signature scheme*.[5] A digital signature is an appendix to a digital document which authenticates the signer. The signature is computed by using a private key, and it is verified by using a public key. If a digital signature is "valid," it proves that it has been computed by someone who knew a given private key. This means that it is impossible for an adversary to forge a valid signature without knowing the private key.

---

[4] See Chapter 9.
[5] The notion of digital signature and public key will be explained in Chapter 9.

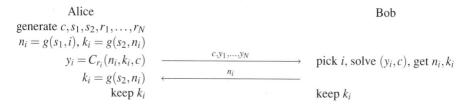

Figure 5.6. Merkle Key exchange protocol using puzzles.

One of the first signature schemes was invented by Ralph Merkle in 1979 (but it was published 10 years later; see Ref. [131]). Basic principles are twofold:

- Each bit x_i of the message is signed by using a one-time secret key k_i: a 1-bit $x_i = 1$ is signed by disclosing the secret key k_i, and the corresponding public key is the image $v_i = h(k_i)$ of the secret key through a one-way function;
- A large set of public keys v_i is authenticated by using a hash tree: each v_i is attached to a leaf of an oriented binary tree, and if a_ℓ and a_r are attached to the two subtrees of a node, we attach $h(a_\ell, a_r)$ to the node where h is a collision-resistant hash function.

The property of the hash tree is that we can authenticate all public keys by authenticating the value attached to the root of the tree only. Therefore, assuming that the root value is authenticated, we sign the message x by disclosing all k_i keys for which $x_i = 1$ and reminding all v_i for other i. Signature verification simply consists in checking that all $h(k_i)$ and reminded v_i lead to the correct root value when attached to the tree[6] (see Fig. 5.7).

One problem with this basic signature scheme is that only 1-bits are signed: the signature verifier is ensured that all 1-bits are authentic, but he is not sure for 0-bits since they could have been substituted to 1-bits. This problem is fixed by preencoding the message. A message m is first encoded into a binary string x in such a way that replacing one or several 1-bit of x by 0-bits leads to an invalid codeword. As an example, Merkle proposed to simply append to m the binary representation c of the number of 0-bits in m: $x = m||c$. We notice that if c' is the binary representation of a number which is greater than c, then there must be at least one position i for which we have $c_i = 0$ and $c'_i = 1$. Since the adversary cannot replace a 0-bit by a 1-bit in x, he cannot increase the number of 0-bit in m by replacing a 1-bit by a 0-bit.

If m has a length of n, then x has a length of $n + \log_2 n$. Hence we need $n + \log_2 n = O(n)$ keys to sign m, and $O(n)$ h-operation in order to sign or verify the signature.

---

[6] As one can see, the main difference between computer science and botanic is that trees are rooted on the top in the former.

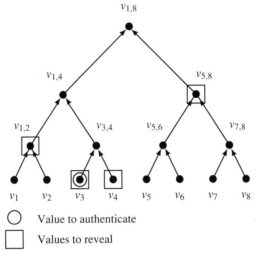

Figure 5.7. Authentication using a Merkle tree.

5.5.2 ⋆*Timestamps and Notary*

Another problem is how to timestamp a digital document in a notary sense: when producing the document together with a timestamp, we aim at proving that the document was deposited as is to a notary at a given date. This problem was addressed by Stuart Haber who actually made a business out of this problem.[7]

Provided that the notary is trusted, the problem is trivial: the notary only has to sign the document and the date. His signature is the timestamp, and verifying the signature consists of checking the signature.

The problem is more complicated when the notary is not trusted. For this, we first need to realize that the notion of time is society-related. A date is a frontier in the timescale which separates two classes of events: events which occur before and events which occur after. We can prove that a document was deposited after a given date by signing the document together with a proof that past societal events occurred. Since depositing a document becomes an event itself, we can prove that it was deposited before another given event by having a linear and linked history of events. Haber and Stornetta proposed the notion of *timestamp linkage* (see Ref. [84]). In this protocol, a notary-like service records sequences of digital documents y_n together with identities (or pseudonyms) of depositors ID_n. It computes sequences of links z_n and issues timestamps. Upon reception of y_n and ID_n, the notary proceeds as follows.

---

[7] See the activities of the Surety Technologies company http://www.surety.com, which is a kind of digital notary.

1. It sends ID_n to the r previous customers $ID_{n-1}, \ldots, ID_{n-r}$.
2. It computes $z_{n-1} = H(L_{n-1})$ where H is a hash function and L_{n-1} was previously computed.
3. It sets L_n to the sequence $((t_{n-r}, ID_{n-r}, y_{n-r}, z_{n-r}), \ldots, (t_{n-1}, ID_{n-1}, y_{n-1}, z_{n-1}))$.
4. It takes the current date and time t_n.
5. It authenticates[8] and sends $[n, t_n, ID_n, y_n, L_n]$ to ID_n. (Note that ID_n will later receive $ID_{n+1}, \ldots, ID_{n+r}$ as well.)
6. Once in a while, e.g. when n is a multiple of k, it publishes (n, z_n, ID_n) in a newspaper.

When someone wants to verify a timestamp y_n, t_n from ID_n, he asks for L_n and $ID_{n+1}, \ldots, ID_{n+r}$. He can retrieve ID_{n-i} from L_n for $i = 1, \ldots, r$. He can thus deduce the r depositors before and after t_n. By contacting them and collecting answers, he will be able to check that previous timestamps are embedded by H in L_n (thus, they happened before), and that the timestamp of L_n is embedded by H in later timestamps (thus happened before as well). He can therefore check the right sequence of events. Going backwards and forwards a sufficient number of times, he will reach published timestamps and will be able to check that they are indeed embedded in a social event like the newspaper. It is actually hard to falsify *a posteriori* a newspaper which has been widely distributed. It is necessary here to use some data from a social event (see Ref. [23]).

5.6   Wireless Communication: Two Case Studies

5.6.1   The GSM Network

GSM (Global System for Mobile communications) is a standard developed by ETSI for mobile wireless communications. It includes security standards. Security objectives are quite low in the sense that they only prevent attacks against the radio channel between the terminal and a fixed base. The main threats are

- usage of the GSM network with a fake or stolen identity,
- monitoring of private communications through the radio channel,
- monitoring of positioning information in the radio channel.

Secure charging of networks use and privacy in the wireless link are thus the main concerns. Neither confidentiality of transmissions in the wired part nor authentication of the network to the terminal are provided in GSM. The GSM security goals thus just consist of protecting confidentiality, anonymity, and authentication of terminals in the wireless part. Two standard interfaces are defined: the A3/8 authentication algorithm and the A5 encryption algorithm. Interfaces are publicly available. As it will be

---

[8] Authentication is performed by a digital signature, which will be studied in Chapter 10.

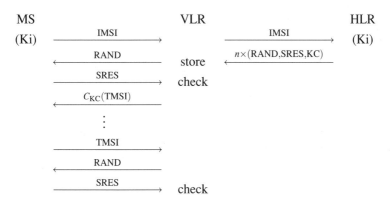

Figure 5.8. GSM authentication.

explained, the A3/8 algorithm itself is not standard: every GSM operator can use its own algorithm. However, the A5 algorithm is standard but secret.[9]

A mobile system (MS) is a combination of a terminal and a security module (the SIM card). The terminal can be manufactured by any company, but the SIM card is manufactured by the service provider who corresponds to a home network: the Home Location Register (HLR). Each MS has an identifier called IMSI. When connecting to a local network, the Visited Location Register (VLR), the IMSI is sent and forwarded to the HLR (see Fig. 5.8). Then, the HLR sends many triplets, which are used in order to authenticate the MS to the VLR. After the first authentication, the VLR gives a temporary identity TMSI to the MS in a confidential way in order to protect its privacy.

For the authentication, the mobile and the network share a long-term 128-bit secret key Ki (integrity key) which is stored in the security module. When a mobile identifies itself, it sends a TMSI (a temporary identity) which protects the real identity. The network sends a random 128-bit challenge RAND to the mobile. The mobile uses A3/8 with inputs Ki and RAND in order to compute SRES and KC. SRES is sent to the network. It is the response to the challenge. The network can perform the same computation and compare the SRES values for authentication. At the end, the mobile is authenticated and both parties have computed a common short-term 64-bit secret key KC. KC is used for encryption. The three values RAND, SRES, and KC make a triplet, which is used by the VLR.

We emphasize that Ki is protected by the security module and the HLR, but KC is a short-term secret key between the device and the VLR. Encryption is performed by the telephone, whereas authentication is performed by the security module. Therefore, A5 must be standard for every VLR and telephone manufacturers, but A3/8 can be specific to a service provider.

---

[9] The version presented in Section 2.8.3 was disclosed, and then broken in Ref. [32]. Interestingly, another secret algorithm—COMP128, which was an A3/8 proprietary algorithm—was disclosed and broken. See http://www.isaac.cs.berkeley.edu/isaac/gsm.html.

For the encryption, the A5/1 algorithm is a standard algorithm for A5. It is actually a pseudorandom generator which is initialized with a 22-bit counter and the 64-bit secret key KC. It generates a 114-bit block which is XORed to the plaintext. This is just a one-time pad with 114-bit block sequences. The heart of A5/1 is explained in Section 2.8.3.

Once the setup phase is complete, confidentiality is ensured. A counter-based stream cipher protects against attempts to erase, swap, or replay packets. However, integrity protection is rather poor. It is easy for an adversary to replace a confidential message x by a message $x \oplus \delta$ for a δ of her choice (even without knowing x). Hence it is hard to say that authentication is protected.

5.6.2   The Bluetooth Network

Bluetooth networks[10] are other nice examples of security infrastructure based on conventional cryptography only. We briefly outline how it works based on the Bluetooth version 1.2 standard (Ref. [4]).

Bluetooth uses several conventional cryptographic algorithms. The core ones are the stream cipher E0 that was described in Section 2.8.4, and the block cipher SAFER+, which is a successor of the block cipher SAFER K-64. They are used in order to define a series of cryptographic algorithms E0, E1, E21, E22, and E3. E0 serves for encryption. E1 serves for peer authentication. E2 (including E21 and E22) is a key generator for authentication. E3 is a key generator for encryption.

E0 was described in Section 2.8.4.

The authentication algorithm E1 works like a MAC. No matter who is the master and who is the slave, authentication can be done in the two directions, so we talk about a "verifier" and a "claimant." E1 takes the 48-bit logical address BD_ADDR of the claimant, a 128-bit random challenge AU_RAND, which is transmitted by the verifier, and a 128-bit "link key" K, which is the secret key. E1 produces a 32-bit response SRES and a 96-bit value ACO (authentication ciphering offset). With this primitive, authentication is quite trivial: the verifier picks a random challenge and sends it to the claimant; the claimant computes the response and sends it to the verifier; the verifier does the same computation and compares the two values. The output of E1 is defined by using SAFER+ twice in a (strange) hash mode. Note that E1 must keep track of successful and unsuccessful authentications. Indeed, E1 starts with a waiting interval whose value is kept in memory. If an authentication is not successful, this value is multiplied by a factor greater than 1. Otherwise, it is divided by a factor greater than 1. The value must further be bounded.

The authentication challenge is generated either by E21 or by E22 depending on what kind of authentication is required. E21 takes a 128-bit random value and a 48-bit

---

[10] Following the Bluetooth folklore, "network" should be replaced by "piconet."

logical address and produces a 128-bit value. E22 takes an additional PIN code of L bytes where $1 \leq L \leq 16$. Note that E21 is a kind of SAFER+ encryption of the address by using the random value as a key, and that E22 is a kind of SAFER+ encryption of the random value by using a combination of the PIN and the address as a key.

Finally, the encryption key is generated by E3. E3 takes as input the 128-bit link key K, a 128-bit random value EN_RAND, and a 96-bit value COF. This value called ciphering offset is either the concatenation of the two logical addresses of the master and the slave, or the ACO value coming from the authentication, depending on what kind of link key is used. It produces a 128-bit value which is linearly shrunk to the required length for giving the encryption key K_c. E3 is defined from SAFER+ in the same hash mode as that of E1.

We can now describe how these primitives are used in order to set up the encrypted channel between two peers.

First of all, the peers negotiate who is the master and who is the slave. Then they have to do some key management through a "pairing protocol," which leads to a secret 128-bit "link key." Typically, this link key is semipermanent and will be used in a future connection so that key management will not be required. Indeed, if the peers are already paired, then the link key already exists on both sides. When a session starts they perform a bidirectional authentication based on this key using E1 as depicted in Fig. 5.9. When they need to start encryption they agree on a key length, derive an encryption key using E3, and encrypt using E0.

When two devices want to set up a pairing, a human user typically has to securely type a random ephemeral PIN code on both devices as depicted in Fig. 5.10. If one device does not have any keyboard, a PIN code can be built in by a manufacturer (on Bluetooth headsets, the PIN code is usually 0000). The key management consists of generating an initialization key, generating a link key, and exchanging the link key. The initialization key is generated using E22 using a PIN code and a 128-bit random value IN_RAND which is communicated by the master to the slave. Then both peers pick a fresh random value LK_RAND and exchange the XOR of this value with the initialization key. They can then compute two keys LK_K with E21 using the two

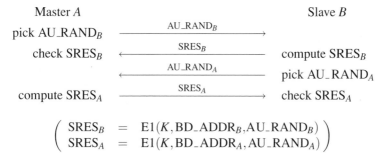

Figure 5.9. Bidirectional authentication protocol in bluetooth.

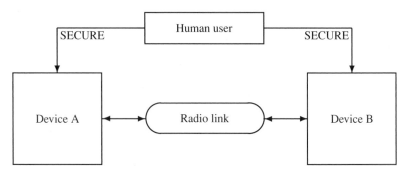

Figure 5.10. Bluetooth pairing.

random values and their addresses and deduce a combination key which is the XOR of both LK_K keys. This combination key serves as the link key. The overall (typical) pairing protocol is depicted in Fig. 5.11. If one device has low memory capabilities, it uses its unit key which is generated once for all as a link key and sends its XOR with the initialization key to the other device which deduces it (see Fig. 5.12).

Obviously, if an adversary listens to the communication in the pairing and authentication protocols and if the PIN code can be found by exhaustive search, then she can easily recover the link key. Since the whole security infrastructure is built on the confidentiality of the link key, security is void in this case. However, peer authentication and key establishment is safe assuming that the pairing is run through a confidential channel.

Like in GSM, once the setup phase is complete, confidentiality is ensured. A clock-based stream cipher protects against attempts to delay, swap, or replay a frame, but not

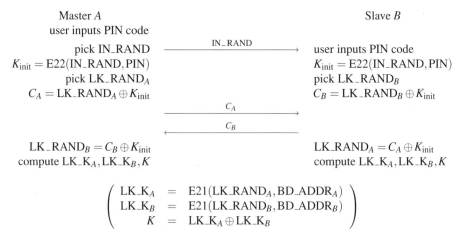

Figure 5.11. A typical pairing protocol in bluetooth.

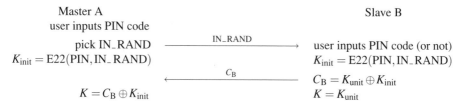

Figure 5.12. A pairing protocol with a device with low capacities.

against attempts to erase frames. Like in GSM, the integrity protection is very poor so frame authentication is not guaranteed.

5.7   Exercises

Exercise 5.1. *We consider an arbitrary secret function f from a finite set C of C challenges to a finite set $\mathcal{R}$ of R responses. We consider an access control scheme in which a server picks a challenge uniformly at random in C and the client sends the corresponding response after one f application. Explain how the chance of cheating increases when looking at access control communications. Describe an attack and compute its probability of success.*

Exercise 5.2. *The Kerberos authentication protocol is presented using secret-key encryption function C_K. Identify the accurate security property which is required here. (Confidentiality? Integrity? Authentication?)*

6

Algorithmic Algebra

Content

Group theory: isomorphism, construction
The ring Z_n: Euclid algorithm, exponentiation, Chinese Remainder Theorem
Finite fields: generators, construction
⋆Quadratic residuosity
Elliptic curves

Basic notions of number theory are briefly exposed in this chapter, as well as a number of useful algorithms on number theory. We encourage the reader to experiment with the algorithms using a symbolic computing software (e.g. Maple, from the University of Waterloo,[1] or Pari/GP from the University of Bordeaux[2]). While conventional cryptography uses simple operations on bitstrings which are built in all microprocessors, public-key cryptography uses computation in algebraic structures. These classical structures are reviewed here.

6.1 Basic Group Theory

6.1.1 Basic Set Theory

We briefly remind here some basic notions and notations from set theory.

A *set* consists of a collection of *elements*. If an element x is in a set A we write $x \in A$. Two sets are equal if they have exactly the same elements. We let $\emptyset$ be the empty set, i.e. the set which has no element. If A and B are two sets, their *intersection* is the set denoted $A \cap B$ of all x which are elements of both A and B. The *union* of A and B is the set denoted $A \cup B$ of all x which are elements of either A or B. If all elements of A are systematically elements of B we say that A is a *subset* of B and write $A \subseteq B$. In order to denote the set of all elements x of A which satisfy a predicate $P(x)$, we write $\{x \in A; P(x)\}$, or simply $\{x; P(x)\}$ when A is clear from the context.

A *function* f may map an element x of A to an element $f(x)$ of a set B. We write $f : A \to B$ to denote that f takes elements of A and maps them into elements of B. We write $f : x \mapsto y$ to denote that $f(x) = y$. In this case we say that y is the *image* of x by f and that x is a *preimage* of y by f. If $I \subseteq A$, we let $f(I)$ denote the set of

---

[1] See http://www.maplesoft.com.
[2] See http://pari.math.u-bordeaux.fr.

all $f(x)$ for $x \in I$. If $J \subseteq B$, we let $f^{-1}(J)$ denote the set of all x such that $f(x) \in J$. To denote the set of all images by f of elements that satisfy the predicate we write $\{f(x); x \in A, P(x)\}$ or $f(\{x \in A; P(x)\})$.

A function can also be considered as a *family*, but for this we use sequence-like notations. A family $(x_i)_{i \in I}$ is essentially a function from I to another set which maps i into an element x_i. The set I is called the *index* set of the family. As an example a *sequence* is a family whose index set is the set of all integers (which may start from zero or one). A *pair* can be viewed as a family of index set $\{1, 2\}$. In this case we just denote (x_1, x_2) instead of $(x_i)_{i \in \{1,2\}}$. Similarly we write (x_1, x_2, x_3) for a *triplet* $(x_i)_{i \in \{1,2,3\}}$. Given two sets A and B we define the *Cartesian product* $A \times B$ as the set of all pairs (x, y) for which $x \in A$ and $y \in B$. We similarly define the set $A \times B \times C$ of all triplets consisting of elements in A, B, and C respectively. For simplicity we consider $\times$ to be associative in the sense that we do not make any difference between $(A \times B) \times C$ and $A \times (B \times C)$. (Formally we would consider $(A \times B) \times C$ as the set of all pairs whose first component is a pair belonging to $A \times B$ and the second one is an element of C.)

Given a family $(A_i)_{i \in I}$ of sets we can define the intersection

$$\bigcap_{i \in I} A_i$$

and the union

$$\bigcup_{i \in I} A_i$$

of all A_i. We also define the Cartesian product

$$\prod_{i \in I} A_i$$

as the set of all families $(x_i)_{i \in I}$ for which $x_i \in A_i$ for all $i \in I$. When all A_i are equal to a single set A we write this product A^I. We also write A^2 instead of $A^{\{1,2\}}$, and more generally A^n instead of $A^{\{1,\dots,n\}}$.

A *binary relation R* between elements of a set A and elements of a set B is formally a subset of $A \times B$. If (x, y) is in this subset, we say that x and y are related by R and denote this by $x R y$. When $A = B$, we say that R is *reflexive* if $x R x$ for all $x \in A$. We say that it is *symmetric* if $x R y$ is equivalent to $y R x$ for all $x, y \in A$. We say that it is *transitive* if $x R y$ and $y R z$ imply $x R z$ for any $x, y, z \in A$. R is an *equivalence relation* if it is reflexive, symmetric, and transitive. In this case, denoting $\text{Cl}(x) = \{y \in A; x R y\}$ as for the "class of x," we have

$$\text{Cl}(x) = \text{Cl}(y) \iff \text{Cl}(x) \cap \text{Cl}(y) \neq \emptyset \iff x R y$$

for all $x, y \in A$. Since $x \in \text{Cl}(x)$ we notice that all $\text{Cl}(x)$ build a *partition* of A, i.e. a collection of subsets $\text{Cl}(x)$ of empty pairwise intersections whose union covers all of

A. In this case we formally call this partition the *quotient* of *A* by *R* and denote it by A/R.

6.1.2 Groups

Formally, a *group* is any set *G* associated to a group law which is a mapping from $G \times G$ to *G*. It thus maps two operands from *G* onto an element of *G*. This law can be denoted either additively (with the $+$ symbol) or multiplicatively (with $\times$, the dot symbol, or even nothing). Using multiplicative notation, this law must fulfill the following group properties.

1. *Closure*: For any $a, b \in G$, ab is an element of *G*.
2. *Associativity*: For any $a, b, c \in G$, we have $a(bc) = (ab)c$.
3. *Neutral element*: There exists a distinguished element *e* in *G* such that for any $a \in G$, we have $ae = ea = a$.
4. *Invertibility*: For any $a \in G$, there exists an element $b \in G$ such that ab and ba are neutral elements.

It is further easy to see that the neutral element *e* is necessarily unique: if *e* and e' are neutral, we must have $e'e = ee' = e'$ because *e* is neutral, and $ee' = e'e = e$ because e' is neutral, therefore $e = e'$. We usually denote this neutral element by 1 (or 0 if the group law is additively denoted). This implies that if *b* is an inverse of *a*, then $ab = ba = 1$. It is not more difficult to see that the inverse of an element is unique: if *b* and b' are both inverse of *a*, we must have $ab = ba = 1$ and $ab' = b'a = 1$. We can then multiply the latter equality by *b* to the right and obtain $(b'a)b = 1.b = b$ which implies $b'(ab) = b$ by associativity, and then $b' = b$. We usually denote by $b = a^{-1}$ the *inverse* of *a* (or $-a$ if the group law is additively denoted, in which case the term *opposite* is more appropriate).

Commutativity means that for any $a, b \in G$, we have $ab = ba$. Usually, additively denoted groups are commutative. When a group is commutative, we say it is an *Abelian group*.

We notice that all products made of a single element *a* are uniquely defined by their number of terms: for instance $(a(a(aa)))a = a(((aa)a)a)$. We can thus uniquely denote it by a^5 (or $5a$ with additive notations). We can also define a^{-n} as the inverse of a^n. (With additive notations, this is denoted $n.a$ as a multiplication of an integer by a group element.)

Here are a few fundamental examples.

- The *trivial group* $G = \{0\}$ defined by $0 + 0 = 0$. There is not much to say about this group.
- The Abelian group **Z** of *relative integers* with the usual addition law. We notice that this is the *free Abelian group* generated by a single element $g = 1$: all elements can be uniquely written ng.

- The *symmetric group* $\mathbf{S}_A$ over a given set A. This is the set of all permutations over A with the composition law which is usually denoted $\circ$. When $A = \{1, 2, \ldots, n\}$, we denote it $\mathbf{S}_n$. Note that this is not an Abelian group when $n \geq 3$.
- The *group* $\mathbf{Z}_n$ *of residues modulo n*. This is the group $\{0, 1, \ldots, n-1\}$ with the additive law

$$(a, b) \mapsto a + b \bmod n.$$

We do not encourage denoting it as $a + b$ in cryptography since this may lead to confusions with other modular additions, or even the regular one.

We recall that $x \bmod n$ denotes the *remainder* in the *Euclidean division* of x by n: computing the division of x by n, we obtain an integral relation $x = qn + r$ with $0 \leq r < n$. The $x \bmod n$ integer is simply r. The quotient q is the greatest integer which is smaller than $\frac{x}{n}$. We can denote it $\lfloor \frac{x}{n} \rfloor$. We can thus write

$$x \bmod n = x - \left\lfloor \frac{x}{n} \right\rfloor \times n.$$

6.1.3 Generating a Group, Comparing Groups

If we take a subset A of a group G, we say that A *generates* G, or is a generator set, if any element of G can be written as a finite product (or sum for additive notations) of elements which are taken only from A or the inverse (or opposite) of elements of A. For instance, $\{1\}$ generates $\mathbf{Z}$ as a group since all relative integers are finite sums of terms all equal to 1 or to -1, the inverse of 1. It also generates $\mathbf{Z}_n$ with the modulo n addition.

A *group (homo)morphism* is a function f from a group G (whose neutral element is 1_G) to a group G' (whose neutral element is $1_{G'}$) with the following properties:

1. If 1_G is the neutral element of G, then $f(1_G)$ is neutral in G';
2. For all $a, b \in G$, we have $f(ab) = f(a)f(b)$ (here, ab is a G-product and $f(a)f(b)$ is a G'-product);
3. For all $a \in G$, we have $f(a^{-1}) = f(a)^{-1}$ (here, a^{-1} is a G-inverse and $f(a)^{-1}$ is a G'-inverse).

We notice that the first and third properties are consequences of the second one.

We can define the kernel $f^{-1}(\{1_{G'}\})$ of f as the reciprocal image of the set $\{1_{G'}\}$ by f: it is the set of all $a \in G$ such that $f(a)$ is neutral in G'. We can also define the image $f(G)$ of f as the set of all elements reached by f. We have the following properties:

- f is injective if and only if $f^{-1}(\{1_{G'}\}) = \{1_G\}$;
- f is surjective if and only if $f(G) = G'$.

When a group morphism is injective and surjective, it is bijective, thus called a *group isomorphism*. In that case we say the groups are *isomorphic*, and considered as having the same group structure.

A *subgroup* of a group G' is a subset G of G' such that

1. G is nonempty,
2. for all $a, b \in G$, we have $ab^{-1} \in G$.

Therefore it is a nonempty subset stable by multiplication and inversion. As an example, $\{1_G\}$ and G are subgroups of G. They are the trivial subgroups. Kernels and images of group morphisms are subgroups. Interestingly, any group G is isomorphic to a subgroup of $\mathbf{S}_G$: we let f be a mapping from G to $\mathbf{S}_G$, defined by $f(a)$ as the permutation over G which maps x onto ax. f is a group morphism which is injective. G is thus isomorphic to the image of this group morphism which is hence a subgroup of $\mathbf{S}_G$. Therefore, any finite group of cardinality n is isomorphic to a subgroup of $\mathbf{S}_n$.

6.1.4 Building New Groups

We can make new groups from others. We can make the *group product* $G \times G'$ of any two groups G and G' as the set of pairs of elements of G and G' with the *product law*:

$$(a, b).(c, d) = (ac, bd).$$

We notice that the notion of product of group is associative since $G \times (G' \times G'')$ is isomorphic to $(G \times G') \times G''$. We can make the product of more groups. We can also define G^n. More generally, for any set A, we can define the group G^A as the set of all functions from A to G.

We can also obtain the *quotient* of an Abelian group G by a subgroup H. With additive notations, we define a congruence in G in the following way: we say that $a, b \in G$ are congruent if $a - b \in H$. We denote $a \equiv b \,(\mathrm{mod}\ H)$. The congruence class of $a \in G$ is the set of all $b \in G$ which are congruent to a. We can easily check that this is $a + H$, the set of all $a + h$ terms for $h \in H$. We then define G/H as the set of all congruence classes. We can easily define additions in G/H by saying that the sum of the class of a and the class of b is the class of $a + b$ which is uniquely defined: if $a \equiv a' \,(\mathrm{mod}\ H)$ and $b \equiv b' \,(\mathrm{mod}\ H)$, then $a + b \equiv a' + b' \,(\mathrm{mod}\ H)$.

The set $n\mathbf{Z}$ of all multiples of n is a subgroup of $\mathbf{Z}$. We can thus define $\mathbf{Z}/n\mathbf{Z}$. As we will see, this group is actually isomorphic to the group $\mathbf{Z}_n$ of residues modulo n that was defined in Section 6.1.2, and we denote $a \equiv b \,(\mathrm{mod}\ n)$ instead of $a \equiv b \,(\mathrm{mod}\ n\mathbf{Z})$.

6.1.5 Fundamentals on Groups

We say that an element a of a finite group G has an *order* n if n is the smallest positive integer such that $a^n = 1$. Note that the order can be infinite, but when the group has a finite number of elements, all the orders of its elements are necessarily finite. We also call *order of a group* its cardinality. We should thus avoid confusion between the order of a group and the order of an element. We recall the famous Lagrange Theorem.

Theorem 6.1 (Lagrange). *In a finite group, the order of an element always divides the order of its group.*

How to compute orders in practice will be addressed in Chapter 7.

It is worth mentioning that we can characterize all finite Abelian groups by the following result.

Theorem 6.2 (Reduction of finite Abelian groups). *Let G be a finite Abelian group. There exists a unique sequence $n_1, \ldots, n_r$ of natural integers such that for all i, n_i is a factor of n_{i+1}, $n_1 > 1$, and G is isomorphic to*

$$\mathbf{Z}_{n_1} \times \cdots \times \mathbf{Z}_{n_r}.$$

6.2   The Ring $\mathbf{Z}_n$

6.2.1   Rings

Formally, a *ring* is an additively denoted Abelian group R with a second law which is multiplicatively denoted and which fulfills the following ring properties.

1. *Closure*: For all $a, b \in R$, $a \times b$ is in R.
2. *Associativity*: $\times$ is associative.
3. *Neutral element*: There exists a neutral element. Since it is necessarily unique, we denote it by 1.
4. *Distributivity*: For any $a, b, c \in R$, we have $a \times (b + c) = ab + ac$ and $(a + b) \times c = ac + bc$.

We notice that distributivity implies that $a \times 0 = 0 \times a = 0$ for any a: we have $a \times 0 = a \times (0 + 0) = a \times 0 + a \times 0$, which can be simplified by $a \times 0$ to yield $a \times 0 = 0$. We thus notice that unless R is the trivial group, 0 must be different from 1: if $1 = 0$, for any a we have $a = a \times 1 = a \times 0 = 0$, thus the group is trivial. We notice that elements are not always invertible with respect to $\times$. 0 is actually not invertible since $0 \times a$ cannot be equal to 1. We can however define the *multiplicative group* denoted R^* as the set of all invertible ring elements. When the multiplicative group consists of R with 0 removed, we say that R is a *field*.

In this book we only consider *commutative rings*: rings for which the multiplication is also commutative.

6.2.2   Definition of Z_n

We have already mentioned the group $\mathbf{Z}_n$. The structure of this group is however richer. It actually has a ring structure.

We already mentioned its additive structure of an Abelian group. We can similarly define the multiplication by

$$(a, b) \mapsto a \times b \bmod n.$$

Once again, we do not suggest writing it $a + b$ since it may introduce confusion.

This is actually a "pedestrian way" to define $\mathbf{Z}_n$. A more intellectual one consists of saying that $\mathbf{Z}_n$ is the quotient ring of ring $\mathbf{Z}$ by the principal ideal $n\mathbf{Z}$ generated by n. We have seen that we can make a quotient of an Abelian group by one of its subgroups. For rings, we quotient by ideals. An *ideal* is a subset I such that

1. I is a subgroup for the addition;
2. for any $a \in I$ and any $b \in R$, we have $ab \in I$.

In this case, quotients are defined similarly as for groups. The multiplication of the class of a by the class of b is simply the class of ab. An arbitrary set A can generate an ideal $\langle A \rangle$: it is simply the set of all ring elements which can be written as a finite combination $a_1 x_1 + \cdots + a_n x_n$ with $a_1, \ldots, a_n \in R$ and $x_1, \ldots, x_n \in A$. When A is reduced to a single element, the ideal is *principal*. The principal ideal generated by n is thus simply the set of all integers for which n is a factor. Making a quotient by this ideal simply means that we further consider all multiples of n as zero elements: we thus reduce modulo n. Classes of residues modulo n are uniquely represented by their representative in $\{0, 1, \ldots, n - 1\}$.

Since we will later make an extensive use of $\mathbf{Z}_n$, it is important to get familiar with it. We will use examples with $n = 35$. As a computation example, we can see that

$$27 + 19 \bmod 35 = 11$$

because $27 + 19 = 46$ and for $46 \bmod 35$, we make the Euclidean division of 46 by 35. We get a quotient of 1 with a remainder of 11 (indeed, $46 = 1 \times 35 + 11$), thus $46 \bmod 35 = 11$. As another example, we have

$$17 \times 22 \bmod 35 = 24$$

because $17 \times 22 = 374$ and the quotient of 374 by 35 is 10 with a remainder of 24 (indeed, $374 = 10 \times 35 + 24$).

For completeness we need to realize that the "pedestrian" and "intellectual" ways really define the same thing! This can be checked by the following properties

$$(a + n\mathbf{Z}) + (b + n\mathbf{Z}) = ((a + b \bmod n) + n\mathbf{Z})$$
$$(a + n\mathbf{Z}) \times (b + n\mathbf{Z}) = ((a \times b \bmod n) + n\mathbf{Z})$$

where $a + n\mathbf{Z}$ is the residue class of a, $(a + n\mathbf{Z}) + (b + n\mathbf{Z})$ means the addition of two residue classes in the "intellectual" sense, and $a + b \bmod n$ is the "pedestrian" addition.

6.2.3 Additions, Multiplications, Inversion

We can then realize that it is computationally easy to make simple operations on large numbers. Let us first look at how additions can be carried out.

We assume that large numbers are represented as bitstrings. For instance, if a and b are ℓ-bit numbers, we can represent them as

$$a = \sum_{i=0}^{\ell-1} a_i 2^i \quad \text{and} \quad b = \sum_{i=0}^{\ell-1} b_i 2^i$$

with $a_i = 0$ or 1 and $b_i = 0$ or 1 for $i = 0, 1, \ldots, \ell - 1$. Fig. 6.1 is an example of an algorithm computing the addition of a and b. This program computes the addition by managing carries from right to left. We can prove it by induction by showing that when entering into loop i, the addition of the truncated parts of a and b is equal to the truncated part of c plus $r.2^i$ and that $r = 0$ or 1, namely

$$\sum_{j=0}^{i-1} a_j 2^j + \sum_{j=0}^{i-1} b_j 2^j = \sum_{j=0}^{i-1} c_j 2^j + r 2^i.$$

Input: a and b, two integers of at most ℓ bits
Output: c, an integer of at most $\ell + 1$ bits representing $a + b$
Complexity: $\mathcal{O}(\ell)$
1: $r \leftarrow 0$
2: **for** $i = 0$ to $\ell - 1$ **do**
3:    $d \leftarrow a_i + b_i + r$
4:    set c_i and r to bits such that $d = 2r + c_i$
5: **end for**
6: $c_\ell \leftarrow r$

Figure 6.1. Addition of big numbers.

It is trivial for $i = 0$. Assuming that this holds for i, we can prove it for $i + 1$ by noticing that

$$\sum_{j=0}^{i} a_j 2^j + \sum_{j=0}^{i} b_j 2^j = \sum_{j=0}^{i-1} a_j 2^j + a_i 2^i + \sum_{j=0}^{i-1} b_j 2^j + b_i 2^i$$

$$= \sum_{j=0}^{i-1} c_j 2^j + r 2^i + a_i 2^i + b_i 2^i$$

$$= \sum_{j=0}^{i-1} c_j 2^j + (a_i + b_i + r) 2^i.$$

The parenthesis $a_i + b_i + r$ corresponds to the new d value. Since a_i, b_i, and r are not greater than 1, the new d is at most 3. Thus, we can compute the Euclidean division of d by 2:

$$d = 2r + c_i.$$

Thus, with the new r value, we have

$$\sum_{j=0}^{i} a_j 2^j + \sum_{j=0}^{i} b_j 2^j = \sum_{j=0}^{i-1} c_j 2^j + c_i 2^i + r 2^{i+1}$$

and $r = 0$ or 1. This completes the induction. Then, the induction equation for $i = \ell$ raises

$$a + b = \sum_{j=0}^{\ell-1} c_j 2^j + c_\ell 2^\ell$$

which means $a + b = c$.

This program uses elementary operations (like the addition of bits). Its complexity is $\mathcal{O}(\ell)$. We can thus compute $a + b$ within a linear time in the sizes of a and b.

If n is a number of exactly ℓ bits, we can compare $a + b$ with n within $\mathcal{O}(\ell)$ operations by comparing bits from left to right until we have a difference. Then, if $a + b$ is greater than n, we can subtract n within $\mathcal{O}(\ell)$ operations. Therefore, if a and b are smaller than n, we can compute $a + b \bmod n$ within $\mathcal{O}(\ell)$ operations.

We can generalize this method for the multiplication. We have indeed two possible iterative algorithms for multiplying a by b. One looks at all bits of b iteratively from the rightmost to the leftmost (see Fig. 6.2), the other does the same from the leftmost to the rightmost (see Fig. 6.3). For multiplication in $\mathbf{Z}_n$, we just have to replace the regular additions by the addition in our group: the addition modulo n.

Input: a and b, two integers of at most ℓ bits
Output: $c = a \times b$
Complexity: $\mathcal{O}(\ell^2)$
1: $x \leftarrow 0$
2: $y \leftarrow a$
3: **for** $i = 0$ to $\ell - 1$ **do**
4:    **if** $b_i = 1$ **then**
5:        $x \leftarrow x + y$
6:    **end if**
7:    $y \leftarrow y + y$
8: **end for**
9: $c \leftarrow x$

Figure 6.2. Multiplication from right to left.

Division is harder but generalizes as well.

Finally, Fig. 6.4 depicts a program performing the *Extended Euclid Algorithm.* This enables us to compute the *greatest common divisor (gcd)* of a and b together with an integral relationship (called *Bezout relationship*)

$$au + bv = \gcd(a, b).$$

The program manipulates three-dimensional vectors $\vec{x} = (x_1, x_2, x_3)$ and $\vec{y} = (y_1, y_2, y_3)$. We can prove by induction that the above algorithm works. We first have to notice that we have

$$x_1 = ax_2 + bx_3 \quad \text{and} \quad y_1 = ay_2 + by_3$$

at any time. Thus, if the program halts, we have $d = au + bv$. Then, we notice that $|y_1|$ decreases at every step 4, since the new y_1 is the remainder of the division of x_1 by y_1,

Input: a and b, two integers of at most ℓ bits
Output: $c = a \times b$
Complexity: $\mathcal{O}(\ell^2)$
1: $x \leftarrow 0$
2: **for** $i = \ell - 1$ downto 0 **do**
3:    $x \leftarrow x + x$
4:    **if** $b_i = 1$ **then**
5:        $x \leftarrow x + a$
6:    **end if**
7: **end for**
8: $c \leftarrow x$

Figure 6.3. Multiplication from left to right.

Input: a and b, two integers of at most ℓ bits
Output: d, u, v such that $d = au + bv = \gcd(a, b)$
Complexity: $\mathcal{O}(\ell^2)$
1: $\vec{x} \leftarrow (a, 1, 0), \vec{y} \leftarrow (b, 0, 1)$
2: **while** $y_1 > 0$ **do**
3:     make an Euclidean division $x_1 = qy_1 + r$
4:     do $\vec{x} \leftarrow \vec{x} - q\vec{y}$ and exchange $\vec{x}$ and $\vec{y}$
5: **end while**
6: $(d, u, v) \leftarrow \vec{x}$

Figure 6.4. Extended euclid algorithm.

thus lesser than $|y_1|$. Thus y_1 eventually reaches zero and the program halts. Finally, we notice that the gcd of x_1 and y_1 remains unchanged throughout the computation since

$$\gcd(x_1, y_1) = \gcd(y_1, x_1 - qy_1).$$

When the computation starts, the gcd of x_1 and y_1 is the gcd of a and b. When the computation ends, the gcd of x_1 and y_2 is the gcd of d and 0 which is d. Therefore the computation eventually halts with $d = \gcd(a, b) = au + bv$. Finally, we prove that the complexity is $\mathcal{O}(\ell^3)$. For this we notice that every loop is of complexity $\mathcal{O}(\ell^2)$ (the complexity of the Euclidean division). We thus have to prove that the maximal number of iterations is $\mathcal{O}(\ell)$. For this, let us consider the sequence $(z_0, z_1, \ldots, z_i)$ of all values taken by y_1. We know that it is a decreasing sequence such that $z_0 < 2^\ell$, $z_i = 0$, and $z_{j+1} = z_{j-1} - q_j z_j$ with

$$q_j = \left\lfloor \frac{z_{j-1}}{z_j} \right\rfloor.$$

Note that q_j can never be zero, but for the first iteration, thus we have $z_{j+1} + z_j \le z_{j-1}$ for $j = 1, 2, \ldots, i - 1$. Let us define $t_i = z_i = 0$, $t_{i-1} = z_{i-1} = d$, and $t_{j-1} = t_{j+1} + t_j$ for $j = i - 1, i - 2, \ldots, 1$. We have $z_j \ge t_j$ for $j = 0, 1, \ldots, i$, thus $t_0 \le 2^\ell$. This t_j sequence is a Fibonacci sequence which resolves into

$$t_j = \frac{d}{\sqrt{5}} \left(\left(\frac{1 + \sqrt{5}}{2} \right)^{i-j} - \left(\frac{1 - \sqrt{5}}{2} \right)^{i-j} \right).$$

Hence

$$2^\ell \ge t_0 \ge \frac{1}{\sqrt{5}} \left(\left(\frac{1 + \sqrt{5}}{2} \right)^{i} - \left(\frac{1 - \sqrt{5}}{2} \right)^{i} \right)$$

which ends up with $i = \mathcal{O}(\ell)$.

For completeness we mention that a more complicated analysis shows that the complexity is actually $\mathcal{O}(\ell^2)$. The proof of this result is out of the scope of this course (see Ref. [112]).

As an important application of the Extended Euclid Algorithm, we can now compute the inversion in $\mathbf{Z}_n$: if we want to invert an element x in $\mathbf{Z}_n$, we run the algorithm with $a = x$ and $b = n$. If the obtained gcd is 1, we get the Bezout relationship $1 = xu + nv$, which means $u \equiv x^{-1} \pmod{n}$. If the gcd is not 1, x and n have a common factor greater than 1, so $xu - qn$ also shares this common factor for any $q \in \mathbf{Z}$, therefore $xu \bmod n$ cannot be equal to 1: x is not invertible modulo n.

As an example, we can invert 22 modulo 35. We run the algorithm with $a = 22$ and $b = 35$. We obtain the following sequence of vectors.

Iteration	$\vec{x}$	$\vec{y}$	q
0	$(22, 1, 0)$	$(35, 0, 1)$	0
1	$(35, 0, 1)$	$(22, 1, 0)$	1
2	$(22, 1, 0)$	$(13, -1, 1)$	1
3	$(13, -1, 1)$	$(9, 2, -1)$	1
4	$(9, 2, -1)$	$(4, -3, 2)$	2
5	$(4, -3, 2)$	$(1, 8, -5)$	4
6	$(1, 8, -5)$	$(0, -35, 22)$	

Thus $1 = 22 \times 8 - 35 \times 5$, and the inverse of 22 modulo 35 is 8.

6.2.4 The Multiplicative Group $\mathbf{Z}_n^*$

Let $\mathbf{Z}_n^*$ denote the multiplicative group of all invertible elements and let $\varphi(n)$ denote its cardinality (called *Euler totient function*). We can prove the following properties of $\mathbf{Z}_n^*$.

Theorem 6.3. *Given an integer n, we have the following results.*

1. *For all $x \in \mathbf{Z}_n$ we have $x \in \mathbf{Z}_n^* \iff \gcd(x, n) = 1$.*
2. *$\mathbf{Z}_n$ is a field if and only if n is prime.*
3. *For all $x \in \mathbf{Z}_n^*$ we have $x^{\varphi(n)} \equiv 1 \pmod{n}$.*
4. *For any e such that $\gcd(e, \varphi(n)) = 1$, then $x \mapsto x^e \bmod n$ is a permutation on $\mathbf{Z}_n^*$, and for all $y \in \mathbf{Z}_n^*$, $y^{e^{-1} \bmod \varphi(n)} \bmod n$ is the only e-th root of y modulo n*

We already proved the first property. For the second one, we recall that $\mathbf{Z}_n$ is a field if and only if $\mathbf{Z}_n^*$ consists of all nonzero elements of $\mathbf{Z}_n$, which means that for any $x = 1, \ldots, n - 1$, we have $\gcd(x, n) = 1$. This holds if and only if n is a prime. For the third property, we notice that if x is a group element of $\mathbf{Z}_n^*$, the Lagrange theorem says that its order is a factor of the cardinality of the group which is $\varphi(n)$. Hence $x^{\varphi(n)} \equiv 1 \pmod{n}$. The last property consists of solving the $x^e \equiv y \pmod{n}$ equation in x. If $\gcd(e, \varphi(n)) = 1$, we know that e is invertible in $\mathbf{Z}_{\varphi(n)}$, so we can compute $d = e^{-1} \bmod \varphi(n)$. Now we can raise the equation to the power d and get $x^{ed} \equiv y^d$ $(\bmod\ n)$. But since $ed \equiv 1\,(\bmod\ \varphi(n))$, $x^{ed} \bmod n$ can be written $x^{1+k\varphi(n)} \bmod n$ which is equal to x. Thus $x \equiv y^{e^{-1} \bmod \varphi(n)} \bmod n$. Conversely, we check that this x is a solution of the equation by raising it, modulo n, to the power e.

6.2.5 Exponentiation

We notice that a modular exponentiation $x^e \bmod n$ does not necessarily require to perform e multiplications. We have much more efficient algorithms. Note that $x^e \bmod n$ can be defined by $x \times x \times \cdots \times x$ (e times) where the multiplications are performed modulo n, so we can adapt the multiplication algorithm of Figs. 6.2 and 6.3 to the exponentiation in $\mathbf{Z}_n^*$ by replacing the regular addition by a multiplication modulo n. Fig. 6.5 is an algorithm which computes the exponentiation "from right to left" because it reads all exponent bits in this direction. Conversely, Fig. 6.6 computes the exponentiation "from left to right." Both algorithms require $O(\log e)$ modular multiplications, thus a complexity of $O(\ell^2 \log e)$. We have many possible improvements of these algorithms. For instance we can read the exponent from left to right in basis B instead of a binary basis. We then need to precompute all $a^j \bmod n$ for $j = 0, \ldots, B - 1$ prior to the loop.

6.2.6 Z_{mn}: The Chinese Remainder Theorem

Exponentiation in $\mathbf{Z}_{mn}$ can also be accelerated by using the following theorem.

Theorem 6.4 (Chinese Remainder Theorem). *Let m and n be two integers such that* $\gcd(m, n) = 1$. *We have*

1. *$f : \mathbf{Z}_{mn} \to \mathbf{Z}_m \times \mathbf{Z}_n$ defined by $f(x) = (x \bmod m, x \bmod n)$ is a ring isomorphism*
2. *$\varphi(mn) = \varphi(m)\varphi(n)$*
3. *$f^{-1}(a, b) \equiv an(n^{-1} \bmod m) + bm(m^{-1} \bmod n)\,(\bmod\ mn)$*

> **Input:** a and n, two integers of at most ℓ bits, an integer e
> **Output:** $x = a^e \bmod n$
> **Complexity:** $\mathcal{O}(\ell^2 \log e)$
> 1: $x \leftarrow 1$
> 2: $y \leftarrow a$
> 3: **for** $i = 0$ to $\ell - 1$ **do**
> 4:   **if** $e_i = 1$ **then**
> 5: $x \leftarrow x \times y \bmod n$
> 6:   **end if**
> 7: $y \leftarrow y \times y \bmod n$
> 8: **end for**

Figure 6.5. Exponentiation from right to left (Square-and-Multiply).

Input: a and n, two integers of at most ℓ bits, an integer e
Output: $x = a^e \bmod n$
Complexity: $\mathcal{O}(\ell^2 \log e)$
1: $x \leftarrow 1$
2: **for** $i = \ell - 1$ downto 0 **do**
3:     $x \leftarrow x \times x \bmod n$
4:     **if** $e_i = 1$ **then**
5:         $x \leftarrow x \times a \bmod n$
6:     **end if**
7: **end for**

Figure 6.6. Exponentiation from left to right (Square-and-Multiply).

To prove the first property, we first observe that $\mathbf{Z}_m \times \mathbf{Z}_n$ is a product ring with unit element $(1, 1)$. The f function then fulfills

$$f(xy \bmod mn) = f(x)f(y)$$

and $f(1) = (1, 1)$, which are the ring morphism properties. Finally, $f(x) = (0, 0)$ implies $x \bmod m = 0$ and $x \bmod n = 0$, which means that x is a multiple of m and n simultaneously. Since m and n have no common prime factor, this means that x is a multiple of mn, so that $x \bmod mn = 0$. Thus the preimage of zero by f in $\mathbf{Z}_{mn}$ is $\{0\}$, which means that f is injective. Now since the cardinalities of $\mathbf{Z}_{mn}$ and $\mathbf{Z}_m \times \mathbf{Z}_n$ are equal, f must be a bijection, hence a ring isomorphism. For the second property, we can see that invertible elements of $\mathbf{Z}_m \times \mathbf{Z}_n$ are elements of $\mathbf{Z}_m^* \times \mathbf{Z}_n^*$, so there are $\varphi(m)\varphi(n)$ many. We have $\varphi(mn)$ invertible elements in $\mathbf{Z}_{mn}$. Since $\mathbf{Z}_{mn}$ and $\mathbf{Z}_m \times \mathbf{Z}_n$ are isomorphic rings, the number of invertible elements must be the same, hence $\varphi(mn) = \varphi(m)\varphi(n)$. Finally, we check the last property by computing the f of the right-hand term. We first reduce it modulo m. We know that for any x, $(x \bmod mn) \bmod m = x \bmod m$, thus we can remove the final reduction modulo mn. Next, the modulo m reduction cancels the second term of the sum $bm(m^{-1} \bmod n)$ which is a factor of m. The remainder is $an(n^{-1} \bmod m) \bmod m$ which is a. The modulo n reduction similarly outputs b. Hence the right-hand term of the last property is actually the preimage of (a, b).

As an example in $\mathbf{Z}_{35}$, we can let $m = 5$ and $n = 7$. If we want to solve $x \bmod 5 = 3$ and $x \bmod 7 = 4$ simultaneously, we compute

$$f^{-1}(3, 4) = \left(3 \times 7 \times (7^{-1} \bmod 5) + 4 \times 5 \times (5^{-1} \bmod 7)\right) \bmod 35.$$

The Extended Euclid Algorithm gives us the following Bezout relationship.

$$1 = (-2) \times 7 + 3 \times 5.$$

Thus $5^{-1} \bmod 7 = 3$ and $7^{-1} \bmod 5 \equiv -2$ which gives us $7^{-1} \bmod 5 = 3$. Hence

$$f^{-1}(3, 4) = (3 \times 7 \times 3 + 4 \times 5 \times 3) \bmod 35 = 123 \bmod 35 = 18.$$

We can check that 18 mod 5 = 3 and 18 mod 7 = 4.

This theorem can be used to compute exponentiation in $\mathbf{Z}_{mn}$ faster. Since $\mathbf{Z}_{mn}$ is isomorphic to the $\mathbf{Z}_m \times \mathbf{Z}_n$ product structure, instead of computing a^e mod mn, we can compute a^e mod m and a^e mod n which gives a^e in $\mathbf{Z}_m \times \mathbf{Z}_n$. Then we can use the Chinese Remainder Theorem to recover a^e mod mn. Since the complexity of exponentiation is cubic in the size of the modulus, assuming that m and n are half of the size of mn, exponentiation in $\mathbf{Z}_m$ costs $1/8$ of the exponentiation price in $\mathbf{Z}_{mn}$, as well as exponentiation in $\mathbf{Z}_n$. Since applying the Chinese Remainder Theorem is quadratic, we speed up the exponentiation by a factor of 4. This method needs however to use the factorization of mn, which is not always available as we will see in the next sections.

For instance, if we want to compute 2^{23} mod 35, we first compute 2^{23} mod 5 and 2^{23} mod 7. For 2^{23} mod 5, we notice that $\mathbf{Z}_5^*$ has a cardinality of 4 since $\mathbf{Z}_5$ is a field (see Section 6.3). Hence the Lagrange theorem implies that 2^4 mod 5 = 1. We can reduce 23 modulo 4, by $23 = 4 \times 5 + 3$, and obtain 2^{23} mod 5 = 2^3 mod 5. It is now easy to compute 2^3 mod 5 which gives 2^{23} mod 5 = 3. Similarly, 2^{23} mod 7 = 2^5 mod 7 = 4. Now we apply the Chinese Remainder Theorem for computing $f^{-1}(3, 4)$ and obtain that 2^{23} mod 35 = 18. If we apply the algorithm of Fig. 6.6, we obtain the following sequence of x values in step 2 with the corresponding bits of $e = 23$

e	1	0	1	1	1
x	1	4	16	9	9

and we terminate with $x = 18$ as well.

We summarize all the above algorithms by the following complexities for computations in $\mathbf{Z}_n$. We assume that all operands are lesser than n.

- Addition: linear in the size of n.
- Multiplication, inversion, gcd: quadratic in the size of n.
- Exponentiation: cubic in the size of n.

6.3   The Finite Field $\mathbf{Z}_p$

6.3.1   Basic Properties of $\mathbf{Z}_p$

We recall that a field is a ring K in which the multiplicative group K^* consists of all nonzero ring elements. This means that all elements but zero are invertible for the multiplication.

In Theorem 6.3 we saw that a ring element x of $\mathbf{Z}_n$ is invertible if and only if the gcd of x and n is 1. When n is prime, all nonzero elements of $\mathbf{Z}_n$ fulfill this property. But if n is composite, we may have a nontrivial factor x, and for all integers y we know that $xy \bmod n$ is a multiple of x, so it cannot be 1. This means that $\mathbf{Z}_n$ is a field if and only if n is a prime integer. In the following, we let p denote a prime integer and focus on the field $\mathbf{Z}_p$.

It is important to emphasize that $\mathbf{Z}_p$ is a *finite field*: we have a finite number of elements in it. This is not the case for classical fields: the field of real numbers $\mathbf{R}$, the field of complex numbers $\mathbf{C}$, the field of rational numbers $\mathbf{Q}$, etc.

Here are a few properties allowing to get familiar with $\mathbf{Z}_p$.

- $\mathbf{Z}_p^* = \{1, \ldots, p-1\}$ since $\mathbf{Z}_p = \{0, 1, \ldots, p-1\}$ and zero is the only noninvertible element;
- $\varphi(p) = p - 1$ since $\mathbf{Z}_p^*$ contains $p - 1$ elements;
- for any $x \in \mathbf{Z}_p^*$, we have $x^{p-1} \equiv 1 \pmod{p}$ since the order of x is a factor of the order $p - 1$ of $\mathbf{Z}_p^*$.

We have the following important result.

Theorem 6.5. *Let p be a prime number. $\mathbf{Z}_p^*$ is a cyclic group with $\varphi(p-1)$ generators.*

We recall that a *cyclic group* is a group which has at least one *generator*, namely an element g such that all group elements are powers of g, i.e. $\mathbf{Z}_p^* = \{1, g, g^2, \ldots, g^{p-2}\}$. Assuming that $\mathbf{Z}_p^*$ is cyclic, it is fairly easy to prove that the number of possible generators is actually $\varphi(p-1)$. For this we can pick a generator g and find conditions on $i = 1, \ldots, p - 2$ for $g^i \bmod p$ to be a generator of $\mathbf{Z}_p^*$. It is a generator if and only if there exists a j such that $g^{ij} \bmod p = g$: it is necessary because a generator must generate g, and it is sufficient because if it generates g, we know that we can generate all elements from g only. Since the exponents of g "live" in $\mathbf{Z}_{p-1}$, $g^{ij} \bmod p = g$ is equivalent to $ij \equiv 1 \pmod{p-1}$. Hence such a j exists if and only if i is invertible modulo $p - 1$. We already know that we have exactly $\varphi(p-1)$ invertible elements modulo $p - 1$, which completes the proof.

6.3.2 ⋆Quadratic Residues

In Theorem 6.3 we saw how to extract e-th roots modulo p of an element $x \in \mathbf{Z}_p^*$ when e is invertible modulo $\varphi(p) = p - 1$: we just have to raise x to the power $e^{-1} \bmod p - 1$. How can we proceed when e is not invertible modulo $p - 1$? In particular, how can we proceed with $e = 2$ which will never be invertible since $p - 1$ is even?[3] As for real numbers, square roots do not always exist (e.g. for negative numbers), and when they do, they come in couples which are the opposite of each other. In finite fields, we call *quadratic residues* the elements which can be written as the square of some other element.

---

[3] We omit the $p = 2$ case here which is trivial.

Input: a quadratic residue $a \in \mathbf{Z}_p^*$ where $p \geq 3$ is prime
Output: b such that $b^2 \equiv a \pmod{p}$

1: **repeat**
2:   choose $g \in \mathbf{Z}_p^*$ at random
3: **until** g is not a quadratic residue
4: let $p - 1 = 2^s t$ with t odd
5: $e \leftarrow 0$
6: **for** $i = 2$ to s **do**
7:   **if** $(ag^{-e})^{\frac{p-1}{2^i}} \bmod p \neq 1$ **then**
8:     $e \leftarrow 2^{i-1} + e$
9:   **end if**
10: **end for**
11: $b \leftarrow g^{-t\frac{e}{2}} a^{\frac{t+1}{2}} \bmod p$

Figure 6.7. The Tonelli algorithm for square roots in $\mathbf{Z}_p^*$.

Let us first state the following theorem.

Theorem 6.6. *Let p be an odd prime number. We have*

1. *$x \in \mathbf{Z}_p^*$ is a quadratic residue if and only if $x^{\frac{p-1}{2}} \bmod p = 1$*
2. *$\frac{p-1}{2}$ quadratic residues in $\mathbf{Z}_p^*$*
3. *that if $p \equiv 3 \pmod 4$, for any quadratic residue $x \in \mathbf{Z}_p^*$, the two square roots of x modulo p are $x^{\frac{p+1}{4}} \bmod p$ and $-x^{\frac{p+1}{4}} \bmod p$*

The last property holds only for $p \equiv 3 \pmod 4$, i.e. when $p + 1$ is a multiple of 4. For other primes p, we generalize this formula by using the Tonelli algorithm in Fig. 6.7.

Proof. We first notice that since $\mathbf{Z}_p$ is a field, the number of possible solutions to the polynomial equation $y^2 - x = 0$ in y is limited to two. For $x \neq 0$, we can even notice that if y is a root, then $-y$ is another different root. Thus the number of solutions for $x \neq 0$ is zero or two. Due to the pigeonhole principle, we infer that all elements of $\mathbf{Z}_p^*$ will be mapped onto the set of all quadratic residues by the square operation as a two-to-one mapping. This proves the second property, namely we have exactly $\frac{p-1}{2}$ quadratic residues in $\mathbf{Z}_p^*$. To prove the first property, we notice that if x is a quadratic residue, we can write $x = y^2 \bmod p$. Then we have

$$x^{\frac{p-1}{2}} \equiv y^{p-1} \equiv 1 \pmod{p}.$$

Thus all quadratic residues are roots of the equation $x^{\frac{p-1}{2}} \equiv 1$. Since we have exactly $\frac{p-1}{2}$ quadratic residues and at most $\frac{p-1}{2}$ roots, this shows that all roots are quadratic residues.

The third property is straightforward: if x is a quadratic residue, let $y = \pm x^{\frac{p+1}{4}} \bmod p$. We have

$$y^2 \equiv x^{\frac{p+1}{2}} \equiv x^{\frac{p-1}{2}} x \pmod{p}.$$

Since x is a quadratic residue, we know that $x^{\frac{p-1}{2}} \bmod p = 1$. This shows that y is a root of x.   □

6.4   Finite Fields

Finite fields are useful in communication systems, and in cryptography in particular. In addition to all $\mathbf{Z}_p$ fields, we have other finite fields. We give without proof the following theorem which characterizes the finite fields.[4]

Theorem 6.7. *We have the following results.*

1. *The cardinality of any finite field is a prime power p^k.*
2. *For any prime power p^k, there exists a finite field of cardinality p^k. p is called the* characteristic *of the field.*
3. *Two finite fields of same cardinality are isomorphic, so the finite field of cardinality p^k is essentially unique. We denote it by $\mathrm{GF}(p^k)$ as Galois field of cardinality p^k.*
4. *$\mathrm{GF}(p^k)$ is isomorphic to a subfield of $\mathrm{GF}(p^{k \times \ell})$.*
5. *$\mathrm{GF}(p^k)$ can be defined as the quotient of the ring $\mathbf{Z}_p[x]$ of polynomials with coefficients in $\mathbf{Z}_p$ by a principal ideal spanned by an irreducible polynomial of degree k: $\mathbf{Z}_p[x]/(P(x))$.*

The last property suggests a way to represent finite fields: in order to define $\mathrm{GF}(p^k)$, we first find an irreducible polynomial $P(x)$ of degree k in $\mathbf{Z}_p[x]$.[5] Then we represent an element of $\mathrm{GF}(p^k)$ as a polynomial in $\mathbf{Z}_p[x]$ of degree at most $k - 1$. Additions are then performed as regular additions modulo p. Multiplications are performed modulo $P(x)$ and modulo p. Then all algorithms of this section generalize to $\mathrm{GF}(p^k)$.

As an example, let us consider GF(4) where $p = 2$ and $k = 2$. We must get an irreducible polynomial of degree 2 in $\mathbf{Z}_2[x]$. We have only four polynomials of degree 2:

- x^2 which is equal to $x \times x$
- $x^2 + 1$ which is equal to $(x + 1) \times (x + 1)$ (remember that $1 + 1 = 0$ in $\mathbf{Z}_2$)
- $x^2 + x$ which is equal to $x \times (x + 1)$
- $x^2 + x + 1$ which is irreducible.

---

[4] For a more complete treatment on finite fields, we suggest the textbook by Lidl and Niederreiter (Ref. [117]).

[5] Picking irreducible polynomials is quite easy. We can for instance pick random polynomials and check irreducibility. Factorization of polynomials is actually easily feasible, so instead of making irreducibility tests, we can directly try to factorize. More elaborate ways are also possible. They can be found in any textbook on finite fields.

Let $P(x) = x^2 + x + 1$ in $\mathbf{Z}_2[x]$. We consider GF(4) as $\mathbf{Z}_2[x]/(P(x))$. Any polynomial over $\mathbf{Z}_2$ can be reduced modulo $P(x)$ into a polynomial of degree at most 1, so we have only four classes of polynomials:

- the class c_0 of polynomials congruent to 0
- the class c_1 of polynomials congruent to 1
- the class c_2 of polynomials congruent to x
- the class c_3 of polynomials congruent to $x + 1$

Therefore GF(4) $= \{c_0, c_1, c_2, c_3\}$. Addition is quite straightforward, as well as multiplication by c_0 or c_1. We however have to explain how to compute $c_2 \times c_2$, $c_2 \times c_3$, and $c_3 \times c_3$. $c_2 \times c_2$ is x^2 which is equal to $x + 1$ after reduction modulo $P(x)$ since $x^2 = x + 1 + P(x)$ thus $c_2 \times c_2 = c_3$. Similarly, we have $x^2 + x = 1 + P(x)$, thus $c_2 \times c_3 = c_1$, and $x^2 + 1 = x + P(x)$, thus $c_3 \times c_3 = c_2$. Here are the addition and multiplication tables.

+	c_0	c_1	c_2	c_3
c_0	c_0	c_1	c_2	c_3
c_1	c_1	c_0	c_3	c_2
c_2	c_2	c_3	c_0	c_1
c_3	c_3	c_2	c_1	c_0

×	c_0	c_1	c_2	c_3
c_0	c_0	c_0	c_0	c_0
c_1	c_0	c_1	c_2	c_3
c_2	c_0	c_2	c_3	c_1
c_3	c_0	c_3	c_1	c_2

We notice that the additive group is isomorphic to $\mathbf{Z}_2 \times \mathbf{Z}_2$ (and not to $\mathbf{Z}_4$!), that c_0 and c_1 are neutral elements for the addition and the multiplication respectively, that all elements but c_0 are invertible, and that GF(4)* is isomorphic to $\mathbf{Z}_3$.

6.5 $\star$Elliptic Curves over Finite Fields

Elliptic curves are odd structures. They are curves of equations like $y^2 = x^3 + ax + b$. This looks like the curve in Fig. 6.8 when x and y are real numbers, depending on the parameters a and b. They are used to define new types of groups for cryptography. For completeness we give all necessary material to implement algorithms on elliptic curves over finite fields.

6.5.1 $\star$Characteristic $p > 3$

Let us first define an *elliptic curve* and *point addition*.

Definition 6.8. *Given a finite field* $\mathbf{K}$ *of characteristic* $p > 3$ *and given* $a, b \in \mathbf{K}$ *such that* $4a^3 + 27b^3 \neq 0$, *we let*

$$E_{a,b} = \{O\} \cup \{(x, y) \in \mathbf{K}^2; y^2 = x^3 + ax + b\}.$$

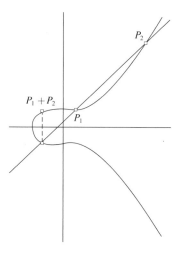

Figure 6.8. Elliptic curve example over the real numbers.

Given $P = (x, y)$, we define $-P = (x, -y)$ and $-\mathcal{O} = \mathcal{O}$. Given $P_1 = (x_1, y_1)$ and $P_2 = (x_2, y_2)$, if $P_2 = -P_1$, we define $P_1 + P_2 = \mathcal{O}$. Otherwise, we let

$$\lambda = \begin{cases} \frac{y_2 - y_1}{x_2 - x_1} & \text{if } x_1 \neq x_2 \\ \frac{3x_1^2 + a}{2y_1} & \text{if } x_1 = x_2 \end{cases}$$

$$x_3 = \lambda^2 - x_1 - x_2$$

$$y_3 = (x_1 - x_3)\lambda - y_1$$

$$P_3 = (x_3, y_3)$$

and $P_1 + P_2 = P_3$. In addition, $P + \mathcal{O} = \mathcal{O} + P = P$ and $\mathcal{O} + \mathcal{O} = \mathcal{O}$.

We further define the discriminant $\Delta = -16(4a^3 + 27b^2)$ and the j-invariant $j = -1728(4a)^3/\Delta$, which can also be expressed as

$$j = 1728\frac{4}{4 + 27b^2/a^3}$$

when $a \neq 0$.

(Note that the $x_1 = x_2$ case in the λ formula implies that $y_1 = y_2$, thus $P_1 = P_2$, and $y_1 \neq 0$. Otherwise we would have had $P_2 = -P_1$.) The definition of point addition may look quite odd. It can be geometrically illustrated as depicted in Fig. 6.8. Actually, $y - y_1 = \lambda(x - x_1)$ is the equation of a straight line which contains P_1. It is the chord which contains P_2 when $P_1 \neq P_2$. It is the tangent to the elliptic curve when $P_1 = P_2$. Since $E_{a,b}$ is an algebraic curve of degree 3, it usually intersects straight lines on three points. The intersection between this line and the curve is defined by

$$(y_1 + \lambda(x - x_1))^2 = x^3 + ax + b$$

by expanding in terms of x we obtain

$$x^3 - \lambda^2 x^2 + (a - 2\lambda(y_1 - \lambda x_1))x + (b - (y_1 - \lambda x_1)^2) = 0.$$

This polynomial equation of degree 3 clearly has three roots whose sum is λ^2. Since x_1 and x_2 are known roots, the third one is simply

$$x_3 = \lambda^2 - x_1 - x_2.$$

It corresponds to the third intersection point. Due to the equation of the line, we notice that $(x_3, -y_3)$ is this third point (see Fig. 6.8). $(x_3, -y_3)$ is therefore on the curve, so P_3 is as well.

We summarize important facts on elliptic curves.

Theorem 6.9. *Given a finite field* $\mathbf{K}$ *of characteristic* $p > 3$ *and given* $a, b \in \mathbf{K}$ *such that* $4a^3 + 27b^3 \neq 0$, *we let* $E_{a,b}$ *be the elliptic curve as defined in Def. 6.8.*

1. $E_{a,b}$ *together with the point addition forms an Abelian group where* $\mathcal{O}$ *is the neutral element.*
2. *For any* a' *and* b', *the group* $E_{a,b}$ *is isomorphic to the group* $E_{a',b'}$ *if and only if there exists some* $u \in \mathbf{K}^*$ *such that* $a' = au^4$ *and* $b' = bu^6$.
3. *Two isomorphic elliptic curves on* $\mathbf{K}$ *have the same* j*-invariant. The converse is true when* $\mathbf{K}$ *is algebraically closed.*

Proof (sketch). To prove the first property, we notice that addition is trivially commutative, with a neutral element $\mathcal{O}$ and that every P point has an opposite $-P$ point such that $P + (-P) = \mathcal{O}$. We already saw that addition is internal in $E_{a,b}$. What remains to prove is associativity. This part can be proven in a sophisticated way or through an exhausting computation.

For the second property we notice that $(x, y) \mapsto (u^2 x, u^3 y)$ defines a mapping from $E_{a,b}$ to $E_{u^4 a, u^6 b}$. We further notice that it is a group isomorphism. The converse is true as well.

For the third property, we notice that if $E_{a,b}$ and $E_{a',b'}$ are isomorphic, then we can write $a' = au^4$ and $b' = bu^6$. Therefore $(b')^2/(a')^3 = b^2/a^3$ and the two curves have the same j-invariant. We omit the proof for the converse result. $\square$

Let $a' = av^2$ and $b' = bv^3$ for some $v \in \mathbf{K}^*$. Obviously, when v is a quadratic residue, it can be written $v = u^2$ and we define an isomorphic group $E_{a',b'}$. One may wonder what happens when v is a not a quadratic residue. Obviously, we obtain another curve whose isomorphism class depends on the isomorphism class of $E_{a,b}$ only. It is actually called the *twist* of the curve. Note that although a curve and its twist share the same j-invariant, they are usually not isomorphic. Their cardinality is actually complementary in the sense of the following theorem.

Theorem 6.10. *Given a finite field* $\mathbf{K}$ *of characteristic* $p > 3$ *and given* $a, b \in \mathbf{K}$ *such that* $4a^3 + 27b^2 \neq 0$, *we let* $E_{a,b}$ *be the elliptic curve defined in Def. 6.8. The twist of* $E_{a,b}$ *is* E_{au^2,bu^3} *for* $u \in \mathbf{K}^*$ *which is not a quadratic residue. We have*

$$\#E_{a,b} + \#E_{au^2,bu^3} = 2\#\mathbf{K} + 2.$$

Proof. For any $x \in \mathbf{K}$, we notice that

- either $x^3 + ax + b$ is a nonzero quadratic residue, or and $u^3(x^3 + ax + b)$ is not a quadratic residue, or
- $x^3 + ax + b$ is not a quadratic residue and $u^3(x^3 + ax + b)$ is a nonzero quadratic residue, or
- $x^3 + ax + b = u^3(x^3 + ax + b) = 0$.

Let $f(x)$ be the number of affine points on $E_{a,b}$ (i.e. all points except $\mathcal{O}$). When $x^3 + ax + b$ is a nonzero quadratic residue, then $f(x) = 2$. When $x^3 + ax + b$ is not a quadratic residue, then $f(x) = 0$. When $x^3 + ax + b = 0$, then $f(x) = 1$. Let $g(x)$ be the number of points on E_{au^2,bu^3} which can be written (ux, y). We notice that $g(x)$ is respectively 0, 2, and 1 in the three cases. Therefore $f(x) + g(x) = 2$ for all x. Since this counts all affine points on $E_{a,b}$ and E_{au^2,bu^3}, we obtain the result. □

Note that since we have a group law, we can define mP for any integer m and any point P and compute mP by the square-and-multiply algorithms which were defined (with multiplicative notations) in Figs. 6.5 and 6.6.

6.5.2 ★*Characteristic Two*

Finite fields of characteristic two are important in practice. For completeness we provide here the definitions and properties related to elliptic curves over these fields.

Let us first recall that given a finite field $\mathbf{K}$ of cardinality 2^m we can define the trace $\text{Tr}_{2^m,2}$ function by

$$\text{Tr}_{2^m,2}(x) = \sum_{i=0}^{m-1} x^{2^i}$$

which is a linear form of $\mathbf{K}$ over $\text{GF}(2)$.

Definition 6.11. *Given a finite field* $\mathbf{K}$ *of characteristic two and given* $a_6 \in \mathbf{K}^*$ *and* $a_2 \in \{0, \gamma\}$ *with* γ *such that* $\text{Tr}_{\#K,2}(\gamma) = 1$, *we let*

$$E_{a_2,a_6} = \{\mathcal{O}\} \cup \{(x, y) \in \mathbf{K}^2; y^2 + xy = x^3 + a_2x^2 + a_6\}$$

be a non-supersingular elliptic curve. Given $P = (x, y)$, we define $-P = (x, x + y)$ and $-\mathcal{O} = \mathcal{O}$. Given $P_1 = (x_1, y_1)$ and $P_2 = (x_2, y_2)$, if $P_2 = -P_1$, we define $P_1 + P_2 = \mathcal{O}$. Otherwise, we let

$$\lambda = \begin{cases} \frac{y_2 + y_1}{x_2 + x_1} & \text{if } P_1 \neq P_2 \\ \frac{x_1^2 + y_1}{x_1} & \text{otherwise} \end{cases}$$

$$\mu = \begin{cases} \frac{y_1 x_2 + y_2 x_1}{x_2 + x_1} & \text{if } P_1 \neq P_2 \\ x_1^2 & \text{otherwise} \end{cases}$$

$$x_3 = \lambda^2 + \lambda + a_2 + x_1 + x_2$$
$$y_3 = (\lambda + 1)x_3 + \mu = (x_1 + x_3)\lambda + x_3 + y_1$$
$$P_3 = (x_3, y_3)$$

and $P_1 + P_2 = P_3$. In addition, $P + \mathcal{O} = \mathcal{O} + P = P$.

We further define the discriminant $\Delta = a_6$ and the j-invariant $j = 1/\Delta$.

We have similar results for group structures.

Theorem 6.12. *Given a finite field $\mathbf{K}$ of characteristic two, let $\gamma \in \mathbf{K}^*$ be such that $\mathrm{Tr}_{\#K,2}(\gamma) = 1$. Given $a_6 \in \mathbf{K}^*$ and $a_2 \in \{0, \gamma\}$, we let E_{a_2,a_6} be the elliptic curve as defined in Def. 6.11.*

1. *E_{a_2,a_6} together with the point addition is an Abelian group of which O is the neutral element.*
2. *For any $a_6' \in \mathbf{K}^*$ and $a_2' \in \{0, \gamma\}$, the group E_{a_2,a_6} is isomorphic to the group $E_{a_2',a_6'}$ if and only if $a_2 = a_2'$ and $a_6 = a_6'$.*
3. *E_{0,a_6} and E_{γ,a_6} are called* twist *of each other. We have*

$$\#E_{0,a_6} + \#E_{\gamma,a_6} = 2\#\mathbf{K} + 2.$$

6.5.3   ⋆*General Results*

We mention an important result that will be used later.[*]

Theorem 6.13 (Hasse 1933). *Let $\mathbf{K}$ be a finite field and E be an elliptic curve on $\mathbf{K}$. We have $\#E = \#\mathbf{K} + 1 - t$ where $|t| \leq 2\sqrt{\#\mathbf{K}}$. t is called the trace of Frobenius.*

Computing $\#E$ is quite technical (but feasible in polynomial time).

For some technical reasons, we define special elliptic curves.

---

[*] See, e.g. Ref [171]

- An elliptic curve is *singular* if its discriminant Δ is zero. We can prove that this is equivalent to the fact that the algebraic equation which defines the elliptic curve has a singular point. We notice that this is excluded by our definitions.
- An elliptic curve is *supersingular* if its trace of Frobenius is multiple of the characteristic of the field. For the characteristic two case, we can prove that it is equivalent to $j = 0$, which is excluded by our definition. For a characteristic $p > 3$, we can prove that it is equivalent to $t = 0$, which implies that $\#E = \#\mathbf{K} + 1$.
- An elliptic curve is *anomalous* if its trace of Frobenius is one. This implies that $\#E = \#\mathbf{K}$.

According to the state of the art of research, these special curves (except anomalous curves of characteristic two) should be avoided for cryptographic use.

6.6 Exercises

Exercise 6.1. *Show that the Caesar cipher is "isomorphic" to the addition of 3 in $\mathbf{Z}_{26}$. Similarly, what is ROT13?*

Exercise 6.2. *Show that the Vigenère cipher can be considered as a block cipher in ECB mode defined by addition in $\mathbf{Z}_{26}^m$.*

Exercise 6.3. *Let a, b, and n be three integers of at most ℓ bits and $n \geq 2^{\ell-1}$. Prove that we can compute $a \times b \bmod n$ within a time complexity of $\mathcal{O}(\ell^2)$.*

Exercise 6.4. *Let a and b be two integers of at most ℓ bits. Prove that we can perform an Euclidean division $a = bq + r$ within a complexity of $\mathcal{O}(\ell^2)$.*

Exercise 6.5. *We define a new cipher. The message space is $\mathbf{Z}_{26}$ (we encrypt arbitrary long alphabetical messages in ECB mode). The key space is $\mathbf{Z}_{26}^* \times \mathbf{Z}_{26}$ with a uniform distribution. Given a key $K = (a, b)$, we define $C(x) = ax + b \bmod 26$.*

   How many possible keys do we have?
   Show that we have perfect secrecy.
   How can we break it with a known plaintext attack?

Exercise 6.6 (Hill cipher). *We define a new cipher. The message space is $\mathbf{Z}_{26}^m$. The key space is the set of all $m \times m$ invertible matrices in $\mathbf{Z}_{26}$.*

   How many keys do we have?
   How can we break it with a known plaintext attack?

Exercise 6.7. *Let p be an odd prime number. Prove that the algorithm in Fig. 6.7 computes square roots in $\mathbf{Z}_p^*$.*

Exercise 6.8. *Let G be the set of all $x \in \mathbf{Z}_{p^2}$ such that $x \equiv 1 \pmod{p}$. Show that G is a multiplicative group, that $L : G \to \mathbf{Z}_p$ defined by $L(x) = \frac{x-1}{p}$ is an isomorphism, that $p + 1$ is a generator of G, and that L is the logarithm in base $p + 1$ in L. Infer that $\varphi(p^2) = p(p-1)$.[6]*

Exercise 6.9. *Considering the reduction modulo p as a group homomorphism on $\mathbf{Z}_{p^\alpha}^* \to \mathbf{Z}_p^*$, prove that $\varphi(p^\alpha) = (p-1)p^{\alpha-1}$.*

Infer that if $p_1, \ldots, p_r$ are distinct prime integers and if $\alpha_1, \ldots, \alpha_r$ are nonzero positive integers, then

$$\varphi(p_1^{\alpha_1} \times \cdots \times p_r^{\alpha_r}) = \prod_{i=1}^{r}(p_i - 1)p_i^{\alpha_i-1}.$$

---

[6] This exercise was inspired by the Okamoto–Uchiyama cryptosystem. See Ref. [143].

7

Algorithmic Number Theory

Content

Primality: Fermat test, Miller-Rabin test
★Primality: Carmichael numbers, Solovay–Strassen test
★Factorization: rho method, $p - 1$ method, elliptic curve method
★Discrete logarithm: baby steps – giant steps, Pohlig–Hellman

This chapter is a continuation of the previous one. Here we see that prime numbers can be efficiently generated, while factorization is intractable to date. We also study the discrete logarithm problem. These are basic tools in public-key cryptography.

7.1 Primality

This section deals with the *prime number generation* problem. We first try to distinguish prime numbers from composite ones by *primality tests*.

We first recall the intuitive method depicted in Fig. 7.1. This algorithm tries to divide the input n by every integer. At each iteration, we perform all possible divisions by integers up to $i - 1$ and obtain x, thus the remaining factors are between i and x. This method has been optimized: since we know that there is no factor of x between 2 and $i - 1$, we know that the remaining factors lie between i and $b = \lfloor \sqrt{x} \rfloor$. Thus we can stop as soon as $i > b$. The worst case occurs when n is prime or a product of two primes of same size, for which we need $\sqrt{n}$ iterations, which is enormous for typical numbers in cryptography. We notice however that this algorithm does more than expected since it prints the factorization of the input instead of just checking whether or not it is prime. Primality tests are nevertheless easier than factorization as will be shown in Section 7.2.

7.1.1 Fermat Test

A first important primality test is the *Fermat test*. We first notice that all prime numbers p are such that for any b with $0 < b < p$, we have $b^{p-1} \equiv 1 \pmod{p}$. This property is known as the *Little Fermat Theorem*. We can thus check the primality behavior of a number n by picking a random b such that $0 < b < n$, and checking whether $b^{n-1} \equiv 1 \pmod{n}$. For all prime numbers, this verification will always succeed. But how about composite numbers?

Input: an integer n
Output: a list of prime numbers whose product is n
Complexity: $\mathcal{O}(\sqrt{n})$ arithmetic operations
1: $b \leftarrow \lfloor \sqrt{n} \rfloor, x \leftarrow n, i \leftarrow 2$
2: **while** $x > 1$ and $i \leq b$ **do**
3:    **while** i divides x **do**
4:       print i
5:       $x \leftarrow x/i$
6:       $b \leftarrow \lfloor \sqrt{x} \rfloor$
7:    **end while**
8:    $i \leftarrow i + 1$
9: **end while**
10: if $x > 1$ then print x

Figure 7.1. Trial Division Algorithm.

One deficiency in the Fermat test is that it checks a necessary, but not sufficient, condition: there are some composite numbers for which the above test has the same behavior as for prime numbers, unless we pick p dividing n. For example, $n = 561 = 3 \cdot 11 \cdot 17$ is such that for all b's which are prime with n, we have $b^{n-1} \equiv 1 \pmod{n}$. This can be proven easily: we notice that $n - 1 = 560 = 2^4 \cdot 5 \cdot 7$ which is a multiple of $3 - 1$, $11 - 1$, and $17 - 1$. Therefore, if b is prime with 3, we have $b^{n-1} \equiv 1 \pmod{3}$ and the same for 11 and 17. Hence, from the Chinese Remainder Theorem we obtain that if b is prime with n we have $b^{n-1} \equiv 1 \pmod{n}$. We study these numbers in more detail in Section 7.1.2.

7.1.2 ⋆Carmichael Numbers

Theorem 7.1. *We call* Carmichael number *any integer n which is a product of at least two pairwise different prime numbers p such that $p - 1$ is a factor of $n - 1$. An integer n is a Carmichael number if and only if it fulfills the Fermat property: for any b that is prime with n, we have $b^{n-1} \equiv 1 \pmod{n}$.*

It follows that the Fermat test cannot be used in order to distinguish prime numbers from composite ones.

Proof. We can easily show that a Carmichael number $n = p_1 \cdots p_r$ fulfills the Fermat property: if b is prime with n, it is prime with any p_i, we have $b^{p_i - 1} \equiv 1 \pmod{p_i}$. Then since $p_i - 1$ is a factor of $n - 1$ we obtain that $b^{n-1} \equiv 1 \pmod{p_i}$. Finally, thanks to the Chinese Remainder Theorem we obtain that $b^{n-1} \equiv 1 \pmod{n}$. This means that unless we pick a b that is already a factor of some unknown prime factor of n, the Carmichael numbers will behave just like a prime number in the Fermat test.

Proving converse result is a bit more technical. We assume that n is such that $b^{n-1} \equiv 1 \pmod{n}$ for any $b \in \mathbf{Z}_n^*$. Let $n = p_1^{\alpha_1} \times \cdots \times p_r^{\alpha_r}$ be the factorization of n where the p_i's are pairwise different prime numbers. We use two lemmata.

Lemma 7.2. *Let G be a group of order n. If p is a prime factor of n, there exists an element of order p in G.*

Lemma 7.3. *Given a finite group G, we call* exponent *of G the smallest integer μ such that $x^\mu = 1$ for all $x \in G$. The exponent is equal to the lcm of all element orders in G. If n is such that $x^n = 1$ for all $x \in G$, then μ must be a factor of n.*

From this we infer that the exponent and the group order have exactly the same prime factors. In our case, G is $\mathbf{Z}_n^*$ (whose order is $\varphi(n)$) and $b^{n-1} \equiv 1 \pmod{n}$ for all $b \in G$, and thus all prime factors of $\varphi(n)$ are factors of $n - 1$. If for some i we had $\alpha_i > 1$, then p_i would be a factor of $\varphi(n)$, and therefore a factor of $n - 1$ as well. But a p_i cannot simultaneously be a factor of n and $n - 1$. Therefore we have that $\alpha_i = 1$ for all i.

We know from the Chinese Remainder Theorem that $\mathbf{Z}_n^*$ is isomorphic to $\mathbf{Z}_{p_1}^* \times \cdots \times \mathbf{Z}_{p_r}^*$. Since $\mathbf{Z}_{p_i}^*$ is a cyclic subgroup of order $p_i - 1$, there must be an element b of order $p_i - 1$, but $b^{n-1} \equiv 1 \pmod{n}$ implies $p_i - 1$ is a factor of $n - 1$ for any i. $\qquad \square$

Proof (Lemma 7.2). We prove this by induction on the order of G. This is trivial when the order is 1. If x is an element of G of order $k > 1$, we first assume that p is not a factor of k. x generates a subgroup H of G of order k, and G/H is a group of order $\frac{n}{k} < n$. Since this is a factor of p, there must be an element yH of order p. It is then easy to see that the order of y must be a multiple of p. This shows that we must have an element x of G of order multiple of p. It is then easy to see that $x^{\frac{k}{p}}$ is of order p. $\qquad \square$

Proof (Lemma 7.3). Let H be the set of all integers μ for which $x^\mu = 1$ for all $x \in G$. It is quite easy to notice that H is a subgroup of $\mathbf{Z}$: it is not empty (it contains the order of G), it is stable with respect to addition and subtraction. Due to a structure property[1] of $\mathbf{Z}$, H must be generated by a single integer μ which is the exponent of G.

We also prove by induction that we can compute the smallest integral power which makes all elements of a subset A vanish by computing the lcm of the orders of all elements in A. $\qquad \square$

---

[1] When considering the smallest nonnegative element μ of H, we can prove that μ spans the whole subgroup H: clearly, all elements spanned by μ are in H; conversely, if $x \in H$, the Euclidean division $x = q\mu + r$ of x by μ tells us that $r = x - q\mu$ is in H as well and $0 \le r < \mu$, but since μ is the smallest nonnegative element of H, then we must have $r = 0$, which means that $x = q\mu$ is spanned by μ.

Finally, Carmichael numbers exist (we have seen $n = 561$ as an example). We further know that there exist an infinite number of such numbers.[2]

7.1.3 ⋆Solovay–Strassen Test

Prime numbers have other properties which can be used by primality tests. For instance, the Euler test says that for primes p and $0 < b < p$, we have

$$b^{\frac{p-1}{2}} \equiv \left(\frac{b}{p}\right) \pmod{p}$$

where $\left(\frac{b}{p}\right)$ is the Legendre symbol. The following theorem tells us that this necessary property is also sufficient (when considering the Jacobi symbol). The Solovay–Strassen primality test is based on it.

Theorem 7.4. *Let n be an odd number. n is prime if and only if for any b such that $0 < b < n$ we have $b^{\frac{n-1}{2}} \equiv \left(\frac{b}{n}\right) \pmod{n}$.*

We recall that $\left(\frac{b}{n}\right)$ is the Jacobi symbol which is defined as follows. Let $n = p_1^{\alpha_1} \cdots p_r^{\alpha_r}$ be the factorization on n into pairwise different odd prime numbers $p_1, \ldots, p_r$. We define

$$\left(\frac{b}{n}\right) = \left(\frac{b}{p_1}\right)^{\alpha_1} \cdots \left(\frac{b}{p_r}\right)^{\alpha_r}$$

where $\left(\frac{b}{p_i}\right)$ is the *Legendre symbol* defined by

$$\left(\frac{b}{p_i}\right) = \begin{cases} 0 & \text{if } b \bmod p_i = 0 \\ 1 & \text{if } b \text{ is a quadratic residue in } \mathbf{Z}_{p_i}^* \\ -1 & \text{if } b \text{ is not a quadratic residue in } \mathbf{Z}_{p_i}^*. \end{cases}$$

It is important to emphasize that the Jacobi symbol can be efficiently computed. This can be done using an algorithm which is very similar to the Euclid algorithm. We actually use the following properties:

1. $\left(\frac{a}{b}\right) = \left(\frac{a \bmod b}{b}\right)$ for b odd,
2. $\left(\frac{ab}{c}\right) = \left(\frac{a}{c}\right)\left(\frac{b}{c}\right)$ for c odd,
3. $\left(\frac{2}{a}\right) = 1$ if $a \equiv \pm 1 \pmod 8$ and $\left(\frac{2}{a}\right) = -1$ if $a \equiv \pm 3 \pmod 8$ for a odd,
4. $\left(\frac{a}{b}\right) = -\left(\frac{b}{a}\right)$ if $a \equiv b \equiv 3 \pmod 4$ and $\left(\frac{a}{b}\right) = \left(\frac{b}{a}\right)$ otherwise for a and b odd.

As an example, we can compute both terms of the test for $b = 362$ and $n = 561$ (a Carmichael number). First we compute $b^{\frac{n-1}{2}} \bmod n = 362^{280} \bmod 561$. We have

---

[2] For more information we recommend Ref. [53].

$\frac{n-1}{2} = 280 = 2^3 \times 35$; thus

$$b^{\frac{n-1}{2}} \bmod n = 362^{2^3 \times 35} \bmod 561$$

$$= \left(\left(\left(362^2\right)^2\right)^2\right)^{35} \bmod 561$$

$$= \left(\left(331^2\right)^2\right)^{35} \bmod 561$$

$$= \left(166^2\right)^{35} \bmod 561$$

$$= 67^{35} \bmod 561$$

$$= 67 \times \left(67^2\right)^{17} \bmod 561$$

$$= 67 \times 1^{17} \bmod 561$$

$$= 67.$$

Here we do not even have to compute the Jacobi symbol since 67 is neither 1 nor -1. We could have computed it without any factorization as follows.

$$\left(\frac{b}{n}\right) = \left(\frac{362}{561}\right)$$

$$\text{(factor 2 isolation)} = \left(\frac{2 \times 181}{561}\right)$$

$$\text{(multiplicativity)} = \left(\frac{2}{561}\right) \times \left(\frac{181}{561}\right)$$

$$(561 \equiv 1 \,(\bmod\, 8)) = \left(\frac{181}{561}\right)$$

$$\text{(quadratic reciprocity)} = \left(\frac{561}{181}\right)$$

$$\text{(modular reduction)} = \left(\frac{18}{181}\right)$$

$$\text{(factor 2 isolation)} = \left(\frac{2 \times 9}{181}\right)$$

$$\text{(multiplicativity)} = \left(\frac{2}{181}\right) \times \left(\frac{9}{181}\right)$$

$$(181 \equiv -3 \,(\bmod\, 8)) = -\left(\frac{9}{181}\right)$$

$$\text{(quadratic reciprocity)} = -\left(\frac{181}{9}\right)$$

$$\text{(modular reduction)} = -\left(\frac{1}{9}\right)$$

$$= -1$$

Parameter: k, an integer
Input: n, an integer of ℓ bits
Output: notification of non-primality or pseudo-primality
Complexity: $\mathcal{O}(k\ell^3)$

1: **if** $n = 2$ **then**
2:     output "prime" and stop
3: **end if**
4: **if** n is even **then**
5:     output "composite" and stop
6: **end if**
7: **repeat**
8:     pick a random b such that $0 < b < n$
9:     **if** $b^{\frac{n-1}{2}} \not\equiv \left(\frac{b}{n}\right) (\mathrm{mod}\ n)$ **then**
10:         output "composite" and stop
11:     **end if**
12: **until** k iterations are made
13: output "pseudo-prime" and stop

Figure 7.2. The Solovay–Strassen Primality Test.

We can also verify the definition with the factorization of n by

$$\left(\frac{b}{n}\right) = \left(\frac{362}{561}\right)$$

$$= \left(\frac{362}{3 \times 11 \times 17}\right)$$

$$= \left(\frac{362}{3}\right) \times \left(\frac{362}{11}\right) \times \left(\frac{362}{17}\right)$$

and $362^{\frac{2-1}{2}} \bmod 3 = 2$, $362^{\frac{11-1}{2}} \bmod 11 = 10$, $362^{\frac{17-1}{2}} \bmod 17 = 16$, thus $\left(\frac{b}{n}\right) = (-1)^3 = -1$.

Instead of proving the previous theorem, we will prove an actually much stronger theorem which is stated as follows.

Theorem 7.5 (Solovay–Strassen 1977 [174]). *Let n be an odd integer. If n is prime, for any $b \in \mathbf{Z}_n^*$ we have $b^{\frac{n-1}{2}} \equiv \left(\frac{b}{n}\right) (\mathrm{mod}\ n)$. Conversely, if n is composite, this equality holds for no more than half of all the possible b values.*

This shows that when n is prime, the primality test in Fig. 7.2 always answers "prime" or "pseudo-prime"; otherwise, it answers "composite" with probability greater than $1 - 2^{-k}$, k being the maximum number of times the test iterates.

Proof. To prove the theorem, we first let n be an odd prime number. The Jacobi symbol reduces to the Legendre symbol, and all b such that $0 < b < n$ are in $\mathbf{Z}_n^*$. We thus only have to prove that b is a quadratic residue if and only if $b^{\frac{n-1}{2}} \equiv 1 \pmod{n}$. We already did it for Theorem 6.6.

The converse is a little more technical.

We assume that the test holds for more than half of the b is in $\mathbf{Z}_n^*$. We notice that the set of all b for which the test holds is actually a subgroup of $\mathbf{Z}_n^*$. (The test predicate is stable by multiplication.) Therefore the probability that the test holds for a random b is one over the index of the subgroup. If the probability is greater than $\frac{1}{2}$, this means that the subgroup is $\mathbf{Z}_n^*$ itself. Therefore the test must hold for all b.

By squaring the test predicate, we notice that this implies $b^{n-1} \equiv 1 \pmod{n}$ for all $b \in \mathbf{Z}_n^*$. Thus n is either prime or a Carmichael number. All we have to do is show that the test predicate cannot hold with Carmichael numbers.

We already know that a Carmichael number is a product of pairwise different prime numbers. Let $n = p_1 \cdots p_r$ be the factorization of n into primes. Seeing $\mathbf{Z}_n^*$ like $\mathbf{Z}_{p_1}^* \times \cdots \times \mathbf{Z}_{p_r}^*$, we can consider all the $b_i = \left(\frac{b}{p_i}\right)$ as independent bits indicating whether b is (as a $\mathbf{Z}_{p_i}^*$ element) a quadratic residue ($+1$) or not (-1). Obviously, $\left(\frac{b}{n}\right)$ is the product of all these independent bits. Due to Theorem 7.1, we know that $p_i - 1$ divides $n - 1$. If $p_i - 1$ divides $\frac{n-1}{2}$, then $b^{\frac{n-1}{2}} \equiv 1 \pmod{p_i}$. Otherwise, $b^{\frac{n-1}{2}} \equiv b_i \pmod{p_i}$. We define $b_i' = \pm 1$ such that $b^{\frac{n-1}{2}} \equiv b_i' \pmod{p_i}$. We know that depending on i only, b_i' is equal to b_i or to 1. Hence b_i' can be written $f_i(b_i)$. Thus for all i we have

$$f_i(b_i) \equiv \prod_{j=1}^{r} b_j \pmod{p_i}.$$

But both sides are $+1$ or -1 and p_i is an odd prime. Therefore this must be an equality. Thus for any b we have

$$f_1(b_1) = \cdots = f_r(b_r) = \prod_{j=1}^{r} b_j.$$

Clearly this cannot happen unless $r = 1$: once we have at least two factors, we know that the b_i's are totally independent, so we can just fix b_i for $i > 1$ and make b_1 change, and we obtain that $f_2(b_2)$ must depend on b_1, which is a contradiction. Hence $r = 1$, which means that n is a prime number. $\square$

7.1.4 Miller-Rabin Test

We conclude this section with the **Miller-Rabin test** which generalizes the Fermat test and the Solovay–Strassen test. It is depicted in Fig. 7.3. We can prove that it always

Parameter: k, an integer
Input: n, an integer of ℓ bits
Output: notification of non-primality or pseudo-primality
Complexity: $\mathcal{O}(k\ell^3)$

1: if $n = 2$ then output "prime" and stop
2: if n is even then output "composite" and stop
3: write $n = 2^s t + 1$
4: **repeat**
5:   pick a random b such that $0 < b < n$
6:   $x \leftarrow b^t \bmod n, i \leftarrow 0$
7:   **if** $x \neq 1$ **then**
8:     **while** $x \neq n - 1$ **do**
9:       $x \leftarrow x^2 \bmod n, i \leftarrow i + 1$
10:       **if** $i = s$ or $x = 1$ **then**
11:         output "composite" and stop
12:       **end if**
13:     **end while**
14:   **end if**
15: **until** k iterations are made
16: output "pseudo-prime" and stop

Figure 7.3. The Miller-Rabin Primality Test.

detects prime numbers, and detects composite ones with a probability greater than $1 - 4^{-k}$.

The Miller-Rabin test consists of successively dividing $n - 1$ by 2 until the result becomes some odd t. Then, we raise b to the power of t, and square it. If we eventually find 1 (as in the Fermat test), we check that the previous value was -1. If it was not, we have found a square root of 1 which is neither $+1$ nor -1, which is a proof of compositeness (see Fig. 7.4).

Theorem 7.6 (Miller-Rabin 1976, 1980 [134, 154]). *Let n be an integer, and let us consider the algorithm in Fig. 7.3 with input n and parameter k. If n is prime, then the algorithm always outputs "prime" or "pseudo-prime." Conversely, if n is composite, the algorithm outputs "composite" with probability greater than $1 - 4^{-k}$.*

This result is proven in Section 7.1.5.

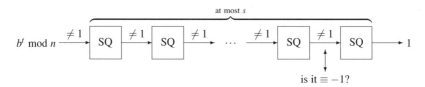

Figure 7.4. The Miller-Rabin test.

7.1.5   ⋆Analysis of the Miller-Rabin Test

Proof. Since the case of even integers is trivial we assume that n is odd and we write $n = 2^s t + 1$.

When n is prime, any b such that $0 < b < n$ is in $\mathbf{Z}_n^*$. We know that $b^{2^s t} \equiv 1 \pmod{n}$. Since $\mathbf{Z}_n$ is a field, we know that the only square roots of 1 are $+1$ and $-1 \bmod n$. Hence either $b^t \equiv 1 \pmod{n}$ or there exists i such that $0 \leq i < s$ and $b^{2^i t} \equiv -1 \pmod{n}$. Therefore none of the k iterations can lead to "composite."

For a composite n, the result is quite technical to prove. We simply mention the following two results.

- If n passes the Miller-Rabin test for b, then n passes the Solovay–Strassen test for b, and so the Miller-Rabin test is at least as efficient as the Solovay–Strassen test.
- One can prove that the probability that the test passes with $b \in \mathbf{Z}_n^*$ is less than $\frac{1}{2}$.

We simply prove the second result. We refer to Ref. [102] for more details. One can easily notice that the set G of b's in $\mathbf{Z}_n^*$ for which the test passes is a subgroup. If we have $G \neq \mathbf{Z}_n^*$, then the result holds since $\#G$ is a factor of $\varphi(n)$. Otherwise, $n = p_1 \cdots p_r$ is a Carmichael number. Let i_j be the smallest i such that $\frac{p_j - 1}{2}$ divides $2^i t$. We know that for any $b \in \mathbf{Z}_n^*$ we have $b^{2^{i_j+1}t} \bmod p_j = 1$ and $b^{2^{i_j}t} \bmod p_j = 1$ if and only if b is a quadratic residue modulo p_j. Let j be the index for which i_j is the greatest and let k be the index different from j for which i_j is the greatest. We know that for any $b \in \mathbf{Z}_n^*$ we have $b^{2^{i_j+1}t} \bmod n = 1$. If $j > k$, for any quadratic nonresidue b modulo p_j, $b^{2^{i_j}t} \bmod n$ is neither $+1$ nor $n - 1$ (which is -1 modulo n) and so the test cannot pass. If $j = k$, for any b with different quadratic residuosity modulo p_j and p_k, $b^{2^{i_j}t} \bmod n$ is neither $+1$ nor $n - 1$ and so the test cannot pass. In both cases, we cannot have $G = \mathbf{Z}_n^*$.   □

7.1.6   Prime Number Generation

It should be noticed that prime numbers can be randomly generated with ease: we can iteratively pick a random number until one primality test responds positively. Due to the following *Prime Number Theorem*, we know that we will eventually end up with a prime number of n bits within $\mathcal{O}(n)$ trials.

Theorem 7.7 (Prime Number Theorem). *Let $p(N)$ denote the number of prime numbers in $\{2, 3, \ldots, N\}$. We have $p(N) \sim \frac{N}{\log N}$ when N increases toward infinity.*

Thus the number of prime numbers of at most ℓ bits is asymptotically equal to $\frac{2^\ell}{\ell \log 2}$, which means that the probability that a random ℓ-bit number is prime is $\Omega(1/\ell)$.

We pick a random ℓ-bit n until it passes a primality test with k iterations. The probability that we do not find a prime number after c trials is $\left(1 - \Omega(\frac{1}{\ell})\right)^c$, which is arbitrarily small with $c = \Omega(\ell)$. The probability p_w that this algorithm lets a composite number pass after c trials is lesser than $c4^{-k}$. Therefore we can pick $k = \Omega(\log \ell)$. We notice that the k factor vanishes in the complexity $\mathcal{O}(c\ell^3)$ because k is negligible with respect to c and most composite numbers are ruled out by the very first iteration.

This algorithm will succeed after $c = \mathcal{O}(\ell)$ trials, which leads to a complexity of $\mathcal{O}(\ell^4)$. In practice, we even make sure that the randomly picked ℓ-bit number n has no small prime factors by construction (e.g. we do not pick even numbers). Hence, the running time is indeed smaller in practice.

7.2 ⋆Factorization

As we saw in Section 7.1, it is easy to recognize prime numbers, and therefore, composite numbers as well. Given a composite number n, it is easy to get a "proof of compositeness" (for instance by exhibiting a number b such that $0 < b < n$ and $b^{n-1} \bmod n \neq 1$). Here "easy" means within a time polynomial in the size of n (namely $\log n$). It is however quite hard to get a nontrivial factor of n in general: no polynomial algorithms (in terms of $\log n$) are known for that.

The first algorithm we think of is based on the *trial division algorithm* depicted in Fig. 7.1: we try to divide n by all integers i from 2 to $\sqrt{n}$ until a factor is found. This algorithm will pull a factor out of n within a complexity of $\mathcal{O}(p)$ arithmetic operations where p is the smallest prime factor of n.[3]

In this section we list a few exponential algorithms which have a better complexity.

7.2.1 ⋆Pollard Rho Method

Pollard Rho algorithm (named after the Greek ρ character) lowers the complexity of trial division from $\mathcal{O}(p)$ down to $\mathcal{O}(\sqrt{p})$ where p is the smallest prime factor of n (see Ref. [149]). The basic idea is the following.

- We take a "random" function f which can be "factorized" by a mod p function for any factor p of n: namely such that $f(x) \equiv f(x \bmod p) \pmod{p}$ for any factor p of n. For example we can take any polynomial function. In practice one always uses $f(x) = x^2 + 1$ which behaves "like a random function" from a heuristic viewpoint.

---

[3] Note that we should consider the complexity of arithmetic operations. But the overhead is negligible in comparison to p since it is polynomial in $\log n$. We will omit it for simplicity, but recall that the complexity unit is an "arithmetic operation" and not an elementary binary operation.

- We take a random x_0, and iterate $x_{i+1} = f(x_i) \bmod n$. Due to the property of the f function, this modulo n computation actually "hides" the modulo p computation: if we define $x'_{i+1} = f(x'_i) \bmod p$ with $x'_0 = x_0$, we obtain that $x'_i = x_i \bmod p$ for any $i > 0$.
- Since $\mathbf{Z}_p$ is a finite set, we expect that the x'_i sequence will at one point enter into a loop. The shape of the sequence will then look like the Greek character Rho (ρ): with a tail and a loop. If f is random, there is no reason for this loop modulo p to correspond to a loop modulo n: for instance, unless n is not a power of p, there exists another prime factor q, and we know from the Chinese Remainder Theorem that the modulo p and modulo q computations are totally independent. So a loop modulo p will rarely synchronize with a loop modulo q.
- This loop is easy to detect by gcd computations. Furthermore, random mappings analysis shows that we can expect the total length of the Rho (the tail and the loop) to be $\mathcal{O}(\sqrt{p})$. This is similar to the *birthday paradox* effect.

In order to detect a loop, we can just iterate the following process:

1: $a \leftarrow x_0, b \leftarrow x_0$
2: **while** $a \neq b$ **do**
3:      $a \leftarrow f(a)$
4:      $b \leftarrow f(f(b))$
5: **end while**

The a register contains x_t and the b register contains x_{2t} in the t-th iteration where $x_0, x_1, \ldots$ is the sequence obtained by iterating f on x_0. Eventually we will find $x_t = x_{2t}$ when t is greater than the tail length and a multiple of the loop length.

In order to do the same with a "hidden computation" in $\mathbf{Z}_p$, we notice that we only have to check equalities. If computations are performed in $\mathbf{Z}_n$, we can check hidden equalities in $\mathbf{Z}_p$ between a and b by computing the gcd of $a - b$ and n. In case of equality, the gcd will be a multiple of p. Hence the algorithm in Fig. 7.5 eventually stops after a number of iterations which is a big $\mathcal{O}$ of the rho length.

> **Input**: n, an integer with a prime factor smaller than B
> **Output**: a nontrivial factor of n
> **Complexity**: $\mathcal{O}(\sqrt{B})$ arithmetic operations
>   1: $x_0 \leftarrow$ random, $a \leftarrow x_0, b \leftarrow x_0$
>   2: **repeat**
>   3: $a \leftarrow f(a) \bmod n$
>   4: $b \leftarrow f(f(b) \bmod n) \bmod n$
>   5: **until** $\gcd(a - b, n) \neq 1$
>   6: output the gcd

Figure 7.5. Pollard Rho Factorization Algorithm.

The first key argument is now to realize that equalities in $\mathbf{Z}_p$ are independent from equalities in $\mathbf{Z}_n$, which means that the case of full equality in $\mathbf{Z}_n$ is negligible. This means that the gcd will be a nontrivial factor of n which contains p.

The second key argument is the complexity analysis: we can prove that if x_0 and f are random, then the rho length is $\mathcal{O}(\sqrt{p})$. Hence the algorithm works within a complexity of $\mathcal{O}(\sqrt{p})$ arithmetic operations where p is the smallest factor of n. In Fig. 7.5 the complexity in terms of an upper bound B on p is given. For all composite numbers, we have $B \leq \sqrt{n}$ so we factorize a general integer n in $\mathcal{O}(\sqrt[4]{n})$.

We use the following result for the complexity analysis.

Lemma 7.8. *Let f be a random function in a set of p elements, and let x_0 be a random element. We iteratively define $x_{t+1} = f(x_t)$ and let $t = 1 + \lfloor \sqrt{2\lambda p} \rfloor$ for a given real λ. The probability that $x_0, x_1, \ldots, x_t$ are pairwise different is less than $e^{-\lambda}$.*

Proof. Since f is random, this probability is

$$p = \prod_{i=1}^{t} \left(1 - \frac{i}{p}\right).$$

Since $\log(1 - x) < -x$ for $0 < x < 1$, $\log p$ is lesser than $-\frac{t(t+1)}{2p}$. Since $t \geq \sqrt{2\lambda p}$, this is smaller than $-\lambda$.   □

As an example, we try to factorize $n = 18923$. We let $f(x) = x^2 + 1$ and $x_0 = 2347$. The iterations yield the data given in Fig. 7.6 and ends by pulling out the factor 127. Then we can see that, indeed, $18923 = 127 \times 149$.

7.2.2 ⋆*Pollard $p - 1$ Method*

The Pollard Rho algorithm works well for numbers n featuring a relatively small factor. We can find another method when n has a prime factor p such that all prime factors of

t =	1	a =	1817	b =	8888	gcd =	1
t =	2	a =	8888	b =	12599	gcd =	1
t =	3	a =	11943	b =	13068	gcd =	1
t =	4	a =	12599	b =	1342	gcd =	1
t =	5	a =	8678	b =	10137	gcd =	1
t =	6	a =	13068	b =	7978	gcd =	1
t =	7	a =	11473	b =	8232	gcd =	1
t =	8	a =	1342	b =	16487	gcd =	1
t =	9	a =	3280	b =	11407	gcd =	1
t =	10	a =	10137	b =	11280	gcd =	127

Figure 7.6. Example of Pollard Rho factorization.

Input: n
Output: a nontrivial factor of n
Complexity: $\mathcal{O}(B)$ arithmetic operations
  1: pick x at random in $\{2, \ldots, n - 1\}$
  2: **if** $\gcd(x, n) \neq 1$ **then**
  3:     output this gcd and stop
  4: **end if**
  5: $i \leftarrow 1$
  6: **while** $\gcd(x - 1, n) = 1$ **do**
  7:     $x \leftarrow x^i \bmod n$
  8:     $i \leftarrow i + 1$
  9: **end while**
 10: **if** $x = 1$ **then**
 11:     fail
 12: **else**
 13:     output $\gcd(x - 1, n)$ and stop
 14: **end if**

Figure 7.7. Pollard $p - 1$ Factorization Algorithm.

$p - 1$ are small. We call it the $p - 1$ method (see Ref. [148]). When all prime factors of $p - 1$ are smaller than B, we say that $p - 1$ is B-*smooth*.

Concretely, we assume that there exists some threshold B such that there exist two prime factors p and q of n such that $p - 1$ is B-smooth and $q - 1$ is not B-smooth. (In most examples, $B = O(\sqrt[4]{n})$ works.) Fig. 7.7 shows the *Pollard $p - 1$ algorithm*. It simply consists of computing $x^{B!} \bmod n$. The modulo p part of this number will be congruent to 1 since $p - 1$ is a factor of $B!$, and therefore $(x^{B!} \bmod n) - 1$ has a common factor p with n which can be found by a gcd computation.

Conversely, if n contains a B-smooth factor p, then for some "B-small" t the $t!$ integer is a multiple of $p - 1$, hence $x^{t!} \equiv 1 \pmod{p}$, which can be detected by computing the gcd of $(x^{t!} \bmod n) - 1$ and n as in the rho method. More precisely, if $p - 1 = p_1^{\alpha_1} \cdots p_r^{\alpha_r}$ is the prime factorization of $p - 1$, we take $\alpha_i p_i = \max_j \alpha_j p_j$. For $t \geq \alpha_i p_i$, we know that for all j we have at least α_j multiples of p_j which are lesser than t, so $p_j^{\alpha_j}$ divides $t!$ for all j, so $p - 1$ divides $t!$. We notice that $\alpha_i p_i$ lies between B and $B \log_2 p$ since $\alpha_i < \log_2 p$. In typical cases, α_j's corresponding to large p_j's are all equal to 1, so $\alpha_i p_i$ is actually the largest prime factor of $p - 1$ which is approximated by B. So t only needs to be slightly larger than B to ensure the property. This is what we meant by "B-small."

It is a bit more tricky to know when the equality modulo p does not imply a full equality modulo n in order to make the algorithm succeed. This is quite easy when n has a prime factor p such that $p - 1$ is B-smooth *and* a prime factor q such that $q - 1$ contains a large prime factor r: when t becomes slightly greater than B, $p - 1$ is a factor of $t!$, but r is not, so unless the multiplicative order of the original x is zero modulo r (which is the case for a negligible fraction of x's), $x^{t!} - 1 \bmod n$ will be a multiple of p but not a multiple of q, so the gcd is nontrivial. More precisely, this will always work for integers n such that

- there exists a prime factor p of n such that all prime factors of $p - 1$ are lesser than B,
- there exists a prime factor q of n such that one prime factor r of $q - 1$ is larger than $B \log_2 n$.

In other cases, the algorithm may never work. For instance, when all prime factors p of n are such that the largest prime factor r of $p - 1$ is the same, $x^{t!}$ will certainly simultaneously vanish modulo all prime factors of n. For instance, for $n = 133 \times 331 = 44023$, $p = 133$ is such that $p - 1 = 2^2 \times 3 \times 11$ and $q = 331$ is such that $q - 1 = 2 \times 3 \times 5 \times 11$. It is easy to see that the smallest factorial number which is a multiple of $p - 1$ is $11!$, just like for $q - 1$. This means that for any initial x whose multiplicative orders in $\mathbf{Z}_p^*$ and $\mathbf{Z}_q^*$ are both multiple of 11 (which is the case for most of the original x), $x^{t!}$ will simultaneously vanish modulo p and modulo q, which gives us no chance to split n with this algorithm. These cases are however quite pathological.

We give the same example as for the rho method: $n = 18923$. (Note that $p = 127$ and $q = 149$ are such that $p - 1 = 2 \times 3^2 \times 7$ and $q - 1 = 2^2 \times 37$, so $r = 37$ is large, and $p - 1$ is B-smooth for $B = 7$.) We pick $x = 2347$. We obtain

$i = 1$	$x = 2347$	$\gcd = 1$
$i = 2$	$x = 1816$	$\gcd = 1$
$i = 3$	$x = 4072$	$\gcd = 1$
$i = 4$	$x = 14891$	$\gcd = 1$
$i = 5$	$x = 18431$	$\gcd = 1$
$i = 6$	$x = 7247$	$\gcd = 1$
$i = 7$	$x = 13590$	$\gcd = 127$

which yields p.

7.2.3 ⋆The Elliptic Curves Method (ECM)

The Pollard $p - 1$ algorithm consists of making hidden computations in a $\mathbf{Z}_p^*$ group of smooth order. Computations in this group are hidden by computations in $\mathbf{Z}_n^*$. We can generalize this algorithm by using other groups, following an idea due to *Hendrik Lenstra* (see Ref. [114]). For instance, by picking $a, b \in \mathbf{Z}_n$, we can consider the elliptic curve $E_{a,b}$ in $\mathbf{Z}_p$ by doing all computations modulo n since the modulo p computations are just "hidden" in the modulo n ones. The order of this group is a random number within the $p + 1 \pm 2\sqrt{p}$ range. If this order happens to be B-smooth, we can apply exactly the same algorithm within a complexity of $\mathcal{O}(B)$ arithmetic operations. The success of this approach thus corresponds to the probability that the order of the $E_{a,b} \bmod p$ group is B-smooth for random a and b, which is estimated to be u^{-u} where $u = \frac{\log p}{\log B}$. Heuristic analysis show that this algorithm has a complexity of $\mathcal{O}(e^{\sqrt{(1+o(1))\log n \log \log n}})$, which is asymptotically smaller than all the factorization complexities that we have seen so far.

The Pollard $p - 1$ algorithm may not work for $B = \sqrt[4]{n}$. In practice, the elliptic curve version will work, because the probabilistic structure of the used group will hide any ill-designed properties of n.

As an example, we have seen that $n = 44023$ could not be factorized with the $p - 1$ method because $44023 = 133 \times 331$ and $133 - 1$ and $331 - 1$ are factors of exactly the same factorial numbers. We can thus try to factorize n with the ECM method.

Let us pick a random a and b. We consider $E_{a,b}$ mod n:

$$y^2 \equiv x^3 + ax + b \pmod{n}.$$

The first problem is to pick a random point X on this curve. It is not quite trivial because we must solve an algebraic equation modulo n whose factorization is assumed to be unknown. So, instead of picking a, b, then X, we pick a, X, then b.

Let us pick $a = 13$ and $X = (x, y) = (23482, 9274)$. We thus have

$$b = y^2 - x^3 - ax \bmod n = 21375.$$

We now have to compute $X_i = i! \cdot X = (x_i, y_i)$ for $i = 1, 2, \ldots$ until we notice that the "hidden point" X_i mod p in $E_{a,b}$ mod p is the infinity point while X_i is not. This necessarily comes from an illegal operation, like a division by a noninvertible element. But note that noninvertible elements in $\mathbf{Z}_n^*$ yield a nontrivial factor of n by gcd computation, which is exactly what we are looking for.

Computing X_1 is easy: $X_1 = X$. To compute X_2, we need to compute $X_2 = 2 \cdot X_1$. For this we compute

$$\lambda = \frac{3x_1^2 + a}{2y_1} \bmod n = 31095$$

and

$$x_2 = \lambda^2 - 2x_1 \bmod n = 18935 \qquad y_2 = \lambda(x_1 - x_2) - y_1 \bmod n = 21838.$$

Next we compute $X_3 = 3 \cdot X_2 = (2 \cdot X_2) + X_2$. We compute $2 \cdot X_2$ by

$$\lambda = \frac{3x_2^2 + a}{2y_2} \bmod n = 41645$$

and

$$x = \lambda^2 - 2x_2 \bmod n = 26093 \qquad y = \lambda(x_2 - x) - y_2 \bmod n = 7008$$

and $(x, y) + X_2$ by

$$\lambda = \frac{y_2 - y}{x_2 - x} \bmod n = 5816$$

and

$$x_3 = \lambda^2 - x - x_2 \bmod n = 15187 \qquad y_3 = \lambda(x - x_3) - y \bmod n = 29168.$$

Next we compute $X_4 = 4 \cdot X_3 = 2 \cdot (2 \cdot X_3)$. We obtain

$$
\begin{array}{ll}
i = 1 & X_1 = (23482, 9274) \\
i = 2 & X_2 = (18935, 21838) \\
i = 3 & X_3 = (15187, 29168) \\
i = 4 & X_4 = (10532, 5412)
\end{array}
$$

In order to compute $X_5 = 5 \cdot X_4 = (2 \cdot (2 \cdot X_4)) + X_4$, we first compute

$$2 \cdot X_4 = (30373, 40140)$$

then

$$2 \cdot (2 \cdot X_4) = (27556, 42335)$$

but when we add up this point and X_4, we need to compute

$$\lambda = \frac{42335 - 5412}{27556 - 10532} \bmod n$$

but the denominator $27556 - 10532 = 17024$ is not invertible modulo n. When trying to invert it with the Euclid algorithm, we end up with the gcd between 17024 and n which is 133, indeed a factor of n.

This kind of algorithm illustrates how computation in an ill-designed structure (namely an elliptic curve over a structure $\mathbf{Z}_n$ which is not a field) can be performed until we stumble upon a computation error which yields an interesting result, here the factorization of n.

7.2.4 ⋆*Fermat Factorization and Factor Bases*

The Fermat factorization algorithm is used to factorize $n = pq$ where $p \approx q$. The purpose is to find a representation of n as the difference of two perfect squares

$n = t^2 - s^2$. Obviously, $t = \frac{p+q}{2}$ and $s = \frac{p-q}{2}$ is one such solution, and we notice that s is small when $p \approx q$. Conversely, if $n = t^2 - s^2$, we have $n = (t+s)(t-s)$, which factorizes n unless $t = s + 1 = \frac{n+1}{2}$. But in this case, s is not small at all since $s \approx \frac{n}{2}$. The algorithm works as follows: we try all possible t values starting from $\lceil \sqrt{n} \rceil$ until $t^2 - n$ is a perfect square s^2. The complexity is $\mathcal{O}(p - q)$ arithmetic operations.

The Fermat method is important because of the following observation: if we happen to find s and t such that $s^2 \equiv t^2 \pmod{n}$ and $s \not\equiv \pm t \pmod{n}$, then $\gcd(s - t, n)$ is a nontrivial factor of n: we notice that $(s - t)(s + t)$ is a multiple of n. So if $\gcd(s - t, n) = 1$, it means that $s + t$ is a multiple of n in which case we have $s \equiv -t \pmod{n}$, but this is not the case. If $\gcd(s - t, n) = n$, we have $s \equiv t \pmod{n}$, but this is not the case either. Hence, $\gcd(s - t, n)$ is a proper factor of n. So we can try to factorize n by looking for nontrivial $s^2 \equiv t^2 \pmod{n}$ relations.

Modern methods use *factor bases*. A factor base is a set B of numbers $p_1, \ldots, p_r$. We say that a number b is a B-number if it can be factorized into a product of numbers which are all in B. This factorization is assumed to be easy to perform. The goal of factor base methods is to get several B-numbers $a^2 \bmod n$. We obtain several relations $a_i^2 \bmod n = p_1^{\alpha_{i,1}} \cdots p_r^{\alpha_{i,r}}$. Once we get a little more than r equations, we consider the vectors $\vec{A}_i = (\alpha_{i,1}, \ldots, \alpha_{i,r})$. Since we have a little more than r vectors of r coordinates, they must be linearly dependent modulo 2. Hence we obtain a linear combination $\sum_{i \in I} \vec{A}_i$, the coefficients of which are all even. Therefore $\left(\prod_{i \in I} a_i \right)^2$ is congruent to a perfect square B-number. This relationship is likely to be a nontrivial $s^2 \equiv t^2 \pmod{n}$ relation which leads to a nontrivial factor of n. It is important to emphasize the three phases of this method:

1. get several $a_i^2 \equiv p_1^{\alpha_{i,1}} \cdots p_r^{\alpha_{i,r}} \pmod{n}$ relations,
2. solve a linear system in GF(2) in order to get an even linear combination of $(\alpha_{i,1}, \ldots, \alpha_{i,r})$ vectors,
3. from the corresponding $s^2 \equiv t^2 \pmod{n}$ relation, get a nontrivial factor of n.

The way the first step is done highly depends on the factorization method.

7.2.5 ⋆*The Quadratic Sieve*

The Quadratic sieve is a factor base method. Let m be the integer part of $\sqrt{n}$. We pick at random $A = X + m$, where X is a small integer. We notice that $A^2 - n = X^2 + 2mX + m^2 - n$. When $X \ll m$, the most important term in this sum is $2mX$ which is approximately $2X\sqrt{n}$. So this is relatively small when compared to n. In particular we may have $A^2 \bmod n = A^2 - n$. Assuming that $A^2 - n$ is b-smooth (namely all prime factors p are lesser than b), we can factorize $A^2 - n$ with the factor base which consists of -1 and all prime numbers lesser than b. (-1 is necessary in order to factorize negative numbers.)

We notice that if p is prime and divides $A^2 - n$, then $A^2 \equiv n \pmod{p}$, therefore n is a quadratic residue modulo p, hence $(\frac{n}{p}) = 1$ when p is odd. Therefore we can just pick B equal to -1, 2, and all prime numbers p lesser than b and for which $(\frac{n}{p}) = 1$.

We have already mentioned that a random integer within the order of magnitude of n is b-smooth with probability u^{-u} where $u = \frac{\log n}{\log b}$. So by picking a totally random A mod n, we obtain a relation with probability u^{-u}. The trick here (due to Carl Pomerance) consists of increasing this probability by decreasing the order of magnitude of A mod n by picking $A = X + m$. A mod n is now within an order of magnitude of $\sqrt{n}$, so u is decreased by one half.

We can heuristically prove that the complexity is $\mathcal{O}\left(e^{\sqrt{(1+o(1))\log n \, \log\log n}}\right)$ when we carefully choose b, as for the ECM method (see Ref. [152]).

As an example, we factorize $n = 527773$. We let $m = 726$, the nearest integer to the square root of n. The list of prime numbers of our factor basis is

$$2, 3, 5, 7, 11, 13, 17, 19, 23, 29, 31, 37, 41, 43, 47, 53, 59, 61, 67.$$

But n is a quadratic residue modulo

$$3, 7, 11, 13, 17, 41, 53, 61, 67$$

only. Therefore we set $B = \{-1, 2, 3, 7, 11, 13, 17, 41, 53, 61, 67\}$. We now try $A = X + m$ with

$$X = 0, +1, -1, +2, -2, +3, -3, \ldots$$

and we test which $A^2 - n$ values are b-smooth. We have

$$
\begin{aligned}
m^2 - n &= -1 \cdot 17 \cdot 41 \\
(m+1)^2 - n &= 2^2 \cdot 3^3 \cdot 7 \\
(m-1)^2 - n &= -1 \cdot 2^2 \cdot 3 \cdot 179 \\
(m+2)^2 - n &= 3 \cdot 11 \cdot 67 \\
(m-2)^2 - n &= -1 \cdot 3 \cdot 11 \cdot 109
\end{aligned}
$$

$$\vdots$$

$$(m+5)^2 - n = 2^2 \cdot 3^3 \cdot 61$$

$$\vdots$$

$$
\begin{aligned}
(m+7)^2 - n &= 2^2 \cdot 3 \cdot 13 \cdot 61 \\
(m-7)^2 - n &= -1 \cdot 2^2 \cdot 3 \cdot 17 \cdot 53
\end{aligned}
$$

$$\vdots$$

$$(m + 10)^2 - n = 3^2 \cdot 7 \cdot 13 \cdot 17$$
$$(m - 13)^2 - n = -1 \cdot 2^2 \cdot 3^2 \cdot 7^2 \cdot 11$$
$$(m + 17)^2 - n = 2^2 \cdot 3 \cdot 7 \cdot 17^2$$
$$(m - 17)^2 - n = -1 \cdot 2^2 \cdot 3^2 \cdot 17 \cdot 41$$
$$(m + 20)^2 - n = 3 \cdot 11 \cdot 13 \cdot 67$$
$$(m + 24)^2 - n = 7 \cdot 11^2 \cdot 41$$
$$(m - 24)^2 - n = -1 \cdot 11^2 \cdot 17^2$$

and so we obtain the following vectors

X	$m + X$	$(m + X)^2 - n$	Factors	Vector
0	726	−697	$-1 \cdot 17 \cdot 41$	$(1, 0, 0, 0, 0, 0, 1, 1, 0, 0, 0)$
1	727	756	$2^2 \cdot 3^3 \cdot 7$	$(0, 2, 3, 1, 0, 0, 0, 0, 0, 0, 0)$
2	728	2211	$3 \cdot 11 \cdot 67$	$(0, 0, 1, 0, 1, 0, 0, 0, 0, 0, 1)$
5	731	6588	$2^2 \cdot 3^3 \cdot 61$	$(0, 2, 3, 0, 0, 0, 0, 0, 0, 1, 0)$
7	733	9516	$2^2 \cdot 3 \cdot 13 \cdot 61$	$(0, 2, 1, 0, 0, 1, 0, 0, 0, 1, 0)$
−7	719	−10812	$-1 \cdot 2^2 \cdot 3 \cdot 17 \cdot 53$	$(1, 2, 1, 0, 0, 0, 1, 0, 1, 0, 0)$
10	736	13923	$3^2 \cdot 7 \cdot 13 \cdot 17$	$(0, 0, 2, 1, 0, 1, 1, 0, 0, 0, 0)$
−13	713	−19404	$-1 \cdot 2^2 \cdot 3^2 \cdot 7^2 \cdot 11$	$(1, 2, 2, 2, 1, 0, 0, 0, 0, 0, 0)$
17	743	24276	$2^2 \cdot 3 \cdot 7 \cdot 17^2$	$(0, 2, 1, 1, 0, 0, 2, 0, 0, 0, 0)$
−17	709	−25092	$-1 \cdot 2^2 \cdot 3^2 \cdot 17 \cdot 41$	$(1, 2, 2, 0, 0, 0, 1, 1, 0, 0, 0)$
20	746	28743	$3 \cdot 11 \cdot 13 \cdot 67$	$(0, 0, 1, 0, 1, 1, 0, 0, 0, 0, 1)$
24	750	34727	$7 \cdot 11^2 \cdot 41$	$(0, 0, 0, 1, 2, 0, 0, 1, 0, 0, 0)$
−24	702	−34969	$-1 \cdot 11^2 \cdot 17^2$	$(1, 0, 0, 0, 2, 0, 2, 0, 0, 0, 0)$

We can now reduce the vectors modulo 2 and try to find linear dependencies. Here, we can simply notice that the vectors for $X = 1$ and for $X = 17$ coincide modulo 2. Indeed, we have

$$727^2 \cdot 743^{-2} \equiv 3^2 \cdot 17^{-2} \pmod{n}.$$

Since $727 \cdot 743^{-1} \bmod n = 223754$ and $3 \cdot 17^{-1} \bmod n = 186273$, we have $223754^2 \equiv 186273^2 \bmod n$ and we notice that $223754 - 186273 = 37481$ and $\gcd(37481, n) = 1013$, which is a nontrivial factor of n. This leads us to the factorization $n = 521 \cdot 1013$.

7.2.6 ⋆*Factorization Nowadays*

The previous methods have been extended to give birth to the more sophisticated *number field sieve method* (NFS), due to Hendrik Lenstra and Arjen Lenstra, which is quite beyond the scope of this book (see Ref. [115]). We simply mention that the NFS complexity is

$$e^{\mathcal{O}\left((\log n)^{\frac{1}{3}}(\log\log n)^{\frac{2}{3}}\right)}.$$

This method becomes substantially better than the previous ones as n increases. (In practice, it becomes better when n reaches 100 to 150 decimal digits.)

As we will see in the next chapters, the ability to factorize large numbers enables to break some cryptosystems. To monitor public progress in this area, factorization challenges were issued by the company RSA Data Security. Every challenge is a large number which is given a tag featuring its length. For instance, RSA155 is the following 155-decimal digits integer.

RSA155 $=$ 10941738641570527421809707322040357612003732945449
20599091384213147634998428893478471799725789126733
24976257528997818337970765372440271467435315933354333897.

This number was factorized on August 22, 1999 by a team of scientists from six different countries, led by Herman te Riele of CWI (Amsterdam). They implemented a network of computers that provided about 8000 mips.year (8000 millions of instructions per second during one year), to discover that RSA155 is equal to

10263959282974110577205419657399167590071656780803806680334193352179071130 7779 $\times$
10660348838016845482092722036001287867920795857598929152227060823719306280 8643

which is a product of two prime numbers. A lot of efforts for a two-line conclusion!

7.2.7 ⋆*Factorization Tomorrow*

At this time, researchers are investigating a new computing model which no longer relies on traditional microprocessors and memories. Instead, it relies on *quantum mechanics*. This model or quantum computing assumes that the *state* of a computing machine can be so isolated from an electromagnetic viewpoint that it can be in a quantum state. Namely, instead of being on a well-defined state, it can be on a superposition of (infinitely) many states associated with a complex weight. The probability that freezing the machine ends up on a given state is the squared norm of the complex weight. Since most people have been educated with well-defined deterministic state machines, this model is clearly against the common intuition. Nevertheless, some experiments show that such machines can be built, but the current state of the art limit them to a dozen of quantum bits of memory. The question whether this model can scale or not is still open today since the more quantum bits we have, the less stable states are.

One advantage of this computing model is the notion of free massive parallelism. With a single quantum bit of memory we can basically do 2^n computations in parallel for any n. One problem is that we cannot collect all results. With some special cases, we can make the results interact (for instance through a discrete Fourier transform) to derive a single result. This case is very well suited to the problem of factorization. Indeed, the Shor algorithm can factorize any integer N within a complexity of $\mathcal{O}((\log N)^2 (\log \log N)(\log \log \log N))$ on a quantum computer. The only remaining problem is to construct a machine with $\log N$ quantum bits of memory.[4]

7.3   Computing Orders in Groups

7.3.1   Finding the Group Exponent

As explained in Section 7.1.2, we recall that the *exponent* of a group is the smallest nonnegative integer λ such that $x^\lambda = 1$ for all x in the group (assuming that the group is multiplicatively denoted). For cyclic groups, the exponent is obviously the order of the group. For instance in $\mathbf{Z}_n$ (which is additively denoted), the exponent is n since n is the smallest x such that $x.1 \equiv 0 \pmod{n}$ and we have $n.x \equiv 0 \pmod{n}$ for any $x \in \mathbf{Z}_n$.

In the case of $\mathbf{Z}_n^*$, λ is denoted $\lambda(n)$ as the *Carmichael function*. We can easily prove that if $n = p_1^{\alpha_1} \cdots p_r^{\alpha_r}$ is the factorization of n, then

$$\lambda(n) = \mathrm{lcm}\left((p_1 - 1)p_1^{\alpha_1 - 1}, \ldots, (p_r - 1)p_r^{\alpha_r - 1} \right)$$

which should be compared to

$$\varphi(n) = (p_1 - 1)p_1^{\alpha_1 - 1} \cdots (p_r - 1)p_r^{\alpha_r - 1}.$$

Finding the exponent of $\mathbf{Z}_n^*$ is not easy. It is actually as hard as factoring n: obviously, the factorization of n allows to compute $\lambda(n)$ by the above formula. The opposite is a little more subtle. Let us assume that we can compute $\lambda = \lambda(n)$ and let us factorize n.

Let us first take an example with $n = pq$ with p and q different primes such that $p \equiv q \equiv 3 \pmod 4$. This way we have $\lambda = 2.\mathrm{lcm}\left(\frac{p-1}{2}, \frac{q-1}{2} \right)$ and the lcm is odd. We know that $x^{\frac{p-1}{2}} \bmod p = 1$ if and only if x is a quadratic residue modulo p, and that $x^{\frac{q-1}{2}} \bmod q = 1$ if and only if x is a quadratic residue modulo q. Hence the two reductions of $x^{\frac{\lambda}{2}} - 1$ modulo p and modulo q are equal with probability $\frac{1}{2}$, namely if the quadratic residuosity is the same for both modulo p and modulo q. This means that we can find factors of n by computing $\gcd(n, x^{\frac{\lambda}{2}} - 1 \bmod n)$ with a random x.

More generally, let us assume without loss of generality that n is odd (we can get rid of even factors by using the Chinese Remainder Theorem) and has at least

---

[4] For more information, see Ref. [140].

two different primes (otherwise, the factorization is easy). Let i be such that λ can be written as $2^i k'$ with k' odd. There is at least a prime factor p of n such that 2^i divides $p - 1$ and $(p - 1)/2^i$ is odd. Obviously, $x \in \mathbf{Z}_n^*$ is a quadratic residue modulo p if and only if $x^{2^{i-1}k'} \bmod p$ is equal to 1. Let q be another prime factor of n. If 2^i does not divide $q - 1$, then we have $x^{2^{i-1}k'} \bmod q = 1$ for all $x \in \mathbf{Z}_n^*$. Otherwise this holds if and only if x is a quadratic residue modulo q. From these two facts (modulo p and q) and the Chinese Remainder Theorem we infer that $x^{2^{i-1}k'}$ modulo p and $x^{2^{i-1}k'}$ modulo q are different with probability $\frac{1}{2}$, but that $x^{2^{i-1}k'}$ is a square root of 1. This means that there is a probability of $\frac{1}{2}$ that $\gcd(x^{2^{i-1}k'} - 1 \bmod n, n)$ yields a nontrivial factor of n for a random $x \in \mathbf{Z}_n^*$. We can iterate this process until we find all factors of n.

Finding an element order is a separate problem. We can first notice that finding element orders implies finding the group exponent. Indeed, the exponent is equal to the lcm of all element orders by Lemma 7.3. Therefore, computing the lcm of orders of a few elements quickly reaches the exponent as the number of elements grows. Therefore, finding the order of an element is at least as hard as computing the group exponent which is equivalent to the factorization problem in the case of $\mathbf{Z}_n^*$.

7.3.2   Computing Element Orders in Groups

As we saw in the previous section, computing element orders is at least as hard as computing the group exponent.

In some particular groups, computation is easy. For instance, in $\mathbf{Z}_n$, we can compute the order of x even though we do not know how to factorize n. The order is the smallest nonnegative k such that $kx \equiv 0 \pmod{n}$, namely such that n divides kx. The order is simply given by the formula $k = \frac{\mathrm{lcm}(n,x)}{x}$.

When the complete factorization of the exponent of a group G is known, it is also easy to compute the order of any group element x: let λ be the exponent of G and let $p_1^{\alpha_1} \cdots p_r^{\alpha_r}$ be the complete factorization of λ (all p_i are pairwise different primes, and all α_i are nonnegative integers). We want to compute the order of $x \in G$. We know that it is a factor of λ. We set $k = \lambda$ as a first approximation for the order of x. For any i from 1 to n, we replace k by k/p_i as long as $x^{\frac{k}{p_i}} = 1$ in G. (We assume the group to be multiplicatively denoted.) At the end we are ensured that k is the smallest nonnegative power of x which is such that $x^k = 1$.

In the case of $\mathbf{Z}_n^*$ we obtain that

> knowledge of the factorization of $\lambda(n)$
>
> $\implies$ ability to compute element orders in $\mathbf{Z}_n^*$
>
> $\implies$ knowledge of $\lambda(n)$
>
> $\iff$ knowledge of the factorization of n

but it is not quite clear whether one of the first two reductions is actually an equivalence or not. We can still suspect that knowledge of $\lambda(n)$ and knowledge of the factorization of $\lambda(n)$ are not equivalent given the hardness of the factorization problem, but this is not so obvious since the integer has a particular form and we have a hint with the extra information of the knowledge of n.

In Section 7.4 we will present an algorithm computing element orders in $\mathcal{O}(\sqrt{\#G})$ time when we do not know $\#G$.

7.4 ⋆Discrete Logarithm

Another problem similar to factorization and widely used in cryptography is the *discrete logarithm problem*: in a multiplicative group G generated by some g, compute an integer x such that $y = g^x$ from $y \in G$. We summarize this by saying that we want to compute $\log_g y$ in G. There are a few variants.

- The order $\#G$ of the group can be available or not.
- Since the logarithm is in unique modulo $\#G$, we can ask for one possible logarithm if $\#G$ is not available.
- The y elements may not necessarily be in G and in that case, the problem consists of distinguishing elements of G from other elements.
- and so on.

Here are some formal problem specifications.

DLP (Discrete Logarithm Problem):
Parameters: a cyclic group G generated by an element $g \in G$
Input: an element y in G
Problem: compute the least integer x such that $y = g^x$
DLKOP (Discrete Logarithm with Known Order Problem):
Parameters: a cyclic group G generated by an element $g \in G$, and the order $\#G$
Input: an element y in G
Problem: compute x such that $y = g^x$

Note that if the order of G is known, then computing the least discrete logarithm and computing one representative are two equivalent problems. We can also consider the problem when the factorization of the order of G is known.

DLKOFP (Discrete Logarithm with Known Order Factorization Problem):
Parameters: a cyclic group G generated by an element $g \in G$, the order $\#G$ and its factorization into prime numbers
Input: an element y in G
Problem: compute x such that $y = g^x$

As an example, we can consider the multiplicative group G generated by some $g \in \mathbf{Z}_n^*$. If $\varphi(n)$ is unknown, it is quite hard to compute the order of g in general. It is also hard to check if a given $y \in \mathbf{Z}_n^*$ is in G or not. If $y \in G$, it is still hard to compute one x such that $y = g^x \bmod n$.

In many cases, we can adapt factorization algorithms to solve all these problems. Here we first see that when $\#G$ and its factorization are known (which is the DLKOFP problem) and when $\#G$ is B-smooth, we can have a simple algorithm within $\mathcal{O}(\sqrt{B})$ arithmetic operations.

7.4.1   *Pollard Rho Method*

The heuristic Pollard Rho factorization algorithm, described in Section 7.2.1, can be adapted to solve the discrete logarithm problem when we are given the order of the group (i.e. the above DLKOP) (see Ref. [150]).

Let G denote the (multiplicatively denoted) group, n denote its order, g and y be two elements of G such that we look for some integer c such that $y = g^c$. The idea consists in managing a sequence of (x, α, β) triplets such that $x = g^{\alpha} y^{\beta}$. The sequence is obtained by some kind of random walk. We expect to loop on the x term of the triplet in $\mathcal{O}(\sqrt{n})$ iterations, so that we obtain an equation of the kind

$$x = g^{\alpha} y^{\beta} = g^{\alpha'} y^{\beta'}$$

which leads us to

$$c = \frac{\alpha - \alpha'}{\beta - \beta'} \bmod n.$$

The random walk is defined by a function $f(x, \alpha, \beta)$ by

$$f(x, \alpha, \beta) = \begin{cases} (x \times g, \alpha + 1 \bmod n, \beta) & \text{if } h(x) = 1 \\ (x \times y, \alpha, \beta + 1 \bmod n) & \text{if } h(x) = 2 \\ (x^2, 2\alpha \bmod n, 2\beta \bmod n) & \text{if } h(x) = 3 \end{cases}$$

where h is a random balanced function from G to $\{1, 2, 3\}$. We can easily see that the property $x = g^{\alpha} y^{\beta}$ is preserved by replacing (x, α, β) by $f(x, \alpha, \beta)$. Analysis shows that this is indeed a random walk so that we are expected to loop on the first term in $\mathcal{O}(\sqrt{n})$. The complete algorithm is detailed in Fig. 7.8.

7.4.2   *Shanks Baby Steps – Giant Steps Algorithm*

We now describe the *Shanks baby step – giant step algorithm* which solves the DLKOP problem within a complexity of $\mathcal{O}(\sqrt{\#G})$. It even solves the DLP problem when we have an upper bound B for $\#G$, within a complexity of $\mathcal{O}(\sqrt{B})$. It is also convenient for finding element orders (which are a kind of discrete logarithm of unity).

> **Input**: g and y in a group G of order n
> **Output**: the logarithm of y in basis g
> **Complexity**: $\mathcal{O}(\sqrt{n})$ group operations
> 1: pick a random function $h : G \longrightarrow \{1, 2, 3\}$
> 2: $\vec{a}, \vec{b} \leftarrow (1, 0, 0) \in G \times \mathbf{Z}_n \times \mathbf{Z}_n$
> 3: **repeat**
> 4: $\vec{a} \leftarrow f(\vec{a})$
> 5: $\vec{b} \leftarrow f(f(\vec{b}))$
> 6: **until** $a_1 = b_1$
> 7: output $(a_2 - b_2)/(a_3 - b_3) \bmod n$ {fail if not possible}

Figure 7.8. Pollard Rho Discrete Logarithm Algorithm.

Let B be $\#G$ (if $\#G$ is not available, B can be any upper bound of $\#G$). We proceed as shown in Fig. 7.9. The algorithm eventually succeeds: if x is the unknown logarithm modulo $\#G$, we know that $x \in \{0, \dots, \ell^2 - 1\}$. It can thus be written $x = i\ell + j$, for which we get the match in the above algorithm. Therefore this algorithm computes the discrete logarithm within $\mathcal{O}(\sqrt{B})$ group operations. (One problem is that it requires $\mathcal{O}(\sqrt{B})$ memory space as well.)

7.4.3 ⋆*Pohlig–Hellman Algorithm*

Here we describe the *Pohlig–Hellman algorithm* (see Ref. [145]). It reduces the computation of a discrete logarithm within a group G (the factorization of the order of which $\#G = p_1^{a_1} \cdots p_n^{a_n}$ is known) into computing discrete logarithms in groups of order $p_1, \dots, p_n$. Combining this reduction with the Shanks baby steps – giant steps algorithm we obtain an algorithm which solves the DLKOFP problem, i.e. which enables the computation of discrete logarithms in a B-smooth ordered group of known factor-

> **Input**: g and y in a group G, B an upper bound for $\#G$
> **Output**: the logarithm of y in basis g
> **Complexity**: $\mathcal{O}(\sqrt{B})$ group operations
> **Precomputation**
> 1: let $\ell = \lceil \sqrt{B} \rceil$ be the size of a "giant step"
> 2: **for** $i = 0, \dots, \ell - 1$ **do**
> 3:   insert $(g^{i\ell}, i)$ into a hash table
> 4: **end for**
> **Algorithm**
> 5: **for** $j = 0, \dots, \ell - 1$ **do**
> 6:   compute $z = yg^{-j}$
> 7:   **if** we have a (z, i) in the hash table **then**
> 8:   yield $x = i\ell + j$ and stop {we get $yg^{-j} = g^{i\ell}$}
> 9:   **end if**
> 10: **end for**

Figure 7.9. Baby Steps – Giant Steps Algorithm.

ization, within a complexity which is essentially $\mathcal{O}(\sqrt{B})$ group operations (plus some extra logarithmic complexity factors).

Let $N = \#G$ of given factorization $N = p_1^{a_1} \ldots p_n^{a_n}$.

We first reduce the discrete logarithm computation to the case of $n = 1$ with the following argument. If x is a discrete logarithm of y, then x is a discrete logarithm of y^{α_i} in the subgroup generated by g^{α_i}. With $\alpha_i = N p^{-a_i}$, the later discrete logarithm is in a subgroup of G of order $p_i^{a_i}$ generated by $g_i = g^{\alpha_i}$, thus a number modulo $p_i^{a_i}$. Conversely, x_i is a discrete logarithm of $y^{Np^{-a_i}}$ modulo $p_i^{a_i}$ in the subgroup generated by $g^{Np^{-a_i}}$, and from the Chinese Remainder Theorem we can reconstruct $x \bmod N$ such that $x \equiv x_i \pmod{p_i^{a_i}}$. We then notice that yg^{-x} is equal to 1. This way we reduce the problem of computing x in G into n problems of computing discrete logarithms in groups of order $p_i^{a_i}$ for $i = 1, \ldots, n$.

To go further we can thus assume that $n = 1$ and $N = p^a$. We will reduce the computation by a computations of discrete logarithms in subgroups of order p.

We proceed by computing x by more precise approximations of x by $x_j = x \bmod p^j$ for $j = 1, \ldots, a$. Note that $x_0 = 1$ is known. Assuming that we know x_{j-1}, we notice that $(yg^{-x_{j-1}})^{p^{a-j}}$ is a power of $g^{p^{a-1}}$, hence of order p. Its discrete logarithm is indeed the next base-p digit of x and enables the computation of x_j. We thus compute the discrete logarithm of $(yg^{-x_{j-1}})^{p^{a-j}}$ and get x_j.

To summarize, we have reduced the computation of x into $a_1 + \cdots + a_n$ discrete logarithm problems in subgroups of orders which are the prime factors of N. Since $a_1 + \cdots + a_n = O(\log N)$, we can combine this reduction with Shanks algorithm and obtain a full algorithm of complexity $\mathcal{O}(\sqrt{B} \log N)$ group operations. The algorithm is shown in Fig. 7.10.

As an example, we want to compute the logarithm of $y = 123$ in base $g = 6$ modulo $p = 125651$. We first check that p is a prime, so $\mathbf{Z}_p^*$ is a cyclic group in which 123 is included. We have $p - 1 = 125650 = 2 \times 5^2 \times 7 \times 359$. We finally check that 6 is a generator of $\mathbf{Z}_p^*$ because $6^{\frac{p-1}{q}} \bmod p \neq 1$ for $q = 2, 5, 7, 359$. So 123 must be a power of 6 modulo p.

Applying the Pohlig–Hellman algorithm, we have to compute the following logarithms.

$$\log_{g^{\frac{p-1}{2}} \bmod p}(y^{\frac{p-1}{2}}), \quad \log_{g^{\frac{p-1}{5^2}} \bmod p}(y^{\frac{p-1}{5^2}}), \quad \log_{g^{\frac{p-1}{7}} \bmod p}(y^{\frac{p-1}{7}}),$$

$$\log_{g^{\frac{p-1}{359}} \bmod p}(y^{\frac{p-1}{359}})$$

Input: g and y in a group G, $\#G = N$ and the complete factorization
$N = p_1^{a_1} \ldots p_n^{a_n}$ such that p_i is prime, $p_i \neq p_j$, and $a_i > 0$ for $1 \leq i, j \leq n$ and $i \neq j$

Output: the logarithm of y in base g

Complexity: $\mathcal{O}(a_1 \sqrt{p_1} + \cdots + a_n \sqrt{p_n})$ group operations

1: **for** $i = 1, \ldots, n$ **do**
2:     $g' \leftarrow g^{N/p_i^{a_i}}$
3:     $g'' \leftarrow g'^{p_i^{a_i-1}}$
4:     $y' \leftarrow y^{N/p_i^{a_i}}$
5:     $y'' \leftarrow y'$
6:     $x_i \leftarrow 0$
7:     **for** $j = 0$ to $a_i - 1$ **do**
8:         $y'' \leftarrow y'^{p_i^{a_i-j-1}}$
9:         compute the discrete logarithm u of y'' in the subgroup of order p_i which is spanned by g''
10:        $y' \leftarrow y'/g''^{u \cdot p_i^{j}}$
11:        $x_i \leftarrow x_i + u.p_i^{j}$
12:    **end for**
13: **end for**
14: reconstruct and yield x such that $x \equiv x_i \pmod{p_i^{a_i}}$

Figure 7.10. Pohlig–Hellman Algorithm.

Let us first compute $\log_{g^{\frac{p-1}{2}} \bmod p}\left(y^{\frac{p-1}{2}}\right)$. We have

$$g^{\frac{p-1}{2}} \bmod p = 6^{62825} \bmod p = 125650, \quad y^{\frac{p-1}{2}} \bmod p = 123^{62825} \bmod p = 125650.$$

Therefore

$$\log_{g^{\frac{p-1}{2}} \bmod p}\left(y^{\frac{p-1}{2}}\right) = 1.$$

Let us now compute $\log_{g^{\frac{p-1}{7}} \bmod p}\left(y^{\frac{p-1}{7}}\right)$. We have

$$g^{\frac{p-1}{7}} \bmod p = 6^{17950} \bmod p = 21153, \quad y^{\frac{p-1}{7}} \bmod p = 123^{17950} \bmod p = 91649$$

so we need to compute $\log_{21153 \bmod p}(91649)$ in a group of order 7. Since 7 is quite small, we can exhaust all powers.

$$21153^0 \bmod p = 1$$

$$21153^1 \bmod p = 21153$$

$$21153^2 \bmod p = 6198$$

$$21153^3 \bmod p = 52301$$

$$21153^4 \bmod p = 91649$$

Therefore

$$\log_{g^{\frac{p-1}{7}} \bmod p}\left(y^{\frac{p-1}{7}}\right) = 4.$$

Let us now compute $\log_{g^{\frac{p-1}{5^2}} \bmod p}\left(y^{\frac{p-1}{5^2}}\right)$. We have

$$g^{\frac{p-1}{5^2}} \bmod p = 6^{5026} \bmod p = 45194, \qquad y^{\frac{p-1}{5^2}} \bmod p = 123^{5026} \bmod p = 34726.$$

We know that this logarithm is in a group of order 5^2. We can have a first approximation (compute the modulo 5 part) by computing $\log_{45194^5 \bmod p}(34726^5)$. We have $45194^5 \bmod p = 10770$ and $34726^5 \bmod p = 55981$, so we need to compute $\log_{10770 \bmod p}(55981)$ in a group of order 5. Since 5 is quite small, we make a logarithm table.

$$10770^1 \bmod p = 10770$$

$$10770^2 \bmod p = 17027$$

$$10770^3 \bmod p = 55981$$

$$10770^4 \bmod p = 41872$$

$$10770^5 \bmod p = 1.$$

Thus $\log_{10770 \bmod p}(55981) = 3$. Therefore $\log_{45194 \bmod p}(34726) \bmod 5 = 3$. So we can take $34726/45194^3 \bmod p = 10770$, and we notice that its logarithm in base 10770 is 1. So we can check that $\log_{45194 \bmod p}(34726) = 3 + 1 \times 5 = 8$. Therefore

$$\log_{g^{\frac{p-1}{5^2}} \bmod p}\left(y^{\frac{p-1}{5^2}}\right) = 8.$$

Let us finally compute $\log_{g^{\frac{p-1}{359}} \bmod p}\left(y^{\frac{p-1}{359}}\right)$. We have

$$g^{\frac{p-1}{359}} \bmod p = 6^{350} \bmod p = 19903, \qquad y^{\frac{p-1}{359}} \bmod p = 123^{350} \bmod p = 101887.$$

We need to compute $\log_{19903 \bmod p}(101887)$ in a group of order 359. For this we need the Shanks algorithm. Let $\ell = \lceil\sqrt{359}\rceil = 19$ be the "giant step." We compute the table of powers of $19903^{\ell} \bmod p$ for powers up to 18:

i	0	1	2	3	4	5	6	7	8	9
$19903^{i\ell} \bmod p$	1	24783	15001	94125	114711	28838	114917	108096	63848	21941
i	10	11	12	13	14	15	16	17	18	
$19903^{i\ell} \bmod p$	71926	56972	122440	84521	81773	80931	71711	5969	38500	

We sort this table into

$(1, 0)(5969, 17)(15001, 2)(21941, 9)(24783, 1)(28838, 5)(38500, 18)(56972, 11)$
$(63848, 8)(71711, 16)(71926, 10)(80931, 15)(81773, 14)(84521, 13)(94125, 3)$
$(108096, 7)(114711, 4)(114917, 6)(122440, 12)$

Next we compute $101887 \times 19903^{-j} \bmod p$ until we hit a value in this table. We compute

$$101887 \times 19903^{-0} \bmod p = 101887$$

$$101887 \times 19903^{-1} \bmod p = 7139$$

$$101887 \times 19903^{-2} \bmod p = 114597$$

$$101887 \times 19903^{-3} \bmod p = 28838$$

which is in the table, corresponding to $i = 5$. So we can check that $\log_{19903 \bmod p}$ $(101887) = 3 + 5 \times 19 = 98$.

Therefore we obtain

$$\log_{g^{\frac{p-1}{359}} \bmod p} \left(y^{\frac{p-1}{359}} \right) = 98.$$

Finally, we obtain that $\log_{g \bmod p}(y)$ is congruent to 1 modulo 2, to 8 modulo 5^2, to 4 modulo 7, and to 98 modulo 359. We can now apply the Chinese Remainder Theorem. We let

$$x = 1 \cdot r_2 + 8 \cdot r_{5^2} + 4 \cdot r_7 + 98 \cdot r_{359} \bmod (p - 1)$$

where

$$r_q = \frac{p-1}{q} \times \left(\left(\frac{p-1}{q} \right)^{-1} \bmod q \right)$$

and we obtain that $\log_{g \bmod p}(y) = x = 23433$.

7.4.4   ⋆*Factor Base and Index Calculus Algorithm*

Factorization algorithms using factor bases can be adapted to the DLKOP problem, which makes some researchers believe that the two problems might have the same intrinsic complexity. This is the *index calculus algorithm*.

To compute the discrete logarithm of y in base g in a group G of known order $\#G$, we first take a factor base $B = \{p_1, \ldots, p_r\}$. The first step consists of getting several B-numbers of the form g^k and to collect $g^{k_i} = p_1^{\alpha_{i,1}} \cdots p_r^{\alpha_{1,r}}$ random relations. When we have $r + c$ relations for a small constant c, we can solve the linear system in $\mathbf{Z}_{\#G}$, which leads to the discrete logarithms of all p_i. Now we can pick a random yg^k until it is a B-number and get the discrete logarithm of y:

1. obtain several $g^{k_i} = p_1^{\alpha_{i,1}} \cdots p_r^{\alpha_{i,r}}$ relations,
2. solve the linear system defined by all $k_i = \alpha_{1,1}x_1 + \cdots + \alpha_{i,r}x_i$ in $\mathbf{Z}_{\#G}$,
3. obtain $yg^k = p_1^{\beta_1} \cdots p_r^{\beta_r}$,
4. infer $\log_g y = \beta_1 x_1 + \cdots + \beta_r x_r - k$.

With a judicious choice of B the complexity of this algorithm in $G = \mathbf{Z}_p^*$ is $\mathcal{O}\left(e^{(c+o(1))\sqrt{\log p \, \log \log p}}\right)$.

As an example, let us compute the discrete logarithm of $y = 123$ in base $g = 7777$ in $\mathbf{Z}_{34631}^*$. We use the factor base $B = \{2, 3, 5, 7, 11, 13\}$. We first collect the relations

$$g^9 \equiv 5^3 \times 11^1 \times 13^1$$
$$g^{109} \equiv 2^2 \times 3^5 \times 5^1 \times 7^1$$
$$g^{130} \equiv 3^1 \times 5^2 \times 11^2$$
$$g^{131} \equiv 2^5 \times 3^1 \times 7^3$$
$$g^{138} \equiv 3^3 \times 5^1 \times 13^1$$
$$g^{161} \equiv 2^5 \times 11^1 \times 13^1$$
$$g^{174} \equiv 2^3 \times 3^7$$
$$g^{185} \equiv 2^1 \times 5^3 \times 7^1 \times 13^1$$

then we write

$$
\begin{pmatrix} 9 \\ 109 \\ 130 \\ 131 \\ 138 \\ 161 \\ 174 \\ 185 \end{pmatrix}
=
\begin{pmatrix}
 & & 3 & & 1 & 1 \\
2 & 5 & 1 & 1 & & \\
 & 1 & 2 & & 2 & \\
5 & 1 & & 3 & & \\
 & 3 & 1 & & & 1 \\
5 & & & & 1 & 1 \\
3 & 7 & & & & \\
1 & & 3 & 1 & & 1
\end{pmatrix}
\times
\begin{pmatrix} x_1 \\ x_2 \\ x_3 \\ x_4 \\ x_5 \\ x_6 \end{pmatrix}
$$

If we extract the sixth and eighth rows, we obtain a matrix with determinant -133 which is invertible modulo $p - 1$. By inverting the matrix, we obtain through computations in $\mathbf{Z}_{p-1}$ that

$$\begin{pmatrix} x_1 \\ x_2 \\ x_3 \\ x_4 \\ x_5 \\ x_6 \end{pmatrix} = \begin{pmatrix} 10918 \\ 5240 \\ 18146 \\ 3187 \\ 13929 \\ 902 \end{pmatrix}$$

which leads to

$$2 = g^{10918} \bmod p$$
$$3 = g^{5240} \bmod p$$
$$5 = g^{18146} \bmod p$$
$$7 = g^{3187} \bmod p$$
$$11 = g^{13929} \bmod p$$
$$13 = g^{902} \bmod p$$

We can finally figure out that

$$yg^{30} \equiv 2^1 \times 5^1 \times 7^1 \times 13^2 \pmod p$$

hence

$$y = g^{-30+10918+18146+3187+2\times902} \bmod p = g^{34025} \bmod p.$$

7.5 Exercises

Exercise 7.1. *We call* strong prime *an odd prime n such that $\frac{n-1}{2}$ is prime as well. Prove that we can (heuristically) generate ℓ-bit strong primes within a time complexity of $\mathcal{O}(\ell^5)$.*

Hint: Make the heuristic assumption that m and $2m + 1$ behave like independent random odd numbers when m is a random odd number.

Exercise 7.2. *Assume we have a table S of n Boolean elements. We consider the five following algorithms.*

Algorithm A:
```
1:  for i = 1 to n do
2:      S[i] ← true
3:  end for
4:  S[1] ← false
5:  for i = 2 to n do
6:      if S[i] then
7:          for j = 2i to n by step of i do
8:              S[j] ← false
9:          end for
10:     end if
11: end for
12: for i = 1 to n do
13:     if S[i] then
14:         print i
15:     end if
16: end for
```

Algorithm B:
```
1:  for i = 1 to n do
2:      S[i] ← true
3:  end for
4:  S[1] ← false
5:  for i = 2 to n do
6:      for j ← 2i to n by step of i do
7:          S[j] ← false
8:      end for
9:  end for
10: for i = 1 to n do
11:     if S[i] then
12:         print i
13:     end if
14: end for
```

Algorithm C:
```
1:  for i = 1 to n do
2:      S[i] ← true
3:  end for
4:  S[1] ← false
5:  for i = 2 to n do
6:      if S[i] then
7:          for j = i + 1 to n do
8:              if i divides j then
9:                  S[j] ← false
10:             end if
11:         end for
12:     end if
13: end for
14: for i = 1 to n do
15:     if S[i] then
16:         print i
17:     end if
18: end for
```

Algorithm D:
```
1:  for i = 1 to n do
2:      S[i] ← true
3:  end for
4:  S[1] ← false
5:  for i = 2 to n do
6:      for j = 2 to i do
7:          if j divides i then
8:              S[i] ← false
9:          end if
10:     end for
11: end for
12: for i = 1 to n do
13:     if S[i] then
14:         print i
15:     end if
16: end for
```

Algorithm E:
```
1:  for i = 1 to n do
2:      S[i] ← true
3:  end for
4:  S[1] ← false
5:  for i = 2 to n do
6:      for j = 2 to √i do
7:          if j divides i then
8:              S[i] ← false
9:          end if
10:     end for
11: end for
12: for i = 1 to n do
13:     if S[i] then
14:         print i
15:     end if
16: end for
```

Each of these algorithms provides the same result. What is this result? What is the complexity of each of these algorithms?

Hint: We admit that the number of prime integers smaller than n is equivalent to $n/\log n$. Infer that the k-th prime is equivalent in magnitude to $k \log k$, and that the sum of the inverses of prime numbers smaller than n is equivalent to $\log \log n$.

Exercise 7.3. *Factor $2^{32} - 1$, $2^{64} - 1$, $3^{32} - 1$.*

Show that $2^8 + 1$ and $2^{16} + 1$ are prime.

Factor $2^{32} + 1$ and $2^{64} + 1$ by any method.

Exercise 7.4. *Using the paradigm which extends the $p - 1$ factorization method into the elliptic curve method, propose an algorithm for finding a prime factor p of n when $p + 1$ is B-smooth.*

Hint: Use the $GF(p^2)^*$ group structure.

Exercise 7.5. *Factorize 530899, 509017, 539377 using the quadratic sieve method.*

⋆Elements of Complexity Theory

Content

⋆**Formal computation:** languages, automata, Turing machines
⋆**Ability frontiers:** computability, decidability
⋆**Complexity reduction:** intractability, NP-completeness, oracles

In Chapter 1 we saw how to formalize secrecy based on information theory with the notion of perfect secrecy. The Shannon Theorem says that secrecy cannot be achieved unless we can afford the technical cost of the Vernam cipher, which is not very practical. The Shannon Theorem was however formulated in the prehistory times of computer science, and the notion of computation complexity did not exist. The security of cryptographic algorithms always relies on a given frontier of computational capability. Shannon implicitly explored the frontier based on information availability. By looking at the foundations of computer sciences, we explore other frontiers in this chapter. We will see that a frontier based on Turing complexity better fits cryptography.

8.1 ⋆Formal Computation

8.1.1 ⋆Formal Languages and Regular Expressions

Formally, a *language* is a set of *words*. A *word* is a finite sequence of characters taken from an *alphabet*. An *alphabet* is a finite set Σ. The basic operation defined on words is *concatenation*. Given two words u and v, we let $u||v$ denote the concatenation of u and v. We can thus let word denote the word (w, o, r, d) as the concatenation of four elementary words which consist of single characters. We also define the *length* of a word which is its number of characters. The length is additive with concatenation (the length of a concatenated word is the sum of the lengths of concatenatees). A special word is the null word ε of length zero. We have the property that $u||\varepsilon = \varepsilon||u = u$ for any word u. Concatenation in the set of all words over the alphabet Σ is thus an associative law for which ε is a neutral element. It is also regular: $u||v = u||w$ or $v||u = w||u$ implies $v = w$ for any words u, v, w.

Alphabets of cardinality 1 are used in order to represent integers: if $\Sigma = \{1\}$, five is represented in *unary* by 11111. In many cases, we use the *binary* alphabet $\Sigma = \{0, 1\}$.

We can manipulate languages by using *regular operations*:

1. concatenation: AB is the language of all words made from the concatenation of a word from the language A and a word from the language B[1];
2. power: A^i is recursively defined as $A^{i-1}A$ with $A^0 = \{\varepsilon\}$;
3. union: $A \cup B$ is simply the union of A and B[2];
4. closure: A^* is the union of all A^i for $i \geq 0$.

We notice that languages over the alphabet Σ are subsets of Σ^*: Σ^* is the set of all words over the alphabet Σ. A *regular language* is a language obtained with the above operations from elementary languages:

1. the empty language $\emptyset$,
2. the null language $\{\varepsilon\}$,
3. all single-character languages $\{a\}$ for $a \in \Sigma$.

For simplicity, we omit braces in operations on languages so that ε denotes $\{\varepsilon\}$, and a denotes $\{a\}$. For instance, the set of odd unary numbers is a regular language over the unary alphabet since it is $1(11)^*$.

8.1.2   *Finite Automata*

A *finite automaton* consists of

1. a finite set Q of *states*,
2. a particular state $q_0 \in Q$ called the *initial state*,
3. a particular subset $F \subseteq Q$ of *final states*,
4. a finite set Σ called the *input alphabet*,
5. a function δ from $Q \times \Sigma$ to Q called the *transition function*.

We recursively extend the δ function on $Q \times \Sigma^*$ by

$$\delta(q, \varepsilon) = q$$

and

$$\delta(q, u||a) = \delta(\delta(q, u), a).$$

If a word u is such that $\delta(q_0, u) \in F$, we say that u is *accepted* by the automaton. The set of all accepted words is the *language accepted by the automaton*.

---

[1] This operation is often called *multiplication*.
[2] This operation is often called *addition*.

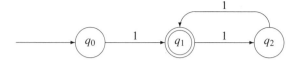

Figure 8.1. Finite automaton which recognizes odd unary numbers.

As an example, we define an automaton which accepts $1(11)^*$ with the unary alphabet $\Sigma = \{1\}$. We take $Q = \{q_0, q_1, q_2\}$ and $F = \{q_1\}$. We define δ by

$$\delta(q_0, 1) = q_1$$
$$\delta(q_1, 1) = q_2$$
$$\delta(q_2, 1) = q_1.$$

Obviously, we reach state q_1 after an odd number of 1 characters. This automaton is depicted in Fig. 8.1. Circles represent states. Double circles represent the terminal states. Transitions are represented by arrows. The arrow with no starting state shows the initial state.

These automata are called *deterministic*, but we also consider *nondeterministic* automata for which δ is simply a subset of $Q \times \Sigma \times Q$ (and not a function of $Q \times \Sigma$ to Q). A word $u = (a_1, \ldots, a_\ell)$ is accepted if there exists a sequence $((q_0, a_1, q_1), \ldots, (q_{\ell-1}, a_\ell, q_\ell))$ of ℓ consecutive transitions (q_{i-1}, a_i, q_i) starting from the initial state q_0, all along the characters a_i of u, and ending on a final state $q_\ell \in F$. As a matter of fact, languages accepted by nondeterministic automata can also be accepted by deterministic ones as the following theorem shows.

Theorem 8.1. *For any nondeterministic finite automaton $\mathcal{A}$, there exists a deterministic finite automaton $\mathcal{B}$ which accepts the very same language.*

Proof. Let $\mathcal{A} = (Q, q_0, F, \delta)$. We let Q' be the set of all subsets of Q and F' be the set of all subsets of Q which contain at least one element of F. We let $q'_0 = \{q_0\}$. We define the deterministic automaton $\mathcal{B} = (Q', q'_0, F', \delta')$ as follows. For any subset q' of Q and any character a, we let $\delta'(q', a)$ be the set of all states r in Q such that there exists at least one state $q \in q'$ such that $(q, a, r) \in \delta$. We now need to prove that $\mathcal{B}$ accepts the very same language as $\mathcal{A}$.

For this we prove by induction (on ℓ) that $\delta'(q'_0, a_1 || \cdots || a_\ell)$ is exactly the set of all states $q_\ell \in Q$ such that there exists a sequence $(q_0, a_1, q_1), \ldots, (q_{\ell-1}, a_\ell, q_\ell)$ of elements of δ: assuming this is true for $q' = \delta'(q'_0, a_1 \cdots a_{\ell-1})$, we know that $\delta'(q'_0, a_1 || \cdots || a_\ell)$ is equal to $\delta'(q', a_\ell)$, which is the set of all r such that there exists at least one $q \in q'$ such that $(q, a_\ell, r) \in \delta$. Therefore, this holds for $\delta'(q'_0, a_1 || \cdots || a_\ell)$ as well by definition of q' and $\delta'(q', a_\ell)$.   □

The following theorem characterizes the languages accepted by some automata.[3]

---

[3] The proof is available in Ref. [92, p. 33] or [19, p. 321].

Theorem 8.2 (Kleene 1956 [83]). *A language is regular if and only if it is the language accepted by a finite automaton.*

8.1.3 ⋆*Beyond Finite Automata Capabilities*

Finite automata do some computations in very simple ways. The output of the computation is the information whether the input word is accepted or not. Regular languages are thus a nice notion of simple computation. It is however not complete because many simple languages are not regular, thus not accepted by finite automata, as shown by the following result.

Theorem 8.3. *The set of all $0^i 1^i$ words for $i \geq 0$ is not a regular language.*

Proof. Let $\mathcal{A} = (Q, q_0, F, \delta)$ be a finite automaton which accepts this language, and let us look for a contradiction. For any i, we let q_i be $\delta(q_0, 0^i)$. Obviously, $\delta(q_i, 1^i)$ is a final state. But since $0^i 1^j$ is not accepted for $i \neq j$, all q_i must be pairwise different. Hence we have an infinite sequence of states $q_0, q_1, \ldots$, which is not possible for finite automata. $\qquad\square$

Finite automata could have been thought of as a good model for computation since all computers are indeed finite automata. What the above result shows is that $0^i 1^i$ cannot be recognized when i is very long, especially when it is much longer than what the computer can store. Therefore this notion does not scale. Furthermore, the finite automaton model does not capture the intuitive notion of complexity since the transition function can be very expensive to implement. This is why we need another model.

8.1.4 ⋆*Turing Machines*

A Turing machine is a simple computer model which formalizes a strong notion of computability. It is defined by

1. a special *blank* character B,
2. an alphabet Σ which does not include B,
3. a finite automaton (Q, q_0, F, δ) on the alphabet $\Sigma \cup \{B\}$,
4. an extension of δ which outputs an element of $\Sigma \cup \{B\}$ and an element of {left, right} in addition to the new state.

A Turing machine has a *tape* which is an infinite sequence of *cells*. Each cell contains an element of $\Sigma \cup \{B\}$. The Turing machine also has a *tape head* which points on a given cell. Originally, the state of the machine is the initial state q_0, the tape head points on the leftmost cell, the leftmost cells are filled with characters of the input word, and all other cells are filled with blank characters. For every move of the machine,

1. the machine reads the pointed cell and applies δ on it,
2. change the state according to the output of δ,

3. print the output character of δ on the pointed cell,
4. move the tape head by one position according to the output of δ (if it points on the leftmost cell, it cannot move to the left).

We say that the Turing machine halts if it happens to enter into a final state. We can define the language accepted by a Turing machine as for finite automata: accepted words are inputs for which the Turing machine halts. Languages which are accepted by one Turing machine are called *recursively enumerable languages*. Note that for words that are not accepted, the Turing machine is not assumed to halt. We can only guarantee that for input words which are accepted, the machine will eventually halt.

As an example we show how to accept the set A of all $0^i 1^i$, which is not a regular language. We first describe how the Turing machine works at a high level. Here are the different states of the Turing machine.

q_0: if the pointed cell is blank, terminate (i.e. accept) if the pointed cell is 1, enter into an endless loop (i.e. reject) otherwise replace the pointed cell by a blank character, move right, and change the state to q_1
   (we have erased the first 0, looking for a 1)

q_1: repeatedly move right until the pointed cell is not 0 if the pointed cell is blank, enter into an endless loop (i.e. reject) otherwise move right and change the state to q_2
   (we have found the first 1, looking for the last one)

q_2: repeatedly move right until the pointed cell is not 1 if the pointed cell is 0, enter into an endless loop (i.e. reject) otherwise move left and change the state to q_3
   (we have gone beyond the last 1, we move back)

q_3: replace the pointed 1 by a blank, move left, and change the state to q_4
   (we have erased the last 1, we move back)

q_4: repeatedly move left until the pointed cell is blank
   (we are moving toward the first nonblank character) move right and change the state to q_0

It is then easy to define the Turing machine. We have $Q = \{q_0, q_1, q_2, q_3, q_4, q_F, q_L\}$ and $F = \{q_F\}$, where q_L is a special state which enters into an endless loop. We have to define $\delta(q, a)$ for each $q \in Q$ and each $a \in \{0, 1, B\}$. This consists of a triplet in $Q \times \{0, 1, B\} \times \{left, right\}$. Here is how δ is defined. (Places with the $-$ character are not used, so we do not define them.)

q	$\delta(q, B)$			$\delta(q, 0)$			$\delta(q, 1)$		
q_0	q_F	$-$	$-$	q_1	B	right	q_L	$-$	$-$
q_1	q_L	$-$	$-$	q_1	0	right	q_2	1	right
q_2	q_3	B	left	q_L	$-$	$-$	q_2	1	right
q_3	$-$	$-$	$-$	$-$	$-$	$-$	q_4	B	left
q_4	q_0	B	right	q_4	0	left	q_4	1	left
q_F	q_F	$-$	$-$	q_F	$-$	$-$	q_F	$-$	$-$
q_L	q_L	$-$	$-$	q_L	$-$	$-$	q_L	$-$	$-$

Although real computers have a finite memory and not an infinite tape, Turing machines are better models than finite automata since the microprocessor is very close to a finite automaton and the memory is virtually infinite from the microprocessor point of view! However, the access model of the memory is not so relevant since we do not need to scan all the memory in order to reach the end.

8.2 ⋆Ability Frontiers

8.2.1 ⋆Standard Computational Models

The Church hypothesis consists of considering that all computable languages over Σ are precisely those that are accepted by some Turing machine. We can even show that adding extra characters in the alphabet does not extend the computational power of Turing machines. We can thus consider that all computable languages over Σ are those that are accepted by some Turing machine with the same alphabet. Languages over a larger alphabet can always be encoded with this alphabet.

When the underlying finite automaton is not deterministic, we obtain a *nondeterministic Turing machine*. We say that a language L is accepted by a nondeterministic Turing machine M if for any word x, we have $x \in L$ if and only if there exists a running of M on x which eventually halts. As we transformed nondeterministic finite automata into deterministic ones, we can represent nondeterministic Turing machines as deterministic Turing machines with two tapes: one regular tape and one read-only tape on which we only move to the right. We use this tape as an additional input which is used in order to decide what is the next state. In simpler words it is interesting to consider a nondeterministic algorithm on input x as a deterministic algorithm on inputs x and r. The input r is sometimes called a *witness* for x being in L. Hence we say that L is accepted by a nondeterministic Turing machine M if for any word x, we have $x \in L$ if and only if there exists a witness r such that $M(x, r)$ eventually halts.

One special case of nondeterministic Turing machines is *probabilistic Turing machines*. Here we consider that the new state of the Turing machine is decided at random, and we consider the probability that the Turing machine halts. Equivalently, we consider r as being a random input, following a given distribution.

Obviously, nondeterministic Turing machines do not extend the notion of computability. Indeed, we can simulate acceptance by a nondeterministic Turing machine by doing an exhaustive search on the random input r with a deterministic Turing machine. The crucial difference, as will be noticed later, is about the complexity.

8.2.2 ⋆Beyond Computability

It is fairly easy to show the limits of computability by proving that there exist languages which are not computable. This can be made by a standard set theory argument.

Since Turing machines over an alphabet Σ are totally defined by a finite set of states and a function δ over finite sets, we define an encoding technique in order to represent pairs (M, x) of Turing machines M and input word x as words over the alphabet $\{0, 1\}$. Let $\langle M, x \rangle$ denote the encoding of (M, x). Let us now consider the language L which consists of all words representing a pair $\langle M, x \rangle$ for which M accepts the word x. We call L the *universal language*. We can easily see that L is computable: we can build a Turing machine A such that for any Turing machine M, M accepts x if and only if A accepts $\langle M, x \rangle$.

Since the set of words is enumerable, the set of all Turing machines is enumerable. Thus, the set of all computable languages is enumerable. But, the set of all languages is not enumerable, which can be proven by a standard *diagonal argument*: let $(w_1, w_2, \ldots)$ be an infinite sequence which contains all words, and let $(M_1, M_2, \ldots)$ be an infinite sequence which contains all Turing machines. Putting these two sequences together makes arbitrary pairs $\langle M_i, w_i \rangle$ of Turing machines and words. Now let L_d be the set of all w_i for which $\langle M_i, w_i \rangle \notin L$. If L_d were a computable language, it would have been accepted by some Turing machine. Let M_j be this machine, and let us consider the corresponding word w_j. By definition of L_d, w_j is in L_d if and only if $\langle M_j, w_j \rangle \notin L$, namely if, and only if M_j does not accept w_j. But since the acceptance language of M_j is L_d, M_j accepts w_j if and only if $w_j \in L_d$, namely if and only if M_j does not accept w_j! This leads us to a contradiction. Hence, no Turing machine can accept L_d.

8.2.3 *Decisional Problems and Decidability*

Limits of computability are even more puzzling when we realize that deciding whether a word is accepted or not cannot be algorithmically decided.

More precisely, we have seen that the above universal language L is computable. Let $\bar{L}$ denote the set of all $\langle M, x \rangle$ pairs for which M does not accept x. We notice that if $\bar{L}$ is computable, there exists a Turing machine M' which can tell us when x is not accepted by M. By using the notations of Section 8.2.2, we can build a new Turing machine which accepts L_d as follows.

1. Enumerate all $\langle M_i, w_i \rangle$ pairs until w_i is the input x
2. Simulate M' on $\langle M_i, x \rangle$

This Turing machine accepts the language L_d (from Section 8.2.2). This contradicts the fact that L_d is not computable. Therefore, $\bar{L}$ is not computable.

This means that the acceptance problem is essentially asymmetric: we have seen that we can make a universal Turing machine which can tell when x is accepted by M, but we cannot make a Turing machine which tells when x is not accepted by M. Telling whether or not a word is accepted is called a *decisional problem*. We have seen that deciding whether a given M accepts a given x is *undecidable*. In particular, it cannot decide whether or not M eventually halts on x. This problem is called the *halting problem*.

8.3 ⋆Complexity Reduction

The most important idea of complexity theory for cryptography is the notion of *problem reduction* with *oracles*. The question of problem reduction aims at proving that a problem A is at most as hard as a problem B by showing that an "efficient" algorithm can solve B when using an imaginary machine (an "oracle") which can solve A. For this we must properly define the notion of efficiency and oracle.[4]

8.3.1 ⋆Asymptotic Time Complexity

Whenever a decision problem is decidable, we can still wonder about the cost of the decision (or how efficiently we can solve it). A decision problem is defined by a language L. An *instance* of the problem is a word x. The problem is to decide whether $x \in L$ or not.

For a Turing machine M which accepts L, and for a word x in L, we consider the number $T_{M,x}$ of steps of M with input x before halting. For all integers n we consider the maximum $T(n)$ of $T_{M,x}$ over all words $x \in L$ with length at most n. We say that M has a *time complexity* of T.

We are usually interested in *asymptotic* complexities, which means about the order of magnitude of the growth of $T(n)$ when n grows. For this we must introduce some standard notations. Given two functions $f(x)$ and $g(x)$ defined over a set of values x which is not upper bounded (i.e. in which x can grow up to infinity), we let

- $f(x) = \mathcal{O}(g(x))$ if there exist two constants $c > 0$ and x_0 such that for any $x \geq x_0$, we have $|f(x)| \leq c|g(x)|$
- $f(x) = \Omega(g(x))$ if there exist two constants $c > 0$ and x_0 such that for any $x \geq x_0$, we have $|f(x)| \geq c|g(x)|$, i.e. if $g(x) = \mathcal{O}(f(x))$
- $f(x) = \Theta(g(x))$ if we have both $f(x) = \mathcal{O}(g(x))$ and $f(x) = \Omega(g(x))$, i.e. if there exist three constants $c_1 > 0$, $c_2 > 0$, and x_0 such that for any $x \geq x_0$, we have $c_1|g(x)| \leq |f(x)| \leq c_2|g(x)|$
- $f(x) = o(g(x))$ if for any $\varepsilon > 0$ there exists a constant x_0 such that for any $x \geq x_0$, we have $|f(x)| \leq \varepsilon|g(x)|$.

We say that M is *linear* if $T(n) = \mathcal{O}(n)$. Similarly, we say that M is *quadratic* (resp. *cubic*) if $T(n) = \mathcal{O}(n^2)$ (resp. $T(n) = \mathcal{O}(n^3)$). We say that M is *polynomial* if there exists an integer d such that $T(n) = \mathcal{O}(n^d)$.

Making a difference between a language which can be accepted in linear time or in quadratic time is somehow arbitrary because it depends on the intrinsic power of the Turing machine: we could have defined another computational model with—say—Turing machines with two tapes instead of one. As we already said, our Turing machine model wastes time in order to move the head from both ends of the tape.

---

[4] For further reading about this section we recommend Ref. [20].

However, by having instant access to the memory, we "only" gain a factor limited to the size of the used memory, which is limited to the size of the input and the size of the intermediate results, which is itself less than the time complexity. This would have defined the same notion of computable languages, but one language which is quadratically computable with a single tape could have become linearly computable with the other. Therefore we only try to distinguish languages which can be accepted within a complexity which grows "smoothly" from others, with a notion of smooth growth which is robust with our notion of Turing machine. As Section 8.3.2 shows, "smooth" means "polynomial" here.

8.3.2 ⋆Complexity Classes P, NP, co-NP

Polynomial growth is quite robust. Actually, if we can make a polynomial-time algorithm (in an intuitive sense) which computes the language, then it can also be implemented on a Turing machine in polynomial time. Therefore the simple Turing machine model is enough in order to distinguish polynomial time algorithms from others. We say that a problem defined by L is *polynomial* if there exists a polynomial Turing machine which accepts L. We let P denote the set of all polynomial languages.

Interestingly, once we know an upper bound on the complexity of a Turing machine, we can transform it into a Turing machine which always halts within this complexity on an acceptance or rejection state. Hence, decision problems become symmetric in deterministic time.

As already seen, nondeterministic Turing machines define the same notion of computability. However, the notion of polynomial languages is very different. We let NP denote the set of all languages which are accepted by a nondeterministic Turing machine in polynomial time. Saying that a language L is accepted by a nondeterministic Turing machine M in polynomial time means that

1. for any word x, we have $x \in L$ if and only if there exists a running of M on x which halts
2. there exists an integer d such that for any word $x \in L$ of length n there exists a running of M on x which halts within a time at most n^d

Obviously, the class P is included in the NP class since deterministic Turing machines are special nondeterministic Turing machines. The question whether P is equal to NP or not is still open. It is considered as one of the most fundamental problems in theoretical computer science.

It should be emphasized that decision problems are no longer known to be symmetric. (Of course, if P = NP, it is symmetric.) We let co-NP denote the set of all languages L such that the complement of L is in NP. The decision problem is obviously symmetric in NP ∩ co-NP: for any language L in this class, there exists a nondeterministic Turing machine M which eventually halts within a polynomial time either on an acceptance or on a rejection or on a failure state such that

1. there exists an integer d such that for any word x of length n and any running of M on x, the machine halts within a time of at most n^d
2. for any word x, the set of all possible final states when running M on x includes either the acceptance or the rejection state, but not both
3. for any word x, we have $x \in L$ if and only if there exists a running of M on x which halts on an acceptance state

The question of whether co-NP is equal to NP or not, i.e. whether the decision problem is symmetric in NP, is still open. It is also considered as one of the most important problems in theoretical computer sciences.

8.3.3 ⋆*Intractability*

We recall that our goal is to formalize what a hard problem is in order to make security rely on a hard problem. In complexity theory, this is the notion of *intractability*. Although this is a quite intuitive notion, it should be emphasized that negative notions, e.g. inability to solve a problem, is hard to define. We rather use reference problems which are believed to be hard and we reduce one problem to the other.

Let Σ be an alphabet and let L_1 and L_2 be two languages over Σ. We say that accepting L_1 reduces (in a Karp sense[5]) in polynomial time to accepting L_2 if there exists a function f over Σ^* which is algorithmically computable in polynomial time and such that for any word x we have $x \in L_1$ if and only if $f(x) \in L_2$. Two languages are *polynomially equivalent* if they reduce to each other.

The case of the NP class is quite interesting. We say that a language L is *NP-hard* if any $L_0 \in$ NP reduces to L in polynomial time. We further say that L is *NP-complete* if $L \in$ NP. Actually, NP-complete languages are such that any language in NP reduces to them. Therefore they have the greatest complexity in NP.

As an example we mention the language SAT of all satisfiable Boolean formulas. Informally, a Boolean formula is defined as a tree in which every inner node is labeled by a Boolean gate AND, OR, or NOT (the latter gate being on nodes with degree one only) and every leaf is labeled by a variable v_i. The formula is satisfiable if there exists an assignment of all variables to `true` or `false` such that the root node is evaluated to `true`. We assume that we have defined an efficient encoding rule over an alphabet in order to represent a Boolean formula. As an example, we can use the prefix encoding

---

[5] From the name of Richard Karp who was, e.g. with Stephen Cook, one of the pioneers in complexity theory in the early seventies.

rule over $\Sigma = \{\cup, \cap, \neg, \text{v}, 0, 1\}$. For instance, $x = \cup \cap \neg\text{v}0 \cup \text{v}1\text{v}10 \cup \neg\text{v}10\text{v}1$ represents

$$((\text{NOT } v_0) \text{ AND } (v_1 \text{ OR } v_{10})) \text{ OR } ((\text{NOT } v_{10}) \text{ OR } v_1).$$

This can be satisfied by the assignment $v_0 = v_1 = v_{10} = \texttt{true}$. Therefore the word x is in SAT.

Obviously, SAT is in NP since we can easily make a polynomial time Turing machine which, for every input x and a witness r which encodes an assignment of variable, checks that x and r are syntactically correct and that the assignment r satisfies x. The following result tells us how acceptance of SAT is hard.

Theorem 8.4 (Cook 1971 [47]). *SAT is NP-complete.*

The idea of the proof consists of taking any language in NP and the corresponding nondeterministic Turing machine. We consider the possible running step histories of the Turing machine as variables, and we define a Boolean formula which checks that the running steps are feasible with the Turing machine. This way we transform any word x into a Boolean formula $f(x)$ in polynomial time, and x is in the language if and only if $f(x) \in$ SAT.

8.3.4 ⋆Oracles and Turing Reduction

Let us define *oracle Turing machines*. An oracle is a Boolean function defined by a language L which corresponds to the decision membership problem. An oracle is "connected" to an input tape which contains a finite set of nonblank words. The input tape contains a query and the oracle answers whether the *query* is in the language or not. An oracle Turing machine is a Turing machine with an additional tape which is the input of an oracle, and special states query, yes, and no. Each time the Turing machine enters into the query state, it instantly moves to a yes or no state depending on the answer of the oracle. (Thus the transition function of the finite automaton does not need to be defined on the query state.) In other words, we use the oracle as a subroutine which answers whether or not the query x_i is in the language L.

Usually, we write L as a superscript. For instance, we can consider the class P^L of languages accepted by an oracle Turing machine, where the latter works in polynomial time and has access to an oracle for the decision problem of membership in L.

We say that accepting a language L_1 reduces (in a Turing sense) in polynomial time to accepting a language L_2 if $L_1 \in P^{L_2}$, i.e. if there exists an oracle Turing machine with an oracle for membership in L_2 which accepts L_1 in polynomial time (see Fig. 2). As an example, we have seen in Section 7.3.2 some Turing reductions related to the problem of computing orders of elements in a group. For example, we have seen that we

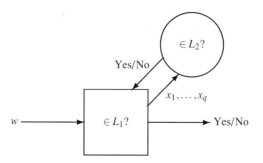

Figure 8.2. Oracle turing machine.

can compute the factorization of n by using an oracle that implements the Carmichael function $\lambda(n)$.

Two languages are *Turing-equivalent* if they reduce to each other in polynomial time.

We have to make two important remarks. First of all, the decision problems are symmetric: if L_1 reduces to L_2, then the complement of L_1 also reduces to L_2 (since the oracle Turing machine is deterministic and the running time is bounded, we just need to wait until the time bound in order to decide whether or not a given word is in L_1). Second, the oracle solves the decision problem of membership in L_2 which is believed to be harder than accepting L_2 in asymmetric cases such as NP-complete problems. For instance, the SAT decision problem is at least as hard as accepting co-SAT. Therefore we can solve both NP (due to the Karp reduction) and co-NP with P^{SAT}. For this reason people believe that NP is not closed under the Turing reduction. Hence we should limit ourselves to NP $\cap$ co-NP as a reference class for intractable problems, which is the case of cryptography.

8.4 Exercises

Exercise 8.1. *Let L be the subset of $\{0, 1\}^*$ of all bitstrings with an even number of bits equal to 1. Prove that it is a regular language by producing a finite automaton which recognizes L.*

Do the same with L equal to the set of all numbers which are congruent to 1 modulo 3 represented in binary notations, i.e. *L is the set of all bitstrings $(a_0, a_1, \ldots, a_n)$ such that*

$$\sum_{i=0}^{n} a_i 2^i \equiv 1 \pmod{3}$$

Let x and y be two integers. Inspiring yourself from the square-and-multiply algorithm from right to left, do the same with L equal to the set of all bitstrings which represent a number which is congruent to x modulo y.

Exercise 8.2. *We represent triplets of integers* (a, b, c) *by bitstrings* $(a_0, b_0, c_0, a_1,$ $b_1, c_1, \ldots, a_n, b_n, c_n)$ *such that*

$$a = \sum_{i=0}^{n} a_i 2^i$$

$$b = \sum_{i=0}^{n} b_i 2^i$$

$$c = \sum_{i=0}^{n} c_i 2^i$$

Prove that the language of all (a, b, c) *triplets such that* $c = a + b$ *is regular.*

Exercise 8.3. *We represent pairs of integers* (a, b) *by bitstrings* $(a_0, b_0, a_1, b_1, \ldots, a_n,$ $b_n)$ *such that*

$$a = \sum_{i=0}^{n} a_i 2^i$$

$$b = \sum_{i=0}^{n} b_i 2^i$$

Derive a Turing machine which takes a pair of integers (a, b) *as an input and outputs a bitstring which represents* $a + b$.

Do the same with the multiplication $a \times b$.

Exercise 8.4. *We represent a graph* G *whose vertices set is* $\{1, 2, \ldots, n\}$ *by its adjacency matrix* M. *Here* M *is of size* $n \times n$ *where* $M_{i,j}$ *is a bit set to one if and only if the* i-*th vertex and the* j-*th vertex are connected by an edge in* G. *The matrix* M *is itself represented by a bitstring of length* n^2 *which is obtained by reading the matrix row by row, column by column. We say that a graph* G *is c-colorable if there exists a mapping* C *from* $\{1, 2, \ldots, n\}$ *to* $\{1, 2, \ldots, c\}$ *such that there exists no edge* (i, j) *such that* $C(i) = C(j)$: *two connected vertices always have different colors.*

We let L *be the language of all 2-colorable graphs. Prove that* L *is in P by deriving an algorithm which yields whether a given graph is 2-colorable or not.*

We let L *be the language of all 3-colorable graphs. Prove that* L *is NP-complete.*

9

Public-Key Cryptography

Content

Diffie–Hellman: asymmetric cryptography, the DH key agreement protocol
★Knapsack problems: NP-completeness, the Merkle–Hellman cryptosystem
RSA: the cryptosystem, attacks against particular implementations
ElGamal Encryption

Interestingly, cryptography was the first application of computer science: after *Alan Turing* created the notion of Turing machine, the very first computer was built in order to break real-life cryptosystems for military purposes. Similarly, the invention of complexity theory—in particular the notion of intractability through NP-completeness—has been directly applied to cryptography in order to invent *asymmetric cryptography*, also called *public-key cryptography*.

This chapter relates to the early foundations of asymmetric cryptography, and modern applications (and attacks).

9.1 Diffie–Hellman

Invention of public-key cryptography is often attributed to Whitfield Diffie and Martin Hellman: in a famous paper (Ref. [59]) which was published in the *IEEE Transactions on Information Theory* journal in 1976, they gave "new directions in cryptography," describing how we can use *one-way functions*, and notions of *trapdoor permutations* in cryptography. A public-key cryptosystem is nothing but a kind of one-way permutation (anybody can encrypt, but cannot decrypt) with a hidden trapdoor which enables the decryption to the legitimate party.

Although this seminal paper played an outstanding role in the area of cryptography, the role of *Ralph Merkle* in the foundations should not be neglected. Merkle submitted his scheme in 1975[1] (discussed in p. 115) which enables the secure communication over an insecure channel. The Merkle Signature Scheme based on hash trees was also made in the late seventies[2]. The Lamport scheme which is given on p. 111 (published in 1979; see Ref. [113]) also illustrates how to make an asymmetric access control protocol from a one-way function.

---

[1] But it was published in 1978 only! See Ref. [129].
[2] But it was rejected for publication, and then published 10 years later. See Ref. [131].

9.1.1 Public-Key Cryptosystems

Formally, a public-key cryptosystem is defined by

- a pseudorandom key generator Gen: this is a probabilistic algorithm which outputs a key pair (K_p, K_s) where K_p is a *public key* and K_s is a *secret key*;
- an encryption algorithm Enc: this is an algorithm (which can be probabilistic) which outputs a ciphertext Y from an input plaintext X and a public key K_p;
- a decryption algorithm Dec: this is an algorithm (which necessarily implements a deterministic function) which outputs the plaintext X from a ciphertext Y and a secret key K_s.

As it will be seen later, the encryption is not necessarily deterministic: we can have several ciphertexts which correspond to the same plaintext. Of course, the cryptosystem should complete the following requirements:

- For any generated key pair (K_p, K_s), any plaintext x, and any possible output y of $\mathrm{Enc}_{K_p}(x)$, we have $\mathrm{Dec}_{K_s}(y) = x$.
- Given the access to specifications, K_p, and a Dec_{K_s} oracle, it is intractable to decrypt a generated ciphertext y without sending the query y to the decryption oracle.

Note that the latter requirement is stated in a very informal way. Indeed, it is very hard to agree on a precise definition of security for public-key cryptosystems. Therefore we first commit on an intuitive notion of security. As we will see several examples of attacks, definitions will become more and more precise (and counterintuitive).

Fig. 9.1 is the Shannon model of encryption revisited for public-key cryptosystems. We can transform an insecure channel into a confidential one with the help of public-key cryptography and an extra channel in order to transmit the public key (usually, the key generator is run by the receiver). It is important to notice that the property required

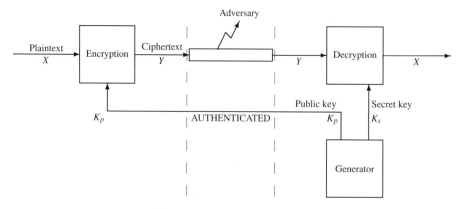

Figure 9.1. Asymmetric Encryption.

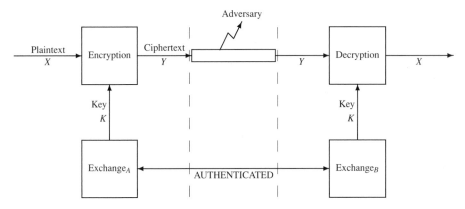

Figure 9.2. Secure Channel Setup by a Key Exchange Protocol.

for this extra channel is not confidentiality, it is indeed authentication; the sender of the encrypted message must be ensured that the public key he uses is the appropriate one.

We clearly see here that encryption and decryption are essentially *asymmetric*: only the recipient of the ciphertext needs to have access to the secret key in order to decrypt. In conventional cryptography, the secret key had to be used for both encryption and decryption, and decryption was essentially the same operation as encryption in an opposite order. Asymmetry is better (here) since we should not have access to a secret in order to be able to encrypt. In addition, the secret key is the secret of a person instead of being the secret of a pair of users.

Of course, this benefit has a cost: public-key cryptosystems are much more involved (both in terms of human being understanding and in terms of computer operations); they are quite rare (Diffie and Hellman did not provide any example of such a cryptosystem: they gave the notion of such a thing without proving it actually existed); as conventional cryptosystems, their security is not guaranteed, and is often more risky to claim.

9.1.2   The Diffie–Hellman Key Agreement Protocol

Although Diffie and Hellman did not provide any example of a public-key cryptosystem, they proposed a concrete *key agreement protocol*. The aim of this protocol is to generate a common secret key between two parties over an insecure (but authenticated) channel which can later be used with conventional cryptography (see Fig. 9.2). This kind of protocol is also often called *key exchange protocol*, but there is no real exchange here since the key is randomly generated.[3]

---

[3] For this some authors distinguish "key exchange," "key transfer," and "key agreement."

A   B

pick x at random, $X \leftarrow g^x$ $\xrightarrow{\hspace{2cm} X \hspace{2cm}}$

$\xleftarrow{\hspace{2cm} Y \hspace{2cm}}$ pick y at random, $Y \leftarrow g^y$

$K \leftarrow Y^x$ $(K = g^{xy})$ $K \leftarrow X^y$

Figure 9.3. The Diffie–Hellman Key Agreement Protocol.

We assume that we have a communication channel between A and B which provides authentication and integrity protection. If A and B want to communicate confidentially over an insecure channel, they must agree on a secret key K in order to use conventional cryptography. For this, we assume that we are given a (multiplicatively denoted) group G equipped with an efficiently computable group law, but some particular other problem which will be defined later is hard. In particular, computing discrete logarithms must be hard. We also assume that we are given an element $g \in G$. Let ℓ be an approximation of $\log_2 \#G$ (for instance, the integer part). Although $\#G$ (or more precisely the order of the cyclic subgroup of G spanned by g) is not necessarily known, ℓ should be public. The protocol works as follows (see Fig. 9.3).

1. A picks a random integer x of ℓ bits, computes $X = g^x$ in G (by using the square-and-multiply algorithm), and sends X to B.
2. B picks a random integer y of ℓ bits, computes $Y = g^y$ in G (by using the square-and-multiply algorithm), and sends Y to A.
3. A computes $K = Y^x$, while B computes $K = X^y$ in G.

Note that when a multiple q of the order of g in G is provided, then we can pick x and y in $\{0, \ldots, q-1\}$. Obviously, if A and B follow the protocol correctly, they end up with the same key K which is $K = g^{xy}$. This protocol must also protect the confidentiality of K, and so it should be hard, given X and Y, to compute $K = X^{\log_g Y}$. This notably implies that computing the discrete logarithm must be hard.

As an example, we can take prime $p = 21489151$ (although p is not large enough to make the computation of the discrete logarithm hard in $\mathbf{Z}_p^*$). We can pick an arbitrary g like $g = 1609879$. Then A picks $x = 3916708$ at random and computes $X = g^x$ mod $p = 13164781$ and sends it to A. Then B picks $y = 16766518$ at random and computes $Y = g^y$ mod $p = 4109137$ and sends it to B. In parallel, B computes $K = X^y$ mod $p = 13275737$. A can also compute $K = Y^x$ mod $p = 13275737$.

We notice that it is important to generate a g with a large order. It is quite hard, in general, to compute the order of an element. (In our example, we can see that $p - 1 = 2 \cdot 3 \cdot 5^2 \cdot 143261$ and that g has the order $3 \cdot 143261$ "only".) We can however generate an appropriate (g, q, p) triplet with a large prime q such that g has an order of q in $\mathbf{Z}_p^*$ by

1. generating a prime q,
2. picking k at random and $p = 1 + kq$ until it is prime,
3. picking g_0 at random and $g = g_0^{\frac{p-1}{q}}$ mod p until it is not 1.

A E B

pick $x, X \leftarrow g^x$ $\xrightarrow{\quad X \quad}$

pick $x', X' \leftarrow g^{x'}$ $\xrightarrow{\quad X' \quad}$

$\xleftarrow{\quad Y \quad}$ pick $y, Y \leftarrow g^y$

$\xleftarrow{\quad Y' \quad}$ pick $y', Y' \leftarrow g^{y'}$

$K_1 \leftarrow (Y')^x$ $(K_1 = g^{xy'})$ $K_1 \leftarrow X^{y'}, K_2 \leftarrow Y^{x'}$ $(K_2 = g^{x'y})$ $K_2 \leftarrow (X')^y$

Figure 9.4. First Man-in-the-Middle Attack in the Diffie–Hellman Key Agreement Protocol.

This ensures that g has an order of q (its order must be a factor of q which is not 1) without having to completely factorize $p - 1$. Note that once we are ensured that g spans a group of prime order q, then we can pick x and y in $\{0, \ldots, q - 1\}$ in the Diffie–Hellman protocol.

We also notice that A and B must communicate over a channel which really provides authentication. Otherwise the Diffie–Hellman protocol is vulnerable to the *man-in-the-middle attack*. Assuming that messages are not authenticated, an adversary E can sit in the middle and run concurrent protocols with A and B as depicted in Fig. 9.4. Then E will share a key with A and B separately although A and B think that they share a key with each other. Here A and B obtain different keys and E continues with an active attack: she decrypts messages coming from one participant, re-encrypts them, and sends them to the other participant. She can also make a more subtle attack in which she no longer has to be active after the key agreement, and A and B obtain the same key. For this we assume that the order of the group G can be written bw with b-smooth (e.g. $b = 1$). In this attack E simply raises X and Y to the power w and get X' and Y' so that A and B obtain the same key K which is a w-th power, i.e. in a subgroup of smooth order. (In the case where $b = 1$, we obtain $X' = Y' = 1$.) E can thus compute K by using the Pohlig-Hellman algorithm. This attack is depicted in Fig. 9.5.

Another important property is the notion of *forward secrecy*. This property means that if any long-term secret key is compromised, then the secrecy of the Diffie–Hellman key will be preserved. Indeed, this key is meant to be used during a session and to be discarded afterward. In the case which is described above, both x and y are *ephemeral* keys which are discarded after the protocol. This means that they cannot be compromised. We can also use a *static* version of the Diffie–Hellman protocol in which x and y are long-term secret keys. This version does not provide forward secrecy since disclosure of x or y eventually compromises K.

A E B

pick $x, X \leftarrow g^x$ $\xrightarrow{\quad X \quad}$

$X' \leftarrow X^w$ $\xrightarrow{\quad X' \quad}$

$\xleftarrow{\quad Y \quad}$ pick $y, Y \leftarrow g^y$

$\xleftarrow{\quad Y' \quad}$ $Y' \leftarrow Y^w$

$K \leftarrow (Y')^x$ solve $X' = g^{x'w}, K \leftarrow y^{x'w}$ $K \leftarrow (X')^y$

$(K = g^{xyw})$

Figure 9.5. Second Man-in-the-Middle Attack in the Diffie–Hellman Key Agreement Protocol.

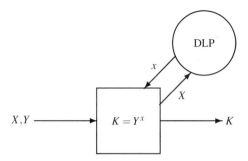

Figure 9.6. Reduction of DHP to DLP.

The Diffie–Hellman problem is stated as follows:

DHP (Diffie–Hellman Problem)
  Parameters: a group G, an element $g \in G$.
  Input: two random elements X and Y in the subgroup of G spanned by g.
  Problem: compute $K = g^{xy}$ where $x = \log_g X$ and $y = \log_g Y$.

(We assume that generating an ℓ-bit integer x and computing $X = g^x$ correctly generates X, and the same for Y.) If this problem is hard, K is confidential.

We would like to compare this problem with other ones. We first focus on the discrete logarithm problem (DLP) that is defined on p. 160. Obviously, if we know how to solve DLP, then we can solve DHP by computing x as the DLP of X and then computing $K = Y^x$. Thus DHP reduces to DLP (see Fig. 9.6). So, if the Diffie–Hellman problem is hard, then the discrete logarithm problem in the subgroup spanned by g is hard as well. DHP is believed to be hard for $G = \mathbf{Z}_p^*$ with a large prime p.

For completeness we also mention the *Decisional Diffie–Hellman problem*, which can be formulated as follows.

DDHP (Decisional Diffie–Hellman Problem)
  Parameters: a group G, an element $g \in G$.
  Input: a triplet (X, Y, K) of elements in the subgroup spanned by g.
  Problem: decide whether $K = X^{\log_g Y}$ or not.

Obviously DDHP reduces to DHP. This problem is also believed to be hard when the subgroup of $G = \mathbf{Z}_p^*$ (for a large prime p) which is spanned by g is large.

9.2 ⋆Experiment with NP-Completeness

Although Diffie and Hellman clearly defined the notion of public-key cryptosystem (by the notion of trapdoor permutation), they did not suggest any example. They did not even prove that such a primitive existed.

In the quest for trapdoor permutations, it is tempting to try to rely on some well-known hard problems. Intuitively, the notion of trapdoor which makes computation easy suggests that the decryption problem must be in the NP class. The hardest problems in the NP class are NP-complete problems. One famous NP-complete problem is the knapsack problem. So it is tempting to try to build a cryptosystem based on a knapsack problem.

9.2.1 ⋆Knapsack Problem

Here is the description of the *subset sum decision problem*.[4]

> DSSP (Decisional Subset-Sum Problem)
> *Input*: a set of integers $\{a_1, \ldots, a_n, s\}$ (represented in binary).
> *Problem*: does a subset of $\{a_1, \ldots, a_n\}$ whose sum is s exist?

Intuitively, the a_i represent the size of packets that we want to put in a knapsack of size s. The question is whether a subset of packets which exactly fits into the knapsack exists or not. This is why we often call this problem the *knapsack problem*.

Theorem 9.1 (Karp 1972). *The language of subset sum problems which are solvable is NP-complete.*

Since deciding whether or not a subset sum problem has a solution is hard, finding a solution to a solvable problem must be hard as well. Hence we can try to build a cryptosystem based on the hardness to find a solution. The problem consists of hiding a trapdoor for the legitimate decryptor.

9.2.2 ⋆The Merkle–Hellman Cryptosystem

The Merkle–Hellman cryptosystem is one of the first examples (or candidates) of a public-key cryptosystem. It was published in 1978 as Ref. [132]. The main idea consists in giving to the knapsack problem a particular form so that the problem becomes trivial, and in hiding this particular form with a secret transformation.

Here, the particular form is *super-increasing knapsacks*. We say that $(b_1, \ldots, b_n, b_{n+1})$ is super-increasing if we have $b_i > \sum_{j=1}^{i-1} b_j$ for $i = 1, \ldots, n + 1$. We notice that if $(b_1, \ldots, b_n, b_{n+1})$ is super-increasing, and if we let $M = b_{n+1}$, then any knapsack problem $(b_1, \ldots, b_n, s)$ modulo M is equivalent to the knapsack problem $(b_1, \ldots, b_n, s)$ over the integers, which is itself quite trivial: we notice that b_n is in the solution sum if and only if $b_n \leq s$, and we then reduce to a subproblem $(b_1, \ldots, b_{n-1}, s')$ with $s' = s$ or $s' = s - b_n$.

---

[4] For more information, see Ref. [72].

The secret transformation which is used in order to hide the super-increasing property is simply a multiplication by a secret key modulo M.

Here is the cryptosystem.

Public parameter: an integer n.
Key generation: choose a super-increasing sequence $(b_1, \ldots, b_n, b_{n+1} = M)$, an integer $W \in \mathbf{Z}_M^*$, and a permutation π of $\{1, \ldots, n\}$.
   Compute $a_i = W b_{\pi(i)} \bmod M$ for $i = 1, \ldots, n$.
Public key: $K_p = (a_1, \ldots, a_n)$.
Secret key: $K_s = (b_1, \ldots, b_n, M, W, \pi)$.
Message: a binary sequence $m = m_1 \cdots m_n$ of length n.
Encryption: $c = m_1 a_1 + \cdots + m_n a_n$.
Decryption: compute $cW^{-1} \bmod M$, solve the super-increasing knapsack problem $x_1 b_1 + \cdots + x_n b_n = cW^{-1} \bmod M$ and let $m_i = x_{\pi(i)}$.

Unfortunately, this cryptosystem was broken a few years later by Adi Shamir (see Ref. [164]). As it was explained later, the security of the Merkle–Hellman cryptosystem does not rely on the full genericity of the NP-complete problem, but on some particular instances which are not necessarily hard. Indeed, the problem can be solved if we can find a small vector in a related lattice.

Mathematically, a lattice is a discrete subgroup of $\mathbf{R}^n$. More intuitively, it is the set of all linear combinations of some given constant vectors, but with only integral coefficients. Finding a small vector (in the sense of Euclidean norm) in a lattice is known to be a hard problem, but which might be easy in many cases. Namely, the famous LLL algorithm can be used to reduce lattices and break cryptosystems like the Merkle–Hellman one.[5]

9.3   Rivest–Shamir–Adleman (RSA)

The first public-key cryptosystem which is still secure and used was invented by Ronald Rivest, Adi Shamir, and Leonard Adleman, the initials of whom led to the name of the cryptosystem: RSA. It was published in 1978 as Ref. [158] in the journal *Communications of the ACM*. Since then, this algorithm has been adapted, generalized, and transformed into several standards. Surprisingly, as it will be seen, although the plain RSA cryptosystem was not broken, many adaptations and standards based on RSA are weak. This raises all the ambiguity of public-key cryptosystems.

9.3.1   Plain RSA Cryptosystem

As depicted in Fig. 9.7, here is how the *plain RSA* algorithm works. (By plain RSA we mean a theoretical algorithm. As it will be seen, this algorithm is not directly usable

---

[5] A survey by Nguyen and Stern on lattices in cryptography is available as Ref. [139].

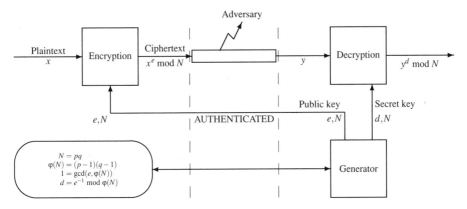

Figure 9.7. Plain RSA Cryptosystem.

since it is described in a mathematical format. We will see that there are many bad ways to use it in practice.)

> *Public parameter*: an even integer s.
> *Setup*: find two random different prime numbers p and q of size $\frac{s}{2}$ bits. Set $N = pq$. Pick a random e until $\gcd(e, (p-1)(q-1)) = 1$. (Sometimes we pick a special e like $e = 17$ or $e = 2^{16} + 1$ and we select p and q accordingly.) Set $d = e^{-1} \bmod ((p-1)(q-1))$.
> *Message*: an element $x \in \{1, \ldots, N-1\}$.
> *Public key*: $K_p = (e, N)$.
> *Secret key*: $K_s = (d, N)$.
> *Encryption*: $y = x^e \bmod N$.
> *Decryption*: $x = y^d \bmod N$.

We notice that the *modulus* N is of s bits. The security will highly depend on this s parameter. In particular, if factoring integers of this size is easy, then RSA is not secure because N is public and factoring N yields p and q, which are enough to enable decryption. Typically, we take $s = 1024$.

It is easy to check that the encryption is deterministic and that if we decrypt $y = x^e \bmod N$, we raise it to the power d modulo N and obtain $x^{ed} \bmod N$. Since $ed \equiv 1 \pmod{\varphi(N)}$, it can be written that $ed = 1 + k\varphi(N)$. We have

$$y^d \bmod N = x^{ed} \bmod N = x^{1+k\varphi\;(N)} \bmod N.$$

For $\gcd(x, N) = 1$, this is x. For $\gcd(x, N) = p$, we can check that it is congruent to x modulo p and modulo q separately, so it is x as well, due to the Chinese Remainder Theorem. For $\gcd(x, N) = q$, we similarly obtain x. Hence y decrypts well into x.

The complexity of the RSA algorithm is quite simple to analyze.

Setup. We have to generate two random primes of $\frac{s}{2}$ bits. We know that this works within a complexity of $\mathcal{O}(s^4)$ elementary operations by using the Miller-Rabin test over random integers. Then, multiplying p and q costs $\mathcal{O}(s^2)$, finding an invertible e costs one gcd computation, hence $\mathcal{O}(s^2)$, and computing d requires an extended Euclid algorithm, hence $\mathcal{O}(s^2)$ as well. In total the complexity is $\mathcal{O}(s^4)$.

Encryption. The encryption costs one full modular exponential, hence $\mathcal{O}(s^3)$. We however often choose e in order to decrease this complexity. For instance, with $e = 17$ or $e = 2^{16} + 1$, the complexity is $\mathcal{O}(s^2)$.

Decryption. The decryption costs one modular exponential, hence $\mathcal{O}(s^3)$.

The security analysis is more tricky. Obviously, the knowledge of p and q is enough to recover the secret key and thus to break the system: we just need to invert e modulo $(p - 1)(q - 1)$. Therefore the factorization of N enables breaking the system. This does not mean that RSA is as strong as factoring is hard, although it is believed to be so. Here are a few problems.

RSADP (RSA Decryption Problem)
  Input: an RSA public key (e, N), an encrypted message y.
  Problem: compute x such that $y = x^e \bmod N$.
RSAKRP (RSA Key Recovery Problem)
  Input: an RSA public key (e, N).
  Problem: compute d such that $x^{ed} \bmod N = x$ for any $x \in \mathbf{Z}_N^*$.
RSAEMP (RSA Exponent Multiple Problem)
  Input: an RSA modulus N.
  Problem: find an integer k such that $x^k \bmod N = 1$ for any $x \in \mathbf{Z}_N^*$ (i.e. $\lambda(N)$ divides k).
RSAOP (RSA Order Problem)
  Input: an RSA modulus N.
  Problem: compute the order of $\mathbf{Z}_N^*$ (i.e. $\varphi(N)$).
RSAFP (RSA Factorization Problem)
  Input: an RSA modulus N.
  Problem: compute the factorization of N.

Obviously, RSADP reduces to RSAKRP. Indeed, the secret key enables the decryption! Reducing the other way is still an open problem: we cannot prove at this time that the secret key is necessary in order to decrypt, nor that decrypting enables the computation of the secret key. What we can prove is that RSAKRP is equivalent to RSAFP (i.e., the knowledge of the secret key is equivalent to the ability to factorize N), which does not mean that decrypting is equivalent to factorizing. For this let us first do the following reductions.

- *RSAKRP reduces to RSAOP.* Clearly, if we can compute the order $\varphi(N)$ which is equal to $(p - 1)(q - 1)$, we can invert e modulo this order and get a d.
- *RSAOP is equivalent to RSAFP.* Clearly, if we can factorize N, we get p and q and we can compute $\varphi(N) = (p - 1)(q - 1)$. Conversely, if we have $\varphi(N)$, we

notice that $\varphi(N) = N - (p + q) + 1$ so p and q are the two roots of $X^2 - (N - \varphi(N) - 1)X + N = 0$. Solving this equation leads to the factorization of N.

- *RSAEMP reduces to RSAKRP.* If we can compute d, then we can get a multiple of $\lambda(N)$, namely $ed - 1$.

So it is sufficient to show that RSAFP reduces to RSAEMP in order to prove that RSAKRP, RSAEMP, RSAOP, and RSAFP are all equivalent. Let us assume that we know an integer k which is a multiple of $\lambda(N)$. The following algorithm factorizes N in a surprisingly similar way to the Miller-Rabin primality test.

1. Let us thus write $k = 2^t r$ with r odd. (We isolate the powers of two.)
2. We pick a random $x \in \mathbf{Z}_N^*$ and we compute $y = x^r \bmod N$. We iterate until $y \neq 1$. (Note that for at least three fourths of the x's which are not quadratic residues modulo p or q, the corresponding y cannot be equal to 1, so we usually do not have to iterate.)
3. If any of y, $y^2 \bmod N, \ldots, y^{2^{t-1}} \bmod N$ is equal to $N - 1$, go back to the previous step and try again. Otherwise, since $y^{2^t} \bmod N$ must be 1, we have found a nontrivial square root z of one.
4. Compute $\gcd(z + 1, N)$ which must be a nontrivial factor of N: either p or q.

(See Fig. 9.8.) Note that if we have, for instance, $\left(\frac{x}{p}\right) = 1$ and $\left(\frac{x}{q}\right) = -1$, then we have $x^{\frac{p-1}{2}} \bmod p = 1$ and $x^{\frac{q-1}{2}} \bmod q = q - 1$. Thus, if $2^i r = \mathrm{lcm}(p - 1, q - 1)$, then $x^{2^{i-1} r} \bmod N$ is equal to 1 modulo p and to $q - 1$ modulo q, hence it is a nontrivial square root of one and the previous algorithm yields p and q. The same holds for $\left(\frac{x}{p}\right) = -1$ and $\left(\frac{x}{q}\right) = 1$. Thus the previous algorithm works for at least half of the x's, and eventually halts with the factorization of N.

Here is the list of reductions that we have proven.

$$\mathrm{RSADP} \Leftarrow \mathrm{RSAKRP} \Leftarrow \mathrm{RSAOP}$$
$$\Downarrow \qquad\qquad \Updownarrow$$
$$\mathrm{RSAEMP} \Rightarrow \mathrm{RSAFP}$$

The problem of whether breaking RSA is equivalent to the factorization of N or not is a famous open problem. Paradoxically, it is a good thing to have no reduction, because one would have been able to use it as a chosen ciphertext attack: using the decryptor as an oracle in a chosen ciphertext attack would have led to the factorization of N, thus

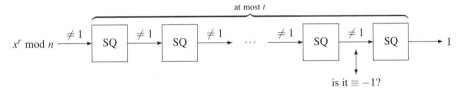

Figure 9.8. Reduction of RSAFP to RSAEMP.

to a secret key recovery. This means that the lack of equivalence between RSADP and RSAFP guarantees that we cannot extract a secret key from a sealed decryption device.

Obviously, breaking RSA means computing e-th roots. Even with $e = 3$, we do not know if computing a cubic root is equivalent to factorizing N in the RSA case, i.e. when $\gcd(e, (p-1)(q-1)) = 1$. We can prove equivalence in some other cases, i.e. when e is not invertible modulo $(p-1)(q-1)$. For $e = 2$, we can prove that computing square roots is equivalent to factorizing N: we just pick a random x, compute $y = x^2 \bmod N$, and compute one square root z of y. If $x \equiv \pm z \pmod{N}$, we just try again. Otherwise we use the Fermat method in order to factorize N. This eventually halts because the square root algorithm has no means to know which are the two square roots which are not interesting (namely x and $N - x$). For $e = 3$, we can similarly prove that computing cubic roots is equivalent to factorizing N when 3 divides $(p-1)(q-1)$.

9.3.2 RSA Standards

PKCS (Public-Key Cryptography Standards) is a set of algorithms published by the RSA Data Security company. Of course, they are based on the RSA algorithm. Here we give details about the encryption scheme of the PKCS#1v1.5 standard. Note that it is now replaced by PKCS#1v2.1 (Ref. [14]) as we will discuss in Section 9.3.8.

We are given a modulus N of k bytes. In order to encrypt a message M of length at most $k - 11$ bytes, we proceed as follows.

1. We generate a string PS of pseudorandom nonzero bytes so that the message concatenated with PS is of length $k - 3$ bytes.
2. We construct the byte string by concatenating a zero byte, a byte equal to 2, PS, another zero byte, and the message. We write this $00||02||\mathrm{PS}||00||M$.
3. This byte string is converted into an integer.
4. We compute the plain RSA encryption.
5. We convert the result into a string of k bytes.

The decryption is then straightforward.

1. We convert the ciphertext into an integer. We reject it if it is greater than the modulus.
2. We perform the plain RSA decryption and obtain another integer.
3. We convert the integer back into a byte string.
4. We check that the string has the $00||02||\mathrm{PS}||00||M$ format for some byte strings PS and M where PS has no zero bytes.
5. We output M.

The 02 byte is used in order to specify that the message is an encrypted message in the RSA format. Some other parts of the PKCS standard use other values for this byte.

9.3.3   Attacks on Broadcast Encryption with Low Exponent

Although the RSA cryptosystem is believed to be quite strong, there are many ways to use it insecurely. One of it is the broadcast encryption with low encryption exponent. Let us assume that one sender wants to broadcast the same message x to n different parties who have public keys $(e, N_1), \ldots, (e, N_n)$ with the same low exponent e. (In many applications, $e = 3$ is suggested, so this hypothesis seems reasonable.) The sender has to send $y_i = x^e \bmod N_i$ to the i-th receiver for $i = 1, \ldots, n$.

Assuming that we have $n > e$, it becomes fairly easy to decrypt all the corresponding ciphertexts $y_1, \ldots, y_n$: Let us assume that all N_i are pairwise relatively primes, which means that no prime factor is used in two different moduli N_i and N_j. (If this does not hold, then the system has indeed other weaknesses.) Let N be the product of all N_i. Due to the Chinese Remainder Theorem, we can compute y such that $y < N$ and $y \equiv y_i \pmod{N_i}$ for all i. This way we have $y \equiv x^e \pmod{N_i}$ for all i, thus $y \equiv x^e \pmod{N}$. However, the natural integer x^e is less than N because x is less than all N_i and N is the product of more than e integers N_i. Since $y < N$ as well, we have indeed $y = x^e$. Then it becomes trivial to extract the e-th root over the natural integers in order to compute x.[6]

9.3.4   Attacks on Low Exponent

Low exponents have several drawbacks. We distinguish low e's from low d's.

When e is low, there exist efficient attacks due to *Don Coppersmith* against various uses of RSA (see Ref. [49]). More precisely, there exists an efficient algorithm in log N which finds roots of a modulo N polynomial equation of degree e as long as one of it is less than $N^{\frac{1}{e}}$. As an application, if a fraction of $\frac{2}{3}$ of the bits of the plaintext are known and $e = 3$, then one can decrypt efficiently. As another application, if two plaintexts differ only in a (known) window of length one ninth of the full length and $e = 3$, one can decrypt the two corresponding ciphertexts.

When d is low, there exists an efficient algorithm due to *Michael Wiener* which enables the recovery of the secret key (see Ref. [185]). It works in typical cases (with p and q of same size) with $d < \sqrt[4]{N}$. This bound can further be improved by using the LLL lattice reduction algorithm.

9.3.5   Side Channel Attacks

There are several ways to get "side information" in order to be able to break RSA. As a first example we mention the *differential fault analysis*. We assume that we can play with the decryptor device as with a black box and we want to retrieve the

---

[6] This simple attack is due to Johan Håstad. See Ref. [87].

secret key. We also assume that this device uses the Chinese remainder acceleration: we know that computing $y^d \bmod N$ can be done within $\mathcal{O}((\log N)^3)$. We can
also compute $y^d \bmod p$ and $y^d \bmod q$ and combine them by the Chinese Remainder Theorem. Since p and q are half size numbers, doing computation modulo p
(or q) requires one eighth of this complexity. The exponent d can further be reduced
modulo $p - 1$, and modulo $q - 1$, and so we get an acceleration by a factor of 8 by
using this trick. Therefore, assuming that the decryptor uses this acceleration trick is
reasonable.

Now we assume that we can physically stress the device (by heat, beams, corrupted
input power or clock signals, etc.) so that the device will make errors. Let us just pick
x and compute $y = x^e \bmod N$ and send y to the decryptor. We assume that we stress
the decryptor so that an error occurs in the modulo p computation, but not in the
modulo q computation. The decryptor will return x' such that $x \equiv x' \pmod{q}$ and
$x \not\equiv x' \pmod{p}$. Therefore, $\gcd(x - x', N) = q$ and we can factorize N and compute
the secret key of the decryptor![7]

This attack is rather an implementation attack in which the adversary gets side
information by quite active attacks.

A more peaceful way to retrieve side information is to measure the computation
time: some microprocessors have a multiplication instruction whose computation time
depends on the input operands. As was shown by Paul Kocher, this information can
be used in order to recover some information about internal computations, and then to
recover the secret keys (see Ref. [103]).

A more sophisticated attack consists in measuring the evolution of the power con-
sumption with time: if we know which program is run by a microprocessor (but we
do not know the key), we can measure with an oscilloscope the power consumed by
the microprocessor for every instruction. The RSA decryption consists of computing a
modular exponentiation to a secret power d. The square-and-multiply method sequentially computes a square and a multiplication for a bit set to 1, or just a square for a bit
set to 0. This is done for every bit of d, sequentially. Presumably, the square operation
and the multiplication will be implemented quite differently, and the power consump-
tion analysis will be able to say when the decryption device makes a multiplication and
when it computes a square. Therefore we will be able to "see" the 0 bits and the 1 bits
of d sequentially! (see Ref. [104]).

This technique can be extended to block ciphers. Assuming that the power depends
on the values of the registers (a memory bit consumes a different power for a bit 0 and
a bit 1), the power analysis can tell what is the Hamming weight (namely the number of
bits set to 1) of all registers. If the computation starts by computing $x \oplus K$ for a secret
K, since we know x and we can get the Hamming weight of $x \oplus K$, by trying several

---

[7] This attack was published in Ref. [35].

x values, we can retrieve K. (Note that this is not that simple in practice since many technical problems must be solved.)

There is yet another example of side channel attack which is due to Daniel Bleichenbacher, from Bell Labs (see Ref. [34]). It is an attack against PKCS#1v1.5. In this scenario, the cleartext is first transformed into a plaintext according to a specific format prior to encryption.[8] After decryption, the format is checked before the clear-text is recovered. The problem is: what about invalid formats? In the first version of PKCS#1v1.5, an invalid format was indicated as an error to the sender of the cipher-text, and this information was useful for adversaries. Actually, adversaries could use the receiver as an oracle which checked the correctness of the format, and the decryption problem would become easy with the help of this oracle by successive approximations.

9.3.6 ⋆Bit Security of RSA

So far we wondered how hard recovering the whole plaintext was. Assuming that it is hard, one can however wonder if recovering a part of it is also hard. As an example, we can ask ourselves what is the security of the least significant bit: how hard is it to recover the least significant bit of the plaintext?

We can prove that recovering this bit is as hard as the decryption problem, by using the notion of Turing reduction. Let us assume that we have an oracle lsbdec which, given a ciphertext y, returns the least significant bit of $x = y^d \bmod N$. First of all, we notice that we can use it to implement an oracle which returns the most significant bit msbdec$(y) = $ msb(x) by observing the following identity.

$$\mathrm{msb}(x) = \mathrm{lsb}(2x \bmod N).$$

Hence

$$\mathrm{msbdec}(y) = \mathrm{lsbdec}(2^e y \bmod N).$$

We can decrypt a given ciphertext y by using the following algorithm.

```
1: a ← 0, b ← N
2: for i = 0 to ⌊log₂ N⌋ do
3:    if msbdec(2^{ie}y mod N) = 0 then
4:       a ← (a + b)/2
5:    else
6:       b ← (a + b)/2
7:    end if
8: end for
9: yield ⌊ a ⌋
```

---

[8] We recall that the cleartext is the message in clear and the plaintext is the input of the encryption algorithm.

We can indeed show that $\mathrm{msb}(2^i x \bmod N) = 0$ if and only if there exists an integer k such that

$$\frac{2k}{2^{i+1}} \le \frac{x}{N} < \frac{2k+1}{2^{i+1}}.$$

So this algorithm simply gets the binary expansion of x/N.

The least (and most) significant bits of the plaintext are thus called *hard core bits* since recovering them can be used to break the cryptosystem. Further studies can additionally show that even approximating those bits, i.e. being able to predict them with a nontrivial advantage, can also be used to break the scheme.

There are bits which are not hard-core, e.g. the Jacobi symbol. Let

$$(-1)^{\mathrm{bit}(x)} = \left(\frac{x}{N}\right)$$

and bitdec be defined as above. We can easily compute bitdec by noticing that

$$(-1)^{\mathrm{bitdec}(y)} = \left(\frac{y}{N}\right)$$

The plain RSA encryption indeed preserves the Jacobi symbol since e is odd and

$$\left(\frac{x^e \bmod N}{N}\right) = \left(\frac{x^e}{N}\right) = \left(\frac{x}{N}\right)^e = \left(\frac{x}{N}\right).$$

9.3.7 ★*Back to the Encryption Security Assumptions*

After having seen all these attacks on public-key encryption schemes, a question remains: what minimal security requirements must such a scheme satisfy? There are so many attack scenarii that we have seen so far that the intuitive notion of encryption security, i.e. that the decryption problem is computationally hard, is not sufficient. For instance the decryption problem could in theory still be hard even though recovering half of the plaintext would be easy, but this would not match our intuition about security. Currently, there are two popular notions of security against three notions of adversaries, leading us to six possible definitions.

First of all, Shafi Goldwasser and Silvio Micali proposed the notion of *semantic security* (see Ref. [77]). This notion intuitively means that the ciphertext leaks no interesting bit of information about the plaintext. This notion is described as a game between a challenger and an adversary. The game runs as follows (see Fig. 9.9).

1. First of all, the challenger and the adversary are given the cryptosystem.
2. The challenger generates a matching pair of public and secret keys and discloses the public one.
3. The adversary selects two plaintexts x_0 and x_1 and sends them to the challenger.

Challenger   Adversary

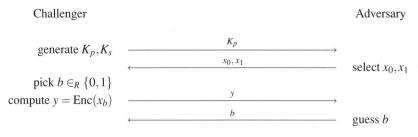

Figure 9.9. Semantic Security Game.

4. The challenger picks uniformly at random a bit b. He encrypts x_b and sends the ciphertext y to the adversary.
5. The adversary tries to guess b.

When the cryptosystem is secure, the adversary cannot guess b with a significant advantage, so we often say that the two messages are indistinguishable. The indistinguishability notion is denoted IND. As it will be explained below, semantic security is denoted IND-CPA.

Note that our definition does not provide so much information to the adversary who only has the public key and a ciphertext. So he cannot do anything but encrypt messages himself. We call this a CPA adversary as for "chosen plaintext attack." The semantic security notion is thus denoted IND-CPA.

Semantic security generalizes the notion of "bit security" to all bits. Indeed, if there is any function bit from the plaintext space to $\{0, 1\}$ such that bitdec(y) is easily computable without the secret key, where bitdec is defined by bitdec(y) = bit(Dec(y)) then we can mount an attack that can win in the semantic security game: the adversary selects two random plaintexts x_0 and x_1 such that bit(x_i) = i for $i = 0, 1$ and deduce b from $b = $ bitdec(y).

Note that all notions of security require that the encryption is nondeterministic. Indeed, if the encryption were deterministic, the adversary would easily encrypt x_0 and x_1 with the public key and compare both results to y. He would be able to guess b with a 100% chance. We can extend this notion of semantic security to adversaries that are given more resources. First of all, we can consider adversaries who can play during "lunch time" with a decryptor. Indeed, prior to the selection of x_0 and x_1, we assume that the adversary can play with a decryption oracle as he likes. After this phase (after lunch), the adversary has no longer access to this oracle. He selects the two plaintexts and plays like in the previous game. This notion of adversary is denoted CCA1 and called "nonadaptive chosen ciphertext attack." The security notion is denoted IND-CCA1.

We have yet another adversary who is more powerful and denoted CCA2 (or simply CCA). Here the adversary keeps access to the decryption oracle even after having received the challenge ciphertext y. The only restriction is that he is not allowed to send y to the oracle. This leads to the stronger security notion IND-CCA.

Another security notion was proposed: the *nonmalleability*, denoted NM. We have a security notion for NM-CPA, NM-CCA1, and NM-CCA depending on which adversary we consider. The nonmalleability is also described by a game which is a little more complicated than the game for semantic security. What is worth keeping in mind is that NM-CCA and IND-CCA are equivalent and that NM-CPA and NM-CCA1 are proven to be stronger security notions than IND-CPA and IND-CCA1 respectively. This leads us to the following matrix of security notions.

	Adversary power		
	CPA	CCA1	CCA
Key recovery	Weaker		
Message decryption			
Bit retrieval			
Indistinguishability			
Nonmalleability			Stronger

Resistance to the strongest attack (key recovery with chosen plaintexts) is the weakest security model. Conversely, resistance to the weakest attack (malleability with CCA) is the strongest security model.

9.3.8 RSA–OAEP

Based on the previous notes and the bad experience of PKCS#1v1.5, the PKCS was updated into PKCS#1v2 with the OAEP preformatting technique. OAEP stands for "Optimal Asymmetric Encryption Padding" and is due to Mihir Bellare and Phillip Rogaway . We describe here the encryption scheme of PKCS#1v2.1 (Ref. [14]).

We are given a modulus N of k bytes and a hash function H which hashes to hLen bytes. We also use a "Mask Generation Function" MGF which is indeed a family of one-way functions such that MGF_ℓ maps a bitstring into a string of ℓ bytes. In order to encrypt a message M, we proceed as depicted in Fig. 9.10.

1. Set an optional label L associated with the message and compute $H(L)$. (This feature is to be used for specific applications. The default value for L, if L is not provided, is the empty string.)
2. Set DB (as for "Data Byte") to the concatenated string $H(L)||00||\cdots||00||01||M$ where we put enough zero bytes (possibly none) in order to get a length of $k - 1 - $ hLen.

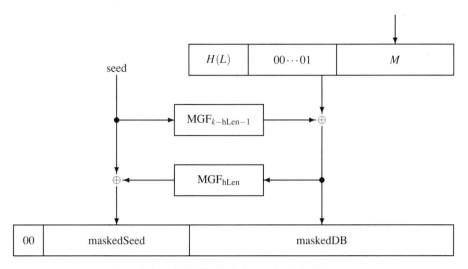

Figure 9.10. OAEP Preformatting for RSA.

3. Pick a random byte string of length hLen denoted seed.
4. Set dbMask to $\text{MGF}_{k-\text{hLen}-1}(\text{seed})$.
5. Set maskedDB to DB $\oplus$ dbMask.
6. Set seedMask to $\text{MGF}_{\text{hLen}}(\text{maskedDB})$.
7. Set maskedSeed to seed $\oplus$ seedMask.
8. Set EM (as for "Encoded Message") to the concatenated string 00||maskedSeed ||maskedDB. Note that this string is of length k.
9. This byte string is converted into an integer.
10. We compute the plain RSA encryption.
11. We convert the result into a string of k bytes.

Note that the OAEP padding is indeed a two-round Feistel scheme. The decryption is then straightforward.

1. We convert the ciphertext into an integer. We reject it if it is greater than the modulus.
2. We perform the plain RSA decryption and obtain another integer.
3. We convert back the integer into a byte string.
4. We parse the string to 00||maskedSeed||maskedDB where maskedSeed is of length hLen.
5. Set seedMask to $\text{MGF}_{\text{hLen}}(\text{maskedDB})$.
6. Set seed to maskedSeed $\oplus$ seedMask.
7. Set dbMask to $\text{MGF}_{k-\text{hLen}-1}(\text{seed})$.
8. Set DB to maskedDB $\oplus$ dbMask.
9. We check that DB has the $H(L)||00||\cdots||00||01||M$.
10. We output M.

The PKCS specifications further suggest a mask generation function MGF1 which is based on a hash function. The $\mathrm{MGF1}_\ell(x)$ string simply consists of the ℓ leading bytes of

$$H(x||00000000)||H(x||00000001)||H(x||00000002)|| \cdots$$

in which x is concatenated to a four-byte counter.

The security proof of RSA-OAEP is far beyond the scope of these lecture notes. We simply mention that it exists with the strongest security notion that we have seen, i.e. IND-CCA, and that its significance was subject to a highly technical controversy.[9]

9.4   ElGamal Encryption

Taher ElGamal initiated a famous family of digital signature schemes which will be discussed in Chapter 10 (see Refs. [63–65]). He also defined a nondeterministic encryption scheme based on the discrete logarithm problem. Here is how it works.

> *Public parameter*: a large prime p, a generator g of $\mathbf{Z}_p^*$.
> *Setup*: generate a random $x \in \mathbf{Z}_{p-1}$, and compute $y = g^x \bmod p$.
> *Message*: an element $m \in \mathbf{Z}_p^*$.
> *Public key*: $K_p = y$.
> *Secret key*: $K_s = x$.
> *Encryption*: pick a random $r \in \mathbf{Z}_{p-1}$, compute $u = g^r \bmod p$ and $v = my^r \bmod p$. The ciphertext is (u, v).
> *Decryption*: Extract the u and v parts of the ciphertext and compute $m = vu^{-x} \bmod p$.

(See Fig. 9.11.) Obviously, the correct encryption followed by a correct decryption recovers the correct message.

One benefit of this scheme is that a single prime number can be used for all users. Hence key setup, encryption, and decryption take $\mathcal{O}(s^3)$ time where $s = \log p$. The drawback is that the ciphertext size is twice the plaintext size.

For security analysis we distinguish the decryption problem from the key recovery problem, as for the RSA cryptosystem.

> EGDP (ElGamal Decryption Problem)
> *Parameters*: a prime number p and a generator g of $\mathbf{Z}_p^*$
> *Input*: a ciphertext (u, v) and a public key y

---

[9] See Refs. [25, 26, 71, 169]. A nice survey is available in Ref. [120].

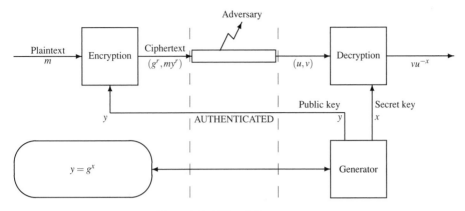

Figure 9.11. ElGamal Cryptosystem.

Problem: compute m such that there exists r such that $u = g^r \bmod p$ and $v = my^r \bmod p$

EGKRP (ElGamal Key Recovery Problem)
    Parameters: a prime number p and a generator g of $\mathbf{Z}_p^*$
    Input: a public key y
    Problem: compute x such that $y = g^x \bmod p$

We notice that being able to decrypt (i.e. solving EGDP) means being able to compute vu^{-x} from u and v. This implies being able to compute u^x as v/m. Obviously, being able to compute u^x from u and g^x is equivalent to the Diffie–Hellman problem as defined on p. 234 DHP with $G = \mathbf{Z}_p^*$.

Let us formally prove that given the public parameters p and g, ElGamal decryption EGDP is equivalent to the Diffie–Hellman DHP problem. First of all, we assume that we have an oracle which solves the Diffie–Hellman problem: given $A = g^a \bmod p$ and $B = g^b \bmod p$, the oracle computes $g^{ab} \bmod p$. We can use this oracle in order to decrypt (u, v) with the public key y. For this we simply give $A = y$ and $B = u$ to the oracle. We obtain $g^{xr} \bmod p$ from the oracle which is $u^x \bmod p$, so we can compute $m = vu^{-x} \bmod p$.

Second, we assume that we have a decryptor oracle which given (u, v) and $y = g^x \bmod p$ computes $vu^{-x} \bmod p$. We can use this oracle in order to solve the Diffie–Hellman problem with A and B: we simply give $u = A$, $y = B$, and take $v \in \mathbf{Z}_p^*$ at random, and we get $vA^{-\log B} \bmod p$ from which we deduce $A^{\log B} \bmod p$.

Similarly, we can prove that the ElGamal key recovery EGKRP problem is equivalent to the discrete logarithm with known order DLP problem as defined on p. 160 with $G = \mathbf{Z}_p^*$. (For $G = \mathbf{Z}_p^*$ with a prime p, DLP and DLKOP are equivalent.)

Here is the list of reductions that we have proven.

$$\text{EGDP} \Leftarrow \text{EGKRP}$$
$$\Updownarrow \qquad\qquad \Updownarrow$$
$$\text{DHP} \Leftarrow \text{DLP}$$

Note that we have variants of the ElGamal encryption with the exclusive or $\oplus$ instead of the multiplication for v: we can define $v = m \oplus (y^r \bmod p)$. This is typically used when adopting the ElGamal encryption over elliptic curves.

9.5 Exercises

Exercise 9.1. *Let $N = pq$ be the product of two odd primes p and q such that 3 divides $\varphi(N)$.*

1. *Under which condition on $p \bmod 3$ and $q \bmod 3$ does 3 divide $\varphi(N)$?*
2. *We call cubic residue modulo N an element x of $\mathbf{Z}_N^*$ such that there exists y such that $x \equiv y^3 \pmod{N}$. Let CR_N denote the set of all cubic residues modulo N.*

   Given a cubic residue $x \in \mathrm{CR}_N$, how many cubic roots of x do we have when $p \equiv 1 \pmod 3$ and $q \equiv 2 \pmod 3$? How many cubic roots do we have when $p \equiv q \equiv 1 \pmod 3$?
   Let y be one cubic root of x. We pick z uniformly at random in the set of all cubic roots of x. Show how $y - z$ may lead to the factorization of N? What is the probability?
3. *Let us assume that we have an oracle which for any $x \in \mathrm{CR}_N$ outputs one cubic root. Show that we can use it in order to factorize N in polynomial time in $\log N$. Deduce that computing cubic roots modulo N is equivalent to factorizing N when 3 divides $\varphi(N)$.*

Exercise 9.2 (Common modulus). *Let us assume that A and B use RSA public keys with the same modulus N but different exponents e_1 and e_2.*

Prove that A can decrypt messages sent to B.

Prove that C can decrypt a message sent to A and B provided that $\gcd(e_1, e_2) = 1$.[10]

Exercise 9.3. *We want to set up the RSA cryptosystem in a network of n users. How many prime numbers do we have to generate?*

We want to reduce this number by generating a smaller pool of prime numbers and making combinations of two of these primes: for each user, we pick a new pair of two of these primes in order to set up his key. Show how one user can factorize the modulus of some other user.

---

[10] This exercise was inspired by Ref. [172].

Show how anyone can factorize all moduli for which at least one prime factor has been used in at least one other modulus.

Exercise 9.4 (Small exponent and known variations). *Let us assume that e = 3 and that we obtain the encryption of two unknown messages x_1 and x_2 for which we know that $x_2 - x_1 = \delta$. Show that we can decrypt both messages by solving polynomial equations.*

Extend this attack for $x_2 = P(x_1)$ where $P(X)$ is a polynomial of low degree.[11]

Exercise 9.5 (Rabin cryptosystem). *Let us consider the following cryptosystem.*

Setup: *find two prime numbers p and q, set $N = pq$, and pick a random $B \in \mathbf{Z}_N$*
Messages: $x \in \mathbf{Z}_N$
Public key: B, N
Secret key: B, p, q
Encryption: $E(x) = x(x + B) \bmod N$
Decryption: *$D(y)$ is one of the four square roots of $\frac{B^2}{4} + y$ minus $\frac{B}{2}$*

Explain how we can compute the square roots in $\mathbf{Z}_N$.

Show that we can make decryption deterministic by adding redundancy in the plaintexts.

Show that the cryptosystem can be broken by a chosen ciphertext attack.

Show that the ability to decrypt is equivalent to the ability to factorize N.[12]

Exercise 9.6. *Let p be a prime number such that $p \equiv 3 \pmod 4$. Let g be a generator of $\mathbf{Z}_p^*$. Given $y = g^x \bmod p$ (with x unknown), how can we efficiently compute the parity bit x mod 2 of x?*

Show that if y is a quadratic residue modulo p, then $y^{\frac{p+1}{4}} \bmod p$ is a square root of y. What is the link between the discrete logarithm of y and the discrete logarithm of $y^{\frac{p+1}{4}} \bmod p$?

We assume that we are given an oracle $\mathcal{O}$ which for any $y = g^x \bmod p$ outputs the second parity bit $\lfloor \frac{x}{2} \rfloor \bmod 2$ of the logarithm of y. Show how to efficiently compute discrete logarithms by using $\mathcal{O}$.

Deduce that for $p \equiv 3 \pmod 4$, computing the second parity bit of the discrete logarithm is polynomially equivalent to computing the discrete logarithm in terms of complexity.

---

[11] This exercise was inspired by Ref. [50].
[12] This exercise was inspired by Ref. [153].

10

Digital Signature

Content

RSA signature: PKCS, ISO/IEC 9796
ElGamal signature family: ElGamal, Schnorr, DSS, ECDSA
⋆Attacks on ElGamal signatures: existential forgery, Bleichenbacher attack
⋆Provable security: interactive proofs, random oracle model

As public-key cryptosystems are the asymmetric alternative to conventional encryption, there is an alternative to MAC algorithms which is the notion of digital signature. With it, a secret key is given to each person, and a corresponding public key is released. The person can sign any document, and anybody else can verify the correctness of the signature. We have already seen in Chapter 5 several signature schemes based on conventional cryptography: the Lamport scheme and the Merkle scheme based on hash trees. We study other schemes based on asymmetric cryptography techniques in this chapter.

10.1 Digital Signature Schemes

Formally, a public-key signature scheme consists of

- a pseudorandom key generator which generates a public key K_p and a secret key K_s;
- a signature algorithm which from each message X and the secret key K_s computes (in a deterministic or a probabilistic way) a signature σ;
- a verification algorithm which from each message X, signature σ, and public key K_p verifies (in a deterministic way) the correctness of the signature

(see Fig. 10.1).

Digital signatures face several security issues.

1. They must provide authenticity and integrity. For this, it must be impossible for anyone who does not have access to the secret key to forge a (X, σ) pair which is valid for the public key. This is called a *signature forgery*.

   Of course this assumption must remain valid even when the adversary gets several valid (X_i, σ_i) pairs, or even when the adversary can choose the X_i and play with the signer as with a black box.

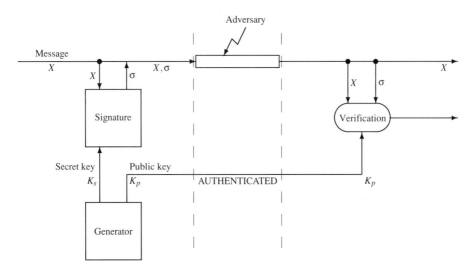

Figure 10.1. Digital signature.

We distinguish several classes of attacks which are listed below from the strongest to the weakest.

- *Total break*: From a public key, the adversary manages to recover the secret key which can be used to forge signatures.
- *Universal forgery*: From a public key, the adversary manages to derive an algorithm which makes it feasible to forge the signature of any message (or random ones).
- *Selective forgery*: The adversary can generate messages X such that she can, from a public key, forge a signature for the selected message. (Note that the target message selection is made *prior* to the knowledge of the public key.)
- *Existential forgery*: From a public key, the adversary is able to create a pair made by a message X and a forged signature, but has no control on which X is output from the attack.

The strongest security requirement corresponds to security against the weakest attack, i.e. the existential forgery attack. This security model was first proposed by Shafi Goldwasser, Silvio Micali, and Ronald Rivest (see Refs. [79, 80]). Conversely, total break is the strongest attack model. So security against this is the weakest security model.

Note that in all attack models we must also discuss the power and access capabilities of the adversary: Is the adversary bounded in space complexity or time complexity? Can the adversary obtain samples of signatures, or query a signing oracle with selected messages? This leads us to similar discussions as for public-key cryptosystems (see Section 9.3.7).

2. They must provide *nonrepudiation*. It must be impossible for the legitimate signer to repudiate his signature. When a signed message (X, σ) is valid, the signer cannot claim that the signature was forged. Indeed, if the signature scheme is secure according to the previous criterion, it is impossible for an adversary to have forged this message, so the signature cannot have been created by

someone else but the secret key holder. Note that this implies that the key holder is restricted to a single person, which is a critical legal issue in the case of signatures. (Encryption does not have the same legal problem.)

Here nonrepudiation relies on the security assumption, and on the hypothesis that no attack is feasible. In most cases we cannot prove that no attack is feasible but only reduce the forgery problem to some other problem we do not know how to solve (yet). In some special signature schemes which can be used in paranoid cases where we do not want to rely on this unstable assumption, an additional protocol makes it feasible for a signer to formally prove that a signature was forged when it happens to be the case. The denial protocol must be such that it is infeasible for the signer to repudiate a signature he created. Most of the time we cannot prove that it is infeasible. We can only argue that it must be hard. But here the debatable assumption is in favor of the signer and not on the verifier, which may be more suitable depending on legal constraints.

10.2   RSA Signature

The original RSA paper (Ref. [158]) proposed a way to use the RSA algorithm as a digital signature scheme. The relationship between public-key cryptosystems and digital signatures is however quite general and not specific to RSA.

10.2.1   From Public-Key Cryptosystem to Digital Signature

Assuming that we have a public-key cryptosystem with a key generator, an encryption algorithm which is deterministic, and a decryption algorithm, we can sign a message by decrypting it. Verification simply consists of encrypting it. Note that here we have a signature with *message recovery*: we do not need to send X together with σ since X can be extracted from σ. So we can replace the verification algorithm by an extraction algorithm. This case is depicted in Fig. 10.2.

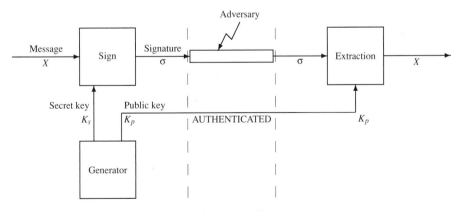

Figure 10.2. Digital signature with message recovery.

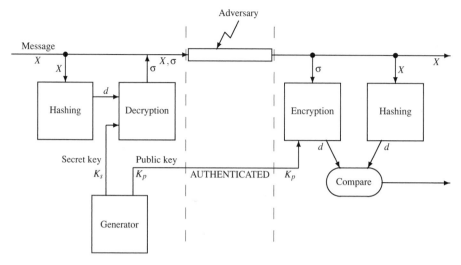

Figure 10.3. Encryption to signature.

In order to limit the size of the signature, we can use a cryptographic hash function before signing. This hash function must however be collision-resistant (otherwise we can have the same signature for two different messages, so a chosen message attack with the first message makes a signature forgery on the second message).

Fig. 10.3 represents the generic transformation of public-key encryption into a signature scheme. Note that it does not provide message recovery. In the following, we however strongly discourage to talk about encryption instead of signature, since the threat model is totally different.

10.2.2 On the Plain RSA Signature

Let $K_p = (N, e)$ and $K_s = (N, d)$ be an RSA key pair for signature. The signature of a message m by using the plain RSA algorithm is simply $\sigma = m^d \bmod N$, as depicted in Fig. 10.4. This suffers from several problems which are mainly due to the RSA properties.

First of all, it is easy for anyone to pick a random σ and to construct $m = \sigma^e \bmod N$ which makes (m, σ) a valid pair. This is an *existential forgery*: we can forge a valid pair, but we have no control on the meaning of the forged message m.

Second, we can easily modify two valid pairs (m, σ) and (m', σ'), for instance by taking $m'' = mm' \bmod N$ and $\sigma'' = \sigma\sigma' \bmod N$. (m'', σ'') is then a new valid pair. This comes from the property of *malleability* of the RSA algorithm.

These security issues can be fixed by cryptographic hash functions. We must at least adapt the plain RSA system in order to prevent these attacks.

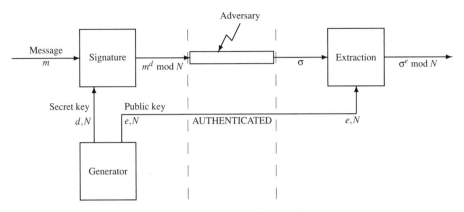

Figure 10.4. Plain RSA signature scheme.

10.2.3   ISO/IEC 9796

The ISO/IEC 9796 (Ref. [10]) was the first international norm which specified a message formatting scheme to be used in order to feed a given signature scheme.[1] The original norm does not specify the signature scheme, but it is RSA in most applications (it can also be the *Rabin scheme*).

The signature of a d-bit message m into a k-bit signature proceeds as follows. (Let us consider that $d \leq 512$ and $k = 1024$ for instance.)

1. We pad m with leading zero bits (at most seven) so that the total length can be cut into a sequence of z bytes $m_z, m_{z-1}, \ldots, m_1$.
2. We extend the message by taking the t rightmost bytes of the infinite sequence
   $$\ldots, m_z, m_{z-1}, \ldots, m_1, m_z, m_{z-1}, \ldots, m_1, \ldots, m_z, m_{z-1}, \ldots, m_1$$
   where t is the smallest size such that $16t \geq k - 1$. (Hence $t = 64$ bytes.)
3. We add redundancy by inserting a byte $S(x)$ to the left of each of the t bytes x of the string, and XOR r onto the z-th rightmost redundancy byte $S(m_z)$. We thus obtain a string of $2t$ bytes, which consists of at least $k - 1$ bits. Here r is one plus the number of zero bits which have been padded at the beginning (hence between 1 and 8), and S is the *shadow function* defined by $S(x_H x_L) = \pi(x_H)\pi(x_L)$ where $x_H x_L$ represents the two hexadecimal digits of x, and π is a permutation defined by
   $$\pi = \begin{pmatrix} 0 & 1 & 2 & 3 & 4 & 5 & 6 & 7 & 8 & 9 & A & B & C & D & E & F \\ E & 3 & 5 & 8 & 9 & 4 & 2 & F & 0 & D & B & 6 & 7 & A & C & 1 \end{pmatrix}.$$
4. We take the $k - 1$ rightmost bits and we pad a one bit to the left and replace the rightmost byte $x = x_H x_L$ by $x_L 6$ in hexadecimal. We thus obtain a formatted string of k bits.
5. We sign the formatted string, for instance by using the plain RSA.

---

[1] Note that it was originally published in 1991.

The extraction scheme is thus performed as follows.

1. We open the signature. (In case of RSA, we raise the signature to the public exponent.)
2. We first check that the signature is of length k and that the rightmost hexadecimal digit is 6.
3. We perform a *message recovery*: we remove the leading bit 1, replace the rightmost two bytes $y_H y_R x_H x_R$ by $y_H y_R \pi^{-1}(y_H) x_H$, obtain $\ldots, x_2, x_1$, take z as the smallest index such that $x_{2z} \oplus S(x_{2z-1}) \neq 0$ (reject if it does not exist) and set r equal to this value (and check that $r \leq 8$), extract $x_{2z}, x_{2z-2}, \ldots, x_2$, and remove the $r - 1$ leftmost bits (reject if they are not equal to zero). We must obtain a message m.
4. Check that the formatting scheme on m leads to the value obtained after opening the signature. (Check the redundancy.)

One important property of this scheme is the *message recovery*: as long as the message m is of length at most d, we do not need to send it with the signature σ: the verification process enables the recovery of m.

As an example, let us consider the message "PAY 1'000'000.-CHF" with $k = 512$. The message (of 18 characters) turns in hexadecimal into

P	A	Y		1	'	0	0	0	'	0	0	0	.	–	C	H	F
50	40	59	20	31	27	30	30	30	27	30	30	30	2e	2d	43	48	46

hence   5040 5920312730303027 3030302e2d434846.   We   have $z = 18$ and we need $t = 32$ bytes. So we take

3127303030273030 302e2d434846||5040 5920312730303027 3030302e2d434846

i.e. the message plus an extra 14 bytes. We then add the S redundancy and get

83315f278e308e30 8e305f278e308e30 8e305c2era2d9843 904892464e509e40
4d595e2083315f27 8e308e308e305f27 8e308e308e305c2e 5a2d984390489246

(note that the z-th redundancy byte is 4e as $S(50)$) and XORing the z-th redundancy byte to $r = 1$ we obtain

83315f278e308e30 8e305f278e308e30 8e305c2era2d9843 904892464f509e40
4d595e2083315f27 8e308e308e305f27 8e308e308e305c2e 5a2d984390489246

and the final operation leads to

83315f278e308e30 8e305f278e308e30 8e305c2era2d9843 904892464f509e40
4d595e2083315f27 8e308e308e305f27 8e308e308e305c2e 5a2d984390489266

which can now feed the plain RSA signature scheme.

10.2.4 *Attack on the ISO/IEC 9796 Signature Scheme

A first surprising attack has been found by Jean-Sébastien Coron, David Naccache, and Julien Stern in Ref. [51] on a slightly modified variant of the ISO/IEC 9796 norm: let us assume that we remove the XOR to r in the third step of the signature. Let us further assume that k is a multiple of 64. For an original message of $d = \frac{k}{2}$ bits, we have $t = z = \frac{k}{16}$. We write $m = m_z \cdots m_2 m_1$. If $m_1 = m_{1H} m_{1L}$ is the least significant byte, we write $u = m_{1L} || 6$ in hexadecimal. The formatted string is

$$((S(m_z) \oplus 1) \text{ OR } 80) || m_z || S(m_{z-1}) || m_{z-1} || \cdots || S(m_2) || m_2 || S(m_1) || u.$$

With the XOR to r removed, following our assumption, the formatted string is

$$(S(m_z) \text{ OR } 80) || m_z || S(m_{z-1}) || m_{z-1} || \cdots || S(m_2) || m_2 || S(m_1) || u.$$

Now if m_z is chosen so that the leftmost bit of $S(m_z)$ is set to 1, and if we choose $m_1 = 66$, the formatted string is

$$S(m_z) || m_z || S(m_{z-1}) || m_{z-1} || \cdots || S(m_2) || m_2 || S(m_1) || m_1.$$

We notice that z is a multiple of 4. So we can choose a special message m of the form

$$m = m_4 m_3 m_2 m_1 || m_4 m_3 m_2 m_1 || \cdots || m_4 m_3 m_2 m_1.$$

We still assume that m_4 is such that the leftmost bit of $S(m_4)$ is set to 1, and that $m_1 = 66$. The formatted string is now

$$S(m_4) || m_4 || S(m_3) || m_3 || S(m_2) || m_2 || 2266 || \cdots || S(m_4) || m_4 || S(m_3) || m_3 || S(m_2) || m_2 || 2266.$$

Let us write

$$x = S(m_4) || m_4 || S(m_3) || m_3 || S(m_2) || m_2 || 2266$$

and $\Gamma = 1 + 2^{64} + 2^{128} + \cdots + 2^{k-64}$. The formatted string is nothing but $x \times \Gamma$, where x is a 64-bit integer. We have 2^{23} messages m_i of this type for which the formatted string is $x_i \times \Gamma$. We can estimate the probability that all prime factors of x_i are less than 2^{16} to be $2^{-7.7}$. Therefore, we may have more than 2^{15} messages for which the x_i factorizes into primes which are less than 2^{16}. We can prove that with less than 200 such messages, we are likely to find four messages m_g, m_h, m_i, m_j such that $x_g \times x_h = x_i \times x_j$. In this case, the signature of message m_j is simply the multiplication of the signatures of m_g and m_h divided by the signature of m_i. We can thus forge a new signature with the signature of m_g, m_h, m_i!

This attack was later transformed and improved into an attack against the real ISO/IEC 9796 norm (see Refs. [51, 81]).

10.2.5   PKCS#1

The PKCS (Public-Key Cryptography Standards) that we saw in Chapter 9 also includes a signature scheme based on RSA. Here we give details about the signature scheme of the PKCS#1v1.5 standard (Ref. [13]).

We are given a modulus n of k bytes. In order to sign a message, we proceed as follows.

1. We hash the message, for instance with MD5, and get a message digest.
2. We encode the message digest and the identifier of the hash algorithm.
3. We pad it with a zero byte to the left, then with many (at least 8) FF bytes in order to reach a length of $k - 2$ bytes, then with a 01 byte. We obtain $k - 1$ bytes.
4. This byte string is converted into an integer.
5. We compute the plain RSA signature.
6. We convert the result into a string of k bytes.

The verification is then straightforward.

1. We convert the signature into an integer. We reject it if it is greater than the modulus.
2. We perform the plain RSA verification and obtain another integer.
3. We convert back the integer into a byte string.
4. We check that the string has the $00||01||FF \cdots FF||00||D$ format for a byte string D.
5. We decode the data D and obtain the message digest and the hash algorithm. We check that the hash algorithm is acceptable.
6. We hash the message and check the message digest.

The PKCS#1v2.1 (Ref. [14]) includes another signature scheme which uses the padding scheme called PSS (as for Probabilistic Signature Scheme), which is similar to the OAEP (Optimal Asymmetric Encryption Padding) (see Section 9.3.8).

10.3   ElGamal Signature Family

In his PhD, Taher ElGamal studied the application of the discrete logarithm in cryptography (see Refs. [63–65]). The ElGamal signature started a dynasty of signature schemes based on the discrete logarithm problem.

10.3.1   ElGamal Signature

The original ElGamal signature scheme is defined as follows. We use a cryptographic hash function H.

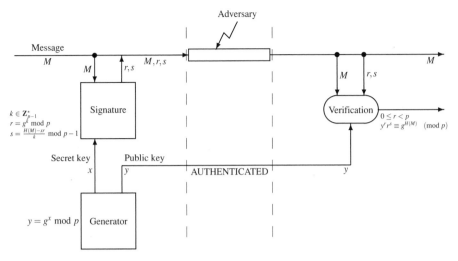

Figure 10.5. ElGamal signature scheme.

Public parameters: a large prime number p, a generator g of $\mathbf{Z}_p^*$.
Setup: generate a random $x \in \mathbf{Z}_{p-1}$ and compute $y = g^x \bmod p$.
Secret key: $K_s = x$.
Public key: $K_p = y$.
Message digest: $h = H(M) \in \mathbf{Z}_{p-1}$.
Signature generation: pick a random $k \in \mathbf{Z}_{p-1}^*$, compute $r = g^k \bmod p$ and $s = \frac{h-xr}{k} \bmod p - 1$, the signature is $\sigma = (r, s)$.
Verification: check that $y^r r^s \equiv g^h \pmod{p}$ and $0 \le r < p$.

(See Fig. 10.5.) We first prove that the signatures are correct: if σ was correctly computed, we have $0 \le r < p$ and

$$y^r r^s \equiv g^{xr+ks} \equiv g^h \pmod{p}.$$

Now we can study the security of this scheme: the difficulty to forge valid signatures.

A signature forgery consists of finding r and s such that $y^r r^s \equiv g^h \pmod{p}$. This is quite easy if we know how to compute the discrete logarithm of y (which is actually the secret key). It is quite easy as well, in general, if we forget the requirement $0 \le r < p$. Indeed, one can just pick $\alpha \in \mathbf{Z}_{p-1}$ and $\beta \in \mathbf{Z}_{p-1}^*$ at random, take $r_p = y^\alpha g^\beta \bmod p$, $s = h/\beta \bmod (p-1)$, and $r_{p-1} = -s\alpha \bmod (p-1)$, then reconstruct r such that $r \bmod p = r_p$ and $r \bmod (p-1) = r_{p-1}$ by using the Chinese Remainder Theorem.

One problem with the plain ElGamal scheme concerns the signature length. Assuming that p is of length 1024 bits, it means that σ is of length 2048 bits (256 bytes), which is quite long.

10.3.2   ★The Bleichenbacher Attack against the ElGamal Signature

We describe here an attack against the ElGamal signature which works for special public parameters. The attack is due to Daniel Bleichenbacher (see Ref. [33]).

Let p and g be the parameters in the ElGamal signature. Let us assume that $p - 1 = bw$ with an integer b which is smooth (namely such that all its prime factors are small). As an example, we can just have $b = 2$, which works for every odd prime p. Let us further assume that we know some relation $g^{1/t} \bmod p = cw$. This is a reasonable assumption if we have $g = b$ (note that the complexity of the exponentiation is decreased if g is small) and $p \equiv 1 \pmod 4$ since we can check that the relation holds for $t = \frac{p-3}{2}$ and $c = 1$: we have

$$(cw)^t \equiv \left(\frac{p-1}{g}\right)^{\frac{p-1}{2}-1} \equiv -g \frac{(-1)^{\frac{p-1}{2}}}{g^{\frac{p-1}{2}}} \equiv g \pmod p$$

since $g^{\frac{p-1}{2}}$ is a square root of 1 which is not 1 (otherwise g would not be a generator) and $(-1)^{\frac{p-1}{2}} = 1$ due to the assumption on $p \bmod 4$.

We will show now that with the assumption that $\frac{p-1}{w} = b$ is smooth and $g^{1/t} \bmod p = cw$, anyone can forge a signature for any message digest h.

- First take $r = cw$.
- Find z such that $y^{wc} \equiv g^{wcz} \pmod p$. This is nothing but the discrete logarithm of $y^{wc} \bmod p$, in basis $g^{wc} \bmod p$, which spans a group of order factor of b. Thus the Pohlig–Hellman algorithm works, thanks to the assumption on b.
- Take $s = t(h - cwz) \bmod (p - 1)$.
- Yield the signature (r, s).

We only have to prove that the signature is valid. First we check that $0 \le r < p$. Next we have

$$y^r r^s \equiv y^{cw}(cw)^{t(h-cwz)} \equiv y^{cw} g^{h-cwz} \equiv g^h \pmod p.$$

Therefore the signature is valid.

The main idea here is to simplify the discrete logarithm problem by raising everything to the power w, so that the underlying subgroup becomes smooth.

We can get rid of this kind of attack by using subgroups of prime order.

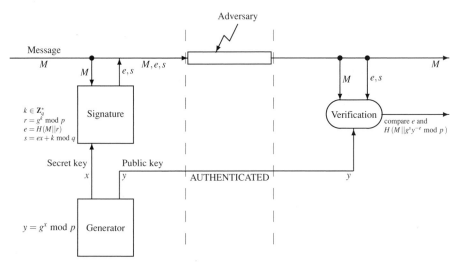

Figure 10.6. Schnorr signature scheme.

10.3.3 Schnorr Signature

In 1989, Claus Schnorr presented a new variant of the ElGamal signature which over-comes the drawbacks that we have seen: a long signature size and the Bleichenbacher attack (but this attack was unknown at that time). (See Ref. [160, 161]). Here is a short description of the Schnorr signature.

> *Public parameters*: pick a (not-too-large, but large enough) prime number q, a large prime number $p = aq + 1$, a generator of $\mathbf{Z}_p^*$ whose a-th power is denoted g (an element of order q).
> *Setup*: pick $x \in \mathbf{Z}_q$ and compute $y = g^x \bmod p$.
> *Secret key*: $K_s = x$.
> *Public key*: $K_p = y$.
> *Signature generation*: pick a random $k \in \mathbf{Z}_q^*$, compute $r = g^k \bmod p$, $e = H(M||r)$, and $s = ex + k \bmod q$, the signature is $\sigma = (e, s)$.
> *Verification*: check that $e = H(M||g^s y^{-e} \bmod p)$.

(See Fig. 10.6.) Here H is a hash function (whose output is smaller than the size of q) and $M||r$ denotes the concatenation of M and r.

We can see here that the signature complexity is very cheap when (k, r) are pre-computed. In addition, the size of the signature is a message digest size plus a modulo q number which can be quite short. We can thus have signatures of size less than 300 bits.

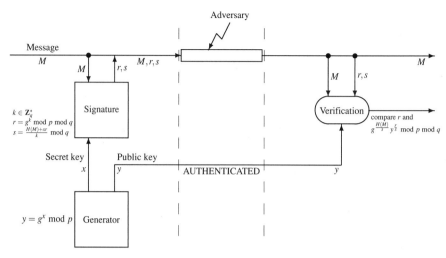

Figure 10.7. DSA.

10.3.4 The Digital Signature Standard (DSS)

DSS (as for Digital Signature Standard) was published as Ref. [7] by NIST, a branch of the American department of commerce, in 1994. It includes a Digital Signature Algorithm (DSA) which is very similar to the Schnorr signature, which led to a juridical controversy.

> *Public parameters*: pick a 160-bit prime number q, a large prime number $p = aq + 1$, a generator of Z_p^* whose a-th power is denoted g (an element of order q).
>
> *Setup*: pick $x \in Z_q$ and compute $y = g^x \bmod p$.
>
> *Secret key*: $K_s = x$.
>
> *Public key*: $K_p = y$.
>
> *Signature generation*: pick a random $k \in Z_q^*$, compute $r = (g^k \bmod p) \bmod q$, and $s = \frac{H(M)+xr}{k} \bmod q$, the signature is $\sigma = (r, s)$.
>
> *Verification*: check that $r = \left(g^{\frac{H(M)}{s} \bmod q} y^{\frac{r}{s} \bmod q} \bmod p\right) \bmod q$.

(See Fig. 10.7.) Here H is the standardized hash function SHA-1 which hashes onto 160 bits.

The signature is still quite short: 320 bits in total. The main difference with the Schnorr signature is the removal of the r in the message to be hashed. This leads to a security problem when we know two messages M and M' such that $q = H(M) - H(M')$. (See Ref. [180]).

10.3.5 ⋆ECDSA

ECDSA (as for Elliptic Curve Digital Signature Algorithm) is yet another variant of the ElGamal signature. It is dedicated to elliptic curves and is directly adapted from DSA. It is a standard from several organizations including NIST and ANSI (see Refs. [3,8]).

Public parameters: we use finite fields of two possible types: either a field of characteristic two or a large prime field. The public parameters consist of the field cardinality q, the selected field representation (in the characteristic two case, i.e. an irreducible polynomial over $\mathbf{Z}_2$), an elliptic curve defined by two field elements a and b, a prime number n larger than 2^{160}, and an element G of the elliptic curve of order n. The elliptic curve equation over $GF(q)$ is $y^2 + xy = x^3 + ax^2 + b$ in the characteristic two case and $y^2 = x^3 + ax + b$ in the prime field case. Public parameters are subject to many security criteria.

Setup: pick an integer d in $[1, n-1]$, compute $Q = dG$. Output $(K_p, K_s) = (Q, d)$.

Signature generation: pick k in $[1, n-1]$ at random and compute

$$(x_1, y_1) = kG$$
$$r = \overline{x_1} \bmod n$$
$$s = \frac{H(M) + dr}{k} \bmod n$$

Here $\overline{x_1}$ is simply a standard way to convert a field element x_1 into an integer. If $r = 0$ or $s = 0$, try again. Output the signature $\sigma = (r, s)$

Verification: check that $Q \neq O$, $Q \in C$, and $nQ = O$. Check that r and s are in $[1, n-1]$ and that $r = \overline{x_1} \bmod n$ for $(x_1, y_1) = u_1 G + u_2 Q$, $u_1 = \frac{H(M)}{s} \bmod n$, and $u_2 = \frac{r}{s} \bmod n$.

(See Fig. 10.8). The H hash function is the same standard hash function as usual, i.e. SHA-1.

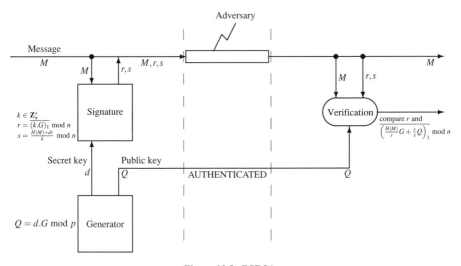

Figure 10.8. ECDSA.

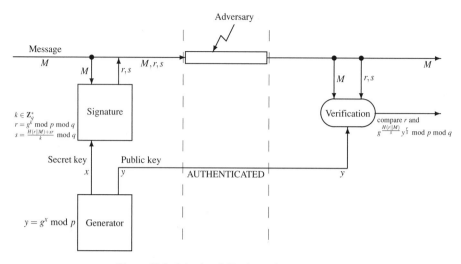

Figure 10.9. Pointcheval–Vaudenay signature scheme.

The difficulty with ECDSA is to deal with objects of many different types: elliptic curve points, field elements, integers, and of course bitstrings. The standard provides extensive details about how to represent and manipulate them.

10.3.6   Pointcheval–Vaudenay Signature

The Pointcheval–Vaudenay signature is yet another variant of DSS with a slight modification: we just have to compute $H(r\|M)$ instead of $H(M)$ (see Refs. [38, 147]). (See Fig. 10.9). This may look as a minor modification. It is actually not: with this modification, we can prove that the signature scheme is secure provided that

1. H behaves like a random function,
2. the discrete logarithm is hard,
3. $k \mapsto (g^k \bmod p) \bmod q$ is a one-way function.

(The last two conditions are actually necessary. The first one is still a reasonable assumption, but may be too strong.) None of the previous signature schemes had this strong security result. As we will see below, the security of the Schnorr signature is close to being formally proven under the hypothesis of the hardness of the discrete logarithm.

This variant was added in the ISO/IEC 14888 norm (Ref. [12]).

10.4   ★Toward Provable Security for Digital Signatures

10.4.1   ★From Interactive Proofs to Signatures

We have seen in Chapter 5 access control protocols with challenge and response. Similar protocols exist with asymmetric keys. They can be transformed into signature schemes.

A   B

pick $k, r = g^k \bmod p$

$\xrightarrow{\hspace{1cm} r\|\text{certificate for } y \hspace{1cm}}$

$\xleftarrow{\hspace{2cm} e \hspace{2cm}}$

pick $e, 1 \le e \le 2^t$

$s = ex + k \bmod q$

$\xrightarrow{\hspace{2cm} s \hspace{2cm}}$

check $ry^e \equiv g^s \pmod{p}$

Figure 10.10. The Schnorr identification protocol.

For instance, the Schnorr signature comes from the Schnorr identification protocol. This protocol is actually performed by the owner of the secret key in order to convince someone that he knows the secret key related to some public key. When we have a *certificate* from a *trusted authority*, stating that the public key is linked to some identity, we have an identification protocol. It works as follows.

Public parameters: p, q, g as in the Schnorr signature.
Setup: compute $K_s = x$ and $K_p = g^x \bmod p$ as in the Schnorr signature.
Interactive proof: in order to prove that A knows K_s to B, they proceed as follows (see Fig. 10.10).
  1. A picks k at random, computes a *commitment* $r = g^k \bmod p$ and sends it to B,
  2. B picks a *challenge* e at random such that $1 \le e \le 2^t$,
  3. A computes the *response* $s = ex + k \bmod q$ and sends it to B,
  4. B checks that $ry^e \equiv g^s \pmod{p}$.

The connection with the Schnorr signature is straightforward: the challenge e is simulated by a hash function with the commitment r and the message.

Let us first consider a simple case where a honest B always accepts when interacting with A. This means that A can compute the response to all potential challenges e, in particular to any two different e_1 and e_2. We can thus transform A into an extractor for the discrete logarithm x of y as follows. Let A generate r, and let us send her e_1. We obtain a successful response s_1 in return. Let us now restart A from the same internal state in order to generate r again, and let us now submit the challenge e_2. We obtain a successful response s_2 in return. Obviously we have

$$r \equiv g^{s_1} y^{-e_1} \equiv g^{s_2} y^{-e_2} \pmod{p}.$$

So $\frac{s_1 - s_2}{e_1 - e_2} \bmod q$ is a discrete logarithm of y in basis g. This means that if A successfully passes all identification challenges then she must be able to compute the discrete logarithm of y. Therefore there is no way for a malicious cheater to impersonate A to B with 100% chances without the ability to solve the discrete logarithm problem. We can prove a much stronger result, namely that there is no way to succeed with probability P without the ability to compute x.

Here is a more precise statement.

Theorem 10.1. *For any $P > 2^{1-t}$, we can transform a prover which succeeds the Schnorr Identification Protocol with a honest verifier with probability P and time complexity T into an algorithm which finds the secret key x in time complexity $O(T2^t/P)$.*

This is the standard way to prove that A must know x, otherwise fail the identification protocol with probability at least $1 - 2^{1-t}$. (Obviously, this statement makes sense when t is small because of the 2^t factor in the complexity reduction.)

The proof works as follows: let us assume that B follows the protocol correctly and that A succeeds with probability P to pass the final check. Clearly A must output a random r which only depends on the initial (random) state ρ of A (so let us denote it $r(\rho)$), and a value s which depends on some e and on ρ (so let us denote it $s(\rho, e)$). The probability is over the distribution of ρ and the distribution of e. Let $\Pr[\rho]$ be the probability of having ρ as an initial state. Let $1_{S(\rho,e)}$ be 1 if the final check succeeds with $r(\rho)$, e, and $s(\rho, e)$, and 0 if it fails. We have

$$P = \sum_{\rho,e} 2^{-t} 1_{S(\rho,e)} \Pr[\rho].$$

Let $N(\rho)$ denote the number of possible e's for which the protocol succeeds. We have

$$P = \sum_{\rho} 2^{-t} N(\rho) \Pr[\rho].$$

Clearly, by splitting the sum for $N(\rho) \le 1$, and $2^t \ge N(\rho) \ge 2$, we have

$$P \le 2^{-t} \Pr[N(\rho) \le 1] + \Pr[N(\rho) \ge 2].$$

Therefore we have

$$P \le 2^{-t} + \left(1 - 2^{-t}\right) \Pr[N(\rho) \ge 2]$$

hence $\Pr[N(\rho) \ge 2] \ge \frac{P-2^{-t}}{1-2^{-t}} \ge \frac{P}{2}$. We transform A as follows.

1. We generate r from a random ρ.
2. For all e's we compute $s(\rho, e)$ and we check if this succeeds.
3. If we have less than two succeeding e's, we try again. Otherwise, we have (e_1, s_1) and (e_2, s_2) such that

$$r \equiv g^{s_1} y^{-e_1} \equiv g^{s_2} y^{-e_2} \pmod{p}.$$

   We thus compute

$$x = \frac{s_1 - s_2}{e_1 - e_2} \bmod q.$$

Since with probability $\Pr[N(\rho) \ge 2]$ we obtain two succeeding e's, and that this probability is greater than $\frac{P}{2}$, this works within a complexity of $\mathcal{O}(2^t/P)$ times the complexity of A and B.

We emphasize that the security proof of the Schnorr identification protocol suffers from

- being meaningful for really small values of t,
- being valid when the verifier is honest only.

The first drawback makes the security result on the signature scheme impossible, because hash functions usually output $t \geq 128$ bits. The second drawback is reasonable for a digital signature, because the message (and therefore how the challenge will be generated out of the commitment) is decided before the commitment is made. However in real identification protocols, we must prove that no verifier can extract any useful information out of this protocol. This is still possible for really small t's, and the reason why it is possible is because we can actually cheat with probability 2^{-t}.

Indeed, we can make a prover A which succeeds with probability 2^{-t} without knowing the secret key:

1. A picks a random e_0 with $1 \leq e_0 \leq 2^t$ and a random $s \in Z_q$,
2. A computes $r = y^{-e_0} g^s \bmod p$ and sends it to B,
3. for any received challenge, A outputs s.

Clearly this succeeds when $e = e_0$. Therefore, if a cheater B can extract some information in order to break the system, we can run it with this cheater and retry every time it fails. Within a complexity factor of 2^t, this simulation with the cheater will break the scheme as well, but without knowing the secret key. Therefore, if a malicious verifier can extract some useful information from the protocol within a complexity $\mathcal{O}(T)$, then there exists an algorithm that produces the same information within a complexity $\mathcal{O}(2^t T)$.

The above argument is valid, for two reasons.

- The commitment is statistically indistinguishable from a right commitment: the distribution of $y^{-e_0} g^s \bmod p$ is clearly uniform in the subgroup spanned by g. Therefore, making a commitment like this will not change the behavior of the malicious verifier.
- The challenge e cannot depend on e_0: the distribution of $y^{-e_0} g^s \bmod p$ is also clearly independent from e_0 thanks to s, which is not revealed at this point. Therefore, the success probability is independent from (r, e), and actually equal to 2^{-t}.

We summarize all these properties by saying that the Schnorr identification scheme is a *zero-knowledge interactive proof* for small values of t. Security for higher values (in particular for the Schnorr signature) is an open problem.

In Chapter 11, we will see other identification protocols (like the Fiat–Shamir or the Guillou–Quisquater protocols). Transformation into signature schemes is straightforward: each time the verifier has to produce something, we generate it from a pseudorandom generator fed with the previous communications and the message to be signed.

10.4.2   ⋆Security in the Random Oracle Model

A further step forward to formal proofs of security was made by Jacques Stern and David Pointcheval. They formally proved the security of the ElGamal signature scheme in what is called the "random oracle model", demonstrating that it is hard for an adversary to existentially forge signatures, even with an access to the signing oracle. Note that this proof holds *on average* over the public parameter choice (i.e. the value of p and g) and not for *any* choice. As a matter of fact, the result by Pointcheval and Stern was presented at the same conference where the attack of Bleichenbacher was presented. (The latter indeed demonstrates that for some choices of p and g it is indeed very easy to forge a signature.) (See Refs. [33, 146]).

This proof technique was later adapted to other signature schemes. It also motivated the Pointcheval–Vaudenay one for which the proof argument works better and for any choice of public parameters. We provide here this demonstration.

The security proof relies on the assumption that the underlying hash function H is replaced by a truly random oracle. This is not a practical model but an idealized approximation of what happens in practice.

Let us formalize the Pointcheval–Vaudenay scheme with a random oracle by the following three algorithms.

Setup $\rightarrow$ (p, q, g, y, x): generate two prime numbers p and g such that q divides $p - 1$, an integer g which spans a subgroup of $\mathbf{Z}_p^*$ of order q. Pick a secret key $x \in \mathbf{Z}_q$. Compute the public key $y = g^x \bmod p$.

Sig$(M) \rightarrow (h, r, s)$: pick a random $k \in \mathbf{Z}_q^*$, compute $r = (g^k \bmod p) \bmod q$, query the oracle with $r \| M$ and obtain $h = H(r\|M)$, and compute $s = \frac{h+xr}{k} \bmod q$, the signature is $\sigma = (h, r, s)$.

Ver(M, h, r, s): query the oracle with $r\|M$ and check that $h = H(r\|M)$ and $r = \left(g^{\frac{h}{s} \bmod q} y^{\frac{r}{s} \bmod q} \bmod p\right) \bmod q$.

We will prove the following theorem.

Theorem 10.2. *We consider the three algorithms Setup, Sig, and Ver as defined above. We assume that the oracle H in the above algorithms is a random oracle which outputs elements of $\mathbf{Z}_q$. We let $\ell - 1$ denote the largest preimage set size for the $k \mapsto (g^k \bmod p) \bmod q$ mapping from $\mathbf{Z}_q^*$ to $\mathbf{Z}_q$. Let ε, T, and Q be arbitrary positive real numbers such that $\varepsilon \gg Q^2 \ell / q$. We say that $\mathcal{A}$ is a (ε, Q, T)-adversary if it is an algorithm which, given the output (p, q, g, y) from Setup, can query Sig or H at most Q times and output within a time less than T a (M, h, r, s) quadruplet such that M was never queried to Sig, and that the probability that Ver accepts the quadruplet is greater* *than ε. We can transform any (ε, Q, T)-adversary into an algorithm which, given the output (p, q, g, y) from Setup, outputs x such that $y = g^x$ mod p, with a complexity $\mathcal{O}\left(\frac{QT}{\varepsilon}\ell \log \ell\right)$, and a probability of success close to 1.*

Note that if $k \mapsto (g^k \bmod p) \bmod q$ looks like a random function, then we have $\ell = \mathcal{O}(\log q)$. Indeed, for a random function over $\mathbf{Z}_q$, there are less than $\frac{q^{c\log q}}{(c\log q)!}$ possible sets of $c \log q$ pairwise different elements and every single set is mapped onto a single value with probability $q^{1-c\log q}$. So the probability that such a set exists is less than $q/(c \log q)!$ This becomes very small for large q.

Proof. Let (M, h, r, s) be the output of $\mathcal{A}$. First of all, we notice that if $r||M$ has never been queried to H (neither directly nor by the Sig oracle), then the probability that $h = H(r||M)$ is $1/q$. If we replace $\mathcal{A}$ by an algorithm which decides to fail if $r||M$ was not queried, the new probability of success is greater than $\varepsilon - 1/q$, which can be approximated to ε. So from now on we assume that $r||M$ was always queried to H.

We also notice that there is no use for $\mathcal{A}$ to query H with some values which are already known, so we assume that every time $\mathcal{A}$ sends some query to H then it was never queried before to H and it cannot be written $r||M$ where M was queried to Sig before and r was a part of the output.

The first step of the proof consists of simulating the two oracles H and Sig by some probabilistic algorithms which produce the same statistic behavior. The simulator works by managing a list of declared $(u, H(u))$ pairs. Initially, the list is empty. Every time the adversary queries an oracle, the simulator uses the defined list, may insert a new pair, and may decide to abort the simulation. We will show that the probability to abort is negligible. Here is how the simulator works.

```
 1: if oracle H is queried then
 2:    let u be the query
 3:    pick a random h
 4:    insert (u, h) in the list
 5:    output h
 6: else
 7:    let M be the query
 8:    pick α, β ∈ Z*_q at random
 9:    r ← (g^α y^β mod p) mod q
10:    s ← r/β mod q
11:    h ← sα mod q
12:    if there is some (r||M, h) pair in the list then
13:       abort the simulation
14:    else
15:       insert (r||M, h) in the list
16:       output (h, r, s)
17:    end if
18: end if
```

Let $L = ((u_1, h_1), \ldots, (u_n, h_n))$ be the list of all known $h_i = H(u_i)$ values. Let L^* be the event that $h_i = H(u_i)$ for $i = 1, \ldots, n$ for the random oracle H. Obviously $\Pr[\text{output } h|L] = \Pr[H(u) = h|L^*]$ when we query H with u in the simulator. It is not more difficult to realize that

$$\Pr[\text{output } (h, r, s)|L] = \Pr[\text{Sig}(M) = (r, s) \text{ and } H(r||M) = h|L^*]$$

(assuming that no u_i is equal to $r||M$ when we query Sig with M in the simulator. Therefore we deduce that except when the simulator aborts, it perfectly simulates the two oracles. Since r is generated with probability up to $\mathcal{O}(\ell/q)$, the $r||M$ is equal to some u_i with probability up to $O(n(\log q)/q)$. The cases which are not simulated thus happen with probability less than $O(Q^2(\log q)/q)$, which can be neglected. We conclude this first step of our proof by saying that the adversary $\mathcal{A}$ running with the simulator will output a valid (M, h, r, s) quadruplet with probability at least $\varepsilon - O(Q^2(\log q)/q)$. By assuming that $\varepsilon \gg Q^2(\log q)/q$ we can simply say that it succeeds with probability at least ε.

The second step is known as the "forking lemma." We assume that every time the simulator for H wishes to pick a random value, it sequentially reads it from a tape ρ which is set up at the beginning. What we will do is run $\mathcal{A}$ with the simulator several times with some modified tape. More precisely, we re-run $\mathcal{A}$ with a tape which starts by the same numbers, but whose content has been overwritten starting from the value which is read at some crucial point. Indeed, for any initial random tape ρ which leads to a valid forgery, there is one crucial moment in the simulator when $r||M$ was a query to the H oracle. (Note that it cannot come from the query to the signing oracle, otherwise it would mean that M was queried to this oracle, which is forbidden.) We number the oracle calls from 1 to Q. Given a random tape ρ, for any i we let ρ_i be the prefix of ρ which consists of all values which have been used before the i-th query. We let $c(\rho)$ be the number of the oracle call when $r||M$ is queried to H. We let $\text{dist}(\rho)$ be $\rho_{c(\rho)}$. We intend to re-run $\mathcal{A}$ with a new tape $\text{dist}(\rho)||\rho'$ where ρ' is a new random sequence. Given a tape ρ we let $\text{succ}(\rho)$ be the event that $\mathcal{A}$ succeeds when initialized with ρ, and $\text{succ}_c(\rho)$ be the event that both $\text{succ}(\rho)$ and $c(\rho) = c$ occur. Note that cutting all possible ρ sequences at the oracle query times leads to a tree structure of depth Q. Given a truncated random tape v, we can consider the probability $f(v)$ that a random tape $\rho = v||\rho'$ leads to a successful run such that $\text{dist}(\rho) = v$. By using Lemma 10.3 we show that

$$\Pr_{\rho}\left[f(\text{dist}(\rho)) > \frac{\varepsilon}{2Q} \,\middle|\, \text{succ}(\rho) \right] \geq \frac{1}{2}.$$

In other words,

$$\Pr_{\rho}\left[\Pr_{\rho'}\left[\text{succ}_{c(\rho)}(\text{dist}(\rho)||\rho') \right] > \frac{\varepsilon}{2Q} \,\middle|\, \text{succ}(\rho) \right] \geq \frac{1}{2}.$$

This means that if we pick a successful ρ, there is a very high chance that $\text{dist}(\rho)||\rho'$ succeeds on the same crucial oracle call with probability at least $\frac{\varepsilon}{2Q}$. Starting from such a ρ, we can try $\frac{2Q}{\varepsilon} \log \ell$ values of ρ', and the probability to get at least one $\text{dist}(\rho)||\rho'$ tape such that $\text{succ}_{c(\rho)}(\text{dist}(\rho)||\rho')$ is at least $1 - \frac{1}{\ell}$. So if we iterate ℓ times, we obtain ℓ tapes with the same crucial oracle call and the same prefix tape with probability at least e^{-1}. To recapitulate, the algorithm works as follows.

1: Pick a random tape ρ until $\mathcal{A}$ succeeds
2: **for** $i = 1$ to ℓ **do**
3:   try $\frac{2Q}{\varepsilon} \log \ell$ values ρ' until $\text{dist}(\rho)||\rho'$ succeeds and $c(\text{dist}(\rho)||\rho') = c(\rho)$
     (if this does not work the algorithm fails)
4: **end for**
5: yield the (M, h, r, s) quadruplets corresponding to the ℓ found values ρ'

This algorithm succeeds with a constant probability and yields ℓ quadruplets. We notice that the crucial oracle call is the one where $r||M$ is queried to H, so all quadruplets have the same r and M. So we have ℓ quadruplets (M, h_i, r, s_i) such that $r = \left(g^{\frac{h_i}{s_i} \bmod q} y^{\frac{r}{s_i} \bmod q} \bmod p \right) \bmod q$.

The third step uses the fact that $k \mapsto (g^k \bmod p) \bmod q$ has no preimage set of size ℓ. This implies that we must have

$$\frac{h_i + xr}{s_i} \equiv \frac{h_j + xr}{s_j} \pmod{q}$$

for some $1 \le i < j \le \ell$. This leads to

$$x = \frac{h_i s_j - h_j s_i}{r(s_i - s_j)} \bmod q.$$

We can try all combinations of (i, j) until this formula gives x.   □

Lemma 10.3. *We consider a finite tree and a mapping* dist *which maps any leaf λ to one of its ancestors* $\text{dist}(\lambda)$. *We call it a distinguished ancestor. We assume we are given a distribution which defines a random descent from the root of the tree to a random leaf λ. We let* $\text{visit}(v)$ *be the event that the descent goes through v, i.e. that v is an ancestor of λ. We let* $\text{succ}(\lambda)$ *be an event related to a leaf λ of the tree. When it occurs we say that λ is successful. We let $p = \Pr[\text{succ}(\lambda)]$ and $\bar{d} = E(\text{depth}(\lambda))$ for a random leaf λ. Finally, we let $f(v) = \Pr[\text{succ}(\lambda)$ and $\text{dist}(\lambda) = v|\text{visit}(v)]$. For any real number $\theta > 0$, we have*

$$\Pr_{\lambda}\left[f(\text{dist}(\lambda)) > (1 - \theta)\frac{p}{\bar{d}} \,\middle|\, \text{succ}(\lambda) \right] \ge \theta.$$

This lemma means that within $\Theta(p^{-1}\theta^{-1})$ trials we can find with high probability a successful leaf λ such that $f(v) > (1 - \theta)p/\bar{d}$ for $v = \text{dist}(\lambda)$, i.e. a subtree in which random leaves are successful with a fixed distinguished ancestor v with probability at least $(1 - \theta)p/\bar{d}$.

Proof. We let G be the set of all good nodes v such that $f(v) > (1 - \theta)p/\bar{d}$. We have

$$\Pr[\text{dist}(\lambda) \notin G | \text{succ}(\lambda)] = \sum_{v \notin G} \Pr[\text{dist}(\lambda) = v | \text{succ}(\lambda)].$$

Since visit(v) is included in dist(λ) = v, we have

$$\Pr[\text{dist}(\lambda) = v | \text{succ}(\lambda)] = \Pr[\text{visit}(v)] \frac{\Pr[\text{succ}(\lambda) \text{ and dist}(\lambda) = v | \text{visit}(v)]}{\Pr[\text{succ}(\lambda)]}$$

$$= \Pr[\text{visit}(v)] \frac{f(v)}{p}.$$

Hence

$$\Pr[\text{dist}(\lambda) \notin G | \text{succ}(\lambda)] \leq \frac{1 - \theta}{\bar{d}} \sum_{v \notin G} \Pr[\text{visit}(v)]$$

$$\leq \frac{1 - \theta}{\bar{d}} \sum_{v} \Pr[\text{visit}(v)].$$

The last sum is equal to $\bar{d}$, thus $\Pr[\text{dist}(\lambda) \notin G | \text{succ}(\lambda)] \leq 1 - \theta$. We deduce $\Pr[\text{dist}(\lambda) \in G | \text{succ}(\lambda)] \geq \theta$. $\qquad\square$

10.5 Exercises

Exercise 10.1. *Show that if we can compute the discrete logarithm of y in the subgroup of* $\mathbf{Z}_p^*$ *spanned by g, then we can break the ElGamal signature, the Schnorr signature, and the DSA signature.*

Exercise 10.2. *Prove that for some pair of two messages M and M',* $q = H(M) - H(M')$ *is a valid prime which can lead to some* (p, q, g) *DSA public parameters. In this case, prove that any signature of M is also a valid signature of M'.[2]*

Exercise 10.3. *In the DSA signature scheme, show that if we can invert the* $k \mapsto (g^k \bmod p) \bmod q$ *function, then we can break the scheme.*

---

[2] This exercise was inspired by Ref. [180].

Exercise 10.4. *Define a signature scheme which is similar to the ElGamal signature scheme, but which uses an elliptic curve modulo p instead of the $\mathbf{Z}_p^*$ group. Precisely describe the setup, signature, and verification algorithms.*
(Hint: Assume that we can easily compute the order of an elliptic curve.)

If we now want to design an algorithm similar to the Schnorr signature, we have to face a new problem. What is this problem?

Exercise 10.5. *Let us assume that a lazy signer has precomputed one (k, r) pair for the DSS signature scheme and that he always uses the same one. Show how to attack him and recover his secret key.*

Exercise 10.6. *Let us assume that a lazy signer has one precomputed (k, r) pair for the Schnorr signature. Each time he needs to sign, he uses the precomputed signature and replaces (k, r) by $(2k \bmod q, r^2 \bmod p)$. What is the complexity gain? Show how to attack him and recover his secret key.*

Exercise 10.7. *The DSA scheme is nondeterministic. Let us assume that the signer now chooses k by using a pseudorandom generator fed with a secret key and the message to be signed. Show that a verifier which has the secret key can efficiently verify the signature.*

Exercise 10.8 (Ong–Schnorr–Shamir). *Precisely define a public-key signature scheme such that there is a common large composite modulus n (of unknown factorization), a public key $K_p = k$, a secret key $K_s = s$ such that $s^2 \equiv -k \pmod{n}$, and where the verification of a signature $\sigma = (x, y)$ consists of checking that $x^2 + ky^2 \equiv H(m) \pmod{n}$.*[3]

(Note: This is insecure. It has been broken by Pollard and Schnorr.)[4]

Exercise 10.9. *Let us assume that we have n ElGamal signatures to verify. We need to check n triplets (M_i, r_i, s_i), where M_i is the message and (r_i, s_i) is the signature. We assume all signatures come from the same signer and correspond to the same public key y and the same p, g parameters.*

What is the complexity of verifying all the signatures sequentially in terms of the size ℓ of p in bits?

---

[3] This exercise was inspired by Ref. [144].
[4] See Ref. [151].

Let A be a set of N pairwise relatively prime numbers from $\mathbf{Z}^*_{p-1}$ which are smaller than B. We pick n pairwise different numbers $a_1, \ldots, a_n$ in A. We define

$$R = r_1^{a_1} \ldots r_n^{a_n} \bmod p$$

$$G = a_1 \frac{H(M_1)}{s_1} + \cdots + a_n \frac{H(M_n)}{s_n} \bmod (p-1)$$

$$Y = a_1 \frac{r_1}{s_1} + \cdots + a_n \frac{r_n}{s_n} \bmod (p-1).$$

Show that $y^Y R \equiv g^G \pmod{p}$ if all signatures are correct. What is the complexity of this computation in terms of n, ℓ, and B? Show that if one signature is incorrect, then this property holds only with a probability at most N^{-2}

11

⋆Cryptographic Protocols

Content

⋆**Zero-knowledge:** Fiat–Shamir, Feige–Fiat–Shamir
⋆**Secret sharing:** threshold scheme, perfect schemes
⋆**Special purpose signatures:** undeniable signatures

In this chapter we review other particular cryptographic protocols. Although they have a minor practical relevance when compared to encryption or signature, they beautifully illustrate how cryptography can be a fun and a highly technical science.

11.1 ⋆Zero-Knowledge

All access control protocols that we have seen so far leak some information (which is not necessarily useful). For instance, password access controls require to disclose the password. Challenge–response protocols aim at proving the knowledge of a password, but require to disclose responses for some given challenges. Complexity theory can however show that it is possible to make access control without disclosing any information through the puzzling notion of *zero-knowledge* proof of knowledge. This is made possible by the power of interaction.

This puzzling concept was first introduced by Shafi Goldwasser, Silvio Micali, and Charles Rackoff in the eighties (see Ref. [78]). The concept of power of interaction was further extended by Adi Shamir who proved that all languages which can be accepted by an interactive proof are actually all languages which can be accepted by a Turing machine limited by a polynomially bounded memory space. This result was stated by the equation IP=PSPACE (for "Interactive Proof" and "Polynomial space"; see Ref. [166]).

11.1.1 ⋆Notion of Zero-Knowledge

In an interactive proof of knowledge, a *prover* aims at convincing a *verifier* that he knows some secret key, by his ability to solve some equations. For instance, he proves that he knows p and q such that $N = pq$ by his ability to compute square roots modulo N. This can be used, for instance, for identification schemes: assuming that the knowledge of p and q such that $N = pq$ is associated to some identity I_N, the prover can prove that he is I_N. The interactive proof of knowledge is defined as follows.

The setup algorithm. This generates a secret key K_s to be given to the prover and a public key K_p to be broadcasted.

The prover and the verifier specifications. It defines two probabilistic algorithms and the interaction between them. At the end, the verifier must accept or reject the proof.

The interactive proof must fulfill the following requirements.

Completeness: If the prover and the verifier behave as specified, the verifier always accepts the proof.

Soundness: There exists a threshold probability τ such that for any probability $p > \tau$, there exists an *extractor* which transforms any possible prover which is accepted by the specified verifier with probability p into an algorithm which outputs the secret key. (The transformation must however be "efficient.")

This intuitively means that any successful cheater must be able to recover the secret. The extractor is actually a machine which can play with the cheater and reset its internal state.

Zero-knowledge: There exists a *simulator* who transforms any verifier (who tries to extract some information from the honest prover) into an algorithm which outputs a possible history of the protocol with the same probability distribution as the history generated by the interaction between the honest prover and the verifier. (The transformation must however be "efficient.")

This intuitively means that if a verifier can use the protocol in order to extract some useful information out of the prover, then he must be able to do the same with the simulator. Therefore he gains no advantage in interacting with the prover: the prover reveals zero-knowledge.

11.1.2 ⋆*The Basic Fiat–Shamir Protocol*

We first give a simplified description of the zero-knowledge protocol which was invented by Amos Fiat and Adi Shamir (see Ref. [68]). This basic version is actually formally equivalent to the original protocol by Shafi Goldwasser, Silvio Micali, and Charles Rackoff (see Ref. [78]).

Setup of public parameters: We generate two prime numbers p and q. We let $n = pq$ and we then erase p and q. We also let t be a security parameter (typically, $t = 20$).

Setup of the keys: The secret key consists of a random element $s \in \mathbf{Z}_n^*$. The public key consists of $v = 1/s^2 \bmod n$.

Protocol: Perform t rounds in which

1. the prover picks a random r and sends a *commitment* $x = r^2 \bmod n$ to the verifier,
2. the verifier sends a random bit e as a *challenge* to the prover,
3. the prover sends the *response* $y = rs^e \bmod n$ to the verifier,
4. the verifier aborts the protocol and rejects unless we have $y^2 v^e \equiv x \pmod{n}$.

After t successful rounds, the verifier accepts.

Prover   Verifier

pick r, $x = r^2 \bmod n$ $\xrightarrow{\qquad v, x \qquad}$

$\xleftarrow{\qquad e \qquad}$ pick $e = 0$ or 1

$y = rs^e \bmod n$ $\xrightarrow{\qquad y \qquad}$

check $y^2 v^e \equiv x \pmod{n}$

Figure 11.1. One round of the basic Fiat–Shamir protocol.

See Fig. 11.1.) This interactive proof is obviously complete: if the prover and the verifier behave as specified, then the final check of each round leads to

$$y^2 v^e \equiv r^2 (s^2 v)^e \equiv r^2 \equiv x \pmod{n}.$$

The difference between the Goldwasser–Micali–Rackoff protocol and this version of the Fiat–Shamir protocol is that the former was stated as a "zero-knowledge proof of membership," i.e. a proof that v is a quadratic residue, and the latter was stated as a "zero-knowledge proof of knowledge," i.e. a proof that the prover owns a square root of v. The latter version is more practical from a cryptographic perspective since one frequently has to identify itself by some kind of proof of ownership. People traditionally say that the protocol is not completely zero-knowledge and does reveal one bit of information: that v is a square. If v was not a square, the protocol would eventually fail. Since distinguishing squares from non-squares is hard in $\mathbf{Z}_n^*$, this is actually one bit of information. This is however not a weakness, because people who want to retrieve information are dishonest verifiers, and people who choose v not to be square are dishonest provers. So we do not really care about what kind of interaction comes out between a dishonest prover and a dishonest verifier.

Soundness is easy: First of all, we notice that if the prover is able to answer the two possible challenges $e = 0$ and $e = 1$ in a single round with commitment x, it means that he can compute y_0 and y_1 such that

$$y_0^2 \equiv x \equiv y_1^2 v \pmod{n}.$$

Therefore, he can produce $z = y_0 / y_1 \bmod n$ such that $z^2 \equiv v \pmod{n}$. Let us now consider a dishonest prover who is able to pass the protocol with probability $p = 2^{-t} + \varepsilon$ and let us construct an extractor. Let p_0 be the probability that the prover is not able to answer both challenges in any round of a protocol. Clearly, we have $p \leq p_0 2^{-t} + (1 - p_0)$, hence

$$p_0 \leq 1 - \frac{\varepsilon}{1 - 2^{-t}} \leq 1 - \varepsilon.$$

Therefore, if we iterate $\frac{1}{\varepsilon}$ rounds, we have a probability greater than $(1 - \varepsilon)^{\frac{1}{\varepsilon}}$ which is approximately $1 - e^{-1}$ that the prover can answer two challenges in a single round. The extractor works as follows: we iterate many times the protocol with a honest verifier. In each round, we reset the prover and we ask the other challenge. If the prover happens to answer both challenges, then we extract z as above, otherwise we keep on running the protocol. Our analysis shows that we have a fair chance of extracting the secret within an order of magnitude of $\frac{1}{\varepsilon}$ iterations.

It is easy to cheat with probability 2^{-t}: in each round, we start by predicting the challenge e_0. Then we generate $x = y^2 v^{e_0} \bmod n$ for a random y and take it as the commitment. If the challenge e chosen by the verifier is equal to e_0, then we can answer it by y. Otherwise it fails.

This inspires the simulator: we play with the malicious verifier by trying to predict e_0 and picking $x = y^2 v^{e_0} \bmod n$ for a random y. The simulator sends x to the verifier and receives e. If $e = e_0$, the simulator can produce y. Otherwise the simulator resets the verifier and tries again. It can be easily checked that both x is uniformly generated among all quadratic residues modulo n. In addition, we can easily check that the generated x in the simulation is independent from e_0. Therefore no malicious verifier can pick e and have it equal to e_0 with probability different from $\frac{1}{2}$. This means that the simulation works with probability $\frac{1}{2}$. If it fails, we can just reset the verifier to the state before the commitment, and try again with other choices for (e_0, y). The generated (x, e, y) protocol history will obviously get the same distribution as for the right interaction between the honest prover and the malicious verifier. Therefore the verifier has no advantage in playing with the real prover (but a complexity factor due to the probability of failures in the simulation of Step 2) and the protocol discloses zero-knowledge.

An additional interesting property of the Fiat–Shamir protocol is that keys can be *identity-based*: in the Schnorr identification protocol, the key was $y = g^x \bmod p$, and we had to produce a certificate that y actually corresponds to some given identity. Here, the certificate can be included in the secret key. Actually, if the certificate issuing authority keeps p and q, it can choose v as the formatted identity string and compute one square root for s to give it to the prover. Here, v is bound to correspond to some identity.

11.1.3   ⋆The Feige–Fiat–Shamir Protocol

The basic Fiat–Shamir protocol has been improved (see Ref. [66]). Here are the specifications of the Feige–Fiat–Shamir protocol.

> *Setup of public parameters*: We generate two prime numbers p and q such that $p \equiv q \equiv 3 \pmod 4$. We let $n = pq$ and we then erase p and q. (Note that -1 is not a quadratic residue modulo both p and q. Therefore the Jacobi symbol $(-1/n)$ is equal to $+1$.) We also let k and t be two security parameters (typically, $k = 5$, $t = 4$).
>
> *Setup of the keys*: The secret key consists of k random elements $s_i \in \mathbf{Z}_n^*$ for $i = 1, \ldots, k$ and k random bits $b_1, \ldots, b_k$. The public key consists of all $v_i = (-1)^{b_i}/s_i^2 \bmod n$. (All v_i are random residues with Jacobi symbol equal to $+1$.)

Prover   Verifier

pick r, $x = \pm r^2 \bmod n$ $\xrightarrow{\quad v_1, \cdots, v_k, x \quad}$

$\xleftarrow{\quad e_1, \cdots, e_k \quad}$ pick $e_1, \cdots, e_k = 0$ or 1

$y = r s_1^{e_1} \cdots s_k^{e_k} \bmod n$ $\xrightarrow{\quad y \quad}$

check $y^2 v_1^{e_1} \cdots v_k^{e_k} \equiv \pm x \pmod{n}$

Figure 11.2. One round of the Feige–Fiat–Shamir protocol.

Protocol: Perform t rounds in which

1. the prover picks a random r and sends a *commitment* $x = \pm r^2 \bmod n$ to the verifier,
2. the verifier sends random bits $e_1, \ldots, e_k$ as a *challenge* to the prover,
3. the prover sends the *response* $y = r s_1^{e_1} \ldots s_k^{e_k} \bmod n$ to the verifier,
4. the verifier aborts the protocol and rejects unless $y^2 v_1^{e_1} \ldots v_k^{e_k} \equiv \pm x \pmod{n}$.

(See Fig. 11.2.) After t successful rounds, the verifier accepts.

This interactive proof is obviously complete: if the prover and the verifier behave as specified, then the final check of each round leads to

$$y^2 v_1^{e_1} \cdots v_k^{e_k} \equiv r^2 (s_1^2 v_1)^{e_1} \ldots (s_k^2 v_k)^{e_k} \equiv r^2 (-1)^{b_1 + \cdots + b_k} \equiv \pm x \pmod{n}.$$

It is also easy to cheat with probability 2^{-k} in each iteration (thus with probability 2^{-kt}): if we can predict the challenge $e_1^0, \ldots, e_k^0$ (which we can with probability 2^{-k}), we can just pick a random response y and compute the commitment $x = \pm y^2 v_1^{e_1^0} \ldots v_k^{e_k^0} \bmod n$ at random. This property is actually used for proving the zero-knowledge property.

Let G be the subgroup of $\mathbf{Z}_n^*$ of all z such that the Jacobi symbol (z/n) is $+1$. We notice that the x generated by the right prover is a random element of G with uniform distribution. If we predict to have a challenge e^0 and we generate x as above, we also obtain a random $x \in G$ with uniform distribution, which is further independent from the guessed challenge e^0: let v^{e^0} denote $v_1^{e_1^0} \ldots v_k^{e_k^0} \bmod n$. We have

$$\Pr_{x,e}[x, e] = \frac{1}{2} \Pr_{y,e}[\pm y^2 = x | v^e, e] = \frac{1}{2} \Pr_y[\pm y^2 = x | v^e] \Pr_e[e] = \frac{1}{\#G} \Pr_e[e].$$

Therefore the generated x is independent from the guessed e^0. One problem is that the challenge e may be chosen by the malicious verifier with an unusual distribution, depending on x. But since x is independent from e^0, which is moreover chosen with the uniform distribution, the probability $\Pr[e = e^0 | x]$ must be 2^{-k}. Therefore if we play with the verifier and make a reset after each failure, we can simulate one round after about 2^k trials. We thus generate (x, e, y) with the same distribution as the real interaction between the honest prover and the same verifier. Therefore the verifier gets no important advantage in playing with the prover: he can just play with the simulator. (The complexity factor is about 2^k because of the potential failures.)

In order to prove the soundness, we first notice that if the dishonest prover can answer to two different questions $e = (e_1, \ldots, e_k)$ and $e' = (e'_1, \ldots, e'_k)$ for the same commitment x, then he can produce y and y' such that

$$x \equiv \pm y^2 v_1^{e_1} \ldots v_k^{e_k} \equiv \pm (y')^2 v_1^{e'_1} \ldots v_k^{e'_k} \quad (\text{mod } n)$$

thus he can solve

$$\pm (y/y')^2 \equiv v_1^{e'_1 - e_1} \ldots v_k^{e'_k - e_k} \quad (\text{mod } n).$$

Since this does not necessarily require the full knowledge of the secret key, we just say that we consider the scheme as broken if one can express a product of the v_i's with powers 0, $+1$, or -1 (with at least one nonzero power) in a $\pm z^2 \bmod n$ way. We have thus proven that provided that this problem is hard, no dishonest prover can answer to two different challenges.

Let us now assume that one prover can pass the protocol with probability $2^{-kt} + \varepsilon$. We can prove that after $\frac{1}{\varepsilon}$ iterations of the protocol there is a fair amount of chance that the prover is able to answer to at least two different challenges in a single round. Therefore an extractor can break the above problem.

11.2   ⋆Secret Sharing

Sometimes, it is necessary to be really paranoid for access control. A typical example is nuclear weapon access. We must not provide access to this dangerous power to anyone who may be the victim of a human failure such as death, insanity, bribery, blackmail, etc. Fiction literature is quite inventive on this issue. For this we thus need to have independent control and backup solutions. Let us say, for example, that access is provided only if one of the following conditions are met

- the president and the head of the parliament agree
- the president and the chief of the army agree
- the vice president, the head of the parliament, and the chief of the army agree
- and others.

This list of conditions actually defines an *access structure*.

Cryptography formalizes this problem as follows: there is an access control secret key S which is *shared* among several participants (each participant has a *share*), and only a few combinations of participants enable the reconstruction of S by putting their shares together. These cryptographic schemes are called *secret sharing schemes*.

We can illustrate it by an easy case: when the key is shared among n participants who all need to cooperate in order to reconstruct S. In this case we can give a random $S_i = X_i$ as a share to the i-th participant for $i = 1, \ldots, n - 1$, and give $S \oplus X_1 \oplus \cdots \oplus X_{n-1}$ to the n-th participant. In this case no proper subset of the n participants can reconstruct S. In fact, no proper subset of the n participants can learn any information about S.

11.2.1 ⋆The Shamir Threshold Scheme

Adi Shamir proposed the first secret sharing scheme with an elaborate access structure (see Ref. [163]). This secret sharing scheme allows to share S among n participants so that any subset of t participants can reconstruct S, but no subset of at most $t - 1$ participants learn any information about S. Here t is called the *threshold*.

We have already seen the $t = n$ case.

Another easy case is $t = 1$: we just give $S_i = S$ as a share to the i-th participant.

Let us start with the $t = 2$ case. We now assume that S is encoded as an element of a field $\mathbf{K}$. We also assume that each participant has a non-zero identity string x_i which is also a field element. Let A be a random element of $\mathbf{K}$ with uniform distribution. We define $S_i = Ax_i + S$. For any user, the share distribution is uniform, and independent of S. Therefore, no single user can reconstruct S. Furthermore, any two users x_i and x_j can reconstruct S by

$$S = S_i - \frac{S_i - S_j}{x_i - x_j} x_i.$$

The system is depicted in Fig. 11.3. For a user who corresponds to x_3, the system is depicted by a straight line which goes through the (x_3, S_3) point, but the user has no clue which line it is. If another user joins (say x_6) they can together reconstruct the straight line and deduce S.

Generalization is now straightforward. We let $A_1, \ldots, A_{t-1}$ be independent randomly distributed field elements. We define $S_i = A_{t-1}x_i^{t-1} + \cdots + A_1 x_i + S$. We can define $P(x) = A_{t-1}x^{t-1} + \cdots + A_1 x + S$ and we have $S_i = P(x_i)$. For any t participants, we have t points (x_i, S_i) on the graph of the polynomial mapping $P(x)$, which is of degree less than t, and therefore we can reconstruct it by interpolation. Indeed, putting the $x_{i_1}, \ldots, x_{i_t}$ shares together, the polynomial is

$$P(x) = \sum_{j=1}^{t} S_{i_j} \prod_{k \neq i_j} \frac{x - x_k}{x_{i_j} - x_k}.$$

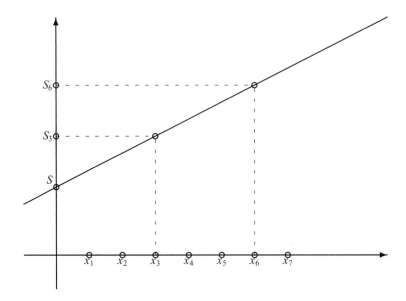

Figure 11.3. Shamir threshold secret sharing scheme with $t = 2$.

(It is easy to check that this polynomial maps x_i onto S_i, therefore $P(x)$ minus this polynomial has at least t roots $x_{i_1}, \ldots, x_{i_t}$. Since it is of degree at most $t - 1$, the difference must be zero, so this must be the $P(x)$ polynomial.) The interpolation now yields $S = P(0)$. Finally, the reconstruction formula is simply

$$S = \sum_{j=1}^{t} S_{i_j} \prod_{\substack{1 \le k \le t \\ k \ne j}} \frac{x_k}{x_k - x_{i_j}}.$$

It is by far more technical to prove that no set of $t - 1$ participants have any knowledge about S. Before doing this, we need more theory.

11.2.2   ⋆Perfect Secret Sharing Schemes

Here we treat the secret S and the shares S_i as random variables. We use again the Shannon entropy.

Definition 11.1. *Let n be an integer and let Γ be a set of subsets of $\{1, \ldots, n\}$. A secret sharing scheme among n participants $P_1, \ldots, P_n$ and based on an access structure Γ is said to be perfect when*

$$\forall A \ (H(S|S_i; i \in A) = 0 \iff A \in \Gamma)$$
$$\forall A \ (H(S|S_i; i \in A) = H(S) \iff A \notin \Gamma)$$

where S is the secret and S_i is the share of P_i.

Intuitively, the access structure is the set of all subsets of participants who can reconstruct S. If a subset A of participants can reconstruct S, putting their shares together provides a zero entropy to S, which is expressed by $H(S|S_i; i \in A) = 0$. The secret sharing scheme is said to be perfect when no subset A of participants which is not in Γ can gain any information on S by putting their shares together, which is expressed by $H(S|S_i; i \in A) = H(S)$. This last condition is very similar to the notion of *perfect secrecy* which was used for encryption.

We can now formalize the security result of the Shamir secret sharing scheme.

Theorem 11.2. *For any threshold t, the Shamir threshold secret sharing scheme is perfect, with the access structure which consists of all subsets of at least t participants.*

We have already seen how to reconstruct S as long as we have at least t shares. Therefore the entropy of S is zero given these shares.

We should now prove that for any $i_1, \ldots, i_{t-1}$, the distribution of S restricted to values of $S_{i_1}, \ldots, S_{i_{t-1}}$ is still uniform. We know (thanks to interpolation) that the function which maps $(S, A_1, \ldots, A_{t-1})$ to $(S, S_{i_1}, \ldots, S_{i_{t-1}})$ is one to one. This means that for any $(s, s_{i_1}, \ldots, s_{i_{t-1}})$, the probability that we have $S = s$ and $S_{i_j} = s_{i_j}$ simultaneously is $(\#\mathbf{K})^{-t}$. Now we have

$$\Pr[S_{i_j} = s_{i_j}; j = 1, \ldots, t-1] = \sum_s \Pr[S = s, S_{i_j} = s_{i_j}; j = 1, \ldots, t-1]$$

$$= (\#\mathbf{K})^{-t+1}$$

and

$$\Pr[S = s | S_{i_j} = s_{i_j}; j = 1, \ldots, t-1] = (\#\mathbf{K})^{-1}.$$

Therefore the distribution of S is still uniform when we fixed $S_{i_1}, \ldots, S_{i_{t-1}}$: we gained no information by having these shares only.

11.2.3 ⋆Access Structure of Perfect Secret Sharing Schemes

An interesting question is for which access structure does a perfect secret sharing scheme exist? We have already seen that it exists for a threshold access structure, thanks to the Shamir scheme. Obviously, if Γ is an access structure for which there exists a perfect secret sharing scheme, Γ must fulfill the following requirement.

For any $A \in \Gamma$ and any B such that $A \subset B$, we have $B \in \Gamma$. (If we can reconstruct S from the shares of A, we can still do it with more shares in B.)

We call this the monotonicity property.

A natural question now is: Is any set of subsets with the monotonicity property an access structure for a perfect secret sharing scheme? This question is addressed in Section 11.2.4.

Before continuing we define the notion of access structure spanned by a given set of subsets. Given a set of subsets Γ_0, we define $\Gamma = \langle \Gamma_0 \rangle$ as the set of all supersets of any set in Γ_0. This clearly has the monotonicity property. It is also clearly the smallest set of subsets with the monotonicity property which includes Γ_0. For this reason we say that Γ is spanned by Γ_0.

11.2.4   ⋆The Benaloh–Leichter Secret Sharing Scheme

The *Benaloh–Leichter* secret sharing scheme enables the construction of a perfect secret sharing scheme for any access structure with a monotonicity property (see Ref. [27]). It works as follows.

1. Given an access structure Γ with the monotonicity property, we first express Γ as an algebraic expression with only $\cup$ and $\cap$ operations from all Γ_i access structures defined as follows: Γ_i is the set of all participant subsets which include the i-th participant. In other words, $\Gamma_i = \langle \{i\} \rangle$.
2. To each subexpression we recursively attach variables in a top–down way:
   - if X is attached to some subexpression $t \cup t'$, we attach X to both t and t',
   - if X is attached to some subexpression $t \cap t'$, we attach a new random variable Y to t and $X - Y$ to t'.
3. For each participant i we collect all variables attached to occurrences of Γ_i, and we define them as the share of the participant.

We have the following result.

Theorem 11.3. *The above construction builds a perfect secret sharing scheme of access structure Γ.*

As an example, let us define a perfect secret sharing scheme among a set of four participants P_1, P_2, P_3, P_4 such that

- P_1 and P_2 can reconstruct the secret,
- P_1 and P_3 can reconstruct the secret,
- P_2, P_3, and P_4 can reconstruct the secret.

Clearly, the access structure expresses into

$$\Gamma = ((\Gamma_1 \cap \Gamma_2) \cup (\Gamma_1 \cap \Gamma_3)) \cup ((\Gamma_2 \cap \Gamma_3) \cap \Gamma_4)$$

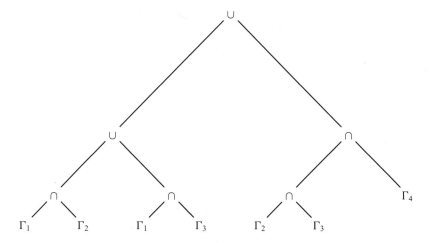

Figure 11.4. Example for an access structure term.

as drawn in Fig. 11.4. We start by attaching S to the whole expression Γ. It is written as a $\cup$ between $(\Gamma_1 \cap \Gamma_2) \cup (\Gamma_1 \cap \Gamma_3)$ and $(\Gamma_2 \cap \Gamma_3) \cap \Gamma_4$. So we attach S to both terms. Similarly, in the former term, we attach S to $\Gamma_1 \cap \Gamma_2$ and $\Gamma_1 \cap \Gamma_3$. We have thus three terms to which S is attached. For the first one $\Gamma_1 \cap \Gamma_2$, we attach W to Γ_1 and $S - W$ to Γ_2. For the second one $\Gamma_1 \cap \Gamma_3$, we attach X to Γ_1 and $S - X$ to Γ_3. For the third one $(\Gamma_2 \cap \Gamma_3) \cap \Gamma_4$ we attach Y to $\Gamma_2 \cap \Gamma_3$ and $S - Y$ to Γ_4. It thus remains to attach Z to Γ_2 and $Y - Z$ to Γ_3. To summarize, we have two occurrences of Γ_1 to which are attached W and X, we have two occurrences of Γ_2 to which are attached $S - W$ and Z, we have two occurrences of Γ_3 to which are attached $S - X$ and $Y - Z$, and we have one occurrence of Γ_4 to which is attached $S - Y$. Therefore we define the share

$$S_1 = (W, X)$$
$$S_2 = (S - W, Z)$$
$$S_3 = (S - X, Y - Z)$$
$$S_4 = S - Y$$

where W, X, Y, Z are independent uniformly distributed random variables. We can, for instance, check that P_1 and P_2 can reconstruct S because they have W and $S - W$. But P_2 and P_3, for instance, cannot reconstruct S because $(S - W, Z, S - X, Y - Z)$ is equivalent to $(S - W, X - W, Y, Z)$ which gives no clue about S.

11.3 ⋆Special Purpose Digital Signatures

In this section we list a few important variants of digital signature schemes.

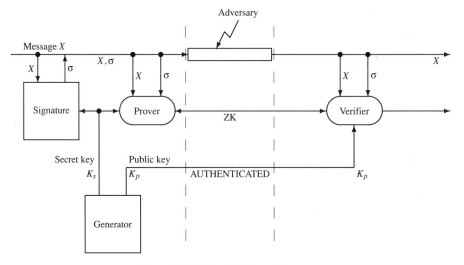

Figure 11.5. Undeniable digital signature.

11.3.1 ⋆Undeniable Signature

In classical digital signature schemes, anyone who has the public key of the signer is able to verify whether a given signature is valid or not. This property is called *universal verifiability*. Sometimes, signers want to keep private their signatures and do not want to have a universally verifiable signature. Another kind of signature proposed by David Chaum and Hans van Antwerpen, called *invisible signature*, makes it impossible for anyone to verify whether the signature is valid or not, and even to associate it to the signer, but a special interactive process which requires the cooperation of the signer would make it possible (see Ref. [45]). In such a case, it could be easy for the signer who wants to deny his signature to simply claim that a signature is invalid. But we want to prevent dishonest signers to repudiate their own signatures. This is why we usually call these signatures *undeniable* signatures. The name may be quite confusing because all signatures are aimed to be undeniable. Indeed, a classical signature is undeniable because of the universal verifiability. Some authors prefer to talk about invisible signatures instead of undeniable signatures, but since the latter is quite widely used we will stick to this name.

Undeniable signatures consist of several algorithms. As for the classical signatures, there is a key pair generation algorithm and a signature algorithm. The verification algorithm is replaced by an interactive protocol between the signer and the verifier as depicted in Fig. 11.5. Actually, the verification is replaced by two protocols: one which is used for the signature confirmation and one which is used for the signature denial. Of course, it is assumed to be impossible to make existential forgeries, and to distinguish valid signatures from invalid ones. Additionally, it must be impossible for the prover to successfully run the confirmation protocol when the signature is invalid, or to successfully run the denial protocol when the signature is valid. Furthermore,

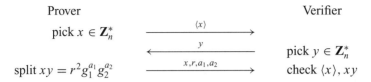

Figure 11.6. MOVA key validation protocol.

malicious verifiers should learn no other information from the protocols but the validity or invalidity of signatures.

As an example we describe here the MOVA scheme designed by Jean Monnerat and Serge Vaudenay which is based on quadratic residuosity.[1] It depends on several security parameters m, t, k, ℓ. In a typical setting we can propose $m = t = k = \ell = 30$.

Key setup. We take two different odd prime numbers p and q and compute $n = pq$. We take two elements $g_1, g_2 \in \mathbf{Z}_n^*$ such that $(g_1/n) = (g_2/n) = -1$, $(g_1/p) = -1$, and $(g_2/p) = +1$. Note that it suffices to use the Chinese Remainder Theorem with a nonquadratic residue (resp. a quadratic residue) in $\mathbf{Z}_p^*$ and a quadratic residue (resp. a nonquadratic residue) in $\mathbf{Z}_q^*$ to make g_1 (resp. g_2). The public key is (n, g_1, g_2). The secret key is p. In order to prove that the generated key is valid, the scheme requires a special protocol. As depicted in Fig. 11.6, this consists of m iterations of the following protocol.

1. The prover picks $x \in \mathbf{Z}_n^*$ at random and sends a commitment to x to the verifier.
2. The verifier picks $y \in \mathbf{Z}_n^*$ at random and sends it to the prover.
3. The prover looks for $r \in \mathbf{Z}_n^*$ and $a_1, a_2 \in \mathbf{Z}_2$ such that $xy \equiv r^2 g_1^{a_1} g_2^{a_2} \pmod{n}$. For this he takes a_1 such that $(xy/p) = (-1)^{a_1}$, a_2 such that $(xy/n) = (-1)^{a_1+a_2}$, and computes a square root r of $xy g_1^{-a_1} g_2^{-a_2} \bmod n$ by using the Tonelli algorithm and the factorization of n. He then reveals r, a_1, a_2 and opens the commitment to x.
4. The verifier checks the commitment for x and that $xy \equiv r^2 g_1^{a_1} g_2^{a_2} \pmod{n}$.

We can prove that this protocol is complete, sound, and zero-knowledge. More precisely, it cannot succeed with probability greater than 2^{-m} if there exists some $z \in \mathbf{Z}_n^*$ which cannot be written $z = r^2 g_1^{a_1} g_2^{a_2} \bmod n$ for $r \in \mathbf{Z}_n^*$ and $a_1, a_2 \in \mathbf{Z}_2$.

Using this process the key holders own some nontrivial character χ over $\mathbf{Z}_n^*$, i.e. some group homomorphism between $\mathbf{Z}_n^*$ and $\{-1, +1\}$ such that $\chi(g_1) = -1$ and $\chi(g_1) = +1$, and he proves that all $\mathbf{Z}_n^*$ can be written $r^2 g_1^{a_1} g_2^{a_2} \bmod n$ for $r \in \mathbf{Z}_n^*$ and $a_1, a_2 \in \mathbf{Z}_2$.

---

[1] We actually describe a particular case based on characters of order 2. See Refs. [135, 136].

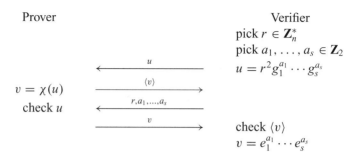

Figure 11.7. MOVA proof of interpolation protocol.

Proof of interpolation. The MOVA scheme requires to prove that given some subset

$$A = \{(g_1, e_1), \ldots, (g_s, e_s)\}$$

of $\mathbf{Z}_n^* \times \{-1, +1\}$, there exists a character χ, i.e. a group homomorphism χ form $\mathbf{Z}_n^*$ to $\{-1, +1\}$ such that $\chi(g_i) = e_i$ for $i = 1, \ldots, s$. In all cases here this character is the Legendre symbol $\chi = (\cdot/p)$, which is computable from the secret key only. We call this a proof of interpolation for A. As depicted in Fig. 11.7, this consists of k iterations of the following protocol.

1. The verifier picks $r \in \mathbf{Z}_n^*$, $a_1, \ldots, a_s \in \mathbf{Z}_2$, computes $u = r^2 g_1^{a_1} \cdots g_s^{a_s} \bmod n$ and sends it to the prover.
2. The prover computes $v = \chi(u)$ and sends a commitment of v to the verifier.
3. The verifier discloses $r, a_1, \ldots, a_s$.
4. The prover verifies that $u = r^2 g_1^{a_1} \cdots g_s^{a_s} \bmod n$ and opens the commitment. (These steps are used in order to make sure that the verifier is honest.)
5. The verifier verifies the commitment and checks that $v = e_1^{a_1} \cdots e_s^{a_s}$.

We can prove that this protocol is complete, sound, and zero-knowledge. More precisely, it cannot succeed with probability greater than 2^{-k} if there exists no character χ for which $\chi(g_i) = e_i$ for $i = 1, \ldots, s$.

Signature algorithm. The signature algorithm is quite simple. Given a message X, we generate $x_1, \ldots, x_t \in \mathbf{Z}_n^*$ by using a generator fed with the hashed value of X. We then compute $y_i = (x_i/p)$ for $i = 1, \ldots, t$. The signature is $\sigma = (y_1, \ldots, y_t)$. (Note that it consists of t bits.) We can show that someone who can distinguish a valid signature from an invalid one can solve the quadratic residuosity problem in $\mathbf{Z}_n^*$, i.e. can distinguish a quadratic residue from a nonquadratic residue with a Jacobi symbol equal to $+1$.

Confirmation algorithm. To confirm a signature $\sigma = (y_1, \ldots, y_t)$ for a message X, we recalculate $x_1, \ldots, x_t$ and then run the proof of interpolation with

$$A = \{(g_1, -1), (g_2, +1), (x_1, y_1), \ldots, (x_t, y_t)\}.$$

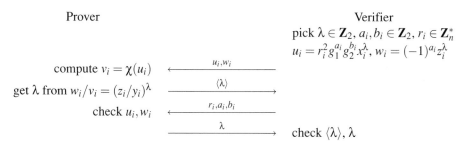

Figure 11.8. MOVA denial protocol.

Denial algorithm. To deny a signature $\sigma = (z_1, \ldots, z_t)$ for a message X, we recalculate $x_1, \ldots, x_t$ and then run the proof of noninterpolation below. As depicted in Fig. 11.8, this consists of ℓ iterations of the following protocol.

1. The verifier picks $r_1, \ldots, r_t \in \mathbf{Z}_n^*$, $a_1, \ldots, a_s, b_1, \ldots, b_s, \lambda \in \mathbf{Z}_2$, computes $u_i = r_i^2 g_1^{a_i} g_2^{b_i} x_i^\lambda \bmod n$ and $w_i = (-1)^{a_i} z_i^\lambda$ for $i = 1, \ldots, t$. He sends the $(u_1, \ldots, u_t)$ and $(w_1, \ldots, w_t)$ to the prover.
2. The prover computes $y_i = (x_i/p)$ and $v_i = (u_i/p)$ for $i = 1, \ldots, t$. Since $w_i/v_i \bmod n$ should be equal to $(x_i/z_i)^\lambda$ for all i and that there must be some i for which $x_i \neq z_i$, the prover can recover λ. In case of inconsistency he picks λ at random. He sends a commitment to λ.
3. The verifier discloses (r_i, a_1, b_i) for $i = 1, \ldots, t$.
4. The prover verifies the consistency with (u_i, w_i) and λ for $i = 1, \ldots, t$. He then opens the commitment.
5. The verifier verifies the commitment and checks that λ is correct.

We can prove that this protocol is complete, sound, and zero-knowledge. More precisely, it cannot succeed with probability greater than $2^{-\ell}$ if the signature is valid.

11.3.2   ⋆Other Special Purpose Digital Signatures

Group signature. We may need to have a signature scheme for a group of participants: we want to certify that someone from a given group has signed a document without disclosing who really did. Group signatures usually require a heavy process for welcoming or revoking members, but have pretty efficient signature and verification schemes.

Ring signature. Some special groups are ad hoc groups. They are not controlled by any means of membership and there is no formal process. Anyone can indeed invent a group by describing who is member and produce a proof that someone from this list did sign a document. (The main drawback is that the proof is pretty long.) These ad hoc groups are called rings.

Blind signature. This signature enables someone to ask a signer to sign the message so that the signer has no means to know what he signed. He only gets insurance that he signed one document, and only one document. One may wonder what kind of applications can have blind signatures. The most important one is digital cash. Privacy in digital cash requires untraceability of the money. Here digital coins are signed by a bank, one by one, in a blind way because customers do not want to have coins which can be traced.

Invisible signature with designated confirmer. We have seen the notion of invisible signatures with undeniable signatures. This was in order to protect the privacy of the signer. One problem remains: the signer can be asked to confirm or deny under threats. In order to have even stronger protection for the signer, another kind of signature prevents him from being able to confirm or deny, but he can designate a third party (e.g. a lawyer) who will be able to do both. Of course, this third party should not be able to forge signatures.

Fail-stop signature. In classical digital signatures, the signer is protected by complexity theory arguments that nobody can forge a signature. Fail-stop signatures are signatures with a stronger protection level: here the signer is protected by information theory arguments. Indeed, even if forging a signature is hard, if it happens to occur, the signer will be able to demonstrate that it is a forgery by solving a problem that he would not have been able to solve in other circumstances.

11.4   ⋆Other Protocols

Cryptography contains some other beautiful dedicated protocols. We give a few examples here.

Escrowed digital cash. We have seen that we can make untraceable digital cash (for more privacy) with blind signatures. The main drawback is indeed the lack of traceability. In order to protect against criminal organizations and prevent money laundering, law enforcement requires having some kind of hidden traceability based on legal request. This makes practical digital cash systems quite complicated.

Electronic votes. Voting schemes are fundamental for democracy. In order to be implemented in an electronic way, we must protect privacy, and prevent the temptation of being corrupted. For this we must both authenticate the voter (in order to avoid double votes) and treat his ballot in an anonymous way. The tricky part is that anonymity must be enforced against a third party, but also against the voter himself: the voter must not be able to prove that he has voted for someone. Interestingly, the protection must remain valid even in the case of a revolution when a dictator could get access to all master secret keys, etc. Adversaries are indeed quite hard to formalize in voting schemes!

Mental Poker. When trying to play a card game (e.g. poker) remotely, there is a big security problem related to card shuffling and distribution: one should make sure that no participant can learn what card was distributed to another participant, one should make sure that no card is distributed twice, and one should make sure that the distribution of card shuffling is as fair as possible. Some protocols can be used in order to share the card deck, to shuffle, to distribute, etc.

Multiparty computation. A more general problem is to make multiparty computation: each participant has a secret value, and we want to compute a function in terms of all secret values, without disclosing the values. In the electronic vote, we want to count the number of occurrences of several values, and hopefully get the majority. We can invent other odd problems: compute the maximum fortune of jealous millionaires who do not want to disclose their fortune, but only to know how much owns the richest; compute perfect matchings out of private requirements in blind date ceremonies, etc.

Broadcast encryption. In pay television, we need to broadcast a signal which is encrypted, and to distribute different keys to the participants in order for them to be able to decrypt.

11.5 Exercises

Exercise 11.1. *An idiot dishonest verifier thinks that giving the challenge $e = 0$ in the basic Fiat–Shamir protocol is useless since the answer $y = r$ does not depend on the secret key. Therefore he decides to always ask $e = 1$.*

Show how a malicious prover can impersonate anyone to this verifier.

Exercise 11.2. *Let us define the following identification scheme. A user U has a secret key which consists of two prime numbers p and q such that $p \equiv q \equiv 3 \pmod 4$. We have $n = pq$ which is public and associated to the identity of U by a certificate. In order to prove the knowledge of the secret key, we can challenge U with a random x. U then computes one square root y of x modulo n, and we can check that it is indeed a square root by raising it to the square.*

Why is it insecure?

Exercise 11.3. *Explain how to transform the Fiat–Shamir protocol into a signature scheme.*

Exercise 11.4 (Guillou–Quisquater zero-knowledge protocol). *We consider the following scheme.*

Setup of public parameters: *take $n = pq$ with p, q primes and an exponent $v \in \mathbf{Z}^*_{\varphi(n)}$.*
Setup of the keys: *for a given prover, define his identity string J, and compute $B = 1/J^{1/v} \bmod n$. The public key is $K_p = (J, v, n)$. The secret key is $K_s = B$.*

Protocol: *perform*

    1. the prover picks a random r and sends $T = r^v \bmod n$,
    2. the verifier sends random d among $1, \ldots, v - 1$,
    3. the prover sends $D = r B^d \bmod n$,
    4. the verifier checks that $T \equiv D^v J^d \pmod{n}$.

Prove that this is a zero-knowledge proof of knowledge of B.[2]

Exercise 11.5. *Construct a perfect secret sharing scheme with the following access structure*

$$\Gamma = \langle \{P_1\}, \{P_2, P_3\}, \{P_2, P_4, P_5\}, \{P_3, P_4, P_5\} \rangle.$$

---

[2] This exercise was inspired by Ref. [82].

12

From Cryptography to Communication Security

Content

Security setup: certificates
Remote access: SSH
Secure Internet transactions: SSL
Security for individuals: PGP

To conclude this book, this chapter shows how to put together materials from the previous ones in order to build cryptographic applications that provide communication security. We illustrate this with a few popular examples.

The main objective is to set up a notion of secure communication session. One example is the (public-key-less) Bluetooth technology which was outlined in Section 5.6.2. We will see some other examples here.

The session usually starts by *peer authentication*, exchange of public-key materials, and goes on with an authenticated key agreement protocol. This ensures that both peers share a common secret key. The secret key is derived into several symmetric secret keys. Then message security, i.e. *message integrity*, *message authentication*, and *message confidentiality*, is ensured by means of MAC and symmetric encryption. Session security additionally requires to ensure the *sequentiality of messages*, i.e. no adversary can replay a message, swap messages, or erase a message. This is usually achieved by means of a synchronized message counter. Some additional security properties may be required, such as

- *Timeliness of message delivery*: a message sender is ensured that his message will be delivered to the right receiver on time;
- *Termination fairness*: peers are ensured to terminate the session in the same state (either termination success or premature abortion);
- *Anonymity*: a peer is ensured that her identity does not leak;
- *Untraceability*: a peer is ensured that the other peer will no later be able to identify her in other sessions;
- *Unlinkability*: peers are ensured that we cannot even realize that two different communication sessions share the same entity;

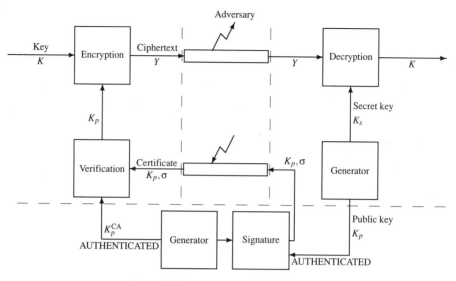

Figure 12.1. Key exchange using certificates.

- *Untransferability*: a peer is ensured that the other peer is not a fake one who hides the real one;
- and so on.

12.1 Certificates

We have seen in Chapter 9 that we can perform a secure key agreement, e.g. by transmitting a key K by using a public-key cryptosystem. This is indeed quite convenient to exchange a common authenticated secret in a client–server protocol because it can later be used in order to set up a secure communication channel. Key agreement protocols however assume that, e.g., we transmitted the public key K_p of the server to the client in an authenticated channel prior to the transmission. This prior authenticated channel could be set up by a common trusted third party (see Fig. 12.1). Indeed, a "certificate authority" (CA) could issue a signature σ for K_p, and the public-key authentication is then guaranteed. The only remaining problems consist in securing the communication of the public key K_p from the server to the certificate authority, and the communication of the authority public key K_p^{CA} to the client (see Fig. 12.2).

Certificates can follow the X.509 standard format. It is also available as the Internet standard RFC 2459 (Ref. [93]). A certificate looks like the one in Figs. 12.3 and 12.4. Fig. 12.3 represents the overall structure, including some information about the issuer of the certificate (here EPFL in Switzerland), the certificate validity period (here between July 2002 and July 2003), and the signature for the certificate (here it is a signature with md5WithRSAEncryption algorithm). Fig. 12.4 provides information about the subject part. (It is put at the place of the . . . in Fig. 12.3.) We can see the subject entity (here an IMAP server for electronic mail boxes in EPFL), its encryption algorithm type (here RSA), and its public key (a modulus and an exponent).

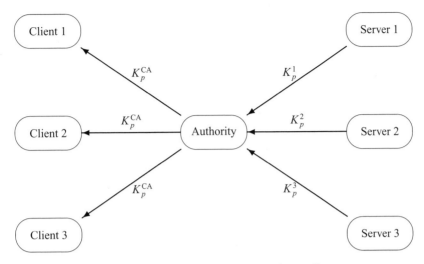

Figure 12.2. Critical secure channels when using certificates.

12.2 SSH: Secure Shell

SSH (as for "Secure SHell") was originally made to enable remote access to a computer in a secure way under UNIX-like operating systems. It was made to be used just like the `rlogin` command (remote login). There is now a series of commercial applications

```
Certificate:
    Data:
        Version: 3 (0x2)
        Serial Number: 212 (0xd4)
        Signature Algorithm: md5WithRSAEncryption
        Issuer:
            C=CH, ST=Vaud, L=Lausanne, O=EPFL,
            CN=EPFL Certification Authority/Email=cert-auth@epfl.ch
        Validity
            Not Before: Jul 11 09:42:05 2002 GMT
            Not After : Jul 11 09:42:05 2003 GMT
        ...
    Signature Algorithm: md5WithRSAEncryption
        a2:ae:a1:b0:f0:24:47:ca:29:b8:78:a6:58:7d:62:3e:25:c9:
        e6:c8:f7:58:99:18:ab:f5:ed:e7:74:7f:a9:4b:5f:07:e3:80:
        a4:68:ea:0a:d2:8f:bb:b7:cc:cc:85:81:d0:15:4a:ee:7e:74:
        f3:be:49:73:bc:4a:ab:22:4e:86:c6:9b:97:d7:4d:16:05:5c:
        69:14:b6:10:36:da:70:64:50:23:4a:33:4c:fe:33:ca:3a:4e:
        cb:c5:9b:28:be:df:b8:30:e7:07:13:d7:e2:88:b2:c2:af:19:
        28:53:7d:39:37:d1:7c:c7:0b:10:3d:12:9d:15:8d:38:dd:6a:
        06:55
```

Figure 12.3. Certificate for a secure IMAP server (overall structure).

```
Subject:
    C=CH, ST=Vaud, L=Lausanne, O=EPFL,
    CN=imapwww.epfl.ch
Subject Public Key Info:
    Public Key Algorithm: rsaEncryption
    RSA Public Key: (1024 bit)
        Modulus (1024 bit):
            00:da:33:16:c5:8b:30:e5:f8:be:4d:43:68:02:e3:
            e4:0e:09:35:72:f4:72:0a:fd:71:6c:79:08:e5:a8:
            31:44:00:f8:e4:72:b1:23:83:6b:b4:f2:85:54:75:
            c7:1e:a0:53:e1:10:b5:e6:85:8a:67:ec:8e:5e:5c:
            6f:c6:b5:95:a0:55:3f:c0:45:8e:54:19:78:6e:40:
            3d:ae:01:55:1c:31:fc:d4:e3:3a:9f:47:a8:6c:25:
            47:f9:87:d5:ab:dc:0b:e3:71:a7:44:03:97:55:86:
            46:d0:48:11:b5:bb:90:fd:d4:c7:25:3b:98:83:20:
            9a:b5:ae:34:23:b8:43:12:71
        Exponent: 65537 (0x10001)
```

Figure 12.4. Certificate for a secure IMAP server (subject part).

based on SSH and a popular open source variant based on the openSSH library.[1] The Linux community is familiar with the ssh command (still for remote login) and scp command (for remote file transfer) since system administrators tend to close all communication ports but the one used by these commands.

12.2.1   Principles of SSH

The principle of SSH is to implement secure (i.e. confidential and authenticated) communication channels in a client–server session. The philosophy of SSH was originally to be user-friendly (ssh had to be used exactly like rlogin), ready to use without any complicated installation, and to be deployed easily. The counterpart was that the security level was not so high, although higher than what was used before. The new release of SSH (known as SSH2) uses public-key infrastructures in order to authenticate servers. This is typically heavy stuff, but the user can easily bypass it: he just has to click "OK" anytime there is a security warning.

When a client wishes to connect to a server, the server sends its public key together with a certificate (if available). The first connection is critical: either the client is able to strongly authenticate the public key, e.g. by checking a certificate or having the user to check the public-key fingerprint, or the client has to trust that the public key is correct. Then the client stores the public key in a file (typically, .ssh/known_hosts). Assuming that this first connection is OK, all future connection to the same server should be secure by comparing the received key with the correct public key from this file. The underlying assumption is that this file has integrity protection. If the key does

---

[1] See http://www.ssh.com and http://www.openssh.org.

not match (for whatever reason), the user has a security warning saying that the public key has changed and that some adversary may be trying to impersonate the server by sending a wrong key. Typically, the user does not care and clicks "OK." This is the major problem of SSH, but remember that the purpose was just to increase the security, not to have a perfect one.

The client and the server run a key agreement protocol such that the server is authenticated, and devise a symmetric key to be used to set up a secure channel. Then, the client is authenticated by a password which is sent through the secure channel.

12.2.2 SSH2 Key Exchange and Authentication

SSH2 uses DSS for server authentication and Diffie-Hellman key agreement for setting up a symmetric session key (previous versions were entirely based on RSA). Both are based on some generator g which generates a subgroup of $\mathbf{Z}_p^*$ of prime order q. Concretely, the clients and the server exchange some "Initial Message" I_C and I_S, and the protocol version V_C and V_S that they support. Then, as illustrated in Fig. 12.5, the key agreement runs as follows.

1. The client picks a random $x \in \{1, \ldots, q - 1\}$, computes $e = g^x \bmod p$, and sends it to the server.
2. The server picks a random $y \in \{1, \ldots, q - 1\}$, computes $f = g^y \bmod p$ and $K = e^y \bmod p$. Then he computes the hashed value H of $V_C \| V_S \| I_C \| I_S \| K_S \| e \| f \| K$ and signs it, where K_S is his public key, and sends K_S, f, and the signature s to the client.
3. The client can verify K_S at this time (e.g. using a certificate or his list of known public keys). Then the client computes $K = f^x \bmod p$, the hashed value H of $V_C \| V_S \| I_C \| I_S \| K_S \| e \| f \| K$, and checks if s is a valid signature for H.

Then the client and the server can use K as a symmetric key for symmetric encryption and MAC. The choice of the algorithms is negotiated between the client and the server. Several encryption schemes are proposed, including triple DES, AES, RC4,

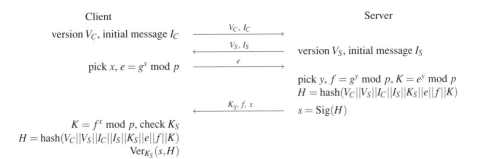

Figure 12.5. Semi-authenticated key exchange in SSH.

and IDEA. The MAC algorithm is typically HMAC based on SHA-1 or MD5. To set up the secure channel, the client and the server derive six keys from K and H. Keys are generated as Gen $(K||H||$string$||$session id$)$ where session id is an identifier for the session and string is a constant which depends on which of the six keys is generated.

- Initial value IV from the client to the server: string $=$ A.
- Initial value IV from the server to the client: string $=$ B.
- Encryption key from the client to the server: string $=$ C.
- Encryption key from the server to the client: string $=$ D.
- Authentication key from the client to the server: string $=$ E.
- Authentication key from the server to the client: string $=$ F.

The generator is defined by taking the first bits of the sequence $k_1||k_2||\ldots$ where

$$k_1 = \text{hash}(K||H||\text{string}||\text{session id})$$

and

$$k_{i+1} = \text{hash}(K||H||k_1||\cdots||k_i).$$

12.3 SSL: Secure Socket Layer

SSL is a famous communication protocol which was first developed by Netscape. It is used in the Internet world. The interface is fairly similar to the TCP/IP one in the sense that applications which need to communicate securely open and close *sockets* in a very similar way so that it is mostly transparent. The most popular versions are SSL version 3.0 and its successor TLS version 1.0 which is the Internet standard RFC 2246 (Ref. [58]). Although SSL is a more popular name, we summarize TLS 1.0 here. SSL/TLS is typically used by Internet browsers in order to communicate securely with HTTP (Hypertext Transfer Protocol) servers. It can also be used by other applications like an e-mail manager willing to connect to a mailbox server. SSL/TLS is designed to be universal and does not rely on a specific cryptographic algorithm choice. The choice of the algorithms, called *cipher suite*, is negotiated between the client and the server at the beginning of a session. We present here a simplified version of SSL.

There are actually two layers of protocols. The lowest is the SSL Record Protocol layer which is on top of TCP and below other high-level communication protocols like HTTP. The other is the SSL Handshake Protocol which is on the same level as the HTTP protocol. The SSL Handshake Protocol is used in order to initiate a session with all the expensive cryptographic protocols such as asymmetric authentication and key agreement. A session can launch several connections which are handled by the SSL Record Protocol. This is really the secure channel which uses only symmetric (i.e. fast) cryptography. As we have seen in the previous chapters, such a channel is possible as long as the two parties previously exchange a symmetric key in an authenticated and confidential way.

For each session, the SSL client and server keep an internal state which contains a session identifier, the peer certificate, the cipher suite choice, and a master secret (a 48-byte symmetric key which is set up at the beginning of the session). It also contains a compression algorithm choice. A session can include several connections. A connection state includes a server and a client nonce, an initialization vector, a sequence number which is incremented for each message, and a set of four secret symmetric keys for MAC and encryption in the two ways: two for the client and two for the server.

The cipher suite specifies the algorithm which is used for peer authentication and key agreement in the handshake protocol, and the symmetric algorithms for encryption and MAC in the record protocol. The latter algorithm pair is often called the "cipher spec." The cipher spec of a session can be changed through the SSL Change Cipher Spec Protocol. It is typically run once at the beginning of the protocol in order to set it up.

An extra protocol, the SSL Alert Protocol, is used to handle alert messages. They can be simple warning alerts or fatal alerts. In the latter case the connection aborts. Other connections in the session can continue, but no new connection can be launched in the session.

12.3.1 Handshake

When a new session starts, the client and the server agree on a protocol version, negotiate a cipher spec, optionally authenticate each other by using certificates, and exchange a key as follows.

1. The client first sends a `ClientHello` message which includes the session identifier, the set of all cipher suites that he can accept, and a nonce to the server.
2. The server responds by sending a `ServerHello` message. This includes the session identifier, the cipher suite he selected in the set of the client, and a nonce. He usually sends his certificate in order to be authenticated. The certificate may include material for a Diffie-Hellman key agreement as explained in Section 12.3.6. Otherwise the server needs to send a specific key exchange message. He may also send a certificate request if he wishes to authenticate the client.
3. Based on this the client may send his certificate if requested by the server. He may also send a key exchange message depending on which key algorithm was selected in the cipher suite. This is the `ClientKeyExchange` message. The client and the server can then compute four symmetric secret keys: two for encryption in one way or another and two for MAC in one way or another.
4. The client sends a protected MAC of all previous handshake messages. This ensures that no messages were lost, swapped, or replayed.
5. Similarly, the server responds by a protected MAC of all previous handshake messages.

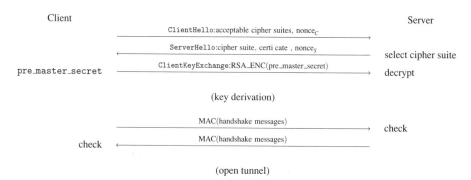

Figure 12.6. A typical SSL handshake.

The client and the server can then communicate through a protected channel.

A typical handshake session is illustrated in Fig. 12.6.

12.3.2   Cipher Suites

A cipher suite includes a key agreement algorithm, a symmetric cipher algorithm, and a hash function. In Figs. 12.7 and 12.8 are a few standard cipher suite definitions for TLS. In addition, an update of TLS integrates AES by specifying the cipher suites of Fig. 12.9 (see Ref. [46]).

We notice that RC4 is the only stream cipher. It is used with two different key lengths: 40 and 128 bits.

All block ciphers use blocks of 8 bytes, except AES which uses 16 bytes. They are all used in CBC mode with an initial vector.

CipherSuite	Key Exchange	Cipher	Hash
TLS_NULL_WITH_NULL_NULL	NULL	NULL	NULL
TLS_RSA_WITH_NULL_MD5	RSA	NULL	MD5
TLS_RSA_WITH_NULL_SHA	RSA	NULL	SHA-1
TLS_RSA_EXPORT_WITH_RC4_40_MD5	RSA	RC4_40	MD5
TLS_RSA_WITH_RC4_128_MD5	RSA	RC4_128	MD5
TLS_RSA_WITH_RC4_128_SHA	RSA	RC4_128	SHA-1
TLS_RSA_EXPORT_WITH_RC2_CBC_40_MD5	RSA	RC2_40	MD5
TLS_RSA_WITH_IDEA_CBC_SHA	RSA	IDEA	SHA-1
TLS_RSA_EXPORT_WITH_DES40_CBC_SHA	RSA	DES40	SHA-1
TLS_RSA_WITH_DES_CBC_SHA	RSA	DES	SHA-1
TLS_RSA_WITH_3DES_EDE_CBC_SHA	RSA	3DES_EDE	SHA-1

Figure 12.7. Standard TLS cipher suites with NULL or RSA key exchange.

CipherSuite	Key Exchange	Cipher	Hash
TLS_DH_DSS_EXPORT_WITH_DES40_CBC_SHA	DH_DSS	DES40	SHA-1
TLS_DH_DSS_WITH_DES_CBC_SHA	DH_DSS	DES	SHA-1
TLS_DH_DSS_WITH_3DES_EDE_CBC_SHA	DH_DSS	3DES_EDE	SHA-1
TLS_DH_RSA_EXPORT_WITH_DES40_CBC_SHA	DH_RSA	DES40	SHA-1
TLS_DH_RSA_WITH_DES_CBC_SHA	DH_RSA	DES	SHA-1
TLS_DH_RSA_WITH_3DES_EDE_CBC_SHA	DH_RSA	3DES_EDE	SHA-1
TLS_DHE_DSS_EXPORT_WITH_DES40_CBC_SHA	DHE_DSS	DES40	SHA-1
TLS_DHE_DSS_WITH_DES_CBC_SHA	DHE_DSS	DES	SHA-1
TLS_DHE_DSS_WITH_3DES_EDE_CBC_SHA	DHE_DSS	3DES_EDE	SHA-1
TLS_DHE_RSA_EXPORT_WITH_DES40_CBC_SHA	DHE_RSA	DES40	SHA-1
TLS_DHE_RSA_WITH_DES_CBC_SHA	DHE_RSA	DES	SHA-1
TLS_DHE_RSA_WITH_3DES_EDE_CBC_SHA	DHE_RSA	3DES_EDE	SHA-1
TLS_DH_anon_EXPORT_WITH_RC4_40_MD5	DH_anon	RC4_40	MD5
TLS_DH_anon_WITH_RC4_128_MD5	DH_anon	RC4_128	MD5
TLS_DH_anon_EXPORT_WITH_DES40_CBC_SHA	DH_anon	DES40	SHA-1
TLS_DH_anon_WITH_DES_CBC_SHA	DH_anon	DES	SHA-1
TLS_DH_anon_WITH_3DES_EDE_CBC_SHA	DH_anon	3DES_EDE	SHA-1

Figure 12.8. Standard TLS cipher suites with Diffie-Hellman key agreement.

DES is used in three variants: a variant limited to 40-bit keys DES40, the regular DES, and triple DES with three keys 3DES_EDE. AES is used with two different key lengths: 128 and 256 bits. RC2_40 is another block cipher with a key of 40 bits.

At the time SSL was developed, the US export restrictions were quite drastic since it required that secret keys were computable by anyone within an effort comparable to an exhaustive search on 40 bits. Corresponding cipher suites are identified by the word "EXPORT" in their name. Actually the algorithms use a secret key which is derived from a 40-bit key and the nonces which prevent dictionary attacks. Corresponding cipher suites still exist because of compatibility reasons.

CipherSuite	Key Exchange	Cipher	Hash
TLS_RSA_WITH_AES_128_CBC_SHA	RSA	AES_128	SHA-1
TLS_DH_DSS_WITH_AES_128_CBC_SHA	DH_DSS	AES_128	SHA-1
TLS_DH_RSA_WITH_AES_128_CBC_SHA	DH_RSA	AES_128	SHA-1
TLS_DHE_DSS_WITH_AES_128_CBC_SHA	DHE_DSS	AES_128	SHA-1
TLS_DHE_RSA_WITH_AES_128_CBC_SHA	DHE_RSA	AES_128	SHA-1
TLS_DH_anon_WITH_AES_128_CBC_SHA	DH_anon	AES_128	SHA-1
TLS_RSA_WITH_AES_256_CBC_SHA	RSA	AES_256	SHA-1
TLS_DH_DSS_WITH_AES_256_CBC_SHA	DH_DSS	AES_256	SHA-1
TLS_DH_RSA_WITH_AES_256_CBC_SHA	DH_RSA	AES_256	SHA-1
TLS_DHE_DSS_WITH_AES_256_CBC_SHA	DHE_DSS	AES_256	SHA-1
TLS_DHE_RSA_WITH_AES_256_CBC_SHA	DHE_RSA	AES_256	SHA-1
TLS_DH_anon_WITH_AES_256_CBC_SHA	DH_anon	AES_256	SHA-1

Figure 12.9. Standard TLS cipher suites with AES.

12.3.3   Record Protocol

When a party needs to send a message (called *application data*) to the other party, it is first split into *fragments* of length at most 2^{14} bytes. Each fragment is treated separately. A fragment is compressed using the compression algorithm of the session (if any). Then we append a MAC to the compressed fragment and we obtain the plaintext. Next, it is encrypted, and the ciphertext is finally sent with an SSL record header.

Upon reception of a record, the header is extracted, the ciphertext is decrypted, the MAC is checked, then extracted, and the remaining is decompressed in order to get the fragment.

When the hash algorithm of the cipher spec is NULL, no MAC is computed, i.e. the MAC length is null. Otherwise, the MAC is simply an HMAC algorithm with the specified hash function. More precisely the MAC of a fragment is computed as

$$\text{HMAC}_{\texttt{MAC\_write\_secret}}\left(\begin{array}{l}\texttt{seq\_num}\\\texttt{TLSCompressed.type, TLSCompressed.version,}\\\texttt{TLSCompressed.length}\\\texttt{TLSCompressed.fragment}\end{array}\right)$$

where MAC_write_secret is the MAC key of the sender, seq_num is the sequence number of the fragment, and remaining fields are the compressed fragment with its actual length and some additional information about the TLS protocol (namely, the compression algorithm) that is being used.

12.3.4   Stream Cipher

The RC4 stream cipher is used as a key-stream generator with one-time pad. The internal state of the generator is kept in the connection state so that the RC4 automaton continuously generates keystreams in order to encrypt the sequence of fragments.

12.3.5   Block Cipher

Since block ciphers are used in CBC mode, the plaintext must be converted into an integral sequence of blocks. For this we append a padding to the plaintext and a padding length of 1 byte. The padding length must be equal to all bytes of the padding, and the total length (the plaintext, the padding, and the padding length) must be a multiple of the block size. When the ciphertext is decrypted, the last byte specifies the length of the padding to be removed. The padding structure is also checked and an error is issued if it is not valid.

Note that the padding does not need to be the shortest one. It can actually be longer in order to hide the real size of the plaintext to a potential adversary.

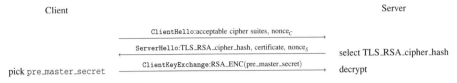

Figure 12.10. TLS key exchange using RSA.

The initial vector (IV) which is used in the CBC mode is a secret pseudorandom value. The IV value for the next record is simply the last ciphertext block so that, like in the stream cipher mode, we can view the sequence of all (compressed and MACed) fragments as a unique plaintext to be encrypted in CBC mode. The very first IV value of a connection is generated together with the secret keys from the nonces and a master secret. (For export cipher suites, the master secret is not used so that IV is not secret at all.)

12.3.6 Master Key Exchange

The key exchange protocol which is specified in the current cipher suite is used in order to set up a pre-master secret. As we have seen in the cipher suites, there are six possible protocols.

RSA: The client chooses the secret and encrypts it using the RSA public key of the server (see Fig. 12.10). This public key must be authenticated in a certificate. Encryption follows the PKCS#1v1.5 standard.

DH_DSS and DH_RSA: These are "fixed Diffie-Hellman" algorithms in which long-term Diffie-Hellman parameters are used. The-Diffie-Hellman parameters p and g are put in the certificate of the server, as well as the Diffie-Hellman public key g^x mod p of the server. The certificate is signed using either DSS or RSA to authenticate the keys. So the client can just take the authenticated Diffie-Hellman parameters from the certificate, pick his Diffie-Hellman public value g^y mod p, and send it to the server in the `ClientKeyExchange` message (see Fig. 12.11).

DHE_DSS and DHE_RSA: These are "ephemeral Diffie-Hellman" algorithms in which the Diffie-Hellman parameters are randomly selected by the client and the server. The server certificate contains either a DSS or a RSA public key. The server can select his chosen Diffie-Hellman parameters and public value $(p, g, g^x$ mod $p)$, hash them with the selected hash function, sign them with

Client   Server

> ClientHello:acceptable cipher suites, nonce$_C$

> ServerHello:TLS_DH_sig_cipher_hash, certificate, nonce$_S$ select TLS_DH_sig_cipher_hash

pick y ClientKeyExchange:g^y mod p pre_master_secret $= g^{xy}$ mod p

Figure 12.11. TLS key exchange using DH_DSS or DH_RSA.

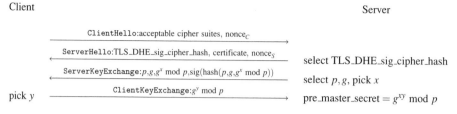

Figure 12.12. TLS key exchange using DHE_DSS or DHE_RSA.

his key and the selected authentication algorithm. The signed parameters are sent in an additional ServerKeyExchange message which immediately follows the ServerHello message. So the client can just take the signed Diffie-Hellman parameters, check the signature by using the authenticated public key from the certificate, pick his Diffie-Hellman public value g^y mod p, and send it to the server in the ClientKeyExchange message (see Fig. 12.12).

DH_anon: This is a particular case of the previous Diffie-Hellman protocols in which the parameters are not authenticated. It does not require any certificate, but it is vulnerable to a man-in-the-middle attack. Like in the ephemeral Diffie-Hellman algorithms, the server selects his chosen Diffie-Hellman parameters and public value $(p, g, g^x$ mod $p)$ and sends them in an additional ServerKeyExchange message. So the client can just take the Diffie-Hellman parameters, pick his Diffie-Hellman public value g^y mod p, and send it to the server in the ClientKeyExchange message (see Fig. 12.13).

12.3.7 Key Derivation

A hash algorithm hash defines a pseudorandom generator P_hash. Given a secret secret and a seed seed, we define a sequence P_hash(secret, seed) by

$$P\text{\_hash}(\text{secret}, \text{seed}) = r_1, r_2, r_3, \ldots$$

where $r_i = \text{HMAC}_{\text{hash}}(\text{secret}, a_i, \text{seed})$, $a_i = \text{HMAC}_{\text{hash}}(\text{secret}, a_{i-1})$, and $a_0 = $ seed.

Client   Server

$\overline{\qquad\qquad \text{ClientHello:acceptable cipher suites, nonce}_C \qquad\qquad}\!\!\!\rightarrow$

$\leftarrow\!\!\!\overline{\qquad\quad \text{ServerHello:TLS\_DH\_anon\_cipher\_hash, nonce}_s \qquad\quad}$ select TLS_DH_anon_cipher_hash

$\leftarrow\!\!\!\overline{\qquad\qquad\quad \text{ServerKeyExchange:}p,g,g^x \bmod p \qquad\qquad\quad}$ select p, g, pick x

pick y $\overline{\qquad\qquad\quad \text{ClientKeyExchange:}g^y \bmod p \qquad\qquad\quad}\!\!\!\rightarrow$ pre_master_secret = g^{xy} mod p

Figure 12.13. TLS key exchange using DH_anon.

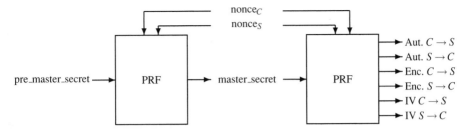

Figure 12.14. Key derivation in SSL.

Given secret secret, a seed seed, and a string label we further define a sequence PRF(secret, label, seed) by

PRF(secret, label, seed) = P_MD5($S1$, label||seed) $\oplus$ P_SHA1($S2$, label||seed)

where $S1$ and $S2$ are the two halves of secret. (If secret has an odd length, its middle byte is both the last byte of $S1$ and the first byte of $S2$.)

PRF is used in order to compute the *master secret*. For this we just take the first 48 bytes of

master_secret = PRF(pre_master_secret, "master secret", nonce$_C$||nonce$_S$).

As illustrated in Fig. 12.14, PRF is also used in order to generate a key block from the master secret as follows.

key_block = PRF(master_secret, "key expansion", nonce$_S$||nonce$_C$)

This key block is the concatenation of the four secret keys and the two initial vectors which are used in the cipher spec.

PRF is also used to compute the two 12-byte MAC of the handshake (one MAC$_C$ from the client, one MAC$_S$ from the server) by

h_handshake = MD5(handshake)||SHA1(handshake)
    MAC$_C$ = PRF(master_secret, "client finished", h_handshake)
    MAC$_S$ = PRF(master_secret, "server finished", h_handshake)

where handshake is the concatenation of all handshake messages.

12.4 PGP: Pretty Good Privacy

Unlike SSL which is dedicated to security of on-line communication, PGP brings security in an off-line way: signature and encryption of e-mails, archives, etc. PGP was first designed by Phil Zimmermann, in the United States, in the nineties. At that time, this country (and some others) looked like a dictatorship from the regulation of cryptography viewpoint. It was basically illegal to prevent authorities from having access to any cleartext by the means of strong cryptography. Several people, like Zimmermann, fought against it by developing appropriate (illegal) software in order to provide access to strong privacy for any individual. Today, rules are more liberal and we can use PGP without betraying the US law.[2]

PGP is available in a commercial and a freeware version. Since there are still strong restrictions for export of cryptographic applications, there is one version to be used within the United States, and another one called PGPi for international usage.[3]

There is also a Gnu version of PGP called GPG as for GnuPGP which is available as the RFC 2440 (Ref. [40]).

12.4.1   Security for Individuals

Due to its origins, PGP is easy to set up without any corporate help. For this reason, certificates do not rely on any authority, we do not use any public parameter, and anyone can freely generate his own key and choose his cryptographic algorithm.

PGP can be used in order to encrypt, decrypt, hash, sign, or verify digital files. These can be archives or just e-mails. Popular algorithms in PGP are IDEA symmetric encryption, RSA encryption or signature, and MD5 hash function. Many other algorithms are available as well.

PGP has a nice feature which enables protecting unreadable files (like ciphertexts, signatures, hashed values, or even cryptographic keys) by encoding them into a readable form. This uses the Radix-64 code, which is also called base64 in the Multipurpose Internet Mail Extensions (MIME) standard (see Ref. [70]). This feature is called the *ASCII armor* in PGP. Files in the ASCII armor format have the .asc file extension.

When PGP is used for e-mails, human beings can usually see which version of PGP, which algorithm, and which key length are used.[4] The PGP software recognizes it by itself, so this is more for transparency and education of users than for making their life complicated. As an example, here is a signed message.

```
-----BEGIN PGP SIGNED MESSAGE-----
Hash: SHA1

PGP makes cryptographic messages readable for human beings.
```

---

[2] See, Ref. [116] for more information about historical details.

[3] Ref. [73] is a reference book for PGP. One can refer to it for more details about using PGP.

[4] Human beings actually could see it, but this feature seems to have disappeared nowadays in versions of PGP, so the user cannot see it by default unless he really asks for it.

```
-----BEGIN PGP SIGNATURE-----
Version: GnuPG v1.2.4 (GNU/Linux)

iD8DBQFBA4c1/LSQdhvwJ58RAjzEAKCXHnwQHNGbX2Bzjo3AMZHABWTW5wCgkx
VLrq22vPs5vlR6RZOf1zEDSF4=
=cVzf
-----END PGP SIGNATURE-----
```

One can see that the message hashed value (using SHA1) was signed by GnuPGP version 1.2.4. If the user asks for the signature verification, the following message is returned.

```
gpg: Signature made Sun 25 Jul 2004 12:11:01 PM CEST using DSA
key ID 1BF0279F
gpg: Good signature from "Serge Vaudenay <serge.vaudenay@epfl
.ch>"
```

So one realizes that the signature is a DSA signature and that the public key is identified in the key ring as belonging to the named person.

When doing a cryptographic operation, PGP may need cryptographic keys which are hardly manageable for a human user. Symmetric keys can be prompted to the user. They are usually derived from a *pass phrase* which is freely chosen by the user by using a hash function.

Asymmetric keys are more problematic since they are in a specific mathematical format. For instance an RSA key is a pair of a modulus and an exponent. We cannot derive them from a human pass phrase. For this, PGP retrieves the key from a *key ring*. The user just needs to provide an identifier for the key to be used. When the key is a secret one, it may be encrypted by a symmetric algorithm. Therefore, PGP needs to ask for the symmetric key by prompting for the corresponding pass phrase.

As an example, here is a listing of a public key ring.

```
vaudenay@lasecpc7:~> gpg --list-public-keys
/home/vaudenay/.gnupg/pubring.gpg
-------------------------------
pub   1024D/1BF0279F 2004-07-25 Serge Vaudenay
<serge.vaudenay@epfl.ch>

pub   1024D/8EB9124A 2004-07-25 Student <student@epfl.ch>

pub   1536R/27295F6B 2004-07-25 Colleague <colleague@epfl.ch>
```

It may look quite cryptic. The second field tells the bit length and the scheme. For instance, 1024D means a 1024-bit key for DSA, 1024g means a 1024-bit key for

ElGamal, and 1536R means a 1536-bit key for RSA. The date of creation as well as the name (e-mail address) of the owner is provided.

PGP makes extensive usage of checksums and cryptographic digests so that bad pass phrases or modified files are easily detected.

12.4.2   Public-Key Management

A user can create his asymmetric keys. He just needs to select the algorithm and key size, and to provide enough randomness for PGP to generate it in a random way. For this, PGP analyzes key strokes on the keyboard (people calls this an "entropy collector") and makes random bits from time intervals between key strokes by using a pseudorandom generator. Once an asymmetric key pair is created, the secret part is encrypted with a symmetric key which is derived from a pass phrase. Both the public key and the encrypted secret key are stored in the corresponding key ring.

PGP provides commands in order to manage key rings: extracting, adding, changing keys, etc. Those commands are as secure and user friendly as possible.

When a user is given a public key from another one, he can insert it in his key ring. At the same time, he determines the level of trust he can attribute to the validity of that key. For instance, if the key was given hand to hand, he can fairly trust that the key is valid. If the key was taken from a Web site through insecure connection, he may give a low confidence to the validity. Additionally, the public key can be certified by a third party that the user trusts, or partially trusts. The *trust path* can of course have more than one intermediate parties. There can be several trust paths to the public key. The public key can be inserted in the key ring with this extra kind of certificate. The user must therefore permanently manage keys with different trust levels and be aware of potential weak trusts.

PGP users have defined the notion of web of trust in which keys are vertices and oriented edges means that one key certified the other one. Trust paths are simply paths in this graph. The shorter the paths the higher the trust confidence.

12.4.3   Security Weaknesses

Since PGP was made in order to be fully controlled by the user, security issues occur when it is not well used. For this a minimal education on cryptography is required in order to securely use it. People must be educated on how to choose and use a pass phrase, on what a key size means, on how the public-key management works, and on how sensitive a key ring can be.

Among one of the weakest point, the key infrastructure heavily relies on trust. The authentication of public keys is not controlled by any central authority (PGP was made in order to avoid it), so depending on how secure an application should be, users really need to authenticate their public keys accordingly.

Also, a key may eventually get compromised (for instance if a pass phrase is intercepted when typing it), and key revocation is ad hoc based. When one wants to revoke his key, he must broadcast a revocation message to any potential user of his public key. Indeed, no central revocation list is available for the same reasons. Of course, one can set up an authority for certification and revocation of PGP keys, but PGP was not done for that and careless users will naturally bypass this feature.

For these reasons PGP is mostly used for small fixed communities in an ad hoc way.

12.5 Exercises

Exercise 12.1. *RC5-CBC-PAD is specified in the informative Internet document RFC 2040. It describes how to pad digital messages (represented as a sequence of bytes) in order to be encrypted via block cipher RC5 in CBC mode. Here is how it works.*

- *Take the message $x_1, \ldots, x_\ell$ as a sequence of ℓ bytes.*
- *Take an integer p such that $\ell + p$ is a multiple of 8 and that $1 \le p \le 8$.*
- *Let $x_i = p$ for $i = \ell + 1, \ldots, \ell + p$.*
- *Take the byte sequence $x_1, \ldots, x_{\ell+p}$ and rewrite it as a block sequence $B_1, \ldots, B_{\frac{\ell+p}{8}}$.*
- *Encrypt the block sequence via RC5 in CBC mode, and obtain the encrypted message $C_1, \ldots, C_{\frac{\ell+p}{8}}$.*

  1. *Show that p is essentially unique and express its value with a mathematical formula.*
  2. *Explain how the C_i are computed.*
  3. *We assume that the receiver of the encrypted message first decrypts in CBC mode, then checks if the padding is correct, and finally extracts the clear text. Carefully explain how all this is performed (for instance by writing a computer program).*
  4. *Given a ciphertext $y = (C_1, \ldots, C_n)$, let $\mathcal{O}(y)$ be equal to 1 if the padding check is correct after the RC5-CBC decryption or equal to 0 otherwise. By using subroutine calls to the $\mathcal{O}$ oracle, write a program which given a block C computes $\mathrm{RC5}^{-1}(C)$.*
     Hint: Submit ciphertexts with the form (R, C) for a carefully chosen block R.
  5. *By using the previous question show how to decrypt any message by having access to $\mathcal{O}$ only.*
  6. *In order to fix the scheme, we decide to encrypt twice with RC5 in CBC mode. Namely, we add an extra step in the previous scheme by re-encrypting $C_1, \ldots, C_{\frac{\ell+p}{8}}$ in CBC mode and obtaining $C'_1, \ldots, C'_{\frac{\ell+p}{8}}$. Make a picture of the encryption scheme. Show that a similar attack holds: we can still decrypt*

any message by having access to an oracle which says whether or not the decrypted message is correctly padded.

7. *Recall how block ciphers are used in order to encrypt SSL fragments. Deduce an attack against SSL.*

Conclude about how to integrate cryptographic schemes.[5]

---

[5] This exercise was inspired by Refs. [21, 41, 182].

Further Readings

The reader familiar with the content of the present textbook may want to have a deeper look at some selected (or missing) topics here. We suggest the following references.

C. Boyd, A. Mathuria. *Protocols for Authentication and Key Establishment*. Springer-Verlag, NY, 2003.
>An excellent textbook on peer authentication and key establishment protocols.

R. Crandall, C. Pomerance. *Prime Numbers: A Computational Perspective*. Springer, NY, 2001.
>This book tells much more on primality tests and factoring algorithms.

M.R. Garey, D.S. Johnson. *Computers and Intractability—A Guide to the Theory of NP-Completeness*. Freeman, NY, 1979.
>This is another fundamental reference about complexity theory. It contains a nice catalog of NP-complete problems.

O. Goldreich. *Modern Cryptography, Probabilistic Proofs and Pseudorandomness*. Algorithms and Combinatorics, vol. 17. Springer-Verlag, NY, 1999.
>A survey on the fascinating area of randomness and the power of interaction. It is more oriented to complexity theory, but it is hard to formally talk about randomness without it.

D. Gollman. *Computer Security*. John Wiley & Sons, NY, 1999.
>An excellent textbook on computer and network security. It is more oriented to the integration and the theory behind. It addresses aspects of security related to hardware, operation systems, networks and distributed systems, and management.

J.E. Hopcroft, J.D. Ullman. *Introduction to Automata Theory, Languages, and Computation*. Addison Wesley, London, 1979.
>This is an outstanding reference on the foundations of computer sciences. It contains necessary information about complexity theory (Turing machines, complexity, intractability).

S. Katzenbeisser. *Recent Advances in RSA Cryptography*. Advances in Information Security, vol. 3. Kluwer Academic Publishers, Boston, 2001.
>This is a complete survey on RSA cryptography.

W. Mao. *Modern Cryptography—Theory and Practice*. Prentice Hall PTR, Upper Saddle River, NJ, 2003.
>An excellent textbook about issues related to what is called "textbook cryptography," or how theoretical cryptography may fail to implement security. It is somewhat a textbook on nontextbook cryptography.

A.J. Menezes, P.C. van Oorschot, S.A. Vanston. *Handbook of Applied Cryptography*. CRC, NY, 1997.

This is a reference textbook. This 780-page book is not meant to be read from the beginning to the end. It is an excellent handbook for finding references, definitions, related topics, *etc.*

M.A. Nielsen, I.L. Chuang. *Quantum Computation and Quantum Information*. Cambridge University Press, Cambridge, 2000.

A reference textbook about current research on quantum computing. It notably includes quantum cryptography and the Shor polynomial time factorization algorithm. If quantum computers become a reality, this might become a classical lecture in every computer science curriculum.

J. Stern. *La Science du Secret*. Odile Jacob, Paris, 1998.

A philosophical dissertation (in French) on cryptography by Jacques Stern. Interesting for people who want to understand the rise of modern cryptography in theoretical computer sciences and the real technical advances which led to modern cryptography.

Bibliography

[1] Advanced Encryption Standard (AES). *Federal Information Processing Standards* Publication #197. U.S. Department of Commerce, National Institute of Standards and Technology, 2001.

[2] ANSI X9.17. American National Standard Institute. Financial Institution Key Management (Wholesale). ASC X9 Secretariat, American Bankers Association, 1986.

[3] ANSI X9.62. Public Key Cryptography for the Financial Services Industry: The Elliptic Curve Digital Signature Algorithm (ECDSA). American National Standard Institute. American Bankers Association, 1998.

[4] Bluetooth. Specification of the Bluetooth System. Version 1.2, November 2003. Available at http://www.bluetooth.org.

[5] Data Encryption Standard (DES). *Federal Information Processing Standard* publication #46–3. U.S. Department of Commerce, National Institute of Standards and Technology, 1999.

[6] DES Modes of Operation. *Federal Information Processing Standard* publication #81. U.S. Department of Commerce—National Bureau of Standards, National Technical Information Service, Springfield, VA, 1980.

[7] Digital Signature Standard. *Federal Information Processing Standard* publication #186. U.S. Department of Commerce, National Institute of Standards and Technology, 1994.

[8] Digital Signature Standard (DSS). *Federal Information Processing Standards* publication #186-2. U.S. Department of Commerce, National Institute of Standards and Technology, 2000.

[9] ETSI. Universal Mobile Telecommunications System (UMTS); Specification of the 3GPP Confidentiality and Integrity Algorithms. Document 2: Kasumi Algorithm specification (3GPP TS 35.202 Version 3.1.2 Release 1999). Available at http://www.etsi.org/.

[10] ISO/IEC 9796. Information Technology—Security Techniques—Digital Signature Scheme Giving Message Recovery. International Organization for Standardization, Geneva, 1991.

[11] ISO/IEC 9797. Data Cryptographic Techniques—Data Integrity Mechanism Using a Cryptographic Check Function Employing a Block Cipher Algorithm. International Organization for Standardization, Geneva, 1989.

[12] ISO/IEC 14888. Information Technology—Security Techniques—Digital Signature with Appendix. International Organization for Standardization, Geneva, 1998.

[13] PKCS#1v1: RSA Cryptography Standard. An RSA Laboratories Technical Report Version 1.5. RSA Laboratories, 1993.

[14] PKCS#1v2.1: RSA Cryptography Standard. RSA Security Inc. Public-Key Cryptography Standards. RSA Laboratories, 2002.

[15] Secure Hash Standard. *Federal Information Processing Standard* publication #180. U.S. Department of Commerce, National Institute of Standards and Technology, 1993.

[16] Secure Hash Standard. *Federal Information Processing Standard* publication #180-1. U.S. Department of Commerce, National Institute of Standards and Technology, 1995.

[17] Secure Hash Standard. *Federal Information Processing Standard* publication #180-2. U.S. Department of Commerce, National Institute of Standards and Technology, 2002.

[18] Specification of the Bluetooth System. Vol. 2: Core System Package. Bluetooth Specification Version 1.2, 2003.

[19] A.V. Aho, J.E. Hopcroft, J.D. Ullman. *The Design and Analysis of Computer Algorithms*. Addison-Wesley, London, 1974.

[20] J.L. Balcázar, J. Díaz, J. Gabarró. *Structural Complexity I*. EATC. Springer, NY, 1988.

[21] R. Baldwin, R. Rivest. The RC5, RC5-CBC, RC5-CBC-Pad, and RC5-CTS Algorithms. RFC 2040, 1996.

[22] J. Bamford. *The Puzzle Palace*. Penguin Books, NY, 1983.

[23] D. Bayer, S. Haber, W.S. Stornetta. Improving the Efficiency and Reliability of Digital Time-Stamping. In *Sequences II: Methods in Communication, Security, and Computer Science*. Springer-Verlag, NY, 1993, pp. 329–334

[24] M. Bellare, R. Canetti, H. Krawczyk. Keyed Hash Functions and Message Authentication. In *Advances in Cryptology CRYPTO'96*, Santa Barbara, CA, Lecture Notes in Computer Science 1109. Springer-Verlag, NY, 1996, pp. 1–15.

[25] M. Bellare, A. Desai, D. Pointcheval, P. Rogaway. Relations among Notions of Security for Public-Key Encryption Schemes. In *Advances in Cryptology CRYPTO'98*, Santa Barbara, CA, Lecture Notes in Computer Science 1462. Springer-Verlag, NY, 1998, pp. 26–45.

[26] M. Bellare, P. Rogaway. Optimal Asymmetric Encryption—How to Encrypt with RSA. In *Advances in Cryptology EUROCRYPT'94*, Perugia, Italy, Lecture Notes in Computer Science 950. Springer-Verlag, NY, 1995, pp. 92–111.

[27] J. Benaloh, J. Leichter. Generalized Secret Sharing and Monotone Functions. In *Advances in Cryptology CRYPTO'88*, Santa Barbara, CA, Lecture Notes in Computer Science 403. Springer-Verlag, NY, 1990, pp. 27–35.

[28] E. Biham, A. Shamir. Differential Cryptanalysis of DES-like Cryptosystems. In *Advances in Cryptology CRYPTO'90*, Santa Barbara, CA, Lecture Notes in Computer Science 537. Springer-Verlag, NY, 1991, pp. 2–21.

[29] E. Biham, A. Shamir. Differential Cryptanalysis of DES-Like Cryptosystems. *Journal of Cryptology*, vol. 4, pp. 3–72, 1991.

[30] E. Biham, A. Shamir. Differential Cryptanalysis of the Full 16-Round DES. In *Advances in Cryptology CRYPTO'92*, Santa Barbara, CA, Lecture Notes in Computer Science 740. Springer-Verlag, NY, 1993, pp. 487–496.

[31] E. Biham, A. Shamir. *Differential Cryptanalysis of the Data Encryption Standard.* Springer-Verlag, NY, 1993.

[32] A. Biryukov, A. Shamir, D. Wagner. Real Time Cryptanalysis of A5/1 on a PC. In *Fast Software Encryption'00*, New York, Lecture Notes in Computer Science 1978. Springer-Verlag, NY, 2001, pp. 1–18.

[33] D. Bleichenbacher. Generating ElGamal Signatures without Knowing the Secret Key. In *Advances in Cryptology EUROCRYPT'96*, Zaragoza, Spain, Lecture Notes in Computer Science 1070. Springer-Verlag, NY, 1996, pp. 10–18.

[34] D. Bleichenbacher. Chosen Ciphertext Attack against Protocols Based on the RSA Encryption Standard PKCS#1. In *Advances in Cryptology CRYPTO'98*, Santa Barbara, CA, Lecture Notes in Computer Science 1462. Springer-Verlag, NY, 1998, pp. 1–12.

[35] D. Boneh, R.A. DeMillo, R.J. Lipton. On the Importance of Checking Cryptographic Protocols for Faults. In *Advances in Cryptology EUROCRYPT'97*, Konstanz, Germany, Lecture Notes in Computer Science 1233. Springer-Verlag, NY, 1997, pp. 37–51.

[36] J. Boyar. Inferring Sequences Produced by Pseudorandom Number Generators. *Journal of the ACM*, vol. 36, pp. 129–144, 1989.

[37] C. Boyd, A. Mathuria. *Protocols for Authentication and Key Establishment.* Springer, NY, 2003.

[38] E. Brickell, D. Pointcheval, S. Vaudenay, M. Yung. Design Validations for Discrete Logarithm Based Signature Schemes. In *Public Key Cryptography'00*, Melbourne, Australia, Lecture Notes in Computer Science 1751. Springer-Verlag, NY, 2000, pp. 276–292.

[39] C. Cachin. *Entropy Measures and Unconditional Security in Cryptography.* Hartung–Gorre, Konstang, ETH Series in Information Security and Cryptography, vol. 1, 1997.

[40] J. Callas, L. Donnerhacke, H. Finney, R. Thayer. OpenPGP Message Format. Internet Standard. RFC 2440, The Internet Society, 1998.

[41] B. Canvel, A. Hiltgen, S. Vaudenay, M. Vuagnoux. Password Interception in a SSL/TLS Channel. In *Advances in Cryptology CRYPTO'03*, Santa Barbara, CA, Lecture Notes in Computer Science 2729. Springer-Verlag, NY, 2003, pp. 583–599.

[42] J.L. Carter, M.N. Wegman. Universal Classes of Hash Functions. *Journal of Computer and System Sciences*, vol. 18, pp. 143–154, 1979.

[43] F. Chabaud, A. Joux. Differential Collisions in SHA-0. In *Advances in Cryptology CRYPTO'98*, Santa Barbara, CA, Lecture Notes in Computer Science 1462. Springer-Verlag, NY, 1998, pp. 56–71.

[44] F. Chabaud, S. Vaudenay. Links between Differential and Linear Cryptanalysis. In *Advances in Cryptology EUROCRYPT'94*, Perugia, Italy, Lecture Notes in Computer Science 950. Springer-Verlag, NY, 1995, pp. 356–365.

[45] D. Chaum, H. van Antwerpen. Undeniable Signatures. In *Advances in Cryptology CRYPTO'89*, Santa Barbara, CA, Lecture Notes in Computer Science 435. Springer-Verlag, NY, 1990, pp. 212–217.

[46] P. Chown. Advanced Encryption Standard (AES) Ciphersuites for Transport Layer Security (TLS). Internet Standard. RFC 3268, The Internet Society, 2002.

[47] S.A. Cook. The Complexity of Theorem-Proving Procedures. In *Proceedings of the 3rd ACM Symposium on Theory of Computing*, Atlanta, GA. ACM Press, NY, 1971, pp. 151–158.

[48] D. Coppersmith. The Data Encryption Standard (DES) and Its Strength against Attacks. *IBM Journal of Research and Development*, vol. 38, pp. 243–250, 1994.

[49] D. Coppersmith. Finding a Small Root of a Univariate Modular Equation. In *Advances in Cryptology EUROCRYPT'96*, Zaragoza, Spain, Lecture Notes in Computer Science 1070. Springer-Verlag, NY, 1996, pp. 155–165.

[50] D. Coppersmith, M. Franklin, J. Patarin, M. Reiter. Low-Exponent RSA with Related Messages. In *Advances in Cryptology EUROCRYPT'96*, Zaragoza, Spain, Lecture Notes in Computer Science 1070. Springer-Verlag, NY, 1996, pp. 1–9.

[51] J.-S. Coron, D. Naccache, J.P. Stern. On the Security of RSA Padding. In *Advances in Cryptology CRYPTO'99*, Santa Barbara, CA, Lecture Notes in Computer Science 1666. Springer-Verlag, NY, 1999, pp. 1–18.

[52] T. Cover, J. Thomas. *Elements of Information Theory*. John Wiley & Sons, NY, 1991.

[53] R. Crandall, C. Pomerance. *Prime Numbers: A Computational Perspective*. Springer, NY, 2001.

[54] J. Daemen, V. Rijmen. *The Design of Rijndael*. Information Security and Cryptography, Springer, NY, 2002.

[55] J. Daemen, L. Knudsen, V. Rijmen. The Block Cipher SQUARE. In *Fast Software Encryption'97*, Haifa, Israel, Lecture Notes in Computer Science 1267. Springer-Verlag, NY, 1997, pp. 149–165.

[56] I.B. Damgård. A Design Principle for Hash Functions. In *Advances in Cryptology CRYPTO '89*, Santa Barbara, CA, Lecture Notes in Computer Science 435. Springer-Verlag, NY, 1990, pp. 416–427.

[57] D.W. Davies, G.I.P. Parkin. The Average Cycle Size of the Key Stream in Output Feedback Encipherment. In *Advances in Cryptology, Proceedings of CRYPTO '82*, 1982, pp. 97–98. Re-edited by Springer, NY, LNCS vol. 1440, 1998.

[58] T. Dierks, C. Allen. The TLS Protocol Version 1.0. Internet Standard. RFC 2246, The Internet Society, 1999.

[59] W. Diffie, M.E. Hellman. New Directions in Cryptography. *IEEE Transactions on Information Theory*, vol. IT-22, pp. 644–654, 1976.

[60] W. Diffie, S. Landau. *Privacy on the Line—The Politics of Wiretapping and Encryption*. The MIT Press, Cambridge, MA, 1998.

[61] H. Dobbertin. The First Two Rounds of MD4 are Not One-Way. In *Fast Software Encryption '98*, Paris, France, Lecture Notes in Computer Science 1372. Springer-Verlag, NY, 1998, pp. 284–292.

[62] H. Dobbertin. Cryptanalysis of MD4. *Journal of Cryptology*, vol. 11, pp. 253–271, 1998.

[63] T. ElGamal. Cryptography and Logarithms over Finite Fields. PhD Thesis, Stanford University, 1984.

[64] T. ElGamal. A Public-Key Cryptosystem and a Signature Scheme Based on Discrete Logarithms. In *Advances in Cryptology CRYPTO '84*, Santa Barbara, CA, Lecture Notes in Computer Science 196. Springer-Verlag, NY, 1985, pp. 10–18.

[65] T. ElGamal. A Public-Key Cryptosystem and a Signature Scheme Based on Discrete Logarithms. *IEEE Transactions on Information Theory*, vol. IT-31, pp. 469–472, 1985.

[66] U. Feige, A. Fiat, A. Shamir. Zero-Knowledge Proofs of Identity. *Journal of Cryptology*, vol. 1, pp. 77–94, 1988.

[67] N. Ferguson, B. Schneier. *Practical Cryptography*. John Wiley & Sons, NY, 2003.

[68] A. Fiat, A. Shamir. How to Prove Yourself: Practical Solutions to Identification and Signature Problems. In *Advances in Cryptology CRYPTO '86*, Santa Barbara, CA, Lecture Notes in Computer Science 263. Springer-Verlag, NY, 1987, pp. 186–194.

[69] J. Franks, P. Hallam-Baker, J. Hostetler, S. Lawrence, P. Leach, A. Luotonen, L. Stewart. HTTP Authentication: Basic and Digest Access Authentication. Internet Standard. RFC 2617, The Internet Society, 1999.

[70] N. Freed, N. Borenstein. Multipurpose Internet Mail Extensions (MIME) Part One: Format of Internet Message Bodies. Internet Standard. RFC 2045, 1996.

[71] E. Fujisaki, T. Okamoto, D. Pointcheval, J. Stern. RSA-OAEP is Secure under the RSA Assumption. In *Advances in Cryptology CRYPTO'01*, Santa Barbara, CA, Lecture Notes in Computer Science 2139. Springer-Verlag, NY, 2001, pp. 260–274.

[72] M.R. Garey, D.S. Johnson. *Computers and Intractability— A Guide to the Theory of NP-Completeness*. Freeman, NY, 1979.

[73] S. Garfinkel. *PGP—Pretty Good Privacy*. O'Reilly, Cambridge, 1995.

[74] H. Gilbert. *Cryptanalyse Statistique des Algorithmes de Chiffrement et Sécurité des Schémas d'Authentification*. Thèse de Doctorat de l'Université de Paris 11, 1997.

[75] H. Gilbert, G. Chassé. A Statistical Attack of the FEAL-8 Cryptosystem. In *Advances in Cryptology CRYPTO'90*, Santa Barbara, CA, Lecture Notes in Computer Science 537. Springer-Verlag, NY, 1991, pp. 22–33.

[76] O. Goldreich. *Modern Cryptography, Probabilistic Proofs and Pseudorandomness*. Algorithms and Combinatorics vol. 17. Springer-Verlag, NY, 1999.

[77] S. Goldwasser, S. Micali. Probabilistic Encryption. *Journal of Computer and System Sciences*, vol. 28, pp. 270–299, 1984.

[78] S. Goldwasser, S. Micali, C. Rackoff. The Knowledge Complexity of Interactive Proof Systems. *SIAM Journal on Computing*, vol. 18, pp. 186–208, 1989.

[79] S. Goldwasser, S. Micali, R.L. Rivest. A "Paradoxical" Solution to the Signature Problem. In *Advances in Cryptology CRYPTO'84*, Santa Barbara, CA, Lecture Notes in Computer Science 196. Springer-Verlag, NY, 1985, p. 467.

[80] S. Goldwasser, S. Micali, R.L. Rivest. A Digital Signature Scheme Secure against Adaptive Chosen-Message Attacks. *SIAM Journal on Computing*, vol. 17, pp. 281–308, 1988.

[81] F. Grieu. A Chosen Messages Attack on the ISO/IEC 9796-1 Signature Scheme. In *Advances in Cryptology CRYPTO'00*, Santa Barbara, CA, Lecture Notes in Computer Science 1880. Springer-Verlag, NY, 2000, pp. 70–80.

[82] L. Guillou, J.-J. Quisquater. A "Paradoxical" Identity-Based Signature Scheme Resulting from Zero-Knowledge. In *Advances in Cryptology CRYPTO'88*, Santa Barbara, CA, Lecture Notes in Computer Science 403. Springer-Verlag, NY, 1990, pp. 216–231.

[83] S.C. Kleene. Representation of Events in Nerve Nets. In *Automata Studies*, C.E. Shannon and M. McCarthy (Eds.), Annals of Mathematical Studies, vol. 34. Princeton University Press, Princeton, 1956, pp. 3–41.

[84] S. Haber, W.S. Stornetta. How to Time-Stamp a Digital Document. *Journal of Cryptology*, vol. 3, pp. 99–111, 1991.

[85] N. Haller. The S/KEY One-Time Password System. RFC 1760, 1995.

[86] N. Haller, C. Metz, P. Nesser, M. Straw. A One-Time Password System. Internet Standard. RFC 2289, The Internet Society, 1998.

[87] J. Håstad. Solving Simultaneous Modular Equations of Low Degree. *SIAM Journal on Computing*, vol. 17, pp. 376–404, 1988.

[88] M.E. Hellman. A Cryptanalysis Time–Memory Trade-Off. *IEEE Transactions on Information Theory*, vol. IT-26, pp. 401–406, 1980.

[89] M.E. Hellman, R. Merkle, R. Schroeppel, L. Washington, W. Diffie, S. Pohlig, P. Schweitzer. *Results of an Initial Attempt to Cryptanalyze the NBS Data Encryption Standard*. Stanford University, September 1976.

[90] H.M. Heys. A Tutorial on Linear and Differential Cryptanalysis. Technical Report CORR 2001–17, Centre for Applied Cryptographic Research, Department of Combinatorics and Optimization, University of Waterloo, 2001. (Also appears in *Cryptologia*, vol. 26, pp. 189–221, 2002.)

[91] F.H. Hinsley, A. Stripp. *Code Breakers*. Oxford University Press, NY, 1993.

[92] J.E. Hopcroft, J.D. Ullman. *Introduction to Automata Theory, Languages, and Computation*. Addison Wesley, London, 1979.

[93] R. Housley, W. Ford, W. Polk, D. Solo. Internet X.509 Public Key Infrastructure Certificate and CRL Profile. Internet Standard. RFC 2459, The Internet Society, 1999.

[94] T. Iwata, K. Kurosawa. OMAC: One-Key CBC MAC. In *Fast Software Encryption'03*, Lund, Sweden, Lecture Notes in Computer Science 2887. Springer-Verlag, NY, 2003, pp. 137–161.

[95] T. Jakobsen, L.R. Knudsen. The Interpolation Attack on Block Ciphers. In *Fast Software Encryption'97*, Haifa, Israel, Lecture Notes in Computer Science 1267. Springer-Verlag, NY, 1997, pp. 28–40.

[96] P. Junod, S. Vaudenay. FOX Specifications Version 1.1. Technical Report EPFL/IC/2004/75, EPFL, 2004.

[97] P. Junod, S. Vaudenay. FOX: A New Family of Block Ciphers. In *Selected Areas in Cryptography'04*, Watterloo, ON, Canada, Lecture Notes in Computer Science 3357. Springer-Verlag, NY, 2005, pp. 114–129.

[98] D. Kahn. *The Codebreakers*. Scriber, 1996.

[99] R.M. Karp. Reducibility among Combinatorial Problems. In *Complexity of Computer Computations*, Plenum Press, New York, 1972. pp. 85–103.

[100] S. Katzenbeisser. *Recent Advances in RSA Cryptography*. Advances in Information Security vol. 3. Kluwer Academic Publishers, Boston, 2001.

[101] J. Kelsey, B. Schneier, N. Ferguson. Yarrow-160: Notes on the Design and Analysis of the Yarrow Cryptographic Pseudorandom Number Generator. In *Selected Areas in Cryptography '99*, Kingston, ON, Canada, Lecture Notes in Computer Science 1758. Springer-Verlag, NY, 2000, pp. 13–33.

[102] N. Koblitz. *A Course in Number Theory and Cryptography*. Graduate Texts in Mathematics 114. Springer-Verlag, NY, 1994.

[103] P. Kocher. Timing Attacks on Implementations of Diffie-Hellman, RSA, DSS, and Other Systems. In *Advances in Cryptology CRYPTO '96*, Santa Barbara, CA, Lecture Notes in Computer Science 1109. Springer-Verlag, NY, 1996, pp. 104–113.

[104] P. Kocher. Differential Power Analysis. In *Advances in Cryptology CRYPTO '99*, Santa Barbara, CA, Lecture Notes in Computer Science 1666. Springer-Verlag, NY, 1999, pp. 388–397.

[105] J. Kohl, C. Neuman. The Kerberos Network Authentication Service (V5). Internet Standard. RFC 1510, 1993.

[106] H. Krawczyk. How to Predict Congruential Generators. In *Advances in Cryptology CRYPTO '89*, Santa Barbara, CA, Lecture Notes in Computer Science 435. Springer-Verlag, NY, 1990, pp. 138–153.

[107] H. Krawczyk. How to Predict Congruential Generators. *Journal of Algorithms*, vol. 13, pp. 527–545, 1992.

[108] H. Krawczyk. LFSR-Based Hashing and Authentication. In *Advances in Cryptology CRYPTO '94*, Santa Barbara, CA, Lecture Notes in Computer Science 839. Springer-Verlag, NY, 1994, pp. 129–139.

[109] H. Krawczyk, M. Bellare, R. Canetti. HMAC: Keyed-Hashing for Message Authentication. RFC 2104, 1997.

[110] X. Lai. *On the Design and Security of Block Ciphers*. ETH Series in Information Processing, vol. 1. Hartung-Gorre Verlag Konstanz, 1992.

[111] X. Lai, J.L. Massey, S. Murphy. Markov Ciphers and Differential Cryptanalysis. In *Advances in Cryptology EUROCRYPT '91*, Brighton, UK, Lecture Notes in Computer Science 547. Springer-Verlag, NY, 1991, pp. 17–38.

[112] G. Lamé. Mentioned in J.O. Shallit, *Historia Mathematica*, vol. 21, pp. 401–419, 1994.

[113] L. Lamport. Constructing Digital Signatures from a One Way Function, Technical Report CSL-98, SRI Intl., 1979.

[114] H.W. Lenstra. Factoring Integers with Elliptic Curves. *Annals of Mathematics*, vol. 126, pp. 649–673, 1987.

[115] A.K. Lenstra, H.W. Lenstra. *The Development of the Number Field Sieve*. Springer-Verlag, NY, 1993.

[116] S. Levy. *Crypto*. Penguin Books, NY, 2001.

[117] R. Lidl, H. Niederreiter. *Introduction to Finite Fields and Their Applications*. Cambridge University Press, Cambridge, 1994.

[118] B. Lloyd, W. Simpson. PPP Authentication Protocols. Internet Standard. RFC 1334, 1992.

[119] M. Luby, C. Rackoff. How to Construct Pseudorandom Permutations from Pseudorandom Functions. *SIAM Journal on Computing*, vol. 17, pp. 373–386, 1988.

[120] W. Mao. *Modern Cryptography—Theory and Practice*. Prentice Hall PTR, Upper Saddle River, NJ, 2003.

[121] J.L. Massey. SAFER K-64: A Byte-Oriented Block-Ciphering Algorithm. In *Fast Software Encryption '94*, Cambridge, UK, Lecture Notes in Computer Science 809. Springer-Verlag, NY, 1994, 1–17.

[122] J.L. Massey. SAFER K-64: One Year Later. In *Fast Software Encryption '95*, Leuven, Belgium, Lecture Notes in Computer Science 1008. Springer-Verlag, NY, 1995, pp. 212–241.

[123] J.L. Massey. Guessing and Entropy. In *IEEE International Symposium on Information Theory*, Tronheim, Norway, 1994, pp. 204.

[124] M. Matsui. Linear Cryptanalysis Methods for DES Cipher. In *Advances in Cryptology EUROCRYPT '93*, Lofthus, Norway, Lecture Notes in Computer Science 765. Springer-Verlag, NY, 1994, pp. 386–397.

[125] M. Matsui. The First Experimental Cryptanalysis of the Data Encryption Standard. In *Advances in Cryptology CRYPTO '94*, Santa Barbara, CA, Lecture Notes in Computer Science 839. Springer-Verlag, NY, 1994, pp. 1–11.

[126] M. Matsui. New Structure of Block Ciphers with Provable Security against Differential and Linear Cryptanalysis. In *Fast Software Encryption '96*, Cambridge, UK, Lecture Notes in Computer Science 1039. Springer-Verlag, NY, 1996, pp. 205–218.

[127] M. Matsui. New Block Encryption Algorithm MISTY. In *Fast Software Encryption '97*, Haifa, Israel, Lecture Notes in Computer Science 1267. Springer-Verlag, NY, 1997, pp. 54–68.

[128] A.J. Menezes, P.C. van Oorschot, S.A. Vanston. *Handbook of Applied Cryptography*. CRC, NY, 1997.

[129] R.C. Merkle. Secure Communications over Insecure Channels. *Communications of the ACM*, vol. 21, pp. 294–299, 1978.

[130] R.C. Merkle. One Way Hash Functions and DES. In *Advances in Cryptology CRYPTO'89*, Santa Barbara, CA, Lecture Notes in Computer Science 435. Springer-Verlag, NY, 1990, pp. 416–427.

[131] R.C. Merkle. A Certified Digital Signature. In *Advances in Cryptology CRYPTO'89*, Santa Barbara, CA, Lecture Notes in Computer Science 435. Springer-Verlag, NY, 1990, 218–238.

[132] R.C. Merkle, M. Hellman. Hiding Information and Signatures in Trapdoor Knapsacks. *IEEE Transactions on Information Theory*, vol. IT-24, pp. 525–530, 1978.

[133] R.C. Merkle, M. Hellman. On the Security of Multiple Encryption. *Communications of the ACM*, vol. 24, pp. 465–467, 1981.

[134] G. Miller. Riemann's Hypothesis and Tests for Primality. *Journal of Computer and System Sciences*, vol. 13, pp. 300–317, 1976.

[135] J. Monnerat, S. Vaudenay. Undeniable Signatures Based on Characters: How to Sign with One Bit. In *Public Key Cryptography'04*, Singapore, Lecture Notes in Computer Science 2947. Springer-Verlag, NY, 2004, pp. 69–85.

[136] J. Monnerat, S. Vaudenay. Generic Homomorphic Undeniable Signatures. In *Advances in Cryptology ASIACRYPT'04*, Jeju Island, Korea, Lecture Notes in Computer Science 3329. Springer-Verlag, NY, 2004, pp. 354–371.

[137] M. Naor, S. Shamir. Visual Cryptography. In *Advances in Cryptology EUROCRYPT'94*, Perugia, Italy, Lecture Notes in Computer Science 950. Springer-Verlag, NY, 1995, pp. 1–12.

[138] R.M. Needham, M.D. Schroeder. Using Encryption for Authentication in Large Networks of Computers. *Communications of the ACM*, vol. 21, pp. 993–999, 1978.

[139] P.Q. Nguyen, J. Stern. The Two Faces of Lattices in Cryptology. In *Proceedings of the International Conference on Cryptography and Lattices (CaLC'01)*, Providence, Rhode Island, Lecture Notes in Computer Science 2146. Springer-Verlag, NY, 2001, pp. 146–180.

[140] M.A. Nielsen, I.L. Chuang. *Quantum Computation and Quantum Information*. Cambridge University Press, Cambridge, 2000.

[141] K.Nyberg, L.R. Knudsen. Provable Security against a Differential Cryptanalysis. *Journal of Cryptology*, Journal version of a paper presented at CRYPTO'92, Santa Barbara, CA, vol. 8, pp. 27–37, 1995.

[142] P. Oechslin. Making a Faster Cryptanalytic Time–Memory Trade-Off. In *Advances in Cryptology CRYPTO'03*, Santa Barbara, CA, Lecture Notes in Computer Science 2729. Springer-Verlag, NY, 2003, pp. 617–630.

[143] T. Okamoto, S. Uchiyama. A New Public-Key Cryptosystem as Secure as Factoring. In *Advances in Cryptology EUROCRYPT'98*, Espoo, Finland, Lecture Notes in Computer Science 1403. Springer-Verlag, NY, 1998, pp. 308–318.

[144] H. Ong, C.P. Schnorr, A. Shamir. An Efficient Signature Scheme Based on Quadratic Equations. In *Proceedings of the 16th ACM Symposium on Theory of Computing*, Washington, D.C. ACM Press, NY, 1984, pp. 208–216.

[145] S. Pohlig, M. Hellman. An Improved Algorithm for Computing Logarithms over GF(q) and Its Cryptographic Significance. *IEEE Transactions on Information Theory*, vol. IT-24, pp. 106–110, 1978.

[146] D. Pointcheval, J. Stern. Security Proofs for Signature Schemes. In *Advances in Cryptology EUROCRYPT'96*, Zaragoza, Spain, Lecture Notes in Computer Science 1070. Springer-Verlag, NY, 1996, pp. 387–398.

[147] D. Pointcheval, S. Vaudenay. On Provable Security for Digital Signature Algorithms. Technical Report LIENS 96-17, Ecole Normale Supérieure, 1996.

[148] J.M. Pollard. Theorems on Factorization and Primality Testing. *Mathematical Proceedings of the Cambridge Philosophical Society*, vol. 76, pp. 521–528, 1974.

[149] J.M. Pollard. A Monte Carlo Method for Factorization. *Nordisk Tidskrift for Informationsbehandlung (BIT)*, vol. 15, pp. 331–334, 1975.

[150] J.M. Pollard. Monte Carlo Methods for Index Computation mod p. *Mathematics of Computation*, vol. 32, pp. 918–924, 1978.

[151] J.M. Pollard, C.P. Schnorr. An Efficient Solution of the Congruence $x^2 + ky^2 = m$ (mod n). *IEEE Transactions on Information Theory*, vol. IT-33, pp. 702–709, 1987.

[152] C. Pomerance. Fast, Rigorous Factorization and Discrete Logarithm Algorithms. In *Discrete Algorithms and Complexity*, D.S. Johnson, T. Nishizeki, A. Nozaki, and H.S. Wilf (Eds.). Academic Press, NY, 1987, pp. 119–143.

[153] M.O. Rabin. Digitalized Signatures and Public-Key Functions as Intractable as Factorization. Technical Report MIT/LCS/TR–212, MIT Laboratory for Computer Science, 1979.

[154] M.O. Rabin. Probabilistic Algorithm for Testing Primality. *Journal of Number Theory*, vol. 12, pp. 128–138, 1980.

[155] A. Rényi. *Probability Theory*. Elsevier, NY, 1970.

[156] R.L. Rivest. The MD4 Message Digest Algorithm. In *Advances in Cryptology CRYPTO'90*, Santa Barbara, CA, Lecture Notes in Computer Science 537. Springer-Verlag, NY, 1991, pp. 303–311.

[157] R.L. Rivest. The MD5 Message Digest Algorithm. RFC 1321, 1992.

[158] R.L. Rivest, A. Shamir, L.M. Adleman. A Method for Obtaining Digital Signatures and Public-Key Cryptosystem. *Communications of the ACM*, vol. 21, pp. 120–126, 1978.

[159] B. Schneier. *Applied Cryptography*. John Wiley & Sons, NY, 1996. French version: *Cryptographie Appliquée*. Vuibert, Paris, 1996.

[160] C.P. Schnorr. Efficient Identification and Signature for Smart Cards. In *Advances in Cryptology CRYPTO'89*, Santa Barbara, CA, Lecture Notes in Computer Science 435. Springer-Verlag, NY, 1990, 235–251.

[161] C.P. Schnorr. Efficient Identification and Signature for Smart Cards. *Journal of Cryptology*, vol. 4, pp. 161–174, 1991.

[162] C.P. Schnorr, S. Vaudenay. Black Box Cryptanalysis of Hash Networks Based on Multi-permutations. In *Advances in Cryptology EUROCRYPT'94*, Perugia, Italy, Lecture Notes in Computer Science 950. Springer-Verlag, NY, 1995, pp. 47–57.

[163] A. Shamir. How to Share a Secret. *Communications of the ACM*, vol. 22, pp. 612–613, 1979.

[164] A. Shamir. A Polynomial Time Algorithm for Breaking the Basic Merkle–Hellman Cryptosystem. In *Proceedings of the 23rd IEEE Symposium on Foundations of Computer Science*, Chicago, IL. IEEE, 1982, pp. 145–152.

[165] A. Shamir. On the Security of DES. In *Advances in Cryptology CRYPTO'85*, Santa Barbara, CA, Lecture Notes in Computer Science 218. Springer-Verlag, NY, 1986, pp. 280–281.

[166] A. Shamir. IP=PSPACE. In *Proceedings of the 22nd ACM Symposium on Theory of Computing*, Baltimore, MD. ACM Press, NY, 1990, pp. 11–15.

[167] C.E. Shannon. Communication Theory of Secrecy Systems. *Bell System Technical Journal*, vol. 28, pp. 656–715, 1969. Re-edited in *Claude Elwood Shannon—Collected Papers*. IEEE Press, New York, 1993.

[168] R. Shirey. Internet Security Glossary. RFC 2828, The Internet Society, 2000.

[169] V. Shoup. OAEP Reconsidered. In *Advances in Cryptology CRYPTO'01*, Santa Barbara, CA, Lecture Notes in Computer Science 2139. Springer-Verlag, NY, 2001, pp. 239–259.

[170] V. Shoup. *A Computational Introduction to Number Theory and Algebra*. Online textbook, 2004. Available at http://shoup.net/ntb.

[171] J.H. Silverman. *The Arithmetic of Elliptic Curves*. Graduate Texts in Mathematics 106. Springer-Verlag, NY, 1986.

[172] G.J. Simmons. A "Weak" Privacy Protocol Using the RSA Crypto Algorithm. *Cryptologia*, vol. 7, pp. 180–182, 1983.

[173] S. Singh. *The Code Book*. Fourth Estate, London, 1999.

[174] R. Solovay, V. Strassen. A Fast Monte-Carlo Test for Primality. *SIAM Journal on Computing*, vol. 6, pp. 84–86, 1977.

[175] J. Stern. *La Science du Secret*. Odile Jacob, Paris, 1998.

[176] J. Stern, S. Vaudenay. CS-Cipher. In *Fast Software Encryption'98*, Paris, France, Lecture Notes in Computer Science 1372. Springer-Verlag, NY, 1998, pp. 189–205.

[177] D.R. Stinson. *Cryptography, Theory and Practice* (2nd Edition). CRC, NY, 2002. French version: *Cryptographie, Théorie et Pratique*, Vuibert, Paris, 2003.

[178] A. Tardy-Corfdir, H. Gilbert. A Known Plaintext Attack of FEAL-4 and FEAL-6. In *Advances in Cryptology CRYPTO'91*, Santa Barbara, CA, Lecture Notes in Computer Science 576. Springer-Verlag, NY, 1992, pp. 172–181.

[179] S. Vaudenay. On the Need for Multipermutations: Cryptanalysis of MD4 and SAFER. In *Fast Software Encryption'95*, Leuven, Belgium, Lecture Notes in Computer Science 1008. Springer-Verlag, NY, 1995, pp. 286–297.

[180] S. Vaudenay. Hidden Collisions on DSS. In *Advances in Cryptology CRYPTO'96*, Santa Barbara, CA, Lecture Notes in Computer Science 1109. Springer-Verlag, NY, 1996, pp. 83–88.

[181] S. Vaudenay. On the Security of CS-Cipher. In *Fast Software Encryption'99*, Roma, Italy, Lecture Notes in Computer Science 1636. Springer-Verlag, NY, 1999, 260–274.

[182] S. Vaudenay. Security Flaws Induced by CBC Padding—Applications to SSL, IPSEC, WTLS. In *Advances in Cryptology EUROCRYPT'02*, Amsterdam, Netherlands, Lecture Notes in Computer Science 2332. Springer-Verlag, NY, 2002, pp. 534–545.

[183] S. Vaudenay. Decorrelation: A Theory for Block Cipher Security. *Journal of Cryptology*, vol. 16, pp. 249–286, 2003.

[184] M.N. Wegman, J.L. Carter. New Hash Functions and Their Use in Authentication and Set Equality. *Journal of Computer and System Sciences*, vol. 22, pp. 265–279, 1981.

[185] M.J. Wiener. Cryptanalysis of Short RSA Secret Exponents. *IEEE Transactions on Information Theory*, vol. IT-36, pp. 553–558, 1990.

Index